POETRY

*Selected Poems* (edited by Ron Padgett, 2007)
*Sun Out* (2002)
*A Possible World* (2002)
*New Addresses* (2000)
*Straits* (1998)
*One Train* (1994)
*On the Great Atlantic Railway: Selected Poems* (1950–1988)
*Seasons on Earth* (1987)
*On the Edge* (1986)
*Selected Poems: 1950–1982* (1985)
*Days and Nights* (1982)
*The Burning Mystery of Anna in 1951* (1979)
*The Duplications* (1977)
*The Art of Love* (1975)
*The Pleasures of Peace* (1969)
*When the Sun Tries to Go On* (1969)
*Thank You and Other Poems* (1962)
*Permanently* (1961)
*Ko, or A Season on Earth* (1960)
*Poems* (1953)

FICTION

*Collected Fiction* (2005)
*Hotel Lambosa* (1993)
*The Red Robins* (1975)

*The*
# COLLECTED
# POEMS
*of*
# KENNETH
# KOCH

*The*
# COLLECTED
# POEMS
*of*
# KENNETH
# KOCH

*The*

# COLLECTED
# POEMS

*of*

# KENNETH
# KOCH

ALFRED A. KNOPF    NEW YORK    2007

THIS IS A BORZOI BOOK
PUBLISHED BY ALFRED A. KNOPF

www.randomhouse.com/knopf/poetry

Originally published in hardcover by Alfred A. Knopf,
a division of Random House, Inc., New York, in 2005.

The poems in this collection previously appeared in the following volumes:
*Thank You and Other Poems*, Grove Press, 1962; *The Pleasures of Peace*, Grove Press, 1969;
*The Art of Love*, Vintage Books, 1975; *The Burning Mystery of Anna in 1951*,
Random House, Inc., 1979; *Days and Nights*, Random House, Inc., 1982; *One Train*,
Alfred A. Knopf, 1994; *Straits*, Alfred A. Knopf, 1998; *New Addresses*, Alfred A. Knopf,
2000; *A Possible World*, Alfred A. Knopf, 2002; *Sun Out*, Alfred A. Knopf, 2002.

Library of Congress Cataloging-in-Publication Data
Koch, Kenneth, 1925–2002
[Poems]
Collected poems / by Kenneth Koch.
p.   cm.
ISBN 978-0-375-71119-0
I. Title

PS3521.027A17 2005
811'.54—dc22      2004063827

Manufactured in the United States of America
Published November 1, 2005
First Paperback Edition, October 2, 2007

# CONTENTS

## THANK YOU AND OTHER POEMS (1962)

## THE PLEASURES OF PEACE (1969)

## THE ART OF LOVE (1975)

## THE BURNING MYSTERY OF ANNA IN 1951 (1979)

A POSSIBLE WORLD (2002)

# A NOTE ON THE TEXT

*The Collected Poems* presents Kenneth Koch's shorter poems more or less in the order of their first appearances in book form. However, the reader who consults the list of other books by Koch in the current volume might wonder why one of those collections seems to be out of sequence and others appear to be unrepresented here.

*Sun Out* was published in 2002, the year of Koch's death, but it begins the current volume because it contains the earliest poems he wished to preserve.

Nine of the eleven poems in *Permanently* were reprinted in *Thank You and Other Poems*, the other two in *The Pleasures of Peace*; they appear under the latter titles here. All the work in *Selected Poems: 1950–1982* and *On the Great Atlantic Rainway: Selected Poems 1950–1988* is also included.

Five other titles—*When the Sun Tries to Go On*; *Ko, or A Season on Earth*; *The Duplications*; *Seasons on Earth* (which combined *Ko* and *The Duplications*); and *On the Edge*—will be gathered in the forthcoming *Collected Long Poems*.

Together, *The Collected Poems* and *The Collected Long Poems* will serve as the definitive editions of Kenneth Koch's major poetic work.

# SUN OUT

Selected Poems 1952–54

# *A Note on* Sun Out

The poems I wrote between 1952 and 1954 are in such a different style from those I wrote afterwards that they never seemed to fit into my books. One did get into *Thank You,* and I included four or five others in my *Selected Poems* of 1994, but I imagine that there they seem more like early oddities than like something that goes with the rest of the poetry. I think their nature will be clearer in a book of their own.

The social and literary context of these poems was the early fifties New York art and poetry world, at least the part of it that I knew. This included the dramatic, splashy, beautiful paintings of Jane Freilicher and Larry Rivers, and Frank O'Hara's seemingly endless inspiration and John Ashbery's eloquent mysteriousness. We poets and painters hung around a lot together, showed each other our works, and were made by this camaraderie very (or more than otherwise) ambitious, envious, emulous, and, I think, lucky. Everyone had an immediately available audience that had no reason not to be critical or enthusiastic. Also I had just spent a year in France, immersed not only in French poetry but in the French language, which I understood and misunderstood at the same time. Words would have several meanings for me at once. *Blanc (white)* was also *blank* and, in the feminine, *Blanche,* the name of a woman. The pleasure—and the sense of new meanings—I got from this happy confusion was something I wanted to re-create in English.

This double or triple quality of words that I imperfectly understood, along with the repetitions, substitutions, and interruptions that for me seemed to go with it, including the abundant use of quotations and exclamations, once I began to hear them all together, constituted a way of using the language that was very stirring to me and seemed to mean a lot. It gave me a strong sensation of speaking the truth; it seemed what had to be said (at least what had to be said by me). If the general sense it made was somewhat clear to me, its individual subjects were less so. When, much later, I came on it, a statement by Wittgenstein seemed to apply: "There are no subjects in the world. A subject is a limitation of the world." Of course everything, once it is written about, even if it's a wild chaos, is bound eventually to become itself a sort of subject. I wanted to keep my subject up in the air as long as possible. For two years, as long as my close relationship to this language lasted, I had the happy sensation of discovery.

*Kenneth Koch*
*June 2002*

# Sun Out

Bananas, piers, limericks
I am postures
Over there, I, are
The lakes of delectation
Sea, sea you! Mars and win-
Some buffalo
They thinly raft the plain,
Common do

It ice-floes, hit-and-run drivers,
The mass of the wind.
Is that snow
H-ing at the door? And we
Come in the buckle, a
Vanquished distinguished
Secret festival, relieving flights
Of the black brave ocean.

# The Chase—First Day

While stealing samples from the grocery store
We knew the green grass blew, and the cabs attempted—
O close to my heart, white days of some invention,
White didn't you know before?

It was a whale that swam, or a ring in the sink then,
The damp nickel among the white
Rainbows (Williams), white didn't I
Know that the mints were going to check you like persons?

Sleet machines!
I approach you like a moth dizzy with materials,
Dick! disk! public peaces of entertainment!
O lonely place-parking under the wonder-falls!

Did the police bend over the taste of peppermint
With the grace of ballet dancers? do the pumps renew?
White might I see you on the whoming dimway
At day and night, and yet win praise of you,
I'll fold my chair in the summer rain,
                    To Jean White.

# Highway Barns, the Children of the Road

Amaryllis, is this paved highway a
Coincidence? There we were
On top of the fuel bin. In the autos
Dusk moved silently, like pine-needle mice.
Often I throw hay upon you,
She said. The painted horse had good news.
Yes, I really miss him, she waves,
She pants. In the dusk bin the fuel reasoned silently.
Amaryllis, is this paved highway a
Coincidence? My ears were glad. Aren't you?
Aren't you healthy in sight of the strawberries,
Which like pine-needle lace fight for dawn fuel?
The white mile was lighted up. We shortened
Our day by two whole tusks. The wind rang.
Where is the elephant graveyard? She missed the pavement.
A load of hay went within speaking distance of the raspberries.
Overture to the tone-deaf evening! I don't see its home.
Prawns fell from that sparkling blue sphere.
The land is coughing, "Joy!" Hey, pavements, you charmers,
When are you going to bring me good news?

# No Biography

If followed to Matador
What Spice Islands!
What I-spy lands. Shush the door,
We shall be calm as a print
Seating not revealing. . . .
Is my filing
The disturbance to liberate the equator,
Master Moon? How literary, you
Fire with excitement.
Yes, but I'm a liar for the week.
By Thailand! is this minute livable?
The Bear replies: Here is my paw,
Living while concealing. . . .
He invited him! Who? Why? Oh,
Speak to me beneath the envelope,
Lie now beneath the roses.
Don't you believe it's true,
The unmanageable seam?
What's that? Stifle
Me! but do not let this go! Where?
Love. He follows a photograph.
I wish I'd the moon,
He knows—what? Sees her? Simply. Dreams!
Though refusals could be lively.
Own this, while with a peculiar . . .
No! you're not going to stamp again?
See
Iron coming late. He's not afraid of overturning the tundra.

# Ellie Campaigns after a Candidate's Defeat

**SHE**

Oh let my mirror pay the bunny-tax,
I'm tired of Shilohs. In from Ping-Pong—?

**ELLIE I**

I see the sighing spray of spring;
The grass is jumping, the roots leap
Phones.

**SHE**

Man comes carrying a tire.

**TOGETHER**

We are the willows beneath the bear rug.

**SHE**

Has any election done less than a wine
Of beastly furniture? and can we be alone,
Is iron? when are the maddening
Steep if consoling fractions of history done

**ELLIE I**

As when by a sign-featured hand? And she shudders

**SHE**

I sent these same ladders into pastures.

**THE CANDIDATE**

The bell of your studio lights
Drove me to ruin. I ran out into advance
But they could not turn round my
Marining out. And I . . .

**THREE GIRLS**

We are three virgins, scansion-hearted,
To whom the words of Shakespeare cry our
Peruvianly-inspired hair . . .

ELLIE I
      O matches!
      The invention of the soundtruck can presume
      The natural limits of rights, but sandy parks
      Are strown by bettors, and the unnatural monsoon
      Casts its ballot eternally for oblivion,

SHE
      Say, of dying parks of velvety orange hair,
      Porches to face death's thrills,
      And the agnostic peaches of today.

# Rapping Along

Greatness on a day
Meant for steadiness and study halls,
Oh can suicide be so near
And the telephone's valence
Our teacher of reaching hills?
And can the policeman's villa
Ever pelt the other fellow
With the wallet of his stars?

In the reversed dream
Grandmother wore an owl; so that
Silver feet made my desk
A drama: then tiny golden snow
At tears, tears! you know collar
Which the windy tree wore. "O my
Reality!" the calm wind swears
Into that.

Long before I raided the ocean
And the leafage had swum
Away; when the broken Piraeos of a bell
Heavens and force. . . . O specks, and dog
"We brang." So their team bust me
In the will, "Frozen Bars,"
Oh way out beyond the leaving cars
Of stay-you-dogs-in-one-place!

# Poem

"Sweethearts from abroad," the madrigal
Sang. When I lay down to sleep
On the team, forest. Future, dear
Elision. Fame said, "She must be Latin."
Within these rooms camels may
Skim a future. Don't shed a tear
My damn darling, on the candle
Which he whom I hate carries. No,
Let him light the niece, sky
And heart picture. Phooey! ice
Below the tram with heaven
In my arms, who cares? a mouse or a dream
Lies waiting upon the divan
For weary to spend its pith
Dreams and calls! the intention
To die asleep, the expansion
Of a moment of inattention
Which an age of plagiarism can never evict—
Oh shame, dear stammered, snow
Where the little clubs are brilliant,
And the fanning park
In lover's track of clacked-up snow;
For mints, your clear summer
And my cold hair! the legs go better.

# Pericles

*Scene 1*

**FRIEND**
I stop and go, Pericles.

**PERICLES**
Because we have come to find this land

**FRIEND**
In the midst of truth,
climates, guitars

**PERICLES**
This breeze is smaller than my mouth

**FRIEND**
O Pericles
what is a leader?

**PERICLES**
How we have grown, dears, since we've been from Greece!

**FRIEND**
How tall a music

**PERICLES**
Lies wasting on the shore.

*Scene 2*

**ANOTHER MAN**
Here I sit.

*Scene 3*

A WOMAN
 Not that the gnat of smallness itself
 has anything to offer the beach
 with and through, without our tears
 as if some tea had raised a blind
 into the concussion of nonsense,
 and a coughing death.

 In Athens I saw twenty-nine old people
 and the sidewalk was faery.
 Oh everywhere the rats struck down ribbons,
 heaven. A slave ship hides my ears.

 O friends
 amid the fornication of signposts
 I saw a new Greece
 arise!


*Scene 4*

FRIEND
 You know. And yet
 he is bothered by the misery of pebbles
 which hat the lovely show
 in which he dies and does appear.
 He: "Take me back to the faucets
 of truth; my mind is a mass."

PERICLES
 Here is freshness and the shore's timeless teeth!


*Scene 5*

FRIEND
 There's no midnight mystery
 and no coconuts here to see,

nothing
but the ocean's sea
which will wash history's tattoos from me;
I hope to live satisfactorily
like a capon that's struck by a tree
and does die gladly
bereft, O large, of his sexuality.
Oh as honey fills the bee
while the waves' orchestra's business spree
sticks its night in your head like a country,
and as the madman throws the flea
to music, helplessly,
here always shall I be
and not in idolatry
but yet superfluous as a ski
in a barge; while the withered air
reduces baneful boughs to everywhere.

PERICLES
Good night, the parachutes have gone to sleep.

FRIEND
I stop and go, Pericles.

*Scene 6*

PERICLES
The air is Chinese!
I felt so strange
the day after tomorrow.
The stops have been removed
and the bottle is filled with leeks.
In the forest a sparring partner
whispers, "We grow."
O maidenhead of today
O maidenhead of yesterday

FRIEND
My lord, I found this face in the sand.

**PERICLES**
  Drop it!

**FACE OF ANOTHER MAN**
  Help!

CURTAIN


*Epilogue*


*(Spoken by the conductor of the orchestra)*

And would it not have been too late
The gas goes on the gas goes off
And we stood there with pure roots
In silence in violence one two one two
Will you please go through that again
The organ's orgasm and the aspirin tablet's speechless spasm.

# The Dead Body

If my entrance is winter,
You won't sunshine the blackboard
And ask the music loins for water—
Oh no, you wouldn't do that!
But if the flowers from outside
Reintegrated the sweet potato,
Then it began to hail,
A cow should lie down in the breezes.
I notice that your harvest
Is bitter. There are lilies
In steerage after the phonograph
Of this afternoon, which is hug me
Tight, ocean! Early in this day they
Met, now it is winter, the sun arcs
Like ruined laundry, a big
Guy, a sweet girl. The moon sings,
"I labeled two entrances beneath her sweater.
And there are two countries for mice.
Fourteen cellars give me cashmere,
Rome, lamplight, and steel.
Now I must go to sleep
Amid the strawberry camps of Morocco."
A stone answered the moon,
Saying, "You certainly make the phone ring
And sheet the town hall
In glorious light, but
Oh, moon, in what rig the trees are
Tonight." There were dancers and
Apples inside the helium observatory
And I again gave my hat
To September's leaning manners—
We sung the flutist, earlier than
The muddy leaves. Explosion happens,
And reminders, the easiest big
World, hobnobbing with the trees
Beside the dam-works. "Hoo hoo hoo,"
Sings the common, "no aviary
Am I." And my knee takes its photograph!
"Life proves nothing,"

Sings the lavatory, imbued with pavements
Of Stonehenges by silences
Which catalogue the rose's. Other playmates ripped out the pictures
And "drave" me my room's orange
To pin. "Open, heaven, their suits
And Chinas, for we are they, now
Especially, among earth's million limes."

# Asunder

Where were you when they handed out teeth?
I struck out in a season of baseball
Toward the legend of apples; I filled
The air with the china's whimpering. Duty
Romanced me through the inches of paper baskets
In the Sunday of charmed ceilings. Why won't you
Be kind? Because I am not here for this session.
I am dancing around a joy-filled coroner. The
Ablative case hates me. The hedges are freezing.
You would look nice in a wastebasket.

I came toward my darling last October
With cams and deceiving optional bracelets
Of sleepy light! She received as in bins
My nervous air of smiling as within her hand
Winter's begun! No, for that bitch in violets
Is britches in voices. Animals
Fill the fear, whose benign April will patch
The sea! Far better than ivory clothes!

2

Now it is Sunday and the leap year is over;
The Polish light is descending a mountain of lawyers
Named cattle, the march is saved
From last Juno ontology. Can the basin reciprocate
African harmony's sleepy films? Negative
Poseidon! O chows. They choose to eat sleepy plates
Of grand opera, times digressing natives,
In clockwork shoes, a medicine to shovel them violets
In the way good counsel cerebrates the scalding shore.

He is the comic fantastic
Tents. The bandleaders notice him
Through the saving brine. A dash of fishes
Summers him. He eats chemicals. They
Dash his bronco into the
Sea of soul confusion. The marginalia
Of his lungs!

What social force upon this easy doorstep
Can or may weather his hatless blimp?
I know you notice that these airy things
Are dogs.

Who heeds the flying violence
Of his pate, and the medicine
Of jam-filled violets, the traffic lights
Of lips?

# When They Packed Up, We Went

O candy Frigidaires, eagles, and paint boxes
Paints are not a loan beneath the Frigidaire. No, here's a pin
To wind some felonous hat-dog on; O sleepiness!
The fainting pine needles of racism oppress my box.
Fuss alone at the theater, maleficent fooeys
Of carolizing.

2

And divinely she gets up
And drives down
Into the bitterest theatres
Of leaves and in a frown
Chic races, mighty heart
Of hands into my tray
She sleeps at last
The acres man gives away.

3

O advancing negress of the moon, beer mug;
Heart without its paleness being entirely grown
Facile with inner meanness, casket filled with sloops,
Nut-head, I see there air eyebrows in your gown, Mrs.
Ann Ann Ann Ann Ann Ann Ann. Ann.

4

The hurricane sanctions him to death like the
Striptease of Lenin described by a leak!
Amidst the white blossoms of her first June growing

Down amidst his throbbing bosom with alacrity!
O the ash cans were foaming with crime! the sea
Was bright with your alimony and chivalry!


5


In the sight of your dagger I refused to fight calmly with myself, expecting
  the nurse of disreason to pick me up and throw me off the gangway,
  O specials! Night, a soda.
O faces, facts, nights on, under, there.


6


When the entrails of my really absolute calm
Seem the crying of my helmet, O-may-snow,
Take me to Texas, where the dogies weeping, "Midnight
Hurts your pants, to fight calmly, desiderata,"
Concentrates me on the deafness of "to go."
In Austin the steel diversity is beautiful
As the auctioning of chemistry sets; I nod
And fill the embarrasing night
With these replies, "I shall never go home in a sweater
And the damning first place
While the conscience reigns
In the trench; rats of Boston!"
A kindly white juror is safe as this bench, while
We sleep through town,
And the bargains go up—

O a great entertainer lies strapped to the down.


7


The dads came up from Boston
With violence in their hearing
And their navels labeled

"The people of Venice,"
And they swiftly ate the dabs
Of tootling disgust. Everybody yelled, "Dads
Are secrets!" and "Any boot
In a brain-stir," but the dads went down
Into the city of blue jeans
And calmness. When Death cried,
"Add!" they began to scream,
"Force, Junior!"; yet time is all.
And nobody kissed the dads
Saturday afternoon, Sunday, and
We spit into the endearing carnival,
Seasons and faces. . . .


8


O candy candy alligator charm
This Louisiana chain into the hall
Without a davenport,
But snow!

# Atlantis Was Original

Too fanned by so tomorrow's ink knot's weak purple
daisy ignorant fan club. He prowl. Pearl. Mid-
nights. Oh. She is, winking their ("Indians' ") fan club
apart. "It merely tempts me, Jason, my heart—" Bed of New Jersey,
and air ink of their clatter: "Mouses." "Breast." "Show
me into him there when all fan clubs start." Her agrees
finds he him as were went there. "My seams we're
every jersey. Silence. It is a purple knockout.

Because we came here, we did not expect to find perfect seasons
and rats raining, into the tunes of everywhere, by gosh!" Mentality
of a the Greeks' closing sentence. Tam to May, "Borrow!" It isn't.
Mighty. And than blue wests a swings gain neutrality, Oh Hen:
"Art eats waves. Gorillas arch coming. He: 'Widest imbecility
of hardest designs few three Mexico—I'm quiet, singable dodger.' Air is
    blind
but not the paw." He is heaving forward then from arrest's
big lozenge: "House, cool middle waking, drive nits and the turrets!"

The shops are comfortably free, and the licensee's net
is everywhere respected, orange paper packages and meant
speech, frowzily frozen, and beautifully free for the inspectors,
so neighborly, of buildings' China, magic ant! "Brings horse to me
lilac respectability jockey-mentioning, shirtwaisted front nylon
bed nicky intelligence. For each smooth occasion, why are you worried
about the railroads?" She sings in tights to the bed-away, rose,
and devilish fringes—Since action's frail in delightful forge her seat.

# Where Am I Kenneth?

## I

Nail Kenneth down
For I fear the crying bloomers
Of a gnome race
They come yessing among the trees
Like your Boston survivor
Nail Kenneth down

Pick Kenneth up
For it is necessary that the sun
Will be a comb of the blue trees
And there's no cough to race
The tumbling seething jenny
Pick him up, put him to work

Amid the freed trees. Is this Boston?
Look around you. Am I Kenneth?
"The changing sighs of her disgust,"
A young man said, "am blue-kneed dust."
Kenneth waddled into a store and said,
"Pick me up," and said, "Apples, down."

## 2

Beyond the costly mountains
Some pills are going to sleep
Frank will cover them with blinding bloomers
Janice appears from multiple nowhere
The sun was a hot disk
How do you spell "dish"?

"The young Ann falls off lie zoom
January ends a room
I am afraid life in a tomb,"

The Doc comes in, "Hi, disk."
"Halo Kenneth, the sunlight is a factory."

Nail Kenneth down
For I fear the shades have gone to sleep
Throw the windows, and hey!
Grace comes, it is a rabbit
A rabbit discovers the triumph's lips
And a tuneless campus is deader than ships


3


With the object of a displaced foot.
Kenneth is reading a novel
Nail us down
Skip the air
The sea is a ship,
And yet a ship of consultation!

So hail the words down, but lead in the air!

(Blue is the air above concentric Lambeth.)

# Without Kinship

*Somewhere on the lawn of Longfellow's House, in Cambridge, Massachusetts.*
*A nightingale leans over her ironing board.*

NIGHTINGALE
  It is small and white.

IRONING BOARD
  Over the pill and far away
  I hot a vision of white
  So mental, that where carpets kneel.

NIGHTINGALE
  Loon, pyramid, shine-shine,
  O bark that has suds, little keel
  In the gemlight, O bibarkcycle—

IRONING BOARD
  Am I then, lady's head,
  Which you have tied unto a knot?

PEBBLE
  Kenneth stands for constancy,
  Roommate for regret;
  Our Christian society for clemency
  To the dancing Sundays of seas' frenetic egret.
  Janice stands for Japanese
  Maple trees, which stream about this yard
  As though a mariner'd come here
  To find his ocean hard.

GIRL PEBBLE
  O Melvin!

PEBBLE
  Charmian!

*(They go together and form a driveway.)*

<br>

### Scene 2

*The Nurse.*

NURSE
These modern gems have laziness;
My hat is his. This Denver sun
Shines on and down
What grassy slopes?
Season! here is the soap factory;
There is the charged balloon.
My grandfather at eighty offered
The stanza a million dollars
That could make him feel as though
He were really a lagoon.
His face is now seldom
More than unscientific explanation
For a rug. Oh, carry me, impossible slug!

*(She lies down, too, and becomes driveway.)*

<br>

### Scene 3

*Roadway, driveway. PATIENCE and HANDY are in their car.*

HANDY
Harrisonville to Spokane
In nine thousand three hundred and sixty-seven
Days, it doesn't seem impossible!

PATIENCE
A storm moderates me this end.

NIGHTINGALE *(from below, as she and her ironing board are now part of the driveway)*
Gazing with hope

**PEBBLE**
This morning upon the

**NURSE**
Foolish capers in the sun

**GIRL PEBBLE**
I understood for the last time

**IRONING BOARD**
How the fan-shaped crisscrosses,
Which speak to everything, are done.

**FOOTBALL** *(comes flying through)*
I gave, for love, my terrifying heart.
Ah, that laughing, papery summer, when we kissed
The leaves of every down, that showed the field
A prayer, and at evening a park.

**HANDY**
Please, Patience, take this green dress!

**PATIENCE**
O branches! where is the collie of happiness?

**EVERYONE**
Woof! Woof!

# Everyone Is Endymion

1

For the two night of my tea nights
Rattrap shop
Hee, he: mouse, supper, and testament,
Column, laying abstractions,
Lemons, pyramid, algebra, and lids
A metropolitan oafness of labor
Fast adhering to light's zone
Asks you to be within socks on
By Rhone-light, a sea of custom
Landslides, fit and pains
Vastly: land, chiffon peanuts,
Nails, pirate, illness, pier-red parks.
She says, "You got me this way sobbing,
Yet all my finds have friends.
At least you can poach me."
Of constancy her landslide by hats.
Such ones met out with hearts
In my love's town, a kangaroo, an ostrich.

2

The blue beer of disunion
United their leading parts
In sanity, and "I" screamed,
"The housekeeper is wet paints
In cure
Crew," when death-adventurer came,
With bears, Afton, burning parts.

O sables, bedroom
Necklaces, and pinch, safe,
Lorry, billboard, asp, and faculty
Limpets, grass, laymen with coffee:
"Didn't we act stupid without our chairs
In the fashion, this afternoon,
Beneath the tree-bellows of everyone?"

# Gypsy Yo-yo

There are ban-dares of "lame" low
Beside "tree" entrance. Hint. Barricades
He ogle. Are the bleeding lifesavers?
Rent hippopotamus! Ave.
Talked savage. In
Says on emp. out
Care, as! bed; free auto tires
Coat, on'd am, O box "e'en" blouse.

# In the Ashes of June

I am waking off in the wooded arms apartments
Of cerebrating trees' bison. I think bicycle
No land. And the gypsy
Gives her knees. The sabbath is over. Choir is dog
Am in roses. Gene-harp I love you
Lanes, oh! more modern than Alaska. Entry
Is tree the strewn
Apartment-ships-bicycle.

Music everywhere bench with Betty
On it.
Paris of ragged sighs! Oh love
The boat. Anchorage. Sweetness. Cordwood. And banana
Sin tree sun tea marrying time
Egypt, interest. As in Havana
It as is as, sweet cigars and swift comment.

"Nary a one can go into the coo
Key clock." I live, I limp. She
Is has and does.
And there anything knows
Mutt; they whistle
"Science and basketball." Prey, parcels
When they "have freed" me.
Tonight. Goodbye. A lantern. Straight top hat.

# Is Nothing Reserved for Next Year, Newlyweds on Arbor Day?

The rosy future
Is a sled all the furniture
You brought inside
What about the whoopee
Flowers and the chief drops

Slide out the window
The vampire the vacuum cleaner
The pocketbook the rags
The rugs I am smiling dear moustache
You are a Chinese laundry

In a garden of orange snow
Nor mind how far the gables go
Neither the red honesty
Oh the music's children
The gun's original behest

I smashed him
Smashed
The dark and darling flowers grow
Behind the living bells
"A sled is all the furniture"

But isn't cups
Cuckoos and formulas
The very fallen street of nuts?
Yes, here's perfumes
Habeus perfumes! My house!

Once, hound street of doors
They said you threw
Eloping ripeness upon the air

O yes, within my sweater
The rosy future

It ripens like cabs
I hope cigars
The yessing nine of an event
For youthful love the oranges
And furies.

# Limits

And the chorus
Of "Wear purple gloves like a sundae"
Circumstances the Afghanistan flowers
The feet under the hue of
The mid-Atlantic,

She has a night simple face,
The accounting for Lambeth,
Lunacies in October,
He wears freezing, he walks writing;
"Your name is Lee

And yet my land
Is on your universe.
Should borrowing expire
And brightness exalt
You would be the campus-horse of sleds,

For whom, as yet, nothing goes on."

2

In the murdersome chorus lines of the snow
An entire bird fell biffing from off a tire;
I see her, old Amy, she puts out the fire
And the trees pull my wings to a celebration
Of almanacs, Rome-air-season, and saids:
"We live at the halt of the universe!"
Are the cups' song; and snowy dignitaries
Fall like laminated paper in wards
I find whims the hospital plate; lingering
To five string, as children-cool eat the climbs
Out Tohu Bohu, for things, in fears, for dogs.
Does anyone hear you smile? Eat the pears and peaches
That Father Ludwig counsels yesterday. Here

Is Firkwild Landing, a notification of stars
On deliberate space, and rational punitive ears
Of a delighted history because I love you.
She was standing beside him in radiance.
He thought, "How can I ever live?" And she,
"The uniform of the gladdest malt is its sureness."


3


Within a tumbling lake you ran brains behind the snow
As though chemise must capture Austria.

To know the symphony of calming death,
O poor weeping oblong!

As if to grow them, the freshness of a wheat
Or holiday dims a granary, the sweet oaf!

# Ohio

"Hi, you ant!"
So encouraged unsoaking bees
With fulfillment
Rosy bikes' age telephone if flowers
Havana-smoking wavy tube
In yo-yos' vicinity crush
Ape dash the wintry season.

"Theory were mentioned
Too bag."

Hispania homogenized
For ankle tablets' tall de-honey
(Inseminate!) Havre in crush wander a "Li"
Pore. Climate Junction.
Cow nigh oat sea estranged
Evening high vastness, laid Z,
In "wild pillow," bench-car mints.

# No Job at Sarah Lawrence

O woebegone snowflakes, a million cold tablets, alas! merry hat, merry
    commonplace, take place Nan marriage is show business
Parade grounds O peace, winter carriage ocean phenomena eagle rain
Banister. Shy people! Europe dent flake easily Montanas
Sherry. Leaf, O loom! seldom
Beside the Greekish wood
A normless kind sweeping dintless carriage
"Moften" would appear. She peaks
Grapes, lines! Man
Toppled, de oh ho yo ho, canary C-foot forests, at now
Oh, harbour; extra lines
Ring at tea foot and certain cows, Oh the bottom
Of a series! how green, camphor, foot ball, Elmer, sing, elbow, sand
    runners, Mediterranean
Armament of tea!

Long long ago, amid the coastlines' breastline magic
Slantline briefcase's
Sweetheart coop llama and sphinx production
O pagans! hear,
Whore, naturalism, simplicity, seduction, amphitheatre,

January, milkmen, hopelessness, and, stare!
Try idea, it is modern, cigars! If blankets
Mutter in cargo, defrayed chests'
Anagram, O coconuts, jujube, and lingo!

Lady, my jungle.
How fond you are of illness,
Elevation, comedy crash beep hooray
Call "ness," life. Sacrilege
Is gnome silver umpire tam, sin,
Sweet to you! Baden
Baden! Lily petals.
We.
Backed through Tulsa, wintry, China's, freshman
Whose queer remark on everything we noticed
Was "Comedy eagle January meditation forehead."
Weird freshman come true delightful rosy night

Sand jumping Samothrace. O peculiar! language,
Scat, rhumba, trireme, manx, silverware, hoop forget! Bogs
Ladylike as the "perfeeect" hornet! Carpet repairs! Oh!
Save me! logs, "hay-pron," forehead, -sail, oh, of slim

Calcium!

# Poem

Roof in me, tone-deaf flail!
Clubfoot, mirror, cacophony!
Orchestra of picture-mail
Seed catalogue of yellow finch-valentines,
Drive mirth to sleep! "Next time."

Four-eyes, November talk-boat!
Swift memory shale questioning
Steep Andes cough tic mentioning
Sabotage quiet pensioning skeet
Buffalo quack nimrod shoots vest key.

O nameplates, foreign till-bow!
Numbers of Crimean Sung
French dog shows' climate speak quietude
Froth Medici Ghent horses, O pock!
Sail me from cart, hooky, and sail!

# Sunshine on January 15

*"This is my hat's weather."*

Opponent disarm firearm
A halo of flowers
Dean London
An apple of early floors
To cope with
Our poor bridge of an
Army of hated flowers,
So goodbye to this environment!

I wish to remember
Their falling fur coats
Whose hair was "too anguished
To limit" the crime wave
Of teased bodies
My loss helps you
Into a hen
And the cheer confabulates once more.

# The Kinkaid Subway

O corpse of March! in my ranch
Automobile subtitles. Ranches reply
Ranches apes to angels,
"Ha ha boxes of apes!" Railings
That lift up to the beautiful city
Apes the tree-bout's limitations for
Niceness ankles ankles today
Soon day. O boxed cool breeze! Mex-
Icans! "I love to climb that valley up in hill
To what oh
Peacock slays then cuckoo hat."
But we met on the open street
If Paris, near the breaking of lemons
Riot. A room. "Bake home," sang the wry weather;
"Yes" is what the went-title said.

"Good morning," sang the Swedish substitute, "at last
The title of drinking water is when
The apple of formlessly crying today
Kenneth sunrise." O about! movement
Ship-easing rags! "I clank," sheep-
Hooded then fire methods, oh! Arch
Of banking! "Wade in minutes," she cried—
Ink peroxide-machine May love you
Doughnut, the Kinkaid Subway,
"Goodbye, goodbye." Music. And then snow.
Oh sing! "His shore finally sees
The angry radiator—back lots ink famous!"

# Guinevere,
# or The Death of the Kangaroo

*Scene: a street, a plaza.*

GUINEVERE
O solids!

GIRAFFE *(moving along the sidewalk)*
Yes, and you know, last evening there were junctures
of drunken breath's dear pink flowers on my lariat.
He put around me. They said, "Denmark and the
vitrines! nameless one!"

WEISSER ELEFANT *(crossing the street toward the GIRAFFE
at right angles)*
I remember.

GUINEVERE *(sings)*
With soles on her shoes,
She takes the gyroscope
Between her fingers,
And, quietly, it spins.

KANGAROO *(waiting at point where the paths of the GIRAFFE and
WEISSER ELEFANT cross)*
The. Oh the the. The. I gave the pillow a cussing sandwich. America
said, "A tree." The manager lay dead. Cuff links.

GIRAFFE *(pausing)*
Listen, darlings, don't be so sassy. Do you remember when Chicago was
only fingertips?

ALL *(sing)*
Though circumstances may collect our iced man!

MAN *(who enters)*
Unpin these benches that you may descry
The leafs beneath them. Lovers know my voice
As that which is or was most at the docks
Before they stopped shipping roses to say *"vivre,"*

O macadam. A child sicklier than restaurant
Waits for the marrying blue of a stiff morning.
We seem to go to run about in a stiff roustabout,
Cuter is the pear of string. Common last touch
Is to die at the nest. Roommate, charm bracelet,
Oh I swear, this is Mexico City.

CHIEFTAIN

He is falling toward me like the charm bracelet
I saw laughing out of the window. At this minute a giraffe
Knows the cow who is offering night my atlas.
The wind, curving from Chinese charm bracelet
To charm bracelet, seems to counsel me, "Dollars,
Feenamint, dollars, gun smoke." After one night
With Dolores, I visited the Huguenot people.

CAPTAIN

Anchors aweigh!

(The plaza with all its occupants floats away; VENUS rises from the waves.)

VENUS

Listen. Listen to the bouquet.
Baby, that placing powder in the pistols,
Married, and placing pistols in the bouquet,
Left me to be long ago at this moment,
Lively the goddess, a headache. A market
Of fleas!

(It is Paris, a Place. VENUS disappears.)

FIRST FLEA

Let go of my left elbow.

SECOND FLEA

That's your potbelly!

A PINK GIRL

I chanced to find these two
Arguing. There were sadly smoke,

Giant cow-guns, shoguns; and, it appears,
A glass page blonder as a neck of blue jeers.

GIRAFFE AND VENUS *(entering together)*
Aren't we a stray couple
From No Land? Oh when
Will catching diseases fly in our plane?

PILOT
Never! Take everyone a box.

*(He passes out little boxes, which, when they are opened, reveal white pieces of paper.)*

WEISSER ELEFANT *(reads)*
"The bench you are sitting on is made of orange boa constrictors which have been treated with piratical chocolate Georgia-bannisters. The Maryland of your face. Despite what you have been, ho ho, the incinerator is not a call girl. Depart before the ice cream melts." Mine is about food!

GUINEVERE *(throwing herself on WEISSER ELEFANT):*
O my lover, my lover!

PILOT
Wait a minute. Read yours.

GUINEVERE *(gazes into VENUS's face)*
"Your head may be paralyzed by lint." Orchids! buzz saws!

ORCHIDS
This is not blood. This is an orchard
Through which you may walk. Like a bug.

BUZZ SAW
Everybody: one, two, three!
Plywood!
Goldsmith!
Sunglasses!

*(The plaza splits in two like an orange. WEISSER ELEFANT eats half of it. On the other half, Guinevere is playing a guitar to the KANGAROO, and playing cards are falling from his pocket. In the slight breeze one can just make out the chorus of neckties. It seems as if the Old World has become the New. A MOUSE enjoys this séance.)*

MOUSE
God plays the guitar
And Religion listens.
The weary squash
Lurks beside the lotus.
See! the glass buildings
Decide nothing.
We are the sobbing world,
Just as they are in the nude.

GUINEVERE *(very loud)*
Photomatic bad living
Gigantic prisms. Beaued. Gee. Leaves!

KANGAROO *(softly)*
Pretty Geneva, pretty Southland, beloved orchestra!

GUINEVERE
I am pink in the nude.

KANGAROO
Yes yes.

GUINEVERE
O Joy!

KANGAROO
Listen. Baccalaureate. Is that
Prometheus?

MAN *(wearing a large mouse head and playing the guitar)*
Only in the bathroom, knees would care
And the table of good red air
Seriously affronts the car
With the yellow daffodils of today.
Somnolent I see an amethyst

Clearing the way for future
Eons, the ragged hoop
And the dippy Fragonard of fluffier days,
Played to the tune of our pablum violin.

GUINEVERE *(throws herself, kissing, against a statue)*
O you, concede that I am the airport!

MAN WITH MOUSE HEAD
America is like an elephant whose baseballs
Are boundaries
Of sunlight. This is peppermint,
That billiard shore. Now she gets,
Like horror, the main idea, a stove that is
Brilliant as the curling raspberries and move to his heart.
O olives, I know your reputation for fairness,
And every pipe dreams of a shirtwaisted kimono
Beyond the callow limousine of the funnies; but Nugent
Drank the Coca-Cola, and Allen left the boudoir
Where Jane lay down like a saint, the music of a thumb
Daring the elate, childless strings.
O mothers, weevil, marketplace of the Sixties,
What is the road to Gary, China?

GUINEVERE
Should industry delay,
Or mice parade? Is that a youth group
Singing: "Daft, weird, kind pennons,
Yo-yos and hills, shirts and displays"?

MAN WITH MOUSE HEAD
O Germany of sofas,
Are we so clear
As beer is harmless?

GIRAFFE
A shoplifting land of railroad pyjamas
Passed my door, evil film stars.
Huguenot! evil girls of film-star plantation!

HIPPO
Yes because we meant to spend the summer;

But now we see the human element
Is merely a white bear, tipping stars
By the briefcase of a violet hand
Meant to inform and believe concatenated
The surface of a wheel-lake or *morgen*
Meaning *morning* in German. Yes I meant
To thumb a ride along the Champs Elysées,
But the sunny Negro
Of handsome stars
Bid for the fingers of my door, and lo! I lay,
The Hippopotamus, sweating as if funny
Water may come true even in the summertime
And—

(*Bang! The HIPPO falls dead.*)

SOMEONE
Pure Pins the Lobster!

(*YELLOWMAY comes in and takes off all Guinevere's clothes; GUINE-VERE puts her clothes back on.*)

GUINEVERE
The shortest way to go home yesterday
He always called the best way.
There's no suffering in a limeade
Of clearer captains, carpenters, and shipwrights
From grains solidly
In the pier. Oh the white shore, the red sea—

(*YELLOWMAY takes her hand; they walk along the seashore.*)

YELLOWMAY
And the works of pineapple.
I have often been a shipmaster
But never a ship. The blow from Tangiers
Never came.

GUINEVERE
Soldiers waiting at my hammock
Counseled me, "Be as back as soot."
Oh nuts, the chairs have gone away.

YELLOWMAY
Paintings of the sea, I won't reveal to you my name is Yellowmay.

MAN *(without the mouse head)*
Or the lobster
That oval
Which I often noticed.
I think,
"Is this a cigar
Or, baby! maybe
The license for a white cigarette,
Given by the shields."
And when the frog becomes a bicycle,
Dear days of pineapple,
Lilac where the giant ripple
Rushes, as past a kangaroo.

KANGAROO
O mournful existence within a matchbox
With a sullen cockatoo
Whose brain beats its own division
And dandy "wawa"—

OCEAN
Oh Sweden is endless! the earliest time to drink.

YELLOWMAY
Are we drinking in chairs like a column?

GUINEVERE
Oh yes, master. Come jinx with the merry columbine!

*(Suddenly it is spring. The HIPPO appears solus, covered with garlands of flowers.)*

HIPPO
Decency of printemps O
Knocks on my pillow!
Houses without a door!
Suitcases which miss my sleeves!
O bears, you, too, on the misty shore
Of the sea, in whose elbows

I hear a moth beginning
To mourn on a blue, beautiful violin.

*(The SKY descends, covering all with blue; from the empty stage comes a song.)*

VOICE FROM EMPTY STAGE
Who cares about them
In a grouping again
Or the poking amethyst
And delicious anthem?
The bread in the butter box
And a dictionary—
The day fears to tell me
Of white screams. Oh, don't you know it,
The marriage of blue-
Bells, America, generous, as white screens
Failing, the magazine basement
Of archways. Water
The generous magazines!

Summery blue daylight
The manner of machines,
Daguerrotype, cigarette store.

*(The dead body of the KANGAROO is dragged across the stage by a two-horse cart.)*

# The Cat's Breakfast

Air-front days

O cardinal the red robes of an angel
Are falling off the winter too
In the season of are we I ate fist
True hail! the sigh's blue
Wheat, wheat
Whose clothes are stationed mines
A lost canals of love

Through reading dance
But where the event's lust
Did not begin quietly, does
Answer on my toes
Winter, weights, seepy ties

Writer, sandbaggery, troths
Freeze the painter
Hams' collectives'
Summers' tunes' qualities

As we are. Nights.
Heat hums, "Airway the madman
Comes: 'too,'" so wish we advance.

# Your Fun Is a Snob

Amnesty store by the facing machine
In the winter of glove
Raiding Western minutes
She spoke low, as a dram,
"On the hinge of a dainty glue
Hundred daisy become a fox
Listen, to what these pinstripes bore
A sin from firewood, up this day
Stump, wheat, end! at my mule team passes
In with love Death Valley."
Through, goodbye mainland!
"These tears, I'm stacking way,"
She whirling smiled, "goodbye," is the plan
Of aspen rain-tinned sunlight, on, "ahem!"

In the next minute the feature is oh
I am backing, science
Halve the apple, plates, come, too.
She is reading in her silk stocking,
La la: "I've got a famous apartment
In cooking. Religion
In the worst ways, that leaves to the basement,
What I know
The handmade height is made you
Is fun, but your fun is a snob."
Agrees, to walk out, illness, the wax taxis,
Reading, "Hopeless mints of lead. . . ." So her
Shy lends night, a helpless manner
Without, in leaflets, to within, often "we're," the crib.

# The Merry Stones

*Scene 1*

*A room in a house by the sea. ROY, a young man, is lying in bed. INGELIL, a young Swedish nurse, is standing at the bedside.*

INGELIL

Lay down and be slumbering. A cabinet is kind. The
music is full of fishes. Have some liberty. Eat colds.
Don't be neglected. Board up the hose. Thank the rip-
tides. Lose collectedness. Break, break the ramps.

ROY

I went to smiling wrists.

INGELIL

Govern the deciding wasps. Age new badness. Sign
Lohengrin. Be out on the Caspian.

ROY

Locks were coming in bananas.
Furniture is necks.
Sacrilege is leaning on tiny horse.
A lamprey, oh, has begun to kiss
The sea.

INGELIL

Use the deigning colors of this cabinet for your windows; only don't,
when the winter comes, complain of the cannon-fare of the horses; for
as surely as hay is tucked into the orphan straw, time will have guess his
last lust in the ephemeral killing bottle. I am a laziness that comes from
a nuttier country; I see to not understand your flailing indecrepitude.
May the blue star of yesterday pink its liberal summit to that head, this

yours, which, like a revolvement, fats the walls with lowing circumvention. Oh, goodbye, normal!

ROY

Farewell, moral, and may the neckerchiefs of humming be kind cousins to your gloom. The illiterate flowers are incompatible with shows.


*Scene 2*

*A room. JIM, a young man, is lying in bed.*

JIM

If I should die, myself,
Give me the wallpaper
And wrap me up around the ceiling,
As if sky to an ornament.
Oh how fitting is my known
Beneath the dense whack of the sheet;

If mattress covers in truth
Were known, ah, steel would be riven!
But I am back to my back
On flowers, like the Chinese river
Sink-you-and-go-long-go-she-go,
And music is everywhere.
I wonder if this knife
Would not slay me like an imbecile
If I let it fall, down snow-light
In registered rocks from here—

*(He seems to stab himself.)*

Oh, lie steep as a swan!
Exaggeration of comments, then help me!

## Scene 3

*A bare stage.*

MASTER OF CEREMONIES *(about forty-five years old)*
Here are the starriest chain-waving starvers
That ever an eyeball sees, O chasing frankness with sleds!

*(Exit M.C.)*

FIRST SHOWGIRL
I am the music bell of doughnuts, ruthful ball,
Beds at night in the Sierras, the beach of brass
That an annoyedly soft breast dims,
And my revealing counsels are foolish with sonnets.

SECOND SHOWGIRL
The least of time's molluscs, and last of the golden hinters
Am I, come down to Seventieth with my scants on!
I am teas
Without formulas! London!

THIRD SHOWGIRL
I am the bashful banditress of beans,
Irritants, Coca-Cola, and steaks.
I lie beyond the built-in Sierra of plates
To see our cares mated to a roach in oblivion!

MASTER OF CEREMONIES *(reenters; he is much younger)*
So seize your hats,
Be merry as a phone,
And cry out at the graying night,
"Oh thou high pajama of happiness!"
Last week
I felt it know you care so cold.

*In the Sierras.*

ELDERLY MAN
  A season is my birthright; for which reason
  Winter is very indebted to hats. We are
  Condemning you to
  Breath under water.

BOB
  But I am a mountain lad! my whole bearing and being
  Calls out for freedom from Fordham.

ELDERLY MAN
  Nevertheless, go under;
  And when you rise, the flowers of heat
  Will open your eyes,
  And you shall see this Sierra
  As the beautiful door to the bust
  Of the highly chlorinate female wind
  Who hides the masculine hills in her boxes;
  The magic of forceful steam
  Will be yours, and the shying parts of airplanes,
  The linked romance of degustation
  And paralysis, to lie on, in the nights of tragic green.

BOB
  I am asea with lust!

ELDERLY MAN
  Yet no more forgotten
  Than a cast-iron ring.
  We are bored by the midday of flowers,
  The Romeo riling amid the wildflowers,
  And the beggar the boar smiling into the flowers.

*Scene 5*

*A hotel room.*

AL *(a young husband)*
   There is another scene than this hotel room!
   Where the boy tries to take his life!
   O monsters, my wife!

NELLIE *(his wife)*
   He is walking the floor in rings!
   I once saw a Swedish stand amid the flowers and throw blood upon
   dancers, while sick man, roving up on the bourgeoisie, held in his hats
   the swan of their hands, as though a telephone rings.

*(Ring. It is a doorbell. Enter BOB.)*

NELLIE *(Throws her arms around AL.)*
   Did you send for the bugles of Lancaster?

# The Days to Solve

There are empty cars of an absolute beauty
Waiting for me beneath the dress
Of day. The lion has shaved,
And hell is willing,
O affair O affair!

Acting summer removes the disk
Of lilac stupidity.
There are sharp reeds in the city
For disintegration.
I watch a love fall. Hills!

Master Chicago! oh the sunlight in milk
Of parenthood! When vichy threw out
Its arrival to blossom saint
And froze the radios like backs
Of cigarette-bards,
Champagne-leaves, Pepper Martin
And true-loves, auto gypsy
Of the ceiling-sink to the Rome we cut
In starlight, delicately alone
Like flag-boys, meeting after sound
Had turned the head blue!

May the gross air be
Sonnet! O bigness!
Grape ships!

Den of mines, use,

There is not a taint on her foot
Made by an it or a madman
Often flowers and shoes' remedy—
Million. Foe in act's hire!

The bread is beautiful beneath the sunlight
Easily medley deep at silence
Sews. As the air is right
By hit's orange graph.

# En l'An Trentièsme de Mon Eage

O red-hot cupboards and burning pavements, alas it's summer my cheeks
    fall into somewhere and alas for the Rainbow Club.
Flowery pins bluejay introspection anagrams. On this day I complete my
    twenty-ninth year! I remember the lovely margarine
And the ack-ack of the Chinese discomfortable antiaircraft bullets
    shouting into the clay weather like a beachball in *Terry and the Pirates,*
A canoe in shorts, or a laughing raincoat of Bessemer steel. What
    lightness it is to be still
Here, among the orange living, like a spine faculty in the harvest diversity
    cup, a red Chinese giraffe that imitates a rose
Like a lover of steel mittens in collarbone harness time, blimp-lovely, and
    hooky players in the green shark
Museum, the sand everywhere around, forming a coat for the naked
    pencils; the last laugh is on me, says air—
O spring! no, summer! O winter!

The coconut magistrate adopted my little sister, "Cousin."
She had always wear a green sweater and toy play in the sybaritic air.
I am trying to clean up the loft, I can do it a lot easier, with blue air
And red seagulls and green crashes. "Cousin" was put among the simple
    cases,
And when she came to see me (that was during my sixteenth summer), I
    said,
Cousin are you glad to be home? and she handed me a lime swimmer.
Boys often ask me my advice on how they can become more sensitive
To orange wagons sunning themselves beside green curbstones, but
    "Cousin" said,
Take this lime advance. Shoe box. We are swimming toward a coffee
    aspirin tablet.
I didn't know what it meant at the time; and when "Cousin" was packed
    away
With the other Christmas ornaments, she asked me once more, California
    lime Swinburne?
But Mother and I laughed at her little cookies and went home. What does
    it mean?
"Chorusgirl" was the name of a dog I had aged seven. I kept him until I
    was nineteen. In nineteen forty-four he reappeared as an ancient cook.
    But one could see the laughing young eyes beneath her (his) gray hair.

And then I touched Coffee Silverware in the Park on her lime-colored
   shoulder, and we kissed
After eating close to a million hamburgers, and drinking bourbon out of
   little hollow glass trees.
That was the advantage of living close to Kentucky! The sedge
   laboratories closed down over New Year's
Day, so Kent and I had to search the barnyard for a light blue accident
Machine; he went to Texas in the same year and founded a shortage
   hospital
Of pure ice, toward which lovely secret purple ladders fell. I sandwiched
In seeing him while I was canoeing through there in the army. Our
Regimental insignia was an ordinary, clean polar bear looking at the sun
As if he were surprised to be in a war. . . . To not hear coconut music
Was all right, but once I did . . . ! O dreams! O nostalgia! A campus of
   cotton roses to detach my wristwatch
Was my dream, and matchsticks the color of yellow real estate, with white
   bearskin gloves
To hold a pink apple! It took place on a bed in New York, a rich
   neighborhood, O coffee-covered sentimentality!

What is your knowledge of the novel? is it happy? are you trying to cover
   up for the green ants? When will the popcorn graduate? The peach's
   mother and father came down to the wedding in fuzz.
Grasping for the boat rail, I inquired after "Cousin" and was showered
   with green lemons. I didn't know you were in love with her! I said to
   Raspberry Corpuscle. He shoved me out into the water.
Amid this blue clothing was I dying or living? how old was I? I had not yet
   published "Fuel Bedrooms," so let me see. . . . Nancy's hands were
   covered with glass sandwiches. She offered me seventeen. I said,
   They're green! She said, Gondolier!
The towers fell down. Mr. Howard, Mrs. Raspberry. Rosemary Character
   Study was holding the candy door wide open for me. . . .
Clean up the happy boats, my son, for we're going to take a vacation
   manuscript. Doctor "Raspberries" to tell me I'm crazy still in the future
   like a white plywood
Airplane. But Jane bought paints! We fractured the coffin-balloon. She
   wore a redbird hat. Alice favored the Cubs. Together they fought with
   tinfoil spoons. A glass of beer-water please!

September. The red photograph-milkmen's clay hods
Plant sybaritic green clay roses through the center of Cow

Museum. "Peanut" arrives in a fur coat. Some more clay?
No thank you, I have to miss the detestable passenger plane
Of agoraphobic candy, which thousands consider a Mississippi
Hairline. Isn't it customary to Presbyterian Hospital? Larks in a motor.
Water, water, water! Heavenly December. O my sovereign, the railroad
    illness!
Aerate the detached choochoo! The leaves fell, greener than grass-
Colored leather. Can I sell you the wheels, sweet European doctor?

Argentine. Italy. Cairo. Myopia. *The Last Supper*. My twenty-sixth
    birthday.

Nudity Silex Kleenex bells June the Empire State Building.
Do you remember France? Can ants be a peasant? When did the daughter
    of Wendell Willkie walk like green lipstick toward the frogs?
Oh why is the weather no signal of gloom, sweet February twenty-
    seventh? The restaurant would not serve licorice, you remember,
To persons under the age of five, and still I love news! Sweet music of
    cement,
Am I a has-been? What? The water is feeling very pretty and green. The
    gunpowder is coughing beside the submarine archway
Of my twenty-ninth birthday, sea lion, cloudburst November! Did the
    bullfrog say he had something he wants to celebrate? Well, come on!
We can't stand here forever smoking bumblebee cigarettes!

# The Man

PENIS

Dancing away from your cars by the frond of the sea I live;
The ramparts are pure rectitude: cut parachutes and deep-sea powdered
    sugar,
A fine run in the silence of the rain—


ARM

          O blue cosmos
Run and financier! Why, there is a France of my up-and-at-them tomb,
A lemon-ray of surreptitious canal sound
Which hops into a series of helpless land.


MIND

I am the mind, dazzling mind reader
Chorus girl in frame-ups landslider
Definition by teacups heavier
Than your Pompeii.


FINGERS

Shorthand the substitute ring me a rose panorama
Climbing western and shirt helpless
The beachless cat. Tomorrow containers!


FOREHEAD

Ocean of Nibelungenlied! Romulus
Satie Mellon canard shoeflex Greene
Dairy farmer. Virus.

NOSE

Oregon bell and carpet.
Leftover silverness. A bell. In a carpet.


EYE

He walks to containers. When the dancing tulip overflows.
The restaurant's a son today. It is sun today.
We throw its overwhelming into the free top that overflows
Blue, violet, purple, everything, the Caribbean ovaries.


OVARIES

What is it? Why am I here?


WRIST

A longer knee events will stop confines orange
Orchestra chocolate logy and snuffly contagious cough.
Reference.


TIBIA

When the foreleg is blue
Covering the lanternslides with fluff country
Panoramic Canada seventieth
Catalogue white swans beer barrel publishing mouse ditch
Wristwatch.


KNEE

With fennel pals the ranch.
The best nights in Arabia. Cotton punches. Rearward actions.
Possibilities will not grumble toward the cheated giraffe
Quietly bursting the cactus with tweezers of cherries,

Just as I cannot remember my norm.
Was bent like this? and is unlike this? Cardboards
Jinglebells and playing cards,
Showing bleachers in light glass.


## KNUCKLES

The benches have always been auctioned.


## SPINE

The backache penny come niche a lesson
Boa constrictor easel pretzel nylon preaches ruffles
Dance elevators less and more dark
Sassafras relieves me foghorn parenthood quietly duck
Penniless master and a nincompoop hallway
Which seasons come into and look.


## HEART

Leopard spots. Why not be a dancer?
Trim summer. Is the hookworm conceived as a relative?
Bust the ocean. In Canada when they say "opera," she brings the nurse.
When silence intimidates the two opium eaters. Rats' legs for breakfast.
Tar and feather the oak tree's builder. Let your mind wander.
Over there. In all kinds of weather. Candy strips them. He builds a glider.
The bell-buoy is a captain. Hate the ocean's builder.
We scream to the sun for kindling wood. Suzanne ignites.
Listen when they say "The peach is hollow"
Because they're lying. Speak of the Renaissance. Describe the feeling
    beneath five layers of snow.
When you are in Romania, be facetious. And they will love you there.
Office furniture. Sailboat's blue mints. Calico shovels. Evening and
    Ireland.
See me handspringing my lookee breast of copper!
The larks bring me,
The dazzling earth has wended

Sunder. I ate lunch in the popularity engine.

She passed the benches. A dog raffle just ended. Your song can't feel the motor. The referee has overalls.

Marching beside me I felt that breast of onion!

Looking into the trees. The afternoon was a sundial. Our wheels came, too.

Suddenly my answer was changed: the shooting lemons ate whiskey a sheep gave a hornet publicity! an architect fell from his office!

Chloroform sat sweetly amused: O ranch houses of green snow

Lectures, castles and rotations. Luminous yet fearless bevel,

What are we? You white bowlegged valleys! I am the happy rose

The working classes have arisen like bright

Seals, and burned the ships whose dark

Indications of blood swing cars by a mere nostalgic smell. Weaken, distinctions,

While passionate light

Darkens the formations. There is a pig on the fortifications.

Remember the star of Bethlehem? Cut dead the commander of the root.

Stand on this pier. Summer now brings its roomy cathexis.

By night the elephant is heard, and by day the water. Now it is day, she must depart. That way they hear nothing. It is a concert.

From far over the desert a crocodile begins. When they called on one another last Easter, it was a rooster. Now a carpet begins to unfold for them.

She wants to be the first. He watches her like a cicada; and when he is no longer interested

The waters flee with them like sundials. The green cities sit down and laugh. To grieve in that climate!

He gives her a pair of angels. They vanish like originals. All is dark . . .

But last summer, I swear,

I heard a voice saying, "Blundering

Coma dancing wild ineptitude, seriousness cars delve orange white

And mother-of-pearl kimonos bleeds delight.

Investing aorta kimono suttee's quietness healthy pianos

Nought handles them for me like shoes."


TEETH

Coldly the knife is Montana

## TORSO

Run by the rink lace

## HIPS

Orchestra when foetal ice

## THIGH

Carnival handball football millionaire
Yes I gave all my gold gives to
The chest, the shoulders, the armpits, the ears, and facial hair

## EAR

We hand together

## FACIAL HAIR

Love and laughter

## ARMPIT

The Earth Mother of silent things

## TOE

Bastinado potato

## SHOULDER

Boiling

## PALM OF THE HAND

Lobster scenario


## HEAD HAIR

And can't one gold give will not
Ecstasy domino shoe foot quiescent


## REAR

Not to banister forever and ever the bare


## SKULL

Rusting of hennaed springtime
Into an act the foot
Wills?


## THUMBNAIL

Yet how can we be silent . . . ?

*The Chase—First Day.* This poem was inspired by the chase for the white whale in *Moby Dick.*

*Highway Barns, the Children of the Road.* "Barns" in the title is, of course, to be read also as "bairns."

*Ellie Campaigns After a Candidate's Defeat.* Ellie goes on campaigning even after Adlai Stevenson's defeat in the presidential race of 1952. "Elecampane" is a sweetmeat and stimulant sometimes referred to in pre-Elizabethan plays.

*Poem/"Sweethearts from abroad."* The "locale" of this poem is the Cedar Bar on a winter night in 1953.

*Pericles.* This play was inspired by a John Cage concert downtown, I think at the Cooper Union, at which the conductor decided to repeat Cage's piece (which was full of silences).

*Guinevere, or the Death of the Kangaroo.* The subtitle is a sort of echo of Hemingway's *Death in the Afternoon.* The Weisser Elefant is from Rilke's poem about the merry-go-round. The Mexican and animal-killing ambience of the work was the result of a short trip I made to Mexico while writing *When the Sun Tries to Go On.*

*Where Am I Kenneth?* Janice in this poem is my first wife, and Frank is Frank O'Hara; "Lambeth" is probably there because the dance "The Lambeth Walk" was popular at the time.

*No Job at Sarah Lawrence.* In 1953 I was looking for a teaching job. This poem was written in response to my failing to get one at Sarah Lawrence.

*The Kinkaid Subway.* The poem seems at least partly about the power of having one's own private subway.

*Your Fun Is a Snob.* The scene is a friend (the painter Jane Freilicher) standing next to a cigarette machine on Third Avenue on a winter day.

*The Man.* I didn't exactly write this as a play—there are no stage direc-
tions—though I can imagine it as one. I was intrigued by the idea of each
of the parts of a person having its say—in the case of the heart, a rather
long one.

# THANK YOU AND OTHER POEMS

# On the Great Atlantic Rainway

I set forth one misted white day of June
Beneath the great Atlantic rainway, and heard:
"Honestly you smite worlds of truth, but
Lose your own trains of thought, like a pigeon.
Did you once ride in Kenneth's machine?"
"Yes, I rode there, an old man in shorts, blind,
Who had lost his way in the filling station; Kenneth was kind."
"Did he fill your motionless ears with resonance and stain?"
"No, he spoke not as a critic, but as a man."
"Tell me, what did he say?" "He said,
'My eyes are the white sky, the gravel on the groundway my sad lament.'"
"And yet he drives between the two. . . ." "Exactly, Jane,

And that is the modern idea of fittingness,
To, always in motion, lose nothing, although beneath the
Rainway they move in threes and twos completely
Ruined for themselves, like moving pictures."
"But how other?" "Formulalessness, to go from the sun
Into love's sweet disrepair. He would fondly express
'Rain trees'—which is not a poem, 'rain trees. . . .'"
"Still, it is mysterious to have an engine
That floats bouquets! and one day in the rear-vision
Mirror of his car we vowed delight,
The insufficiency of the silverware in the sunlight,
The dreams he steals from and smiles, losing gain."

"Yet always beneath the rainway unsyntactical
Beauty might leap up!" "That we might sing
From smiles' ravines, 'Rose, the reverse of everything,
May be profaned or talked at like a hat.'"
"Oh that was sweet and short, like the minuet
Of stars, which would permit us to seem our best friends
By silver's eminent lights! For nature is so small, ends
Falsely reign, distending the time we did
Behind our hope for body-work, riding with Kenneth."
Their voicing ceased, then started again, to complain
That we are offered nothing when it starts to rain
In the same way, though we are dying for the truth.

# Summery Weather

One earring's smile
Near the drawer
And at night we gambling
At that night the yacht on Venice
Glorious too, oh my heavens
See how her blouse was starched up.
"The stars reminded me of youse."
"His lip sticks out. His eye is sailing.
I don't care what happens
Now," she says,
"After those winters in Florida!"
As for a pure dance
With oranges,
"All my factories
Need refilling,"
The corpse said, falling down between them.
"Okay okay
Here's a banana and a bandana
The light on a bright night,
With which, to finish, my personal challenge."
Oh how she admired him!
Lovely are fireworks;
Given, the shirts have a sale
To themselves; but
The wind is blowing, blowing!

# The Brassiere Factory

Is the governor falling
From a great height?
Arm in arm we fled the brassiere factory,
The motion-boat stayed on the shore!
I saw how round its bottom was
As you walked into southern France—
Upon the light hair of an arm
Cigar bands lay!
I kissed you then.  Oh is my bar
The insect of your will?  The water rose,
But will the buffalo on
The nickel yet be still?
For how can windows hold out the light
In your eyes!
Darling, we fled the brassiere factory
In forty-eight states,
Arm in arm,
When human beings hung on us
And you had been arrested by the cloths
Were used in making, and I said, "The Goths
Know such delight," but still we fled, away
Into a dinner atmosphere
From all we knew, and fall asleep this day.
O maintenance men, with cruel eyes,
Then arm in arm we fled the listless factory!
The music changed your fingers' ends to pearl,
I punched you, you foolish girl,
For thanks to the metronome we got out alive, in the air
Where the sun filled us with cruelty!
There's what to do
Except despair, like pages! and laugh
Like prawns, about the sea!
Oh arm in arm we fled the industry
Into an earth of banks
And foolish tanks, for what bare breasts might be.

# The Bricks

The bricks in a wall
Sang this song
"We shall not fall
The whole day long
But white and small
Lie in abandon."

Then the fair maid
Passed with her love
And she to him said,
"There are stars above
Where they have been laid
Let us lie in abandon."

Then the wolf came
With his teeth in abandon
And the lion came
With his teeth in abandon
And they ravaged and he came
To the white stone

And he kissed the field's grass
And he lay in abandon.
"I forget if she was
Or he was the stone
Or if it was the animals,"
And, "Everything comes soon."

# January Nineteenth

I

Houses do not fail to sing in a ghostly way among themselves.
"I felt foolish in the fishmarket of white horses." "She hands me the
    pleasant nucleus."
"The French parliament have grouped themselves around silence." Yes,
    the houses sing!
"The ear sails itself into the wintry custom of door telephones!" Wintry
    lake!
Bassinets leak through the covers of ice-dripping magazines
Of Clark Bar kindness, in the midst of Romeo My Telegraph Street. Like
    a wheel of cigars
Unfinished by Perseus, the coconut bra parts with chilblains
The unbanished sidewalk, where secret members of the Tear walk.
    O boisterousness!
"She wears a tiara of idleness, she has cocoa on her chair-bonnet;
Each of her children is worth sixteen dollars a million, her hat is in
    Nebraska;
Her feet are in South Fort Worth, Texas, and the ale manufacturers
Are agreed to cut criss-crosses in green upon the lilac statue of her
    milliner—"
So—"my strength."
"The cheerleaders have penciled the bathtubs with the words 'Maine
    State'
So as not to be bothered by her prettiness, her booths have become a
    sidewalk, her eyes a dove
On the cover of Plinth Magazine, and her groceries the weather
In red and green; the weather is costly and marvelous!" The shoe slips,
    and the eye comes, off,
But the basket of circuses is still free on the arm of the sanctified circus
    deliverer,

Whose swift speeches cancel our leaves for seventy weeks. "Bakery of
  coffee gloves!
Oh Lorna Doone fizzled the dazzling icicle-pencil
By sheer blue shirts." My hill! "Let's turn to the pathway of potatoes!"


2


Buttes-Chaumont pleased Aragon; the fire department say, "Flint is our
  religion."
The bone Andes are still pledging facial Switzerland to Peruvian intestinal
  prisms
Too coffee-like to replace the face; but then that tissue paper is their
  business. Our replica
Of all this is the sunset, a basilica of friendly brassieres—
The government of Switzerland may not be overcome by gonorrhea!
Finland wants "boats." The sheep want to go to Finland.
"Sand will not make you a very thrilling overcoat," the house said to me;
Our peach tree sat down. "Chalk was dreaming of the lightning and
  thunder."

The hilt of the swords! the hilt of the swords!
The sheep tree, the lightning and thunder!
Powder writes another novel to itself:
Passengers, adroit pyramids, and blue triremes!
Oh how I hate to "Gogol"! Now, baby sweater!
The Green Cab Sighs have fallen in love.

# Desire for Spring

Calcium days, days when we feed our bones!
Iron days, which enrich our blood!
Saltwater days, which give us valuable iodine!
When will there be a perfectly ordinary spring day?
For my heart needs to be fed, not my urine
Or my brain, and I wish to leap to Pittsburgh
From Tuskegee, Indiana, if necessary, spreading like a flower
In the spring light, and growing like a silver stair.
Nothing else will satisfy me, not even death!
Not even broken life insurance policies, cancer, loss of health,
Ruined furniture, prostate disease, headaches, melancholia,
No, not even a ravaging wolf eating up my flesh!
I want spring, I want to turn like a mobile
In a new fresh air! I don't want to hibernate
Between walls, between halls! I want to bear
My share of the anguish of being succinctly here!
Not even moths in the spell of the flame
Can want it to be warmer so much as I do!
Not even the pilot slipping into the great green sea
In flames can want less to be turned to an icicle!
Though admiring the icicle's cunning, how shall I be satisfied
With artificial daisies and roses, and wax pears?
O breeze, my lovely, come in, that I mayn't be stultified!
Dear coolness of heaven, come swiftly and sit in my chairs!

# To You

I love you as a sheriff searches for a walnut
That will solve a murder case unsolved for years
Because the murderer left it in the snow beside a window
Through which he saw her head, connecting with
Her shoulders by a neck, and laid a red
Roof in her heart. For this we live a thousand years;
For this we love, and we live because we love, we are not
Inside a bottle, thank goodness! I love you as a
Kid searches for a goat; I am crazier than shirttails
In the wind, when you're near, a wind that blows from
The big blue sea, so shiny so deep and so unlike us;
I think I am bicycling across an Africa of green and white fields
Always, to be near you, even in my heart
When I'm awake, which swims, and also I believe that you
Are trustworthy as the sidewalk which leads me to
The place where I again think of you, a new
Harmony of thoughts! I love you as the sunlight leads the prow
Of a ship which sails
From Hartford to Miami, and I love you
Best at dawn, when even before I am awake the sun
Receives me in the questions which you always pose.

# Aus Einer Kindheit

Is the basketball coach a homosexual lemon manufacturer? It is suspected
  by O'Ryan in his submarine.
When I was a child we always cried to be driven for a ride in that
  submarine. Daddy would say Yes!
Mommy would say No! The maid read *Anna Karenina* and told us secrets.
  Some suspected her of a liaison with O'Ryan. Nothing but squirrels
Seemed to be her interest, at the windows, except on holidays, like Easter
  and Thanksgiving, when
She would leave the basement and rave among the leaves, shouting, I am
  the Spirit of Softball! Come to me!
Daddy would always leave town. And a chorus of spiders
Would hang from my bedroom wall. Mommy had a hat made out of pasty
  hooks. She gave a party to limburger cheese.
We all were afraid that O'Ryan would come!
He came, he came! as the fall wind comes, waving and razing and swirling
  the leaves
With his bags, his moustache, his cigar, his golfball, his pencils, his April
  compasses, and over his whole
Body we children saw signs of life beneath the water! Oh!
Will he dance the hornpipe? we wondered, Will he smoke a cigar
  underneath eleven inches of ocean? Will he beat the pavement
Outside our door with his light feet, for being so firm? Is he a lemon
  Memnon?
O'Ryan O'Ryan O'Ryan! The maid came up from the basement, we were
  all astonished. And she said, "Is it Thanksgiving? Christmas? I felt
A force within me stir." And then she saw O'Ryan! The basketball coach
  followed her up from the cellar. He and O'Ryan fight!
No one is homosexual then! happily I swim through the bathtubs with my
  scarlet-haired sister
Z. ("O women I love you!" O'Ryan cried.) And we parked under water.
  Then, looking out the window,
We saw that snow had begun to fall, upon the green grass, and both shyly
  entered the new world of our bleached underwear. Rome! Rome!
Was our maid entertaining that limburger cheese, or my mother? has the
  passageway fallen asleep? and can one's actions for six years be called
  "improper"?

I hope not. I hope the sea. I hope cigars will be smoked. I hope it from
   New York to California. From Tallahassee to St. Paul.
I hope the orange punching bag will be socked, and that you'll be satisfied,
   sweet friend. I hope international matrimony, lambent skies, and "Ship,
   ahoy!"
For we're due to be dawned on, I guess.

# Spring

Let's take a walk
In the city
Till our shoes get wet
(It's been raining
All night) and when
We see the traffic
Lights and the moon
Let's take a smile
Off the ashcan, let's walk
Into town (I mean
A lemon peel)

Let's make music
(I hear the cats
Purply beautiful
Like hallways in summer
Made of snowing rubber
Valence piccalilli and diamonds)
Oh see the arch ruby
Of this late March sky
Are you less intelligent
Than the pirate of lemons
Let's take a walk

I know you tonight
As I have never known
A book of white stones
Or a bookcase of orange groans
Or symbolism
I think I'm in love
With those imaginary racetracks
Of red traced grey in
The sky and the gimcracks
Of all you know and love
Who once loathed firecrackers
And license plates and
Diamonds but now you love them all
And just for my sake
Let's take a walk

Into the river
(I can even do that
Tonight) where
If I kiss you please
Remember with your shoes off
You're so beautiful like
A lifted umbrella orange
And white we may never
Discover the blue over-
Coat maybe never never O blind
With this (love) let's walk
Into the first
Rivers of morning as you are seen
To be bathed in a light white light
Come on

# In Love with You

O what a physical effect it has on me
To dive forever into the light blue sea
Of your acquaintance! Ah, but dearest friends,
Like forms, are finished, as life has ends! Still,
It is beautiful, when October
Is over, and February is over,
To sit in the starch of my shirt, and to dream of your sweet
Ways! As if the world were a taxi, you enter it, then
Reply (to no one), "Let's go five or six blocks."
Isn't the blue stream that runs past you a translation from the Russian?
Aren't my eyes bigger than love?
Isn't this history, and aren't we a couple of ruins?
Is Carthage Pompeii? is the pillow the bed? is the sun
What glues our heads together? O midnight! O midnight!
Is love what we are,
Or has happiness come to me in a private car
That's so very small I'm amazed to see it there?


2


We walk through the park in the sun, and you say, "There's a spider
Of shadow touching the bench, when morning's begun." I love you.
I love you fame I love you raining sun I love you cigarettes I love you love
I love you daggers I love smiles daggers and symbolism.


3


Inside the symposium of your sweetest look's
Sunflower awning by the nurse-faced chrysanthemums childhood
Again represents a summer spent sticking knives into porcelain
    raspberries, when China's
Still a country! Oh, King Edward abdicated years later, that's
Exactly when. If you were seventy thousand years old, and I were a pill,

I know I could cure your headache, like playing baseball in drinking-
    water, as baskets
Of towels sweetly touch the bathroom floor! O benches of nothing
Appear and reappear—electricity! I'd love to be how
You are, as if
The world were new, and the selves were blue
Which we don
When it's dawn,
Until evening puts on
The gray hooded selves and the light brown selves of . . .
Water! your tear-colored nail polish
Kisses me! and the lumberyard seems new
As a calm
On the sea, where, like pigeons,
I feel so mutated, sad, so breezed, so revivified, and still so unabdicated—
Not like an edge of land coming over the sea!

# Poem

And so unless
I'm going to see your face
*Bien* soon
What's the point in everything
Going on this
Way like a chimney
Or a pint of marriage a
Western carriage
Cold and drear
Like an Afric foe
Whose stretcher bearer
Is starving while
Feeding him greens?
Yesterday you said
Today you'd say
If tomorrow has
Gone to bed (as in Proust)
Because of the rings
And the lilac weather
Of a gift;
You promised, as
The stars were
Green and blue
Points, a red and white gift; yesterday,
As I say, it was all very
Clear; and yes glitters
Upon the carriage
In green briars
And modesty, not
A baby carriage! I wish
Tears, together,
South, university, winter—
Not: jesting with
Summer, very free. I know.
I know it is white than
When hourly the grape undone

By fox's gift; and
Then too you must know
It's not really
The faculty for wishing
To stone me with paper—
Here's a kiss from today

# Farm's Thoughts

Hay, passion stilled the
Cool and charming disk.
Straw, I know you think I'm rude
And yet it's true: the sun's wrong.
How sweetly the weeks turned
The whole month of September.
Do I believe in you?
Does the rye believe in you?
The sunlight will last all day.
Rye, I think you are mistaken
There. Straw, kiss me. Never, hay.
The sunlight may go wrong
And create a wilderness; a wilderness
Will never create hay. Back me up, then—
The elements create a waterfall.
With vim and vigor, straw,
To avoid being stern I'll
Catapult past the green fruit
Fallen beside honor's mesh. Fresh
Green lives seem to spawn there.
The sun shines down through
Violet-besprinkled fields;
Dawn acts with a club, and we agree on everything
Long beforehand. It's the dew, hay . . .

I am the horse, alive and everything.
On the merry-go-round I made you happy as anything.
In these harvest fields they kick my body like a plaything.

I am the panther, soda fountain of the zoo;
I will represent exoticism here on the farm with you.

I am the elephant, the last laugh of hips.
I land smiling from an Africa of ships.

Near the dirt door, on the road to the farmhouse,
Please pick me up, hold me in your hands, a chicken! not a mouse,

Not a chipmunk, not a lizard, not a cow . . .
Sherbet dreams of me in winter: dairy cow.

Mother farmhouse, residual axis,
Please hear the mushroom phantom sweet
Queer clear voice of the dog-sweets
Left abandoned by a rigorous monster after . . .

Let not civilization enter! Green, draw the curtain.

Morning sweetly shines down on us pigs.
In the afternoon when the rake separates
Diet from dust, the friendly germ will separate some of us
From each other, and heads will be laid in earth.
The best thing a pig can hope for is sun.
When, shyly, in the morning, heads come forth
From the sty, we believe in everything
The air sets forth—mud, green, and trees—if the sun is shining;
If not, then it's a day like any other, a finger stuck in the earth
Like smoke, and the cold breeze of the mud, the deadly hammer
Crashing our skulls for the unreciprocating worm.

In the headlands we heard a murmur. It was the goats! We, the goats,
Wish you, Barbara and Mitchell, a happy stay on the farm.
Drink plenty of goat's milk every morning
And you will grow big and strong
Like the clouds over Mount Sinai, when Moses stood there.
We goats know our Biblical history!
Here is a red-and-blue book in which you can read
About China, and the opera in the Romance countries. Be kind
To goats, and always remember to speak in the morning
Nicely to one another, so as not to ruin the day,
Which might otherwise be spent in cursing and thrashing
As the farmer sometimes does, your Uncle Peter;
Then he kicks tin cans and pulls the beards of us goats.
It is only our love of this environment which helps us to bear
Him. We've never been anyplace else. And we send you a
Kiss.

The horses are real, Mitchell! Oh, what fun we'll have!

Get those goddamn children out of the kitchen, Uncle Lillian,

Or I'll grind them up and feed them to the pigs!

The horror of night
Descends on the cottage,
And only the goat-hair
Is visible, gleaming in the starlight.
The hay is silent. The meadow is overturned,
And the green
Where the children play
Is also the pigs' thatched cottage
Where they roost
In peace and seem
To cry past the straw and the rye to abandoned goodness,
Which is really only another word for
Feathers . . .

      Hi! Kra! Kray! Croak!
Creek! Creek! Fresh water, bleep,
Another day. Haul off and chicken
Every chicken, to chicken chicken, sorrow-pigs!

Filmed in the morning I am
A pond. Dreamed of at night I am a silver
Pond. Who's wading through me? Ugh!

I love you, hay.

I love you, straw.

And so I am the sun.
Don't you wish it about everything?

The pavement that streams past you on the wall.
My laughter is inherited from you all.
The yellow leaves and the green ones know my will.

I am the barefoot hill.

Mitchell, we'll go barefoot.

Hurry into me, the sweet day.
O leaves, can't you find another environment?

Something befriends me and hurts
At the corners of each thing I love.

It looks beautiful out.

Well, to be honest, as the color green,
I can only gather it all in once more and then let it out; this shall be seen
At the end of your stay. Something grows up to become a concert,
And at last the world finds him, the color grey
Accedes to red; and at the lost inn, where many pigs
Have stayed, the doorknobs when they're blue are stones;
In the midst of yellow a word may drop
Which brings it orange.

I am the color blue, on a board in the room.

Bzz, buzz, what beautiful shirttails!

Oh how through the air my beloved Master Bee sails!

# Geography

I

In the blue hubbub of the same-through-wealth sky
Amba grew to health and fifteenth year among the jungle scrubbery.
The hate-bird sang on a lower wing of the birch-nut tree
And Amba heard him sing, and in his health he too
Began to sing, but then stopped. Along the lower Congo
There are such high plants of what there is there, when
At morning Amba heard their pink music as gentlemanly
As if he had been in civilization. When morning stank
Over the ridge of coconuts and bald fronds, with agility
Amba climbed the permanent nut trees, and will often sing
To the shining birds, and the pets in their stealth
Are each other among, also, whether it be blue (thhhh) feathers
Or green slumber. Africa in Amba's mind was those white mornings he
   sang
(thhhh) high trala to the nougat birds, and after
The trenches had all been dug for the day, Amba
Would dream at the edge of some stained and stinking pond
Of the afternight music, as blue pets came to him in his dreams;
From the orange coconuts he would extract some stained milk,
Underneath his feet roots, tangled and filthy green. At night
The moon (zzzzzz) shining down on Amba's sweet mocked sleep.

2

In Chicago Louis walked the morning's rounds with agility.
A boy of seventeen and already recognized as a fast milkman!
The whizz and burr of dead chimes oppressed the
Holocaustic unison of Frank's brain, a young outlaw
Destined to meet dishonor and truth in a same instant,
Crossing Louis' path gently in the street, the great secret unknown.

The fur rhubarb did not please Daisy. "Freddie," she called,
"Our fruit's gang mouldy." Daisy, white cheeks with a spot of red
In them, like apples grown in paper bags, smiled
Gently at the fresh new kitchen; and, then, depressed,
She began to cover the rhubarb with her hands.


4

In the crushy green ice and snow Baba ran up and around with
   exuberance!
Today, no doubt, Father and Uncle Dad would come, and together they
   three would chase the whale!
Baba stared down through the green crusty ice at the world of fish
And closed his eyes and began to imagine the sweet trip
Over the musky waters, when Daddy would spear the whale, and the wind
Blow "Crad, crad!" through Uncle Dad's fur, and the sweet end
Of the day where they would smile at one another over the smoking
   blubber
And Uncle Dad would tell tales of his adventures past the shadow bar
Chasing the white snow-eagle. Baba ran
Into the perfect igloo screaming with impatience, and Malmal,
His mother, kissed him and dressed him with loving care for the icy trip.


5

Ten Ko sprinted over the rice paddies. Slush, slosh, sloosh!
His brother, Wan Kai, would soon be returned from the village
Where he had gone . . . (Blue desire! . . . )


6

Roon startled her parents by appearing perfectly dressed
In a little white collar and gown.

Angebor lifted himself up so he might stare in the window at the pretty
   girl.
His little hands unclenched and dropped the coins he had saved for the
   *oona*.
He opened wide his eyes, then blinked at the pretty girl. He had never
   seen anything like that.
That evening, when it whitened in the sky, and a green
Clearness was there, Maggia and Angebor had no *oona*.
But Angebor talked with excitement of what he had seen, and Maggia
   drank *zee'th*.


7


The little prisoner wept and wailed, telling of his life in the sand
And the burning sun over the desert. And one night it was cool
And dark, and he stole away over the green sand to search for his parents.
And he went to their tent, and they kissed him and covered him with
   loving-kindness.
And the new morning sun shone like a pink rose in the heavens,
And the family prayed, the desert wind scorching their cool skin.


8


Amba arose. Thhhhhhh! went the birds, and clink clank cleck went
The leaves under the monkeys' feet, and Amba went to search for water
Speaking quietly with his fresh voice as he went toward Gorilla Lake
To all the beasts. Wan Kai lifted his body from the rice mat
When his brother Ten Ko came running in. "They have agreed in the
   village,"
He said. Win Tei brought them tea. Outside the rain
Fell. Plop, plop. Daisy felt something stir inside her.
She went to the window and looked out at the snow. Louis came up the
   stairs
With the milk. "Roon has bronchitis," said the American doctor,
"She will have to stay inside for ten days during this rain." Amba
Sneaked away, and wanted to go there again, but Maggia said he could not
   go again in this rain
And would be sure to lose the money for the *oona*. Baba stared

At the green and black sea. Uncle Dad stood up in the boat, while Baba
Watched Father plunge his harpoon three times in the whale. Daisy
  turned
Dreamily around, her hand on her cheek. Frank's boot
Kicked in the door. Amba wept; Ahna the deer was dead; she lay amid her
  puzzled young.
The sweet forms of the apple blossoms bent down to Wehtukai.
The boat split. Sun streamed into the apartment. Amba, Amba!
The lake was covered with gloom. Enna plunged into it screaming.

# The Circus

1

We will have to go away, said the girls in the circus
And never come back any more. There is not enough of an audience
In this little town. Waiting against the black, blue sky
The big circus chariots took them into their entrances.
The light rang out over the hill where the circus wagons dimmed away.
Underneath their dresses the circus girls were sweating,
But then, an orange tight sticking to her, one spoke with
Blue eyes, she was young and pretty, blonde
With bright eyes, and she spoke with her mouth open when she sneezed.
Lightly against the backs of the other girls waiting in line
To clock the rope, or come spinning down with her teeth on the line,
And she said that the circus might leave—and red posters
Stuck to the outside of the wagon, it was beginning to
Rain—she said might leave but not her heart would ever leave
Not that town but just any one where they had been, risking their lives,
And that each place they were should be celebrated by blue rosemary
In a patch, in the town. But they laughed and said Sentimental
Blonde, and she laughed, and they all, circus girls, clinging
To each other as the circus wagons rushed through the night.

2

In the next wagon, the one forward of theirs, the next wagon
Was the elephants' wagon. A grey trunk dragged on the floor . . .

3

Orville the Midget tramped up and down. Paul the Separated Man
Leaped forward. It rained and rained. Some people in the cities
Where they passed through were sitting behind thick glass
Windows, talking about their brats and drinking chocolate syrup.

## 4

Minnie the Rabbit fingered her machine gun.
The bright day was golden.
She aimed the immense pine needle at the foxes
Thinking Now they will never hurt my tribe any more.

## 5

The circus wagons stopped during the night
For eighteen minutes in a little town called Rosebud, Nebraska.
It was after dinner it was after bedtime it was after nausea it was
After lunchroom. The girls came out and touched each other and had fun
And just had time to get a breath of the fresh air of the night in
Before the ungodly procession began once more down the purple
    highway.

## 6

With what pomp and ceremony the circus arrived orange and red in the
    dawn!
It was exhausted, cars and wagons, and it lay down and leaped
Forward a little bit, like a fox. Minnie the Rabbit shot a little woolen
    bullet at it,
And just then the elephant man came to his doorway in the sunlight and
    stood still.

## 7

The snoring circus master wakes up, he takes it on himself to arrange the
    circus.
Soon the big tent floats high. Birds sing on the tent.
The parade girls and the living statue girls and the trapeze girls
Cover their sweet young bodies with phosphorescent paint.

Some of the circus girls are older women, but each is beautiful.
They stand, waiting for their cues, at the doorway of the tent.
The sky-blue lion tamer comes in, and the red giraffe manager.
They are very brave and wistful, and they look at the girls.
Some of the circus girls feel a hot sweet longing in their bodies.
But now is it time for the elephants!
Slowly the giant beasts march in. Some of their legs are clothed in blue
    papier-mâché ruffles.
One has a red eye. The elephant man is at the peak of happiness.
He speaks, giddily, to every one of the circus people he passes,
He does not know what he is saying, he does not care—
His elephants are on display! They walk into the sandy ring . . .

8

Suddenly a great scream breaks out in the circus tent!
It is Aileen the trapeze artist, she has fallen into the dust and dirt
From so high! She must be dead! The stretcher bearers rush out,
They see her lovely human form clothed in red and white and orange wiry
    net,
And they see that she does not breathe any more.
The circus doctor leaves his tent, he runs out to care for Aileen.
He traverses the circus grounds and the dusty floor of the circus entrance,
    and he comes
Where she is, now she has begun to move again, she is not dead,
But the doctor tells her he does not know if she will ever be able to
    perform on the trapeze again,
And he sees the beautiful orange and red and white form shaken with
    sobs,
And he puts his hand on her forehead and tells her she must lie still.

9

The circus girls form a cortege, they stand in file in the yellow and white
    sunlight.
"What is death in the circus? That depends on if it is spring.

Then, if elephants are there, *mon père*, we are not completely lost.
Oh the sweet strong odor of beasts which laughs at decay!
Decay! decay! We are like the elements in a kaleidoscope,
But such passions we feel! bigger than beaches and
Rustier than harpoons." After his speech the circus practitioner sat down.

10

Minnie the Rabbit felt the blood leaving her little body
As she lay in the snow, orange and red and white,
A beautiful design. The dog laughs, his tongue hangs out, he looks at the
  sky.
It is white. The master comes. He laughs. He picks up Minnie the Rabbit
And ties her to a pine tree bough, and leaves.

11

Soon through the forest came the impassioned bumble bee.
He saw the white form on the bough. "Like rosebuds when you are
  thirteen," said Elmer.
Iris noticed that he didn't have any cap on.
"You must be polite when mother comes," she said.
The sky began to get grey, then the snow came.
The two tots pressed together. Elmer opened his mouth and let the snow
  fall in it. Iris felt warm and happy.

12

Bang! went the flyswatter. Mr. Watkins, the circus manager, looked
  around the room.
"Damn it, damn these flies!" he said. Mr. Loftus, the circus clerk, stared at
  the fly interior he had just exposed.

The circus doctor stood beside the lake. In his hand he had a black
  briefcase.

A wind ruffled the surface of the lake and slightly rocked the boats.

Red and green fish swam beneath the surface of the water.
The doctor went into the lunchroom and sat down. No, he said, he didn't
   care for anything to eat.
The soft wind of summer blew in the light green trees.

# The History of Jazz

The leaves of blue came drifting down.
In the corner Madeleine Reierbacher was reading *Lorna Doone.*
The bay's water helped to implement the structuring of the garden hose.
The envelope fell. Was it pink or was it red? Consult *Lorna Doone.*
There, voyager, you will find your answer. The savant grapeade stands
Remember Madeleine Reierbacher. Madeleine Reierbacher says,
"If you are happy, there is no one to keep you from being happy;
Don't let them!" Madeleine Reierbacher went into the racing car.
The racing car was orange and red. Madeleine Reierbacher drove to Beale
  Street.
There Maddy doffed her garments to get into some more comfortable
  clothes.
Jazz was already playing in Beale Street when Madeleine Reierbacher
  arrived there.
Madeleine Reierbacher picked up the yellow horn and began to play.
No one had ever heard anything comparable to the playing of Madeleine
  Reierbacher.
What a jazz musician! The pianist missed his beats because he was so
  excited.
The drummer stared out the window in ecstasy at the yellow wooden
  trees.
The orchestra played "September in the Rain," "Mugging," and "I'm Full
  of Love."
Madeleine Reierbacher rolled up her sleeves; she picked up her horn; she
  played "Blues in the Rain."
It was the best jazz anyone had ever heard. It was mentioned in the
  newspapers. St. Louis!
Madeleine Reierbacher became a celebrity. She played with Pesky
  Summerton and Muggsy Pierce.
Madeleine cut numerous disks. Her best waxings are "Alpha Beta and
  Gamma"
And "Wing Song." One day Madeleine was riding on a donkey
When she came to a yellow light; the yellow light did not change.
Madeleine kept hoping it would change to green or red. She said, "As long
  as you have confidence,
You need be afraid of nothing." Madeleine saw the red smokestacks, she
  looked at the thin trees,

And she regarded the railroad tracks. The yellow light was unchanging.
    Madeleine's donkey dropped dead
From his mortal load. Madeleine Reierbacher, when she fell to earth,
Picked up a blade of grass and began to play. "The Blues!" cried the
    workmen of the vicinity,
And they ran and came in great numbers to where Madeleine Reierbacher
    was.
They saw her standing in that simple field beside the railroad track
Playing, and they saw that light changing to green and red, and they saw
    that donkey stand up
And rise into the sky; and Madeleine Reierbacher was like a clot of blue
In the midst of the blue of all that sky, and the young farmers screamed
In excitement, and the workmen dropped their heavy boards and stones in
    their excitement,
And they cried, "O Madeleine Reierbacher, play us the 'Lead Flint Blues'
    once again!"

O railroad stations, pennants, evenings, and lumberyards!
When will you ever bring us such a beautiful soloist again?
An argent strain shows on the reddish face of the sun.
Madeleine Reierbacher stands up and screams, "I am getting wet! You are
    all egotists!"
Her brain floats up into the lyric atmosphere of the sky.
We must figure out a way to keep our best musicians with us.
The finest we have always melt into the light blue sky!
In the middle of a concert, sometimes, they disappear, like anvils.
(The music comes down to us with sweet white hands on our shoulders.)
We stare up in surprise; and we hear Madeleine's best-known tune once
    again,
"If you ain't afraid of life, life can't be afraid for you."
Madeleine! Come back and sing to us!

2

Dick looked up from his blackboard.
Had he really written a history of the jazz age?
He stared at his television set; the technicolor jazz program was coming
    on.
The program that day was devoted to pictures of Madeleine Reierbacher

Playing her saxophone in the golden age of jazz.
Dick looked at his blackboard. It was a mass of green and orange lines.
Here and there a red chalk line interlaced with the others.
He stared attentively at the program.

It was a clear and blue white day. Amos said, "The calibration is finished.
  Now there need be no more jazz."

In his mountain home old Lucas Dog laughed when he heard what Amos
  had said.
He smilingly picked up his yellow horn to play, but all that came out of it
  was steam.

# Collected Poems

### BUFFALO DAYS

I was asleep when you waked up the buffalo.

### THE ORANGE WIVES

A mountain of funny foam went past.

### GREAT HUMAN VOICES

The starlit voices drip.

### COLORFUL HOUR

A few green pencils in a born pocket.

### EXPRESSION

New little tray.

### SLEEP

The bantam hen frayed its passage through the soft clouds.

### A MINERAL WICK

Town soda.

### SOMEWHERE

Between islands and envy.

CECELIA

Look, a cat.


THE SILVER WORLD

Expands.


JEWELRY SEVENTHS

Minor wonders.


AN ESKIMO COCA-COLA

Three-fifths.


THE EXCEPTION PROVES THE RULE

Eight-fifths.
Nine-fifths.
Three-fifths.
Six-fifths.


THE WATER HOSE IS ON FIRE

Grapeline.


THE LINGERING MATADORS

Eskimo City.


EGYPT

Passiveness.

IS THERE A HOUSE INSIDE THAT FUEL ENGINE?

Extra aging will bring your craft over against the rosy skies.


WHY WEREN'T THEY MORE CAREFUL?

Actions.


PEANUT BUTTER CANDY

Ichthious.


THE BRINDLE COWS

Dairy farm, dairy farm,
H-O-T
H-E-A-D.


IN THE MERRY FOAM

Ask them for the blue patience of lovers.


MY MIXUP

The cherries after a shower.


MILKWEED EMBLEMS

The chambered nautilus is weak.


SUPPOSE

Red and white riding hoods.

**THE GREEN MEDDLER**

Aged in the fire.

**A HOUSE IN MISSISSIPPI**

Who stole all my new sander supplies?

**WICKED OBJECTS**

Aeroliths.

**FRESH LIMES**

A couple's bedroom slippers.

**THE WINDOW**

The chimney.

**PAINTED FOR A ROSE**

The exacting pilgrims were delighted with yellow fatigue.

**NOONS**

Bubbles.

**ROOMS**

Simplex bumblebees.

### IN THE RANCHHOUSE AT DAWN

O corpuscle!
O wax town!

### THE OUTSIDES OF THINGS

The sky fold, and then the bus started up.

### THE BLACK LION

Never stop revealing yourself.

### IN THE COAL MUD

At breakfast we could sob.

### THE HAND-PAINTED EARS OF DEATH

Oh look inside me.

### ALABAMA

Alabama!

# Pregnancy

Inside the pomegranate is the blue sky.

We have been living out the year in Wisconsin.
Sometimes it rains there—tremendous green drops!

We smiled up at the snow—how tremulously! Still . . .

Death is better . . .

The hog leafed through the almanac.

If there is a difference between fortune and misfortune
Which you do not catch immediately, just remember
The house of the orange and yellow squirrels, or the three pigs,
Any house which has easily distinguishable animals in it,
And remember that all animals are unfortunate.
"Yet every animal is fortunate," spoffed the mineral water
From its light green bottle on the Western tea leaves store shelf.
A bossy cow came and stood in the door;
Her hide was mangy. And then we saw the fire extinguisher. Man is
    unhappy!
A Western boy came and took the bossy cow away.
The Western boy was dressed in leather knickers, and his lean face was
    brown;
A smile played there as he looked at the sissy flowers
And led the bossy cow away to the range. In the cow's mind, pastures of
    green
Were replacing the brown architecture of the store.

Under the archways I could see the yellow pulverization
Of all you had meant to put into Paris—but they were a failure,
Your statues! your stores! and your triumphal arches!
You should have put in mere little shops selling dry goods and trumpets,
With here and there a tree and a necktie, the arch of someone's foot
Who turns out not to be beautiful, but extremely civilized, and a
    showerbath, which turns red

On certain nights, showering the green busses of my favorite city with
    cold blood! Oh ask me again
What you should do, and I will tell you differently! Ask me!

Shall any laundry be put out to dry
With so many yellow and orange sequins falling through the air?

Yes, the donkey has become very corpulent.

Will the blue carpet be sufficiently big to cover the tennis court?

Down the street walked a midget. "She's a good looker, hey?"
He said to a passer-by. O tremulous stomach!

We've been spending the winter in Paris . . .

It rains on the sweater . . .

I've a dog in my stomach!

The dogs moved delicately
On the yellow squares,
And if they sat down to play cards
Weren't they happier than we are?

I am at present owner
Of a great chain of dog-supply stores,
So naturally I hope that your child is a dog . . .

O son! or daughter!
Will you ever forgive
Your maddened daddy
For imagining a doggie
In place of a baby?

Out on the range
The blue sky is changing
To black, and the baby

Cows are rehearsing
Their lives by eating.

Near a blaze of straw
Sit the drooping cowhands;
One has on a red hat,
The other has a blue one.
They look at the babies and mothers.

Do you not think they are thinking
Thoughts like mine? O Paris,
France! with the coffee of your
Cafés, I feel life has arrived
For me! Where are you, city?

It rains on the dachshund
And the collie;
On the beach the red, green, and orange
Crustaceans are moved . . .
Tell me, sons of Atlantis, what will happen next?

# The Artist

Ah, well, I abandon you, cherrywood smokestack,
Near the entrance to this old green park! . . .

*

Cherrywood avalanche, my statue of you
Is still standing in Toledo, Ohio.
O places, summer, boredom, the static of an acrobatic blue!

And I made an amazing zinc airliner
It is standing to this day in the Minneapolis zoo . . .

Old times are not so long ago, plaster-of-paris haircut!

*

I often think *Play* was my best work.
It is an open field with a few boards in it.

Children are allowed to come and play in *Play*
By permission of the Cleveland Museum.
I look up at the white clouds, I wonder what I shall do, and smile.

Perhaps somebody will grow up having been influenced by *Play*,
I think—but what good will that do?
Meanwhile I am interested in steel cigarettes . . .

*

The orders are coming in thick and fast for steel cigarettes, steel cigars.
The Indianapolis Museum has requested six dozen packages.
I wonder if I'd still have the courage to do a thing like *Play*?

I think I may go to Cleveland . . .

*

Well, here I am! Pardon me, can you tell me how to get to the Cleveland
  Museum's monumental area, *Play*?

"Mister, that was torn down a long time ago. You ought to go and see the
  new thing they have now—*Gun*."
What? *Play* torn down?
"Yes, Mister, and I loved to climb in it too, when I was a kid!" And he
  shakes his head
Sadly . . . But I am thrilled beyond expectation!
He liked my work!
And I guess there must be others like that man in Cleveland too . . .

So you see, *Play* has really had its effect!
Now I am on the outskirts of town
And . . . here it is! But it has changed! There are some blue merds lying in
  the field
And it's not marked *Play* anymore—and here's a calf!
I'm so happy, I can't tell why!
Was this how I originally imagined *Play*, but lacked the courage?

It would be hard now, though, to sell it to another museum.
I wonder if the man I met's children will come and play in it?
How does one's audience survive?

*


Pittsburgh, May 16th. I have abandoned the steel cigarettes. I am working
  on *Bee*.
*Bee* will be a sixty-yards-long covering for the elevator shaft opening in
  the foundry sub-basement
Near my home. So far it's white sailcloth with streams of golden paint
  evenly spaced out
With a small blue pond at one end, and around it orange and green
  flowers. My experience in Cleveland affected me so
That my throat aches whenever I am not working at full speed. I have
  never been so happy and inspired and
*Play* seems to me now like a juvenile experience!

*


June 8th. *Bee* is still not finished. I have introduced a huge number of red
  balloons into it. How will it work?
Yesterday X. said, "Are you still working on *Bee*? What's happened to your
  interest in steel cigarettes?"

Y. said, "He hasn't been doing any work at all on them since he went to Cleveland." A shrewd guess! But how much can they possibly know?

\*

November 19th. Disaster! *Bee* was almost completed, and now the immense central piece of sailcloth has torn. Impossible to repair it!

December 4th. I've gone back to work on *Bee!* I suddenly thought (after weeks of despair!), "I can place the balloons over the tear in the canvas!" So that is what I am doing. All promises to be well!

December 6th. The foreman of the foundry wants to look at my work. It seems that he too is an "artist"—does sketches and watercolors and such . . . What will he think of *Bee*?

\*

Cherrywood! I had left you far from my home
And the foreman came to look at *Bee*
And the zinc airliner flew into *Play*!

The pink balloons aren't heavy, but the yellow ones break.
The foreman says, "It's the greatest thing I ever saw!"
Cleveland heard too and wants me to come back and reinaugurate *Play*.

I dream of going to Cleveland but never will
*Bee* has obsessed my mind.

\*

March 14th. A cold spring day. It is snowing. *Bee* is completed.

\*

O *Bee* I think you are my best work
In the blue snow-filled air
I feel my heart break
I lie down in the snow
They come from the foundry and take *Bee* away
Oh what can I create now, Earth,

Green Earth on which everything blossoms anew?
"A bathroom floor cardboard trolley line
The shape and size of a lemon seed with on the inside
A passenger the size of a pomegranate seed
Who is an invalid and has to lean on the cardboard side
Of the lemon-seed-sized trolley line so that he won't fall off the train."

*

I just found these notes written many years ago.
How seriously I always take myself! Let it be a lesson to me.
To bring things up to date: I have just finished *Campaign*, which is a
    tremendous piece of charcoal.
Its shape is difficult to describe; but it is extremely large and would
    reach to the sixth floor of the Empire State Building. I have been
    very successful in the past fourteen or fifteen years.

*

*Summer Night*, shall I never succeed in finishing you? Oh you are the
    absolute end of all my creation! The ethereal beauty of that
    practically infinite number of white stone slabs stretching into the blue
    secrecy of ink! O stabs in my heart!

. . . .Why not a work *Stabs in My Heart*? But *Summer Night*?

January. . . . A troubled sleep. Can I make two things at once? What
    way is there to be sure that the impulse to work on *Stabs in My Heart*
    is serious? It seems occasioned only by my problem about finishing
    *Summer Night* . . . ?

*

The *Magician of Cincinnati* is now ready for human use. They are twenty-
five tremendous stone staircases, each over six hundred feet high, which
will be placed in the Ohio River between Cincinnati and Louisville, Ken-
tucky. All the boats coming down the Ohio River will presumably be
smashed up against the immense statues, which are the most recent work
of the creator of *Flowers, Bee, Play, Again* and *Human Use*. Five thousand
citizens are thronged on the banks of the Ohio waiting to see the installa-
tion of the work, and the crowd is expected to be more than fifteen times
its present number before morning. There will be a game of water baseball

in the early afternoon, before the beginning of the ceremonies, between the Cincinnati Redlegs and the Pittsburgh Pirates. The *Magician of Cincinnati*, incidentally, is said to be absolutely impregnable to destruction of any kind, and will therefore presumably always be a feature of this part of the Ohio. . . .

*

May 16th. With what an intense joy I watched the installation of the *Magician of Cincinnati* today, in the Ohio River, where it belongs, and which is so much a part of my original scheme. . . .

May 17th. I feel suddenly freed from life—not so much as if my work were going to change, but as though I had at last seen what I had so long been prevented (perhaps I prevented myself!) from seeing: that there is too much for me to do. Somehow this enables me to relax, to breathe easily. . . .

*

There's the *Magician of Cincinnati*
In the distance
Here I am in the green trees of Pennsylvania.

How strange I felt when they had installed
The *Magician*! . . . Now a bluebird trills, I am busy making my polished stones
For *Dresser*.

The stream the stone the birds the reddish-pink Pennsylvania hills
All go to make up *Dresser*
Why am I camping out?
I am waiting for the thousands of tons of embalming fluid
That have to come and with which I can make these hills.

*

## GREATEST ARTISTIC EVENT HINTED BY GOVERNOR

Reading, June 4. Greatest artistic event was hinted today by governor. Animals converge on meadow where artist working.

## Converge on Meadow Where Working

## Artist Hinted, Same Man

. . . the *Magician of Cincinnati*

## Three Years

October 14th. I want these hills to be striated! How naive the *Magician of Cincinnati* was! Though it makes me happy to think of it. . . . Here, I am plunged into such real earth! Striate, hills! What is this deer's head of green stone? I can't fabricate anything less than what I think should girdle the earth. . . .

### Photograph

### Photograph

### Photograph

Artist who created the *Magician of Cincinnati*; Now at work in Pennsylvania; The Project—*Dresser*—So Far.

\*

Ah! . . .

\*

## Tons

## Silicon, Grass And Deer-head Range

Philadelphia. Your voice as well as mine will be appreciated to express the appreciation of *Dresser*, which makes of Pennsylvania the silicon, grass and stone deer-head center of the world. . . . Artist says he may change his mind about the central bridges. Fountains to give forth real tar-water. Mountain lake in center. Real chalk cliffs. Also cliffs of clay. Deep declivities nearby. "Wanted forest atmosphere, yet to be open." Gas . . .

\*

## Photograph

## Sketch

## Dedication Ceremony

## Goes Swimming in Own Stream

## Shaking Hands with Governor

## Color Picture

## The Head of the Artist

## The Artist's Hand

## STACK OF ACTUAL BILLS NEEDED TO PAY FOR PROJECT

Story of *Dresser*

## PENNSYLVANIA'S PRIDE: *DRESSER*

Creator of *Dresser*

\*

## STILL SMILING AT FORGE

Beverly, South Dakota, April 18. Still smiling at forge, artist of *Dresser* says, "No, of course I haven't forgotten *Dresser*. Though how quickly the years have gone by since I have been doing *Too*!" We glanced up at the sky and saw a large white bird, somewhat similar to an immense seagull, which was as if fixed above our heads. Its eyes were blue sapphires, and its wings were formed by an ingenious arrangement of whitened daffodil-blossom parts. Its body seemed mainly charcoal, on the whole, with a good deal of sand mixed in. As we watched it, the creature actually seemed to move. . . .

August 4th . . . Three four five, and it's finished! I can see it in
 Beverly . . .

\*

## BEVERLY HONORS ARTIST. CALLED "FOUNDING FATHER"

Beverly, South Dakota, August 14 . . .

## MISSISSIPPI CLAIMS BIRTHPLACE

## HONORS BIRTHPLACE

BIRTHPLACE HONORS HELD

*

INDIANS AND SAVANTS MEET TO PRAISE *WEST WIND*

*PAT* HONORED

*PAT* AND *WEST WIND* HONORED

*

June 3rd. It doesn't seem possible—the Pacific Ocean! I have ordered
sixteen million tons of blue paint. Waiting anxiously for it to arrive.
How would grass be as a substitute? cement?

*

# Fresh Air

At the Poem Society a black-haired man stands up to say
"You make me sick with all your talk about restraint and mature talent!
Haven't you ever looked out the window at a painting by Matisse,
Or did you always stay in hotels where there were too many spiders
     crawling on your visages?
Did you ever glance inside a bottle of sparkling pop,
Or see a citizen split in two by the lightning?
I am afraid you have never smiled at the hibernation
Of bear cubs except that you saw in it some deep relation
To human suffering and wishes, oh what a bunch of crackpots!"
The black-haired man sits down, and the others shoot arrows at him.
A blond man stands up and says,
"He is right! Why should we be organized to defend the kingdom
Of dullness? There are so many slimy people connected with poetry,
Too, and people who know nothing about it!
I am not recommending that poets like each other and organize to fight
     them,
But simply that lightning should strike them."
Then the assembled mediocrities shot arrows at the blond-haired man.
The chairman stood up on the platform, oh he was physically ugly!
He was small-limbed and -boned and thought he was quite seductive,
But he was bald with certain hideous black hairs,
And his voice had the sound of water leaving a vaseline bathtub,
And he said, "The subject for this evening's discussion is poetry
On the subject of love between swans." And everyone threw candy hearts
At the disgusting man, and they stuck to his bib and tucker,
And he danced up and down on the platform in terrific glee
And recited the poetry of his little friends—but the blond man stuck his
     head
Out of a cloud and recited poems about the east and thunder,
And the black-haired man moved through the stratosphere chanting
Poems of the relationships between terrific prehistoric charcoal whales,
And the slimy man with candy hearts sticking all over him
Wilted away like a cigarette paper on which the bumblebees have
     urinated,
And all the professors left the room to go back to their duty,
And all that were left in the room were five or six poets

And together they sang the new poem of the twentieth century
Which, though influenced by Mallarmé, Shelley, Byron, and Whitman,
Plus a million other poets, is still entirely original
And is so exciting that it cannot be here repeated.
You must go to the Poem Society and wait for it to happen.
Once you have heard this poem you will not love any other,
Once you have dreamed this dream you will be inconsolable,
Once you have loved this dream you will be as one dead,
Once you have visited the passages of this time's great art!

2

"Oh to be seventeen years old
Once again," sang the red-haired man, "and not know that poetry
Is ruled with the sceptre of the dumb, the deaf, and the creepy!"
And the shouting persons battered his immortal body with stones
And threw his primitive comedy into the sea
From which it sang forth poems irrevocably blue.

Who are the great poets of our time, and what are their names?
Yeats of the baleful influence, Auden of the baleful influence, Eliot of the
    baleful influence
(Is Eliot a great poet? no one knows), Hardy, Stevens, Williams (is Hardy
    of our time?),
Hopkins (is Hopkins of our time?), Rilke (is Rilke of our time?), Lorca (is
    Lorca of our time?), who is still of our time?
Mallarmé, Valéry, Apollinaire, Eluard, Reverdy, French poets are still of
    our time,
Pasternak and Mayakovsky, is Jouve of our time?

Where are young poets in America, they are trembling in publishing
    houses and universities,
Above all they are trembling in universities, they are bathing the library
    steps with their spit,
They are gargling out innocuous (to whom?) poems about maple trees
    and their children,
Sometimes they brave a subject like the Villa d'Este or a lighthouse in
    Rhode Island,

Oh what worms they are! they wish to perfect their form.
Yet could not these young men, put in another profession,
Succeed admirably, say at sailing a ship? I do not doubt it, Sir, and I wish
    we could try them.
(A plane flies over the ship holding a bomb but perhaps it will not drop
    the bomb,
The young poets from the universities are staring anxiously at the skies,
Oh they are remembering their days on the campus when they looked up
    to watch birds excrete,
They are remembering the days they spent making their elegant poems.)

Is there no voice to cry out from the wind and say what it is like to be the
    wind,
To be roughed up by the trees and to bring music from the scattered
    houses
And the stones, and to be in such intimate relationship with the sea
That you cannot understand it? Is there no one who feels like a pair of
    pants?


3


Summer in the trees! "It is time to strangle several bad poets."
The yellow hobbyhorse rocks to and fro, and from the chimney
Drops the Strangler! The white and pink roses are slightly agitated by the
    struggle,
But afterwards beside the dead "poet" they cuddle up comfortingly
    against their vase. They are safer now, no one will compare them to the
    sea.

Here on the railroad train, one more time, is the Strangler.
He is going to get that one there, who is on his way to a poetry reading.
Agh! Biff! A body falls to the moving floor.

In the football stadium I also see him,
He leaps through the frosty air at the maker of comparisons
Between football and life and silently, silently strangles him!

Here is the Strangler dressed in a cowboy suit
Leaping from his horse to annihilate the students of myth!

The Strangler's ear is alert for the names of Orpheus,
Cuchulain, Gawain, and Odysseus,
And for poems addressed to Jane Austen, F. Scott Fitzgerald,
To Ezra Pound, and to personages no longer living
Even in anyone's thoughts—O Strangler the Strangler!

He lies on his back in the waves of the Pacific Ocean.


4

Supposing that one walks out into the air
On a fresh spring day and has the misfortune
To encounter an article on modern poetry
In *New World Writing*, or has the misfortune
To see some examples of some of the poetry
Written by the men with their eyes on the myth
And the Missus and the midterms, in the *Hudson Review*,
Or, if one is abroad, in *Botteghe Oscure*,
Or indeed in *Encounter*, what is one to do
With the rest of one's day that lies blasted to ruins
All bluely about one, what is one to do?
O surely one cannot complain to the President,
Nor even to the deans of Columbia College,
Nor to T. S. Eliot, nor to Ezra Pound,
And supposing one writes to the Princess Caetani,
"Your poets are awful!" what good would it do?
And supposing one goes to the *Hudson Review*
With a package of matches and sets fire to the building?
One ends up in prison with trial subscriptions
To the *Partisan*, *Sewanee*, and *Kenyon Review*!


5


Sun out! perhaps there is a reason for the lack of poetry
In these ill-contented souls, perhaps they need air!

Blue air, fresh air, come in, I welcome you, you are an art student,
Take off your cap and gown and sit down on the chair.

Together we shall paint the poets—but no, air! perhaps you should go to
   them, quickly,
Give them a little inspiration, they need it, perhaps they are out of breath,
Give them a little inhuman company before they freeze the English
   language to death!
(And rust their typewriters a little, be sea air! be noxious! kill them, if you
   must, but stop their poetry!
I remember I saw you dancing on the surf on the Côte d'Azur,
And I stopped, taking my hat off, but you did not remember me,
Then afterwards you came to my room bearing a handful of orange
   flowers
And we were together all through the summer night!)

That we might go away together, it is so beautiful on the sea, there are a
   few white clouds in the sky!

But no, air! you must go . . . Ah, stay!

But she has departed and . . . Ugh! what poisonous fumes and clouds!
   what a suffocating atmosphere!
Cough! whose are these hideous faces I see, what is this rigor
Infecting the mind? where are the green Azores,
Fond memories of childhood, and the pleasant orange trolleys,
A girl's face, red-white, and her breasts and calves, blue eyes, brown eyes,
   green eyes, fahrenheit
Temperatures, dandelions, and trains, O blue?!
Wind, wind, what is happening? Wind! I can't see any bird but the gull,
   and I feel it should symbolize . . .
Oh, pardon me, there's a swan, one two three swans, a great white swan,
   hahaha how pretty they are! Smack!
Oh! stop! help! yes, I see—disrespect for my superiors—forgive me, dear
   Zeus, nice Zeus, parabolic bird, O feathered excellence! white!
There is Achilles too, and there's Ulysses, I've always wanted to see them,
And there is Helen of Troy, I suppose she is Zeus too, she's so terribly
   pretty—hello, Zeus, my you are beautiful, Bang!
One more mistake and I get thrown out of the Modern Poetry
   Association, help! Why aren't there any adjectives around?
Oh there are, there's practically nothing else—look, here's *grey, utter,*
   *agonized, total, phenomenal, gracile, invidious, sundered,* and *fused,*

*Elegant, absolute, pyramidal,* and . . . Scream! but what can I describe with these words? States!

States symbolized and divided by two, complex states, magic states, states of consciousness governed by an aroused sincerity, cockadoodle doo!

Another bird! is it morning? Help! where am I? am I in the barnyard? oink oink, scratch, moo! Splash!

My first lesson. "Look around you. What do you think and feel?" *Uhhh* . . . "Quickly!" *This Connecticut landscape would have pleased Vermeer.* Wham! A-Plus. "Congratulations!" I am promoted.

OOOhhhhh I wish I were dead, what a headache! My second lesson: "Rewrite your first lesson line six hundred times. Try to make it into a magnetic field." I can do it too. But my poor line! What a nightmare! Here comes a tremendous horse,

Trojan, I presume. No, it's my third lesson. "Look, look! Watch him, see what he's doing? That's what we want you to do. Of course it won't be the same as his at first, but . . ." I demur. Is there no other way to fertilize minds?

Bang! I give in . . . Already I see my name in two or three anthologies, a serving girl comes into the barn bringing me the anthologies,

She is very pretty and I smile at her a little sadly, perhaps it is my last smile! Perhaps she will hit me! But no, she smiles in return, and she takes my hand.

My hand, my hand! what is this strange thing I feel in my hand, on my arm, on my chest, my face—can it be . . . ? it is! AIR!

Air, air, you've come back! Did you have any success? "What do you think?" I don't know, air. You are so strong, air.

And she breaks my chains of straw, and we walk down the road, behind us the hideous fumes!

Soon we reach the seaside, she is a young art student who places her head on my shoulder,

I kiss her warm red lips, and here is the Strangler, reading the *Kenyon Review*! Good luck to you, Strangler!

Goodbye, Helen! goodbye, fumes! goodbye, abstracted dried-up boys! goodbye, dead trees! goodbye, skunks!

Goodbye, manure! goodbye, critical manicure! goodbye, you big fat men standing on the east coast as well as the west giving poems the test! farewell, Valéry's stern dictum!

Until tomorrow, then, scum floating on the surface of poetry! goodbye for a moment, refuse that happens to land in poetry's boundaries! adieu, stale eggs teaching imbeciles poetry to bolster up your egos! adios, boring anomalies of these same stale eggs!

Ah, but the scum is deep! Come, let me help you! and soon we pass into the clear blue water. Oh GOODBYE, castrati of poetry! farewell, stale pale skunky pentameters (the only honest English meter, gloop gloop!) until tomorrow, horrors! oh, farewell!

Hello, sea! good morning, sea! hello, clarity and excitement, you great expanse of green—

O green, beneath which all of them shall drown!

# Thanksgiving

What's sweeter than at the end of a summer's day
To suddenly drift away
From the green match-wrappers in an opened pocketbook
And be part of the boards in a tavern?

A tavern made of new wood.
There's an orange-red sun in the sky
And a redskin is hunting for you underneath ladders of timber.
I will buy this tavern. Will you buy this tavern? I do.

In the Indian camp there's awful dismay.
Do they know us as we know they
Know us or will know us, I mean a—
I mean a hostile force, the month of May.

How whitely the springtime is blossoming,
Ugh! all around us!
It is the brilliant Indian time of year
When the sweetest Indians mate with the sweetest others.

But I fear the white men, I fear
The rent apple blossoms and discarded feathers
And the scalp lying secretly on the ground
Like an unoffending nose!

But we've destroyed all that. With shocking guns.
Peter Stuyvesant, Johnny Appleseed,
We've destroyed all that. Come,
Do you believe right was on either side?

How would you like to be living in an Indian America,
With feathers dressing every head? We'd eat buffalo hump
For Thanksgiving dinner. Everyone is in a tribe.
A girl from the Bep Tribe can't marry a brave from the Bap Tribe. Is that
democracy?

And then those dreary evenings around the campfires
Listening to the Chief! If there were a New York
It would be a city of tents, and what do you suppose

Our art and poetry would be like? For the community! the tribe!
No beautiful modern abstract pictures, no mad incomprehensible
Free lovable poems! And our moral sense! tribal.
If you would like to be living in an Indian America
Why not subscribe to this newspaper, *Indian America?*

In Wisconsin, Ben, I stand, I walk up and down and try to decide.

Is this country getting any better or has it gotten?
If the Indian New York is bad, what about our white New York?
Dirty, unwholesome, the filthy appendage to a vast ammunition works,
     I hate it!
Disgusting rectangular garbage dump sending its fumes up to suffocate
     the sky—
Foo, what fumes! and the scaly white complexion of her citizens.
There's hell in every firm handshake, and stifled rage in every look.
If you do find somewhere to lie down, it's a dirty inspected corner,
And there are newspapers and forums and the stinking breath of
     Broadway
To investigate what it feels like to be a source of stench
And nothing else. And if one does go away,
It is always here, waiting, for one to come back. And one does come back,
As one comes back to the bathroom, and to a time of suffering.

Where else would I find such ardent and graceful spirits
Inspired and wasted and using and used by this horrible city,
New York, New York? Can the Pilgrims' Thanksgiving dinner really
     compare to it?
And the Puritans? And the single-minded ankle-divided Indians?
No, nothing can compare to it! So it's here we speak from the heart,
And it's rotting so fast that what we say
Fades like the last of a summer's day,
Rot which makes us prolific as the sun on white unfastened clouds.

# Permanently

One day the Nouns were clustered in the street.
An Adjective walked by, with her dark beauty.
The Nouns were struck, moved, changed.
The next day a Verb drove up, and created the Sentence.

Each Sentence says one thing—for example, "Although it was a dark rainy
     day when the Adjective walked by, I shall remember the pure and sweet
     expression on her face until the day I perish from the green, effective
     earth."
Or, "Will you please close the window, Andrew?"
Or, for example, "Thank you, the pink pot of flowers on the window sill
     has changed color recently to a light yellow, due to the heat from the
     boiler factory which exists nearby."

In the springtime the Sentences and the Nouns lay silently on the grass.
A lonely Conjunction here and there would call, "And! But!"
But the Adjective did not emerge.

As the adjective is lost in the sentence,
So I am lost in your eyes, ears, nose, and throat—
You have enchanted me with a single kiss
Which can never be undone
Until the destruction of language.

# Down at the Docks

Down at the docks
Where everything is sweet and inclines
At night
To the sound of canoes
I planted a maple tree
And every night
Beneath it I studied the cosmos
Down at the docks.

Sweet ladies, listen to me.
The dock is made of wood
The maple tree's not made of wood
It is wood
Wood comes from it
As music comes from me
And from this mandolin I've made
Out of the maple tree.

Jealous gentlemen, study how
Wood comes from the maple
Then devise your love
So that it seems
To come from where
All is it yet something more
White spring flowers and leafy bough
Jealous gentlemen.

Arrogant little waves
Knocking at the dock
It's for you I've made this chanson
For you and that big dark blue.

# You Were Wearing

You were wearing your Edgar Allan Poe printed cotton blouse.
In each divided up square of the blouse was a picture of Edgar Allan Poe.
Your hair was blonde and you were cute. You asked me, "Do most boys
    think that most girls are bad?"
I smelled the mould of your seaside resort hotel bedroom on your hair
    held in place by a John Greenleaf Whittier clip.
"No," I said, "it's girls who think that boys are bad." Then we read
    *Snowbound* together
And ran around in an attic, so that a little of the blue enamel was scraped
    off my George Washington, Father of His Country, shoes.

Mother was walking in the living room, her Strauss Waltzes comb in her
    hair.
We waited for a time and then joined her, only to be served tea in cups
    painted with pictures of Herman Melville
As well as with illustrations from his book *Moby Dick* and from his novella
    *Benito Cereno*.
Father came in wearing his Dick Tracy necktie: "How about a drink,
    everyone?"
I said, "Let's go outside a while." Then we went onto the porch and sat on
    the Abraham Lincoln swing.
You sat on the eyes, mouth, and beard part, and I sat on the knees.
In the yard across the street we saw a snowman holding a garbage can lid
    smashed into a likeness of the mad English king, George the Third.

# Locks

These locks on doors have brought me happiness:
The lock on the door of the sewing machine in the living room
Of a tiny hut in which I was living with a mad seamstress;
The lock on the filling station one night when I was drunk
And had the idea of enjoying a nip of petroleum;
The lock on the family of seals, which, when released, would have bitten;
The lock on the life raft when I was taking a bath instead of drowning;
The lock inside the nose of the contemporary composer who was playing
    the piano and would have ruined his concert by sneezing, while I was
    turning pages;
The lock on the second hump of a camel while I was not running out of
    water in the desert;
The lock on the fish hatchery the night we came up from the beach
And were trying to find a place to spend the night—it was full of
    contagious fish;
The lock on my new necktie when I was walking through a stiff wind
On my way to an appointment at which I had to look neat and simple;
The lock on the foghorn the night of the lipstick parade—
If the foghorn had sounded, everyone would have run inside before the
    most beautiful contestant appeared;
The lock in my hat when I saw her and which kept me from tipping it,
Which she would not have liked, because she believed that naturalness
    was the most friendly;
The lock on the city in which we would not have met anyone we knew;
The lock on the airplane which was flying without a pilot
Above Miami Beach on the night when I unlocked my bones
To the wind, and let the gales of sweetness blow through me till
    I shuddered and shook
Like a key in a freezing hand, and ran up into the Miami night air like a
    stone;
The lock on the hayfield, which kept me from getting out of bed
To meet the hayfield committee there; the lock on the barn, that kept the
    piled-up hay away from me;
The lock on the mailboat that kept it from becoming a raincoat
On the night of the thunderstorm; the lock on the sailboat
That keeps it from taking me away from you when I am asleep with you,
And, when I am not, the lock on my sleep, that keeps me from waking and
    finding you are not there.

# Variations on a Theme
# by William Carlos Williams

1

I chopped down the house that you had been saving to live in next
    summer.
I am sorry, but it was morning, and I had nothing to do
and its wooden beams were so inviting.

2

We laughed at the hollyhocks together
and then I sprayed them with lye.
Forgive me. I simply do not know what I am doing.

3

I gave away the money that you had been saving to live on for the next ten
    years.
The man who asked for it was shabby
and the firm March wind on the porch was so juicy and cold.

4

Last evening we went dancing and I broke your leg.
Forgive me. I was clumsy, and
I wanted you here in the wards, where I am the doctor!

# Thank You

Oh thank you for giving me the chance
Of being ship's doctor! I am sorry that I shall have to refuse—
But, you see, the most I know of medicine is orange flowers
Tilted in the evening light against a cashmere red
Inside which breasts invent the laws of light
And of night, where cashmere moors itself across the sea.
And thank you for giving me these quintuplets
To rear and make happy . . . My mind was on something else.

Thank you for giving me this battleship to wash,
But I have a rash on my hands and my eyes hurt,
And I know so little about cleaning a ship
That I should rather clean an island.
There one knows what one is about—sponge those palm trees, sweep up
    the sand a little, polish those coconuts;
Then take a rest for a while and it's time to trim the grass as well as
    separate it from each other where gummy substances have made
    individual blades stick together, forming an ugly bunch;
And then take the dead bark off the trees, and perfume these islands a bit
    with a song. . . . That's easy—but a battleship!
Where does one begin and how does one do? to batten the hatches?
    I would rather clean a million palm trees.

Now here comes an offer of a job for setting up a levee
In Mississippi. No thanks. Here it says *Rape or Worse*. I think they must
    want me to publicize this book.
On the jacket it says "Published in Boothbay Harbor, Maine"—what a
    funny place to publish a book!
I suppose it is some provincial publishing house
Whose provincial pages emit the odor of sails
And the freshness of the sea
Breeze. . . . But publicity!
The only thing I could publicize well would be my tooth,
Which I could say came with my mouth and in a most engaging manner
With my whole self, my body and including my mind,
Spirits, emotions, spiritual essences, emotional substances, poetry,
    dreams, and lords
Of my life, everything, all embraceleted with my tooth
In a way that makes one wish to open the windows and scream "Hi!" to
    the heavens,

136

And "Oh, come and take me away before I die in a minute!"

It is possible that the dentist is smiling, that he dreams of extraction
Because he believes that the physical tooth and the spiritual tooth are one.

Here is another letter, this one from a textbook advertiser;
He wants me to advertise a book on chopping down trees.
But how could I? I love trees! and I haven't the slightest sympathy with
     chopping them down, even though I know
We need their products for wood-fires, some houses, and maple syrup—
Still I like trees better
In their standing condition, when they sway at the beginning of
     evening . . .
And thank you for the pile of driftwood.
Am I wanted at the sea?

And thank you for the chance to run a small hotel
In an elephant stopover in Zambezi,
But I do not know how to take care of guests, certainly they would all
     leave soon
After seeing blue lights out the windows and rust on their iron beds—I'd
     rather own a bird-house in Jamaica:
Those people come in, the birds, they do not care how things are kept
     up . . .
It's true that Zambezi proprietorship would be exciting, with people
     getting off elephants and coming into my hotel,
But as tempting as it is I cannot agree.
And thank you for this offer of the post of referee
For the Danish wrestling championship—I simply do not feel
     qualified . . .
But the fresh spring air has been swabbing my mental decks
Until, although prepared for fight, still I sleep on land.
Thank you for the ostriches. I have not yet had time to pluck them,
But I am sure they will be delicious, adorning my plate at sunset,
My tremendous plate, and the plate
Of the offers to all my days. But I cannot fasten my exhilaration to the
     sun.

And thank you for the evening of the night on which I fell off my horse in
     the shadows. That was really useful.

# Lunch

The lanternslides grinding out B-flat minor
Chords to the ears of the deaf youngster who sprays in Hicksville
The sides of a car with the dream-splitting paint
Of pianos (he dreamt of one day cutting the Conservatory
In two with his talent), these lanternslides, I say,
They are— The old woman hesitated. A lifesaver was shoved down her
    throat; then she continued:
They are some very good lanternslides in that bunch. Then she fainted
And we revived her with flowers. She smiled sleepily at the sun.
He is my own boy, she said, with her glass hand falling through the
    sparkling red America of lunch.

That old boilermaker she has in her back yard,
Olaf said, used to be her sweetheart years back.
One day, though, a train passed, and pressed her hard,
And she deserted life and love for liberty.
We carried Olaf softly into the back yard
And laid him down with his head under the steamroller.
Then Jill took the wheel and I tinkered with the engine,
Till we rolled him under, rolled him under the earth.
When people ask us what's in our back yard
Now, we don't like to tell them, Jill says, laying her silver bandannaed
    head on my greened bronze shoulder.
Then we both dazzle ourselves with the red whiteness of lunch.

That old woman named Tessie Runn
Had a tramp boyfriend who toasted a bun.
They went to Florida, but Maxine Schweitzer was hard of
Hearing and the day afterwards the judge adjourned the trial.
When it finally came for judgment to come up
Of delicious courtyards near the Pantheon,
At last we had to let them speak, the children whom flowers had made
    statues
For the rivers of water which came from their funnel;
And we stood there in the middle of existence
Dazzled by the white paraffin of lunch.

Music in Paris and water coming out from the flannel
Of the purist person galloping down the Madeleine

Toward a certain wafer. Hey! just a minute! the sunlight is being rifled
By the green architecture of the flowers. But the boulevard turned a big
   blue deaf ear
Of cinema placards to the detonated traveler. He had forgotten the blue
   defilade of lunch!

Genoa! a stone's throw from Acapulco
If an engine were built strong enough,
And down where the hulls and scungilli,
Glisteningly unconscious, agree,
I throw a game of shoes with Horace Sturnbul
And forget to eat lunch.

O launch, lunch, you dazzling hoary tunnel
To paradise!
Do you see that snowman tackled over there
By summer and the sea? A boardwalk went to Istanbul
And back under his left eye. We saw the Moslems praying
In Rhodes. One had a red fez, another had a black cap.
And in the extended heat of afternoon,
As an ice-cold gradual sweat covered my whole body,
I realized, and the carpet swam like a red world at my feet
In which nothing was green, and the Moslems went on praying,
That we had missed lunch, and a perpetual torrent roared into the sea
Of my understanding. An old woman gave us bread and rolls on the street.

The dancing wagon has come! here is the dancing wagon!
Come up and get lessons—here is lemonade and grammar!
Here is drugstore and cowboy—all that is America—plus sex, perfumes,
   and shimmers—all the Old World;
Come and get it—and here is your reading matter
For twenty-nine centuries, and here finally is lunch—
To be served in the green defilade under the roaring tower
Where Portugal meets Spain inside a flowered madeleine.

My ginger dress has nothing on, but yours
Has on a picture of Queen Anne Boleyn
Surrounded by her courtiers eating lunch

And on the back a one of Henry the Eighth
Summoning all his courtiers in for lunch.

And the lunchboat has arrived
From Spain.
Everyone getting sick is on it;
The bold people and the sadists are on it;
I am glad I am not on it,
I am having a big claw of garlic for lunch—
But it plucks me up in the air,
And there, above the ship, on a cloud
I see the angels eating lunch.
One has a beard, another a moustache,
And one has some mustard smeared on his ears.
A couple of them ask me if I want to go to Honolulu,
And I accept—it's all right—
Another time zone: we'll be able to have lunch.
They are very beautiful and transparent,
My two traveling companions,
And they will go very well with Hawaii
I realize as we land there,
That dazzling red whiteness—it is our desire . . .
For whom? The angels of lunch.

Oh I sat over a glass of red wine
And you came out dressed in a paper cup.
An ant-fly was eating hay-mire in the chair-rafters
And large white birds flew in and dropped edible animals to the ground.
If they had been gulls it would have been garbage
Or fish. We have to be fair to the animal kingdom,
But if I do not wish to be fair, if I wish to eat lunch
Undisturbed—? The light of day shines down. The world continues.

We stood in the little hutment in Biarritz
Waiting for lunch, and your hand clasped mine
And I felt it was sweaty;
And then lunch was served,
Like the bouquet of an enchantress.
Oh the green whites and red yellows
And purple whites of lunch!

The bachelor eats his lunch,
The married man eats his lunch,
And old Uncle Joris belches
The seascape in which a child appears
Eating a watermelon and holding a straw hat.
He moves his lips as if to speak
But only sea air emanates from this childish beak.
It is the moment of sorrows,
And on the shores of history,
Which stretch in both directions, there are no happy tomorrows.
But Uncle Joris holds his apple up and begins to speak
To the child. Red waves fan my universe with the green macaw of lunch.

This street is deserted;
I think my eyes are empty;
Let us leave
Quickly.
Day bangs on the door and is gone.

Then they picked him up and carried him away from that company.
When he awoke he was in the fire department, and sleepy but not tired.
They gave him a hoseful of blue Spain to eat for lunch,
And Portugal was waiting for him at the door, like a rainstorm of evening
    raspberries.

It is time to give lunch to my throat and not my chest.
What? either the sting ray has eaten my lunch
Or else—and she searches the sky for something else;
But I am far away, seeming blue-eyed, empirical . . .

Let us give lunch to the lunch—
But how shall we do it?
The headwaiters expand and confer;
Will little pieces of cardboard box do it?
And what about silver and gold pellets?
The headwaiters expand and confer:
And what if the lunch should refuse to eat anything at all?
Why then we'd say be damned to it,
And the red doorway would open on a green railway
And the lunch would be put in a blue car
And it would go away to Whippoorwill Valley

Where it would meet and marry Samuel Dogfoot, and bring forth seven
  offspring,
All of whom would be half human, half lunch;
And when we saw them, sometimes, in the gloaming,
We would take off our mining hats and whistle Tweet twee-oo,
With watering mouths staring at the girls in pink organdy frocks,
Not realizing they really were half edible,
And we would die still without knowing it;
So to prevent anything happening that terrible
Let's give everybody we see and like a good hard bite right now,
To see what they are, because it's time for lunch!

# Taking a Walk with You

My misunderstandings: for years I thought "muso bello" meant "Bell
   Muse," I thought it was a kind of
Extra reward on the slotmachine of my shyness in the snow when
February was only a bouncing ball before the Hospital of the Two Sisters
   of the Last
Hamburger Before I Go to Sleep. I thought Axel's Castle was a garage;
And I had beautiful dreams about it, too—sensual, mysterious
   mechanisms; horns honking, wheels turning . . .
My misunderstandings were:
1) thinking Pinocchio could really change from a puppet into a real boy,
   and back again!
2) thinking it depended on whether he was good or bad!
3) identifying him with myself!
4) and therefore every time I was bad being afraid I would turn into
   wood . . .
5) I misunderstood childhood. I usually liked the age I was. However, now
   I regard twenty-nine as an optimum age (for me).
6) I disliked Shelley between twenty and twenty-five.
All of these things I suppose are understandable, but
When you were wearing your bodice I did not understand that you had
   nothing on beneath it;
When my father turned the corner I misunderstood the light very much
On Fifty-fifth Street; and I misunderstood (like an old Chinese restaurant)
   what he was doing there.
I misunderstand generally Oklahoma and Arkansas, though I think I
   understand New Mexico;
I understand the Painted Desert, cowboy hats, and vast spaces; I do
Not understand hillbilly life—I am sure I misunderstand it.
I did not understand that you had nothing on beneath your bodice
Nor, had I understood this, would I have understood what it meant; even
   now I
(Merry Christmas! Here, Father, take your package) misunderstand it!
Merry Christmas, Uncle Leon! yes, here is your package too.

I misunderstand Renaissance life; I misunderstand:
The Renaissance;
Ancient China;
The Middle Atlantic States and what they are like;
The tubes of London and what they mean;

Titian, Michelangelo, Vermeer;
The origins of words;
What others are talking about;
Music from the beginnings to the present time;
Laughter; and tears, even more so;
Value (economic and esthetic);
Snow (and weather in the country);
The meaning of the symbols and myths of Christmas.
I misunderstand you,
I misunderstand the day we walked down the street together for ten
    hours—
Where were we going? I had thought we were going somewhere. I believe
    I misunderstand many of the places we passed and things you said . . .
I misunderstand "Sons of Burgundy,"
I misunderstand that you had nothing painted beneath your bodice,
I misunderstand "Notification of Arrival or Departure to Be Eradicated
    Before Affection of Deceased Tenant."
I understand that
The smoke and the clouds are both a part of the day, but

I misunderstand the words "After Departure,"
I misunderstand nothingness;
I misunderstand the attitude of people in pharmacies, on the decks of
    ships, in my bedroom, amid the pine needles, on mountains of cotton,
    everywhere—
When they say paralytic I hear parasite, and when they say coffee I think
    music . . .
What is wrong with me from head to toe
That I misinterpret everything I hear? I misunderstand:
French: often;
Italian: sometimes, almost always—for example, if someone says,
    "Fortunate ones!" I am likely to think he is referring to the fountain
    with blue and red water (I am likely to make this mistake also in
    English).
I misunderstand Greek entirely;
I find ancient Greece very hard to understand: I probably misunderstand
    it;
I misunderstand spoken German about 98% of the time, like the
    cathedral in the middle of a town;

I misunderstand "Beautiful Adventures"; I also think I probably
    misunderstand *La Nausée* by Jean-Paul Sartre . . .
I probably misunderstand misunderstanding itself—I misunderstand the
    Via Margutta in Rome, or Via della Vite, no matter what street, all of
    them.
I misunderstand wood in the sense of its relationship to the tree; I
    misunderstand people who take one attitude or another about it . . .
Spring I would like to say I understand, but I most probably don't—
    autumn, winter, and summer are all in the same boat
(Ruined ancient cities by the sea).

I misunderstand *vacation* and *umbrella*,
I misunderstand *motion* and *weekly*
(Though I think I understand "Daytime Pissarros"
And the octagon—I do not understand the public garden) . . .

Oh I am sure there is a use for all of them, but what is it?
My misunderstandings confuse Rome and Ireland, and can you
Bring that beautiful sex to bear upon it?
I misunderstand what I am saying, though not to you;
I misunderstand a large boat: that is a ship.
What you are feeling for me I misunderstand totally; I think I
    misunderstand the very possibilities of feeling,
Especially here in Rome, where I somehow think I am.
I see the sky, and sails.
(I misunderstand the mustard and the bottle)
Oh that we could go sailing in that sky!

What tune came with the refreshments?
I am unable to comprehend why they were playing off key.
Is it because they wanted us to jump over the cliff
Or was one of them a bad or untrained musician
Or the whole lot of them?
At any rate
San Giovanni in Laterano
Also resisted my questioning
And turned a deaf blue dome to me
Far too successfully.
I cannot understand why you walk forwards and backwards with me.

I think it is because you want to try out your shoes for their toes.
It is Causation that is my greatest problem
And after that the really attentive study of millions of details.

I love you, but it is difficult to stop writing.
As a flea could write the Divine Comedy of a water jug. Now Irish mists
   close in upon us.
Peat sails through the air, and greenness becomes bright. Are you the
   ocean or the island? Am I on Irish soil, or are your waves covering me?
St. Peter's bells are ringing: "Earthquake, inundation, and sleep to the
   understanding!"
(American Express! flower vendors! your beautiful straight nose! that
   delightful trattoria in Santa Maria in Trastevere!)
Let us have supper at Santa Maria in Trastevere
Where by an absolute and total misunderstanding (but not fatal) I once
   ate before I met you.
I am probably misinterpreting your answer, since I hear nothing, and
   I believe I am alone.

# The Railway Stationery

The railway stationery lay upon
The desk of the railway clerk, from where he could see
The springtime and the tracks. Engraved upon
Each page was an inch-and-a-half-high T
And after that an H and then an E
And then, slightly below it to the right,
There was COLUMBUS RAILWAY COMPANY
In darker ink as the above was light.
The print was blue. And just beneath it all
There was an etching—not in blue, but black—
Of a real railway engine half-an-inch tall
Which, if you turned the paper on its back,
You could see showing through, as if it ran
To one edge of the sheet then back again.

To one edge of the sheet then back again!
The springtime comes while we're still drenched in snow
And, whistling now, snow-spotted Number Ten
Comes up the track and stops, and we must go
Outside to get its cargo, with our hands
Cold as the steel they touch. Inside once more
Once we have shut the splintery wooden door
Of the railway shack, the stationery demands
Some further notice. For the first time the light,
Reflected from the snow by the bright spring sun,
Shows that the engine wheel upon the right
Is slightly darker than the left-side one
And slightly lighter than the one in the center,
Which may have been an error of the printer.

Shuffling through many sheets of it to establish
Whether this difference is consistent will
Prove that it is not. Probably over-lavish
At the beginning with the ink, he still
(The printer) had the presence of mind to change
His operating process when he noticed
That on the wheels the ink had come out strange.
Because the windows of the shack are latticed
The light that falls upon the stationery

Is often interrupted by straight lines
Which shade the etching. Now the words "Dear Mary"
Appear below the engine on one sheet
Followed by a number of other conventional signs,
Among which are "our love," "one kiss," and "sweet."

The clerk then signs his name—his name is Johnson,
But all he signs is Bill, with a large B
Which overflows its boundaries like a Ronson
With too much fluid in it, which you see
Often, and it can burn you, though the *i*
Was very small and had a tiny dot.
The *l*'s were different—the first was high,
The second fairly low. And there was a spot
Of ink at the end of the signature which served
To emphasize that the letter was complete.
On the whole, one could say his writing swerved
More than the average, although it was neat.
He'd used a blue-black ink, a standing pen,
Which now he stuck back in its stand again.

Smiling and sighing, he opened up a drawer
And took an envelope out, which then he sealed
After he'd read the letter three times more
And folded it and put it in. A field
Covered with snow, untouched by man, is what
The envelope resembled, till he placed
A square with perforated edges that
Pictured a white-haired President, who faced
The viewer, in its corner, where it stuck
After he'd kissed its back and held it hard
Against the envelope. Now came the truck
Of the postman "Hello, Jim." "Hello there, Bill."
"I've got this—can you take it?" "Sure, I will!"

Now the snow fell down gently from the sky.
Strange wonder—snow in spring! Bill walked into
The shack again and wrote the letter *I*
Idly upon a sheet of paper. New
Ideas for writing Mary filled his mind,
But he resisted—there was work to do.
For in the distance he could hear the grind

Of the Seventy-Eight, whose engine was half blue;
So, putting on a cap, he went outside
On the tracks side, to wait for it to come.
It was the Seventy-Eight which now supplied
The city with most of its produce, although some
Came in by truck and some was grown in town.
Now it screams closer, and he flags it down.

# The Islands

Triplets
Do you ever think of
    the good times
When my sleeves
You see, the pilot said,
The king offered me the Admiralty
Islands as a reward for the sludge but the
Motors were filled with steamy juice and
Wouldn't start. My friend Harry
Tried to dry them out by opening
The motor cover and letting the hot wind blow
In, all to no avail—so you see
We just sat there, the way
You and your girlfriends did in the
What you say and
                        A child, weak
With fatigue, wandered up to the
Airplane and there was a smell of joss.
We couldn't let that go on on
Flower Island, so Andy hauled this
Kid up to Pilot Lodge where he
Confessed that he had
Other jealous men
Glanced into the air
You have no right
Thing like that—old
Ways forbid but meanwhile
What sunlight and motor not still
Then that smell again—
With just a tiny piece of her we got up
The child smiled
"I wish you steamy joys"
Then I knew
We wouldn't make the islands
I was shivering
Harry's arm was just a stump
The joss had eaten it
As hot nails    opened into blue

The earth had melted away.

Inside you I feel a revision
Of all my ideals
Day open like a tin-can—We
Smelled, suddenly,
Some joss      its
Smell was mingled with that
Of wet mud—Harry
Stood up and tried to
Guide the airplane
Closer to the ship—He had
A long pole      looked funny      The captain
Bearded man of fifty-six who
Five days afterwards      ,      we already
Accustomed to
Told Harry      he a "blockbuster" or
"Bookworm"      Then onto
Deck stepped
A Chinese miss
Named "Jolie."

"Sylvia was just a child when I began my career on the
But such a dreamer! she would lean back against her—"
The charms being five
I am happiest
When I am with you
Some say she dropped a baby on the island
What has it all to do
You hurt my prunes again
Let me have a look at it
For five cents a trip you can get the
Whole skedaddle triremed
Stick
You're so sweaty
Because I have no arms
Everything is twice as difficult for me
            for you
Harry put rice all over his face
Picked up the scissors

And acted crazy
But the consul wanted the girl
And said he would have to go back to Zululand
On the next ship.
She was tan and brown and slippery
He had a baby by her anyway.
The baby was named Voss
And fought for the U.S. Navy
At Sarapatee—  "I tried to get
It             into the clear."

We moved up
A little closer
    still couldn't make out what
They were saying.   Ed smelled joss
"Is that all they DO out here?"
"Ho, no, Eddie, not at all—
These people are . . ."
Her smell sweet
The sea    lilac of angry fudge

Couldn't keep bringing those
Carpenter tools
                    every day
Back to the plane     without
At some time     attracting
The attention of the
Major, who, naturally, would have
Like to know what was
Going on
              found her attractive
Wanting her in his cabin at night
He would find all kinds of ways
Attract her attention       for example
Sending up flags     green
Or red       dark harbor
                          lilypads
Over her door
And along path to her
                    The father
An old man with rice in his ear
Never taken sedative

In eighty-nine years on the island,     once
Made all the cadets wear golden hats
And take them off to her
As she passed . . . And thus he accomplished
He so ardently
Desired?   Bee stings
She scratched him
He found her "cute" but
The sergeant, Leonard,
Would often find him
"Not really a disgrace
To the service, but
My God a comment on
Something how true!" lying stretched out
In the purple tide flaked
With dawn spots
Covered with bruises and
Slashed—   "As if she
Were trying
Make a woman out of me, Sergeant.
God!"  Innuendoes
He thought of but never said,    as
"You should raise welts on her, Sir"—
A good idea he hadn't
The boycott
Famous old word misused again
And the local nut
Who had gasped with pleasure on half the island

"Promiscuity
Is not attractive—Go home from the dance—"
Not from the native dance!
She was a silver
Blade    and he was like a hammer
Roses    cannon    dawn
Night flushed syringe
"What did you say
We don't have any of those
On this island . . ."

Then
The Colonel took her

Over again
Find his silver eagle attractive
Better than a bug
                    dawn
                        the shore
I wish you hadn't reduced
What? did the milk—
A dog lay    breathing
But half dead
We can't do anything
Invitations    already out

Are you descended from those
People, Voss?
Half

Half a sunset      "fire-tossed horse"
Cannonade       the smell of farts
Disintegrated by breeze
Come—       Nineteen years I'll be an old woman
Can't abide you
The business parlors
Appealed to him much more
                                  that
Green cloth on the tables
"Better than native girls"
More minimal
The sea's light blue wash
"They scratched him up, it was weird
As if they had never seen a man before
On the island . . ."
Said he had a good time
Home sitting on the swing       worst
Old time no plenty come back
    the
Horse farting
Why I could hardly stare a white girl in the face
Shit on calf
Sorry,   I—
                then realized ridiculous
Talk

Perhaps won't mind doesn't know
                    I am
Roses, bridge, her forehead
Even a great one
The cow drops
Memory of her name no I white rose I
Send me back you see
Never, Dad
Soldered up
   for repeal
Meanwhile she was running
Wonder how those
Tout-blankety   native girls—
Voss!
Your own mother
No, boy, I'm not going
To sit around while that   !
Am Lieutenant Governor
Greaseball!
Kill him!
Dropped into the sea
When they unwrapped it
Found her earrings
             and his cloth
"Maple leafs" as well as
The naked body of a sixteen-year-old boy
Completely defaced with scratches
Like a "torpedo"
"When I think that that might
Have happened to me"—
Sunlight
Crutches
Someone named "Lillian Liberty"

Vile old iron ways

# The Departure from Hydra

As I was walking home just now, from seeing
Margaret and Norris off (though Peter,
An Englishman whom Norris had met yesterday,
Went back to change his clothes, and missed the boat)
As I came home along the little street
Without a name on which the only theatre,
The movie theatre, on Hydra is,
Called "The Gardenia" or just plain "Gardenia,"
The street which they today are tearing up
And carrying new stones in to replace
The ones they're tearing up, though it may be
They are the same stones, put in different order
Or in a different way, as I was walking,
With the heat of the day just over, at five-thirty,
I felt quite good, but then felt an awareness
Of something in my legs that might be painful
And then of some slight tension in my jaws
And slight pains in my head; instead of despairing
And giving all thought of pleasure up, I felt
That if I could write down all that I felt
As I came walking there, that that would be
A pleasure also, and with solidity.
I passed a mule—some men were loading up
His fellow-mule with packets—and I stared
At his wide eyes and his long hard flat nose
Or face, at which he turned away his eyes
And stamped his right hoof nervously. I felt
Guilty, a member of a higher species
Deliberately using my power against
A natural inferior because
Really I was afraid that he might kick
When I came past; but when he seemed upset
Then I felt guilty. Then I looked ahead
And saw a view of houses on the hill,
Particularly noticing one red one
And thinking, Yes, that is a part of what
I feel, of the variety of this walk;
Then my mind blurred somewhat, I turned and came
Down this small narrow alley to my home.

As I came in, reviewing the ideas
Which had occured to me throughout my walk,
It suddenly came to me that maybe Peter
Had missed the Athens boat deliberately;
After all, Margaret was not sure that she
Wanted to accompany him and Norris
On a walking trip on Poros, and Norris had said
He wanted to stay with Margaret, so that Peter
Was disappointed, since he and Norris had planned
That very morning to take such a walking trip,
And he, Peter, had been the most excited
Of all, about it. But now since Margaret and Norris
Were going into Athens, what was there for Peter
To do, why should he take the boat at all,
Even though he'd planned to, to stop at Poros?
Except, of course, to act on some marginal chance
That Norris might get off with him and walk,
Or on the strength of previous expectations,
Emotional impetus lingering. If not,
Perhaps his going to change was just an excuse
To avoid an actual confrontation with Norris
In which he would have to say, "No, I'm not going
Unless you'll come on the walking trip!" but he knew,
Peter, that Norris wanted to stay with Margaret
And that therefore speaking to him would only result
In a little pain and confusion, since both were quite drunk,
Having planned their trip to Poros over beer all morning;
And also, of course, it might result in his getting,
In spite of himself, on the boat, by the talk confused
And not thinking clearly (whereas if he walked away
He had only, really, to wait till the boat had left—
Then he could come back down and think it over,
Surely to find he didn't regret too much
Not getting the boat, because after all the reason
He'd wanted to take the boat had long been gone).
For a human situation often leads
People to do things that they don't desire
At all, but they find that what they did desire
Has somehow led them to this situation
In which not to do that which is proposed
Seems inconsistent, hostile, or insane,
Though much more often very unfriendly; then too

Sometimes it chiefly is a lack of time
To explain how things have changed that leads one, waving
One's hands, aboard a ship that bodes one ill.
To walk away as Peter did is one way
Of avoiding such situations—another way
Is never to deceive or have high hopes
For foolish things; to be straight with oneself,
With one's own body, nature, and society,
To cast off everything that is not clear
And definite, and move toward one desire
After another, with no afterthoughts.
Living in this way one avoids the sudden
Transports of excitement Peter felt
When Norris mentioned a Poros walking tour.
For surely if Peter's natural desires
Had all been satisfied, if his life were running
Smoothly sexually, and if his health
Were excellent and his work going well,
He scarcely would have gotten so excited
At the mere thought of walking around Poros;
This sort of thing, however, often happens
To people from Northern countries, not just Peter,
And perhaps if one is English, Norse, or Swedish,
Danish, Finnish, Swiss, or North American,
One cannot avoid a certain amount of tension,
A certain quavering in the hand which reaches
For a ripe peach or the shoulder of a girl,
One whom, as one walks back from going swimming,
One thinks that one could eat, she's so delicious,
But only thinks it for a little while
(This thought itself is such a Northern one!
A Southerner would think about a place
Where he could go and jump on top of her)—
In any case, then, Northerners find it hard
To avoid such sudden excitements, but the English,
And especially the upper class, are worst of all,
Because besides their climate that's oppressed them
There's also been a restrictive upbringing,
Manners around the house perhaps too severe
For children—I am speaking of those English
Who escape from "class" and become bright or artistic,
The ones one sees on places like this island.

(These sudden outbursts of enthusiasm, of course,
Are often much admired by other people,
Particularly some not very smart ones,
Who think however they're very sensitive
And what they most admire is "vitality"
Which they think things like outbursts are a sign of,
And they can bore you far into the night
With telling you how wonderful some Dane
Or Norsky is, when you could be asleep
Dreaming of satisfying your desires
With persons who are always very warm,
Tender, and exciting—but, awake!
They're talking still, and though your sickly smile
Gets sicklier every moment, they go on:
"Hans suddenly got the idea to
Inundate Denmark. He is wonderful!"
"Oh, marvelous! Where does one go to meet him?"
"I'll give you his address. He has a farm
Where he stays in the summer; he loves animals,
But sometimes when he drinks a lot he beats them
And says that he can understand their language."
"How marvelous!" "And here's his city address:
Beschtungen aber Bass Gehundenweiss
996." "Goodnight." But Peter is
Not an exaggerated case like that,
And not a nagging bore who talks of such
People, but he has "outbursts" all the same.
It is true, in a sense these outbursts are
Difficult to discriminate from real
Vitality, which everyone esteems
These days because of man's oppressed position
In modern society, which saps his strength
And makes him want to do what everyone else does,
Whereas some man who says, "Let's pitch the glasses
Against the lamppost" is likely to be praised
By some low-IQ person who is there
As being really vital, ah he's wonderful.
Vitality, however, usually
Appeals to an answering vital force in others
And brings about making love or great events,
Or it at least gives pleasure—I can't judge
Vitality in any way but the way

It gives me pleasure, for if I do not get
Pleasure from life, of which vitality
Is just the liquid form, then what am I
And who cares what I say? I for one don't.
Therefore I judge vitality that way.)
But Peter, after having this idea
Of a walking trip on Poros, must have felt
That in walking around in the sun all day on an island
About which he knew nothing, there might come
Some insight to him or some relaxation,
Some feeling the way an Italian feels all the time,
Or perhaps not, perhaps he never does;
Peter at any rate was probably not
Conscious of an Italian at the time
He thought with pleasure about the walk on Poros,
But there he was, faced with Norris and Margaret
An hour before the boat came in, and Norris
Was saying "Maybe not." One mistake of Peter,
Or, rather, difficulty, a common one
In such enthusiasms, is that since
One's enthusiasm is motivated by submerged
Feelings and so its object isn't clear
To anyone, it is most likely that
Though they respond excitedly at first,
Partly because excitement is so communicable,
Others, when they think over what you've planned,
Will see it in a greyer light, unless of course
They have the same neuroses that you have,
In which case a whole lifetime might be built
Upon one of these outbursts. Norris, probably,
In drinking with Peter, wanted more than anything
To be agreeable, whereas Peter wanted
To "do" something unusual, not necessarily
Pleasing to Norris, not necessarily displeasing;
Norris, I should imagine, then, once he
Was out of Peter's company, since he'd known him
A very short time, was lacking the chief impulse
That motivated him when he agreed
To take a tour with Peter; therefore Margaret,
Speaking to Norris when he was alone
And saying she did not want to take the trip,
Found he immediately agreed with her,

Expressed some doubts at least, and said all right,
The trip was off then, he'd explain to Peter;
Peter, of course, was very surprised by this,
But still he must have been used to it because
The way that Norris and Margaret acted was based
On laws of human conduct which endure;
And since that outburst surely was not his first,
Peter was probably accustomed to
That sort of outcome of his impulses
And said to himself, "Ah, they don't understand,"
But probably knew inside that there was something
Seriously the matter with him. So when he left
The table and said, "I'm going to get my things,"
It was with a certain tension that he left,
Indicative of the fact he'd not come back,
And of the fact that he knew he would not avoid
Self-doubts because he avoided the useless boat trip;
Of course he wouldn't think he should have gone
But wonder why things had been the way they were.
It was these deeper worries in his mind,
I think, that kept him from leaving even sooner
With the same excuse, rather than a hope that Norris
Would change his mind again. Deep thoughts make helpless
Men for small undertakings. Well, perhaps
The last is speculation, but the rest
Seems surely true. I smiled, and closed the door.

# THE PLEASURES OF PEACE

# Sleeping with Women

Caruso: a voice.
Naples: sleeping with women.
Women: sleeping in the dark.
Voices: a music.
Pompeii: a ruin.
Pompeii: sleeping with women.
Men sleeping with women, women sleeping with women, sheep sleeping
    with women, everything sleeping with women.
The guard: asking you for a light.
Women: asleep.
Yourself: asleep.
Everything south of Naples: asleep and sleeping with them.
Sleeping with women: as in the poems of Pascoli.
Sleeping with women: as in the rain, as in the snow.
Sleeping with women: by starlight, as if we were angels, sleeping on the
    train,
On the starry foam, asleep and sleeping with them—sleeping with
    women.
Mediterranean: a voice.
Mediterranean: a sea. Asleep and sleeping.
Streetcar in Oslo, sleeping with women, Toonerville Trolley
In Stockholm asleep and sleeping with them, in Skansen
Alone, alone with women,
The rain sleeping with women, the brain of the dog-eyed genius
Alone, sleeping with women, all he has wanted,
The dog-eyed fearless man.
Sleeping with them: as in *The Perils of Pauline*
Asleep with them: as in Tosca
Sleeping with women and causing all that trouble
As in Roumania, as in Yugoslavia
Asleep and sleeping with them
Anti-Semitic, and sleeping with women,
Pro-canary, Rashomon, Shakespeare, tonight, sleeping with women
A big guy sleeping with women
A black seacoast's sleeve, asleep with them
And sleeping with women, and sleeping with them
The Greek islands sleeping with women
The muddy sky, asleep and sleeping with them.
Sleeping with women, as in a scholarly design

Sleeping with women, as if green polarity were a line
Into the sea, sleeping with women
As if wolverines, in a street line, as if sheep harbors
Could come alive from sleeping with women, wolverines
Greek islands sleeping with women, Nassos, Naxos, Kos,
Asleep with women, Mykonos, miotis,
And myositis, sleeping with women, blue-eyed
Red-eyed, green-eyed, yellow reputed, white-eyed women
Asleep and sleeping with them, blue, sleeping with women
As in love, as at sea, the rabbi, asleep and sleeping with them
As if that could be, the stones, the restaurant, asleep and sleeping with
    them,
Sleeping with women, as if they were knee
Arm and thigh asleep and sleeping with them, sleeping with women.
And the iris peg of the sea
Sleeping with women
And the diet pill of the tree
Sleeping with women
And the apology the goon the candlelight
The groan: asking you for the night, sleeping with women
Asleep and sleeping with them, the green tree
The iris, the swan: the building with its mouth open
Asleep with women, awake with man,
The sunlight, asleep and sleeping with them, the moving gong
The abacus, the crab, asleep and sleeping with them
And moving, and the moving van, in London, asleep with women
And intentions, inventions for sleeping with them
Lands sleeping with women, ants sleeping with women, Italo-Greek or
    Anglo-French orchestras
Asleep with women, asleep and sleeping with them,
The foam and the sleet, asleep and sleeping with them,
The schoolboy's poem, the crippled leg
Asleep and sleeping with them, sleeping with women
Sleeping with women, as if you were a purist
Asleep and sleeping with them.
Sleeping with women: there is no known form for the future
Of this undreamed-of view: sleeping with a chorus
Of highly tuned women, asleep and sleeping with them.
Bees, sleeping with women
And tourists, sleeping with them
Soap, sleeping with women; beds, sleeping with women
The universe: a choice

The headline: a voice, sleeping with women
At dawn, sleeping with women, asleep and sleeping with them.
Sleeping with women: a choice, as of a mule
As of an island, asleep or sleeping with them, as of a Russia,
As of an island, as of a drum: a choice of views: asleep and sleeping with
  them, as of high noon, as of a choice, as of variety, as of the sunlight, red
  student, asleep and sleeping with them,
As with an orchid, as with an oriole, at school, sleeping with women, and
  you are the one
The one sleeping with women, in Mexico, sleeping with women
The ghost land, the vectors, sleeping with women
The motel man, the viaduct, the sun
The universe: a question
The moat: a cathexis
What have we done? On Rhodes, man
On Samos, dog
Sleeping with women
In the rain and in the sun
The dog has a red eye, it is November
Asleep and sleeping with them, sleeping with women
This June: a boy
October: sleeping with women
The motto: a sign; the bridge: a definition.
To the goat: destroy; to the rain: be a settee.
O rain of joy: sleeping with women, asleep and sleeping with them.
Volcano, Naples, Caruso, asleep and sleeping, asleep and sleeping with
  them
The window, the windrow, the hedgerow, irretrievable blue,
Sleeping with women, the haymow, asleep and sleeping with them, the
  canal
Asleep and sleeping with them, the eagle's feather, the dock's weather, and
  the glue:
Sleeping with you; asleep and sleeping with you: sleeping with women.
Sleeping with women, charming aspirin, as in the rain, as in the snow,
Asleep and sleeping with you: as if the crossbow, as of the moonlight
Sleeping with women: as if the tractate, as if d'Annunzio
Asleep and sleeping with you, asleep with women
Asleep and sleeping with you, asleep with women, asleep and sleeping
  with you, sleeping with women
As if the sun, as of Venice and the Middle Ages' "true
Renaissance had just barely walked by the yucca
Forest" asleep and sleeping with you

In China, on parade, sleeping with women
And in the sun, asleep and sleeping with you, sleeping with women,
Asleep with women, the docks, the alley, and the prude
Sleeping with women, asleep with them.
The dune god: sleeping with women
The dove: asleep and sleeping with them
Dials sleeping with women; cybernetic tiles asleep and sleeping with them
Naples: sleeping with women; the short of breath
Asleep and sleeping with you, sleeping with women
As if I were you—moon idealism
Sleeping with women, pieces of stageboard, sleeping with women
The silent bus ride, sleeping with you.
The chore: sleeping with women
The force of a disaster: sleeping with you
The organ grinder's daughter: asleep with bitumen, sunshine, sleeping
    with women,
Sleeping with women: in Greece, in China, in Italy, sleeping with blue
Red green orange and white women, sleeping with two
Three four and five women, sleeping on the outside
And on the inside of women, a violin, like a vista, women, sleeping with
    women
In the month of May, in June, in July
Sleeping with women, "I watched my life go by" sleeping with women
A door of pine, a stormfilled valentine asleep and sleeping with them
"This Sunday heart of mine" profoundly dormoozed with them
They running and laughing, asleep and sleeping with them
"This idle heart of mine" insanely "shlamoozed" asleep and sleeping with
    them,
They running in laughter
To the nearest time, oh doors of eternity
Oh young women's doors of my own time! sleeping with women
Asleep and sleeping with them, all Naples asleep and sleeping with them,
Venice sleeping with women, Burgos sleeping with women, Lausanne
    sleeping with women, hail depth-divers
Sleeping with women, and there is the bonfire of Crete
Catching divorce in its fingers, purple sleeping with women
And the red lights of dawn, have you ever seen them, green ports sleeping
    with women, acrobats and pawns,
You had not known it ere I told it you asleep with women
The Via Appia Antica asleep with women, asleep and sleeping with them
All beautiful objects, each ugly object, the intelligent world,
The arena of the spirits, the dietetic whisky, the storms

Sleeping with women, asleep and sleeping with them,
Sleeping with women. And the churches in Antigua, sleeping with women
The stone: a vow
The Nereid: a promise—to sleep with women
The cold—a convention: sleeping with women
The carriage: sleeping with women
The time: sometimes
The certainty: now
The soapbox: sleeping with women
The time and again nubile and time, sleeping with women, and the time
    now
Asleep and sleeping with them, asleep and asleep, sleeping with women,
    asleep and sleeping with them, sleeping with women.

# Irresistible

Dear miles of love, the Solomon barefoot machine is quinting! dial aster, dial aster!

The ornery bench of wet state painters is minnowing into the dew! phosphorus seems like music lessons.

O bestiary of whose common childhood wings put the dials' acreage jollily into place, kneading

Together the formative impulses of a shirt front. O Crimea!

Sweet are the uses of adversity and. Sea lions dash through an impulse and. The keynote is yellow

Basement. My suffrage has created this hippopotamus. Welcome!

Welcome to the Greek lesson, infinitesimal shelves! art! this yowl is Beethoven

Speaking silence orangutan armament flute tea angel. What! O clear remains of luck's dial!

Ill men have no energy. Quonset hut! Backgammon inside the persimmon garage factory

Of knee length portmanteaux, Canadians! Win, win with Doctor Einstein! Once

Coffee laughed in boiling sleeves, Chicago lakefront. O pullman trade of keys!

Wednesday Bryn Mawr create the college shirt lesson peanut armada. Ah, coo!

Everything matronly impulses. Sophomore we stare at the sea. Love is a big bunch of laundry. My eye is a radish. In Labor Day

Comedies momentary openings jump oak trees by the by grape soda. Goodbye, Beethoven! Net

Whales jump about, decide, decide! The opera house of K. K. Clothes

C.C. April does and goes, A. Rainboat wink, ha!

Surely surely surely the sea has suffragettes' nailpolish kinky kimonos' calcium cogentness! Weights!

The plaza of hirsute wishes has now stumbled into the waste

Secede paper street arf crossing car canoe boxing frog liverwurst

Pajamas equalitarianism pool-game sissiness Calderon Shakespeare. The sea limps!

Copper April wire has dean bazooka quiescent her chair foot. Haven't you met

Lionel Food? After the archery pond soda left shirt bonita. We haven't met at the carpet-ball game.

Dials of Nice! Your cork fume is showing! thou dazzling beach! O honest
   peach Cyrano de Bergerac of golf pins!
Wednesday my hand, Tuesday my face, Wednesday the beautiful blue
   bugle; after all,
Water hasn't nearly concealed its pennies under the discrete lumberyard
Of calcium grasshoppers, nearer than a railroad train to pinkest shoes
Airing the youthful humps of there each so a big hatbox of myself! The
   siren punch, the match box, and
The kittens! Oysters, believe in the velvet kimono. And Monday my feet
   are cookies.
Thursday exams. Saturday silver officers. Friday a bowl of Queen Anne
   porridge. Paste me to a bar!
Dear miles of love, the Solomon barefoot machine is quinting! And faster
   and faster
The blue rose company believes the white air waves to be getting farther
   and farther away from yellow!
When December fig newtons steer through the enraged gas station
Of lilacs, bringing the crushed tree of doughnuts a suitable ornament
Of laughing bridgework pliable as a kilt in the muddiness of this
   November
Scene starring from juxtapositioning April languor, oceans
Breathless with the touch of Argentina's lilac mouse beat in quicksand
Solitude "we cling to me" and backness, O badness, refuse calico
Evidence in a cheese timelessness, on banners of soda, amid limits, cliffs,
Indians' real estate, clay, peat archery, glazed quarrels, pinks,
Clocks, pelts of cloisters, green gasworks, unlimited miracle Irish teens'
Asquith, Gorboduc, and Sensation, opened with the cheers of an article of
   commerce
To a "brandished" and "ill" pasteboard canoe of lumber
Fresher than an orchestra's hateful years of guest walk, the dachshund at
   midnight hung
Beside the green lanterns at Wilted Notch Point; eyes climb through the
   horses and amid the chair beans!
Coffee officers gamble on the lantern painting icicles and the pyramid!
The cloister of rafters is too tear-bitten to canoe blue Afghan mouse.
Earache, earache! its sunshine is brighter than life insurance—
Climates! Lovebirds, rooftops! "I've just brought them in from Africa."
The country club brings airplanes for canoes. It is spring. Old hairpins
   scrub strawberries.
Cereal says, "Mazy combs." There are cup birds swimming beside the
   mask fleet.

Winter is a normal A.C. pockets. Harvest I'll hymnbook. With cocoa-jest.

Cuthbert is racing by Arf Arf Swimmer. She's gentle clearing. Arf Arch cupboard amid the clouds.

Tree mussed gossamer Atlantic ouch toupées hearing book P.S. castiron pasteboard hearing aid in glove society fingers'

Alaska with bounce. "I am a raincoat cupboard of earaches and glass wainscots amid the dreary garden of graves unhumorous, bitten as green"—What winter

Hard to close. Manual training is life in China.

My legs aren't a chair; the silver sandpaper is mumbling "Storm! confess!"

# West Wind

It's the ocean of western steel
Bugles that makes me want to listen
To the parting of the trees
Like intemperate smiles, in a
Storm coat evangelistically ground
Out of spun glass and silver threads
When stars are in my head, and we
Are apart and together, friend of my youth
Whom I've so recently met—a fragment of the universe
In our coats, a believable doubling
Of the fresh currents of doubt and
Thought! a winter climate
Found in the Southern Hemisphere and where
I am who offers you to wear,
And in this storm, along the tooth of the street,
The intemperate climate of this double frame of the universe.

# We Sailed the Indian Ocean for a Dime

We sailed the Indian Ocean for a dime
And went into Africa for a penny
Refreshing Argentina
Rewarded us with many silver cars
For our toy train    We went to Kansas City
In the hope of finding quarters there
But instead we sailed the Manila Sea
Old sea pencils without landing quarters
Five dollars drew us to Tangiers
We had saved up enough dimes to purchase the bill
There it lies all crisp and green and light
Take it pick it up in your hands it is mine

We spent the five dollars in Biarritz in seven minutes
But at least we had a good meal and now we set sail
I've heard that Milwaukee is full of dimes and quarters
And that Cincinnati is the place for half dollars
I can see all that silver I can see it and I think I want it
Can see the sunlight lighting those silver faces
In far-off Cincinnati
The slim half dollars lying in the leaves
In the blue autumn weather behind the Conservatory of Music
Oh give me the money
That I may ascend into the sky
For I have been on so many boats and trains
While endlessly seeking the summits of my life!

# The Young Park

Hands picked
On her blossoms.
The young park was sad.

In the meadow the dog sat waiting for a shed.
The daisy flowers bloomed and laughed.
That cockroach's fever was bitter.
He worked in the landau.
Margaret's face became all cloaked with linen
When she saw the young park dying among the green trees, and answered
The young men who were always so desperately at her side: "You see
What will happen to us if I let you do what you've been
Trying. . . . ?" Mrs. Cockroach bowed pleasantly
To the hat bear. The sheep were all ado. "I bite,"
Said the happy cockroach.
In the meadows and in the park a dog sat cloaked in red woolen fuzz.
He had on a tennis court jacket.
He smelled like a steamship. His green eyes were red.
"You are all hot and heavy and yellow with crying," Jean said.
The bat made their voices ring. The plane spun
Down into yo-yos of dizzying aspirin chaffinch.

In sixteen times at the plate
Young Park had made only one hit.
He dug his feet into the gridiron.
The sky was a white lobster.

Of a perfect strike! Young Park
Relaxed and struck lights from the ax.
He exaggerated among the boats.
His engine was scooting for victory.

"It is the imagination of dance addicts,"
Young Park said with one hand
As he held the door open for the new
Manager of the Hens with the other. "That's decorum!"

Had the young park forgotten how to forgive, was that her difficulty?
The men rose up and tried to be forgiven in the park.

Then the wet moss became something you must try to forget.
I am afraid it is all over with the young park.

"What do I care? Men tell me I am fooling.
In the summer my foot sticks because it is snowing
The ancient regime of reason and the moss is crumbling
Beneath the penitential feet of frisky dogs. Following
My destiny I should die at the age of seventeen, but how can I
Live out this year? The marriage van is grumbling
At my feet its maddened "Try!" O Life! and mine a mixture
Of husky trees and the oil from a baddened car. O disassembled
Garden walls, mayn't you give your pity to a young park?

This is how Oswald became famous.
His whole conduct was dissimulated:
He changed his name to Fred Smith

And spent his summers in Young Park
Perfecting boiler engines
In the free laboratory they supplied there.
However the Foundation stipulated
No one named Oswald shall be, by Young Park,
Granted the use of its facilities
Without paying, but be obliged to pay six cents
For each kilowatt hour exacted of the lamps
And bulbs of the Young Park Seed and Tree Grant Foundation Free
    Laboratory Stationary Fund Facilities Buildings. . . .

In Young Park the coppery city girl felt cold,
So she took all her clothes off except
Her gloves and ran into the water with Mr. Southland.

Above the stones
Young Park spoke to the people in a dead language.
He cautioned them to watch out for sparks
From Oswald's shoes. Then he gave them the baseball glove
For which they had been waiting for fifteen years.

"These traffic lamps have colors that would be perfect for cigarettes," the
    young park said.

The automobile club had changed its location again, and was now located in the zoo.

At the zoo the automobile club was disregarded, everyone stared into the chicken cages.

Then one night the young giraffe became hurt, and the Zoo River was dammed up.

A boat came down the Zoo River. Inside the boat was Dame Oswald.

That boat came to the dam; Dan Cupid played on his quiver; Dame Oswald was left out at the door of the automobile club.

Dame Oswald fell in love with a bear cub she saw whose cage had been left open; and then she reboarded ship with the bear cub.

The next day the zoo reopened its gates to the physical education inspector. He decreed that Zoo River must be reopened.

Thus the automobile club floated out to sea, and the terrible truth of dust is at ease again.


Oswald's victory in the Paris sweepstakes has just been announced; and there is a rumor that he is coming home again.

A grain of sand floats down to the catchy bottom of summer.

At noon the pelvises walk into the green hospital and speak: "The young park is dead.

Young Park has just been killed in a prize fight. Young Park has been ravaged and destroyed by fire."


But here comes Oswald! What an air he has about him!

He looks as though he's raving mad, and there is Margaret on his arm!

I think they are having a bite of cheese before going into the delicatessen.

Stop them and ask them for the news from over there.

There's that dog in a red jacket!

Oswald is really crazy!

Bicycles, the moon and the stars. The seashore.

Look! he's all dressed up, but his mouth is foaming! Aaaahhhhhhhh!


Quick, let's get away from here! You can borrow my blue bicycle.

I'll ride slowly down to sea on my orange-and-red one.

The immense men ride swiftly away on green bicycles, because the young park is dead.

"Wait a moment!"


"At night, when everything is yellow and green,
You too can come alive
If you believe in me."

# Poem

The thing
To do
Is organize
The sea
So boats will
Automatically float
To their destinations.
Ah, the Greeks
Thought of that!
Well, what if
They
Did? We have no
Gods
Of the winds!
And therefore
Must use
Science!

# Three Short Poems

### HEANORUPEATOMOS

Unroll this enrollment.
There, you see—
And now we have done.

And back to another day in the bars of Paris.

### AN X-RAY OF UTAH

Valley! my whole head is a valley! valley! valley!

### RELIGIOUSLY

There is rain in my heart and a boat in the harbor
Greece submerged in the sea      The blue light on its waters
A child wanders in torn clothes crying Vacation!

# Dostoevski's *The Gambler*

Dostoevski's *The Gambler*
Lay on the table.
I opened to page one:
Neshish stroggen baihoosh.

Mantegna's white sculpture,
*The Tail of a Dolphin*,
Lay slumbering in Italy;
The sea it was blue.

Don Mozart's *Concerto*
*Alexander von Wertheim*,
*The Fifth*, for piano
And table legs, bouncers and flute

Was silent, on separate pages.
A painting of bankruptcy spilt through the walls;
Its yellow and gray
Exposed it as a goldfish Juan Gris.

My sailboat has crashed
Against a wall,
My domino is spattered with black
Mud. But where is the hashish of Toledo?

# Hearing

Hear the beautiful tinny voices of the trumpets
Beside the rushing sound of the great blue waterfall;
See the guns fire, then hear the leaves drop to the ground;
Lie back in your chair—and now there is the clatter of pennies!
The familiar scraping noise of the chair feet on the ground,
As if a worm had grown six feet tall! And here is the worm,
And hear his softly scraping noise at the forest gate.
In the Bourse the diamonds clink and clank against each other,
And the violet airplane speaks to the farmland with its buzz
From high in the air, but you hear the slice
Of shears and watch the happy gardener's face whiten
As he hears the final throbs of his failing heart.
All is not stillness—far from it. The tinny
Trumpets renew their song among the eglantine's
Too speciously gracious brilliance, and a hen drops
An egg, with infinite gentleness, into the straw.

Who is this young man with the tremendous French horn in the garden
With a lady in lilac bending her head to catch each note
That flows, serene and unbidden, from the silvery throat?
I think they are strangers here. Stones fall in the pool.
She smiles, she is very witty, she bends too far, and now we hear
The sound of her lilac dress ripping in the soft summer air.

For it is summer! Hear the cool rush of the stream and the heavy black
Vocalism of leaves in the wind. A note then comes, arises
In the air, it is a glass in which a few warm drops of rain
Make music; there are roars and meows, turkeys and spaniels
Come running to the great piano, which, covered with pearls,
Gives extra, clinking sounds to your delighted ears;
And the dogs bark, and there is the little thrilled silence of snails. . . .
Above all else you hear the daisies being torn apart
By tremendous bumblebees who have come here from another
    Department!
"Wisteria tapping the house, so comes your blood. . . ."

Now rain, now this earth streams with water!
Hear the tooting of Triton among the clouds
And on the earth! See the trumpets of heaven floating toward us

Blaring among the wet masses of citron and vermilion wings!
They play "Put down the cushion on the chair,
Put down the cushion on the chair, put down
The cushion, put it down, put the cushion down on the chair,
Ra ta ta. . . ." The young man's French horn is wet, it makes a different
    noise,
The girl turns her face toward him and he hears strings (it is another tear
    in her dress!).
In the kitchen the sound of raspberries being mashed in the cream
Reminds you of your childhood and all the fantasies you had then!
In the highest part of an oak tree is a blue bird
Trilling. A drying friend reads *Orlando Furioso*
Sitting on a beach chair; then you hear awnings being stretched out!
A basso sings, and a soprano answers him.
Then there is thunder in a clear blue sky,
And, from the earth, a sigh: "This song is finished."

# A Poem of the Forty-Eight States

I

O Kentucky! my parents were driving
Near blue grass when you became
For me the real contents of a glass
Of water also the first nozzle of a horse
The bakery truck floating down the street
The young baboon woman walking without a brace
Over a fiord

The electric chair steamed lightly, then touched
Me. I drove, upward,
Into the hills of Montana. My pony!
Here you are coming along with your master!
Yet I am your master! You're wearing my sweater.
O pony, my pony!

As in a dream I was waiting to be seventh
To smile at my brothers in the happy state of Idaho
Each and every one of them condemned to the electric chair!
What have we done? Is it a crime
To shoe horses? Beside a lemon-yellow stream
There seemed to be compact bassoons,
And I was happy and a crackerjack.

My stovepipe hat! Perhaps you think I am Uncle Sam?
No, I am the State of Pennsylvania. . . .
O hills! I remember writing to a city
So as to be contented with my name
Returning in the mails near the mark "Pennsylvania"!

"Somewhere over that hill is Georgia."
What romance there was for me in the words the old man said!
I wanted to go, but was afraid to wander very far.
Then he said, "I will take you in my wagon of hay."
And so we rode together into the Peach State.
I will never forget that day, not so long as I live,
I will never forget the first impressions I had in Georgia!

In Zanesville, Ohio, they put a pennant up,
And in Waco, Texas, men stamped in the streets,
And the soldiers were coughing on the streetcar in Minneapolis,
    Minnesota.
In Minocqua, Wisconsin, the girls kissed each other and laughed,
The poison was working in Monroe, Illinois,
And in Stephanie, New Hampshire, burning fragments were thrown up.

It was the day of the States, and from Topeka, Kansas,
To Lumberville, New York, trees were being struck
Down so they could put the platforms up. However I lay struck
By sunlight on the beach at Waikiki, Hawaii . . .
Why can't Hawaii be one of the United States?
Nothing is being celebrated here; yet the beaches are covered with sun . . .

Florida, Vermont, Alabama, Mississippi!
I guess that I will go back to the United States.
Dear friend, let's pack our bags and climb upon the steamer!
Do not forget the birds you have bought in the jolly land of France,
They are red white orange yellow green and pink and they sing so sweetly,
They will make music to us upon the tedious ocean voyage.

Tedious! How could I have said such a thing?
O sea, you are more beautiful than any state!
You are fuller and bluer and more perfect than the most perfect action.
What is a perfect action?
In the streets of Kokomo a cheer goes up,
And the head of the lion is cursed by a thousand vicissitudes.

Indiana! it is so beautiful to have tar in it!
How wonderful it is to be back on a trolley car, ding dong ding!
I think I will wander into the barbershop and get my hair cut!
Just hear the slice of the scissors, look at the comb!
Now to be once more out in the streets of Indiana
With my hair much shorter, with my neck smelling of talcum powder!

O lucky streetcar wires to be able to look at me, and through whom I can
     see the sun!

I did not know there was so much sun in North Dakota!
But the old man who is telling me about it nods his head and says yes.
I believe him because my skin is peeling. Now I see people going to the
     voting booth.
The voting wagon is red and wooden, it stands on wheels where it is
     anchored to the curb.
I had no idea there were so many old men and old women in North
     Dakota,
But the old man who is explaining things to me says that each is above
     voting age.




4


I cannot remember what all I saw
In northern Florida, all the duck we shot.

You have asked me to recall Illinois,
But all I have is a handful of wrinkles.

Perhaps you would like me to speak of California,
But I hope not, for now I am very close to death.

The children all came down to see the whale in Arkansas,
I remember that its huge body lay attached to the side of the river.




5


O Mississippi joys!
I reckon I am about as big and dead as a whale!
I am slowly sinking down into the green ooze
Of the Everglades, that I feared so much when I was a child!
I have become about as flat as the dust on a baseball diamond
And as empty and clear as the sky when it is just-blue
And you are three, and you stand on the rim of the zone of one of the
     United States

And think about the forty-seven others; then in the evening
Air you hear the sound of baseball players, and the splash of canoes!
You yourself would like to play baseball and travel, but you are too young;
However you look up into the clear flat blue of the evening sky
And vow that you will one day be a traveler like myself,
And wander to all the ends of the earth until you are completely
    exhausted,
And then return to Texas or Indiana, whatever state you happen to be
    from.
And have your death celebrated by a lavish funeral
Conducted by starlight, with numerous boys and girls reading my poems
    aloud!


6


O Charleston! why do you always put me in the mood for kidding?
I am not dead yet, why do you make me say I am?
But I think I am growing older, my shoes are falling off,
I think it must be that my feet are getting thinner and that I am ready to
    die.
Here comes my pony from Montana, he is a mere skull and crossbones,
And here is the old man who told me about North Dakota, he is a little
    baby,
And here is Illinois, and here is Indiana, I guess they are my favorite
    states,
I guess I am dying now in Charleston, South Carolina.
O Charleston, why do you always do this . . . Gasp! Goodbye!


7


In Illinois the trees are growing up
Where he planted them; for he has died.
But I am the one who originally intended to read
You the fast movements. Now we will hear the *Brandenburg*
*Concertos.* Now we will go up in an
Airplane. Steady . . . The poet of America, Walt Whitman, is dead.
But many other poets have died that are reborn

In their works. He also shall be reborn,
Walt Whitman shall be reborn.

8

I did not understand what you meant by the Hudson Tunnel,
But now I understand, New Jersey, I like it fine,
I like the stifling black smoke and the jagged heave-ho of the trains,
I like the sunlight too at the end of the tunnel, like my rebirth in the
    poems of Kenneth Koch,
I like the way the rosy sunlight streams down upon the silver tracks,
I like the way the travelers awake from their dreams and step upon the
    hard paving stone of the station,
But I reckon what I should like best would be to see Indiana again,
Or Texas or Arkansas, or Alabama, the "Cotton State,"
Or Big Rose Pebble Island off the coast of Maine
Where I used to have so much fun during the summer, cooking and
    kidding and having myself a good time,
I like Pennsylvania too, we could have a lot of fun there,
You and I will go there when Kenneth is dead.

# The Scales

Ann sat at the piano singing scales—
First the full-throated, evening-fated DO
(Self-consciousness to start at the right place
And get it low enough) and then the RE
With a slight rising, more secure by now
As to where in absolute sound that tone should fall;
Then, with dark half-disordered thoughts of self
Fighting from the the subconscious yet still willing
To be at last soothed by that music, MI;
Then with relief and a half smile breathed FA,
Then the demanding, round, full-throated SOL,
Which like the earlier note struck harmonies
In language not related to its place
In the parade of monosyllables,
Each with a tone; then, with eyes lighted, LA,
As if she had discovered something as
Delightful as the sound itself, yet more
Related to the world; then, scorning this,
A high, dry, light, and chiefly abstract TI
(Though thoughts were fighting here, despite the spelling,
And odors of hot smoke; but yet the struggle
Over the previous note made this one simpler
As a bright light distracts one from less light,
Or at least makes one capable of behaving,
Inspired, as if the lesser light weren't there,
One's eyes stung with the brightness of the other
And one's intention fortified by pain,
Defeat, and wish for purity; one has
The strength to go on there); at last a full,
Sweet-throated, evening-weighted, though much higher
Than that before it, more like afternoon
In just that moment when day turns to dark,
With pleasure at the ending, plus some strain
At feeling this impurity, oh full
Of all she had so far accomplished, DO.
Starting again, yet this time with the DO
With which she had concluded previously,
She sings it now, but weights it differently,
Which now is a beginning, not an end;

And, like the second step of the next flight
After the first, which leads one out of darkness,
Yet surely to a height one cannot go
Without divine assistance, she sings RE,
Which though it's higher than the last seems darker,
As if foreboding, still a lesser note;
Then, with more gaiety this time, a MI
That makes her think of roses, afternoons
When light is on the tea set, not so much
Conscious this time of an identity
As such, but an identity in things,
Or, rather, hovering round them—no, it's this:
This MI is a possible me sensed only in song,
Not hearty like the other with real doubt
Of earth and death; and now a lightsome FA,
Easy as feathers; then a trilling SOL
Which is to the last MI as is a detour
Which leads one to the sun; and then, as if
Song had no sound, one thrilling highest LA,
A whispered TI, and, coughing at the DO,
She clears her throat and starts this scale again,
Which she sings easily; a cool, clear TI
This time, and a high, lovely, round, full DO,
Like a small rose. Taking this rose again
She starts another scale with it; this time
A thrill is in her voice, for such beginning
Is dangerous, and she may never reach
The end of this third scale. Her confidence
In singing DO is balanced by a touch
Of gloom, or sign of strain, in the third RE,
And then a sense of real pain in the MI
(Self-consciousness, but now of a new kind—
As if she asked herself, "Can *I* do this?"),
Although it sings delightfully, then FA,
Attended by some tension toward its end
As if she felt she had to catch it up
And harden it, for fear that it would be
Too flabby-soft after what came before;
And then, with her whole spirit glowing, SOL,
Just right; and when, as on some garden steps
Whitewashed and lovely, one at last can see

The tulips washed above, blazing in red
And yellow, blue, and violet, and feels
Almost too weak to take those final steps
But yet is primed with energy by the beauty
That lies above, she mightily sang LA
(And here she gave up everything to God,
Or Fate, or chance, or Muses, or whatever,
And let her voice go, simply, if it would),
Then a delicious, light, high, spacious TI,
And, marvelous! one pure, celestial DO.
From this DO she descended: DO, TI, LA
(How strange it sounded, as if it were wrong!),
SOL, FA, MI, RE, DO!
Then down again from that relaxing DO
Quite in the middle: DO, TI, LA, SOL, FA
(Much easier, descending), MI, RE, DO;
Then taking up that DO again, still down,
And down again, DO, TI, LA, SOL, FA, MI,
RE, DO. And then, as if she wished to try
How deep her voice would go, she started DO,
TI, LA from there, but at the FA she choked,
Her face turned purple—something in her throat
Had split: she hemorrhaged; and, in three hours, died.

# Ma Provence

En ma Provence le blé est toujours vert
Et les filles sont jolies
Elles ne meurent pas elles vous aiment à la folie—en ma Provence.

Bills break the breakfast teacups and the sun
Shines darkly over the bill-ware
She writes it out in enervating prose
"In my Provence, my rose."

# Coast

Entwime this shower like a wave, cool elbows!
Amagansett syringe Calabria loop pajamas!
Total beloved flirt pool pajamas
Network sleep Anta photoplasm karmas.
Yes, I have Peruvian Tory plasmas!
Ope! evenings of arrogant dancing sleepies?
Cousin sylfur. Asleep? No.

How? Well, it's like this—
Pargis ulpy sleets at nine-pa
And show much to greep lah.
Toostoo? The gree da doomp cherry
It was three o'clock in the shah
But only nigh-den in the cours, ha?
On empulating. Shuzzup, he is dreenkp.
And,

Hoof morning dairy, alive, airy
Shahzump, has
"We cuzznt shay up too lade" cars
And fleas. Lem go kamma glurp. Ah,
Good morning! For nothing you expect
Shall interfere with this day's airy tines
To fork you music over heartfelt lines
If you can forget how tired we were last night.

Deceiving elf! Fazzum garra maggle twad. Enkh!
I should have known, cow mar a graceful beach stube, hats.
She lives here, appar, as in a throat
Buzz argam. Stop that, Tommy, I'm really awake!

Awake! awake! Azza magger gazump fazgul, eelmp
Oorp. Don't kid! I'm ready! See? Arzump.
And she appears
Attired in her beautiful white hair. *Dove è andata?*
Or, rather, *dove andiamo?* RIzzzzzzzzzzzzzzzzzzzz.

Chapter Forty. The Big Fish.
Then we went sailing, my taste duchess

End I, O frost unconscitude
Met, as agong puréed silver
Shazzle. Ooooohze, uhmp.
God dam somebody lib with.
Discovered silver.
Mahzgod limp.
Shoe.
Im-kazim.

Dear, wake up, we are—uh uh, no, ahzinnnnnnnng
Pajamas
Some panther azing Christ pajamas
Who to? not my sing? weeks, yes,
Entire frost go by
Before you'll wake up. . . . Himazzer beach
Izza grade painer—

O Puerto Com, goodbye!

# Some South American Poets

## Jorge Guinhieme (1887–)

### BOILING WATER

The boiling water, Father, and princely teacher
Whose first reckoning with boiling water
The teeth of the far center will vindicate for seeds
Of us who have lost the first battle!
That boiling water is the dream
Of Jorge Guiells of the Civil Guard—
Every night he washes his passion in it,
Hoping that it will not rub off on the white ribs of Sevilla.
His mother watches him. With five ribs for screen
The dusty night darkens what he has willed.

### CABANA AILANTHUS

At the Cabana Ailanthus when night breezes are stilled
One old commonwealth teacher remains fastened to his desk.
Through the night come the sounds of the frog
As if someone, or as if an entire people, had learned a Romance language.

### OBSCURITY

When the dark night obscures of our tiny village the immense and topless
   steeple
Then we heard the bells ring out, for fear that some men might entrance
   not gain
To their preferred Eastern lights. But a fountain of anachronistic feathers
Darkens the blood of the priest gown before speechlessly he utter the
   ungracious words.

*FROM* THE STREETS OF BUENOS AIRES

ROSEWAY

O unfeigned laughter of a fine young girl—
Or even of one not so fine—
Young girl, that is the essential thing,
And laugh unfeigned—
But how can you not be fine beneath your roses?


CABANA DE TURISTAS, CALLE DE SUENOS (DREAMS)

Here, where there are tourists
Gathered, let us carry
From one of them to another
The money from their country
That they may see
We do not wish it for ourselves
But only that they may share with one another
What they have.


PLEASURE STREET

When all are sleeping
The staccato of those not sleeping
Is a mysterious graph on which
The mathematics teacher studies nightly
To find the stars.


CALLE ROSA

Roseway, oh lovely girl,
Your face is like a tulip.
I have tulip* too, my lovely girl,
And happily will mingle them with yours.


* "Tulip" is in English in the original.—*Trans.*

*FROM* STREETS

More open to the light
Than many little streets
This one on which I met you
Carrying a basket of light
To the sea, is my preferred one of
All the little by-ways of the city.


## Luis De Calliens (1918–)


CANCION DE NOCHE

A catacomb of feathers
Boiling. A frame.
The steep frame of ducks' loves roiling
Together the fantastic pathways.

Now a drumstick of night,
Two Indians on a highway—
One stricter than a feather,
The other, clasped by might.


TO A DREAM

Chuckle out, great planned song
Of the ages!
Laugh ages henceforth to be so free!
We are the ones who knew you in
Your star-spangled babyhood—
We are the perusers of your eternal rose!


THE MORGAN LIBRARY

I, Luis de Calliens, Spanish teacher
And South American poet, as I am known,

See now in Nueva York this Morgan Library
Spattered by the mutual funds of her bloody night.
The rich in Nuena de Cangias do not build libraries
And the poor carry a network of berries into the future's light.


## Luis Cariges (1922–)


### PERIPHER-ARGENTINE

How many stories, bought from love and rain,
This testimony winks to see. Above
These Herculean heights,
Peripher-Argentine,
And far above the desecrated woodlands
And the hopeless farmlands
And the testimonials of bright Western night
A human voice begins a styptic melody
Corroded by your blossoms
Indifferent to the month
And year of every star—
O Argentine!


### BESOS

My mouth, a cascade of kisses!
And, purely below me, your mouth too,
An equal cascade of remembrance, farms of bliss,
Evidence, preoccupation, evening stars,
Truly, reversing our tables,
When, at dusk, we reform
Trees to their original grandeur,
As nude as each other's stars.


### MUSIC

A song creates its own music.

## Juan Garcia (1940–)

### PLAINT

O rolling mountains of my native fascist unconscious mother!
O divine transcendence of some future impassioned stream!
When the souls of the billionaires shall lie streaming in the bloodied
Banknotes of a whorish fantasma, whose plucked grace notes the hideous
    transactor no longer
Imbues with the maleficent horror of death's magnificent scream!

What, O rolling native mountains whose fascist resistances
Strike against the mutinied hearts of mothers, of orphans, of knees
Of silence, what are your invocations, to me, and to my mother poets,
What emblems do you carry for us? when shall we strike the DOLLARO
    from the hideous mustang of our homes?

### ODE TO GUINHIEME

When shall we strike the dollaro, magnificent poet, betrayer of your class?
When shall we tear the mould-headed thread-ribbed dollaro to pieces?
Speak, Guinhieme, if you know . . . but you do not know, and you will not
    speak. You spew wildly into your lunch!

## Vactha (193?–)

### CAMPANHO

Roll, little garden fields, away!
No longer the garden, they insist
As proper for a muse. This time, however, once peruse
The mist and that fair fountain
Which is reflected there
As in the early starlight
Over Buenos Aires
It begins to rain.
First drops!

Brilliant little baby, walk
Across the portico. There, a smiling mama
Will take you in her arms. You will smile.
And I too shall smile. And in this poem I shall enshrine you forever!

## The Hasos in Argentine Poetry

The essence of Argentinian poetry is the *hasos*, or fallen limb. I do not know if my English readers will get a clear idea of this structural element of poetry without some further words of explanation. *Hasosismo*, or the "art of the fallen limb," a technique which was buried deep in the history and classicism of the poetry of our Argentine, is recently brought into the foreground by works of masters who have seen what long was hidden, that to be authentically new the poet is obliged to find poetic elements which are authentically old—that is, authentically *his own*. For we do not exist in the new, but in the permanent—where all is both old and new—and it is the poet's task precisely to remind us of this condition. The "art of the fallen limb," insofar as it can be separated from the Argentinisms of prosodic and syllabic ramifications, may be, I suppose, briefly said to be *the art of concealing in one line what has been revealed in the previous line*. Younger practitioners and, above all, explicators of the *hasosismo* have made often the error of seeing this function as the reverse of what it actually is: the revelation in one line of what was concealed in the preceding—or, the concealing in one line of what is to be revealed in the next. This is not hasosismo: this is fancy and the commonest and most ordinary of poetic and all narrative processuses. HASOSISMO IS THE MYSTERY OF NIGHT COVERED BY THE DAY; IT IS NOT THE DAY, WHICH IS REVEALED AFTER BEING HIDDEN IN THE NIGHT. The difference here is one of heights to plains. San Baz has *hasosismo*; Cediz does not. Juanero is a million miles from having it. In Batorje it is supreme.

*Guinhieme**

* *Hasosismo* is difficult to illustrate, since by its very nature it tends to cover its own tracks. Furthermore, in translation much is necessarily to be lost, but the attempt is worth making, since this heartstone of poetry deserves to be known beyond our language. Here are some examples from the middle work of Batorje:

The streets of the city are shining, wet with light
In the dark and dry forgetfulness of rivers . . .

*Motion of Trees* (1932)


You give me your hand; it is white with pointed
Forests accepting the horizon . . .

*Moon Breed* (1936)


We stand in clouds. The highest tree, far beneath us
Our underwater stamina muddies toward her true contempt.
Indians once walked along this grit with plastic bells
Whose trees only her final simplicity can chide . . .

*Modern* (1943)


In San Baz can be found experiments in using the *hasos* within the line, rather than in succeeding lines. The inspiration from Batorje seems self-evident:

Sweet dreams! dry daylight sounds without feeling or image—

SAN BAZ, *October on the Railroad* (1960)


I look at you. Oceans of beer gush from the left side of my collar
bone.

SAN BAZ, *Madam* (1964)


Garcia, in attempting to use the *hasos* politically, has, I think, essentially weakened its poetic function, but some of his examples have a notable strength:

The Fascists have tied up their mistresses:
One set of brawny men kicking another in the teeth!

JUAN GARCIA, *The Mistresses of Garcia* (1962)

They have befouled us
With the perfumes of exultation.

JUAN GARCIA, *Homage* (1964)

Calliens, in perhaps too academic a way, has praised the *hasos* in verses using it themselves. Of the long (200 lines) poem, these verses are characteristic:

A small brain, you are a wide heart;
A great inspirer, you seek only liquids;
Sainthood, O Hasos, the bed-land of America!
A street without silence, you are the steel one;
My heart without drama, you pet the mammal dog;
O Hasos, my clear observation!

CALLIENS, *In Praise of Hasos* (1961)

An example of what *hasos* is NOT, though it has sometimes been thought to be:

A dark congregation of valleys
Suddenly brings us the sea.

LUIS CEDIZ, *Atalanta* (1943)

From my own work, in conclusion, two examples, one of which I believe to have the *hasos*, the other not:

The dark pagan of the sea
Rolls endlessly into our childhood . . .

*Flavinia* (1936)

Mountains reverberate; seas roar
For the Christhood in which they believe.

*Otros Cristos* (1957)

J.G.

# Reflections on "Hasosismo"

*Hasosismo* in a pure state mocks the punditism of the masters. Guinhieme's "hasosismo" is no more the pure form that appeared in Lope than is Guilha's "structured license." Neither modern writer has bothered to do his scholarship well. Both have confused a linguistic particularity with a technic structure of design.

*Hasosismo*, as we encounter it in Lope and in certain of his contemporaries, is no more than a fixed, and academically fixed and predetermined way of avoiding the vulgar and over-explicit in every instance. One characteristic function of this kind of esthetico-literary lèse-majesté is the avoiding of revealed nakedness, a gently clothing over of all that is too barely and openly flung before the reader's eyes.

In Gomero and Pepite this one aspect of true *hasosismo*, which to Guinhieme is *hasosismo* itself and entire, was stressed at the expense of the whole and true concept, which no longer seemed to fit an age of vulgarity and expansion. Gomero's "hasosismo" was the artist's replique to a time which he found too vulgar to share his concerns and certainly his visions. The thing stated was immediately hidden: it is an art of the standstill. We feel the anguish of his time in this technique.

This is not all of *hasosismo*. To Guinhieme and to others of a modern time, a time which feels itself more anguished perhaps than that of a Gomero or a Pepite, this one use of *hasosismo* necessarily appeals. The mistake is forgiven as soon as it is understood. But the term is vulgarized in the process. Of all the foci of Argentine esthetics it is this one (*hasosismo*) which it most imports, perhaps, to retain in purity. For true *hasosismo* has reference to both diction and structure. Without this knowledge the student of Lope is fatally handicapped before he has begun.

*Omero Pecad*, STUDIES FOR A LEFTIST UNIVERSITY, Buenos Aires, 1963.

HOMAGE

A long line of lyricists
Starting with Lope
Move toward the station—
Listen to them shouting!
Look at their breeziness!
They have befouled us
With the perfumes of exultation!

Listen to them praising!
Whom do they praise now?
Francisco Franco!
Demagogues and Popes!
Look at them grazing!
What do they feed on now?
Aspirations, hopes!

Ah let us destroy them
Immediately!
Cut up their breeches!
Turn them into baloney!
Feed them to the pigs, when
Darkness is approaching!
Lyricist! Hash! Over here!

JUAN GARCIA


## OCTOBER ON THE RAILROAD

A pure blue sun in the sky! the red leaves fall.
Some of the yellow ones are still holding on to their branches.
And in the distance I hear the engine roar.
October on the railroad! Sometimes, like a rhinoceros,
Fierce and angry, the gray locomotive will come
Tearing the leaf-beds to pieces, and at other times
The engine is gentle, a lakeside hotel
Perhaps, where one's mistress is staying.
One longs to see her—is it a dream?
Sweet dreams! dry daylight sounds without feeling or image
Consult the atlas of a goodbye! And now the train!
Will it take me to Switzerland, do you think? Bavaria?
That depends, O stems, upon your road . . .

GARCIA SAN BAZ


## MADAM

I look at you. Oceans of beer gush from the left side of my collar bone
And down my sides, until they form a crystal pool at my feet

In which children are swimming. I push them back and to one side.
Perhaps to love you only it has been given
To me, lady beyond many sorrows. Perhaps you are not of the Mistresses
    of Garcia
Or of Streets Which Are Waving Goodbye. But I love you. Straw sailors
Come out of my brow. They coast in that fresh sea sky.

GARCIA SAN BAZ


## MEADOWS

Prairies outside dormant cities, America of dreams!
There is no reason for you to be without collarbone.
Without dentistry, yes, they have killed him many times,
But not the definitive movies which showed him rolling
In a pirate flag uphill. No, I am not explaining
Too much. I think you walk quietly to me.
Do you remember what our feeling was
Before we took positions up? Then, quietly walking over
Was all we asked of life. Perhaps the days
Were shorter then, though they are not long now.
Perhaps the only thing we said was Yes
To a dreamy tyrant who has enslaved us now
In the boughs of a tree. The pig raved and slept.
In trains we have been shorter than our pampas.

GARCIA SAN BAZ

# Seine

Hounded by Central Islip till the end
Of pyrethmetic days, and onward wishing
Oh that he like me and she like me too,
And the green arboretum bush waving
And the elephant in his noose waving
And the deaths saying goodbye—
Hello to the Death Family!
Here is mother, father, and here is Nell:
She is looking very bright and pretty in her nasturtiums
And the sea wall caves down—
Exit Roland with Angelica *in braccia: Come?*
Says Orlando, you expect to find a bathroom
In these mountains? Come on, now, father, now.
And the Greece temperature change index that day
Floogled all the way bottom to a chortled bottom,
I began to rain confidence on the eastern shore
When the Egyptian confidence room opened, she looked pretty
She had him eating nasturtiums out of a symbolic tube
Of yesterday's restored brush-stroke emblems, whose
Pie only God could call a "more than gift."
There were selected ways and "island gift"
And "party pris" and all other conduct emblems
Toward a future and then toward a future
And then her neck toward a future—if you call "the limited way."
And maybe after all that is right. Maybe the alert dock hound
Scimitar evening is "frigolescent"—I think you look pretty
With me; she had him call in hallways
With busted floors, and when he gave the album
Of wasted flowers to her mother, she
Began to dance, as if Okie's Delicatessen were shifted Paris.
But cannot come easily to the true meaning,
Which is "he topped her puberty"? No,
Another bale to want about Ann Jeffries.
Then she began to slip up, down the beaches
Where cookies had been laid. To her the colonel
Was just a human mattress, but the sea
Was dialectic brilliance. They all lived family
Style in a huge straw hut in the Barbados
Where Dad worked out fifteen hours a day as a steward

In a psychiatric shipping firm
Down St. Louis Avenue. Melanie took up the fluffy powder
And smashed it into the clothesline towel. Damn Bernie,
She said. And the ocean keeps flashing
Signs of hope, or "perfection is a bottle of iced tea"
As the lost ranger said, when Uncle Ernie
Was smashed to doom beside the oceanic cave
And Martha came back to her babies above land, with this sad news.
Come on, Ariel, I'm tired of dippy
Parties and your slow-down repartee.
There is only one great comic born every five million "antons," said
    Uncle Ernie,
But Pam said, " 'You're the ivory lord, of me."
And the balls were hit out into the infield
And the outfield, and Bernie kept looking for the
Ball which Bettie had bit which had a white necktie painted on it
And he said There is only one great comic born every five
Million "epons," it was impossible to see the Mediterranean
In her waving bush, since Fred had deleted the ikons
From the coffee machine. I began to catch on at last, and opened,
Myself, a King Kong Fruit Store. We have
A great comic among us, Beirut Radio said—
You who are truly my friend would never welcome
A personal appearance that betrayed me like this one
For no sooner had the beautiful wolfhound princess entered the Microbe
    Hotel
But that Dr. Factory began to strut and scratch. He said, Welcome
To fruit-bar, but Edna was so cold
From being in the bottle plant, and the Ant Riviera was closed
For feeding period, so there was nothing
To do but come out clothed as ducks,
Which is what we did, and which caused the trouble
You are hearing about now in the radio report
From Radio Free Biarritz which I have on my cufflinks
As a kind of "Sunday emblem," which you are,
In fact, committed to no more than lightning,
But lightning which populates the future
Still can leave a frigid old cow in Banff
And so I say Let all the images stored up by the flashing towels
Be a passionate party to that ship's constant loneliness
As it triples its fuels by emptying one pale guitar—
Unless you are synthetic and can drop silver from gold.

The Medicine Man told me. As a cow drops into the future
From the past. He smiles. The bettered ivory on the keys
Begins to braise her eyes with some Smetana,
And she turns toward the grizzled orphan with a cussword
Standing on the lips of the cornflakes which she has brought you from the
    mountains
Where the answer was found, by one old goat, in her lipstick.
Smear, smear, said the old Bavarian gush-hound;
And let us too smear the ways
Of this dachshund hemorrhage Rapunzel ivory princess
Who promises everything and does everything for the profit
Of two long ivory staves, which she finds in the mountains
So that when after the sun has set the ship is still there
And all preparations are being made for the werewolf to collapse in a
    movie,
Still there is the dead stock-still response of the whispering
Of the sea, and the flat land past desire. America
Remembers it, an orange, pubescent with desire. The old
Doctor disremembers it, and pulses with a swallow-tail recuperation.
    "Day is yet nigh!"
"The night is yet harmless!" "Nameless, oh you, all-absorbent!"

The spoons, though puzzled, in surprise mentioned the baccalaureate
To the weak Mexican town, who, immediately nestling
With a coccyx-less elephant, defied them to repeat it on the
Horse, which they did next day, unrelenting,
Until Venice had to be thoroughly searched for a powder to dry
When their noggins began to wink, stirred by the future excellence
Of tiled oil-catchers, which, when they were ferreting
The priests kept dumping into their unused viola da gambas
Notched for excellence, and purple violins when they went prinking
About the outskirts for these reeds pure notices of choice
To the intelligences of the Rapunzels of another era;
My own selection from the feed of heaven is climate,
Choice, and the feed of these heavenly bars
Which the oysters strafed all night above the climate
Which was making these bars drive crazy, and apes and chimpanzees
Also into the reputed gulf which—here he was interrupted
By a change of powder. Nutmeg Carson has gotten in the game!
These jewels which the boat slips through the water
And which are reputed "nephew" "palfrey" and "hem"
Still could have been manufactured by a greater

Emblem than your poor dope of a cloud.
If these passionate sleeves fondled colors in choices
Until the civics absolutely went another way
Then there are ices and sleeps and aloes—
The dwarf is a greater man; but the heap is a greater.

Now one old general comes here to say
His prayers above the city. Someone is dropped into a crater
And here someone Egyptian goes to sleep. An idiot is born in Parigi,
And an ivory stove is wheezed about in Paris. A man begins to cry
At the thought of the baby, and a woman begins to grieve
At the formation of an intelligence without a nerve.
Closer together, the humorless blossoms can signify
Only the return peanut of a mateless tennis match—
How curious to be dead beneath a sky
In which everything remarkable is hidden—except for the flocks
Of the birds, and an occasional Numa
(Someone's name), blue jewels, and the raucousness of grasshoppers
Closing the jalousies into Olga Park
Where the bunnies lie about like extreme craters
Strewn by the cashiered parallax of jolting
When there were no more tears in the canal.
And now a baby brings an apple. The rabbi sleeps.
The hirsute rainbucket of phosphorescence is decapitated
By the coolness of a sigh—or by the cruelty of a lamb.
It is right, but the secret was before
On the left, and before the end of last month
She played with a jewel. Now, in the winter, it is removed from her mouth
Where an ice hockey game dropped the calves of the girls' legs
So far below freezing the defilade deprived me of the right to wish that it
    was not my chopper
But the sea that was going down.

Maybe it is a land of oblongs
For which you have been pining all your days
Next to the stove museum where Ann brought Henry
And said Look at the clouds, Henry; see how the sky plays
Tricks with the ordinary person's vision; and Henry's okeys
Surprised the madam because they were so sheer,
So useless, finally, for understanding
If he liked the glass dales or not, because he had been tempted
Previously to renounce the bluish black top hat which she had

Purchased for him Saturday midnight the Giudecca
He said I needn't look so good in that
As you suppose, or as chiffon supposes. The sea
Was turgid with fuming tumescence; it was squealing
Like an itemized tribune of flatulent glass dolls and kisses
Through a chimney, in the skyway, or lip outline mark
Where the dollar bills first established their mastery
Always coming down on the fir tree seeking white bread
Which the farmer had promised them in some distant time
Before the pure colonnades existed, at the left was the laundry
And on the right was the sty—there was a continual *va et vient*
Between the two columns of porphyry,
A nicety for when the purple-coated monster apples did come
Bearing a pension for the silence, which she hated.

It is moonlight now
Over the bears.
Father Bear is tired, and he says to Mother Bear,
"The island is becoming too small for our twelve little fishing boats;
I would like to establish a concession on the mainland, which would like
To concede me oblongs." Mother Bear hopped about in the silence
Of the fresh blue air, and she glanced at Father
Over her shoulder. He looks like a Catholic priest, she imagined,
Or, as when I first saw him dancing in Yugoslavia,
He looks like Judas Priest. And Mamma Bear said, "Worthington,
Worthington, you have been on the island too long;
It is time for us to think about the little ones,
The everpresent and omnivorous baby bears,
Who are coming up every year as a result of our screwing,
Of them we must think and of bear job opportunities
Which I agree would be greater on the mainland."

I grow tired of this absurd simplicity as quickly as you do,
But it represents the truth. If bears' concerns
Are not exactly identical with human ones,
Yet it's only by human analogies that we can understand them.
She placed a red hot moccasin on the table and was gone.

A difference between me and you—
You are abjectly hopeful in a steamy kind of way,
Whereas I am pure flawed crystal, able to share my light
With a universe which is pure flawed eyeball. I wonder at

The exaggerations to which occasions force
You; and I marvel
At the bracelet which you bring
Into the charmed circle of the bullfight when you say:
"The test of prudence is a life of need
To spend outside the Bauhaus. It is kind,
But not imprudent, to attack with a certain variety of orange rind
The devastate vicinity canals—I've got that wrong—
The deadly fascination of canals—no, that's wrong either—
Devastating vicinity of canals
Is what I meant, but that is not right anyway
Since 'what I mean' is never what I meant
Except in some inferior phosphorous sense
Which includes the twelve meanings of the verb 'to be.' Are you still
      listening—?"
And you go on and on and on
And I am still listening because I marvel at what you say,
They are my own thoughts exactly, I have been dead for six years
And you have been bearing high the red torch of tradition,
You alone are doing it, there is no one else—
Well, put it down, I am coming back to life,
I am tired of living in the earth and dishes
A little blue rabbit has been doing the dishes
And I am longing for the turtles,
The turtles of fascination which I once saw on the plates,
And the rabbit hearts that vanished from the piers.

Perhaps it is the wrong word, kindness,
For the revolting way we treat each other
On Fridays and Sundays, though on Saturday night
All seems to be going well, the doorbell the incinerator
The childish rat; and you lean over a parking bench to say,
It is well, that the clouds smeared with ugliest cinnamon mirror
An "exuberant" sky, then said that was the wrong word,
Shyness, for the way we act about the dwarf
In the white suit, who is always going into the coast
Food station as if it were a mixture
Of paradise and the seven brassieres' hell. A mystery to awaken
Some morning would be this fluting, which is constantly imperceptible
Although the roofs do their insane best not to resist it,
And you at last are well away on the trail

Which you love. Even the little pears could not prevent it
Nor the giant apples lying across the trail. They said, You need a building,
A large one, a canoe hut diverged with apple blossoms;
We smiled at the old wet men and went our way
Toward the wet women; each had been alive at least thirty years;
The parking beach was deserted; a kind of crisscross
Of flags and passageways could doubt the trees' maturity;
A single person could never become transparent on that beach;
The days shove under; a millionaire leaves his legs
For the benefit of science; the car fashion institute is roped in
By delicate oblongs. Some slow marble clickings drift unconsciously
    toward the sea
Of idiotic markings, made by a change
In the weather, from red to chlorine swill. My aunt,
The Countess of Freitagen, always used to call it
"The cruelest animal," because of the way it behaved
In a stiff collar, although the dirtiest water
Could never find it to put its foot in it in the silly
Repeating islands. There at least we had a chance to gasp
And sunbathe for fifteen seconds, just then the monsoon
Began to collect its annual tariff of ptomaine animals and teacups
Which the frizzled breeze was flinging into the channels
Of a poodle's heart, whose master was a mistress
Of fortunate clouds—that day, lay pink and white and chuckled
Out, the sweet men of the sea. To harm this legion
Jessica accounted a heinous crime, but Beo-grime was redundant
With ectoplasmic gripes. Look, he said, this whole silence of the tundra
As measured with a fish's thigh, sheer global
Different acrimony—how high can you go in a canoe? And Julian said,
That would depend on your astronomy. Both brothers leaped into the
    *Please Me*
And rose high over the lumps of dough which Fish-Bath had left spread
    about the co-stars
Whose names Tim took rapidly writing down—Amos, Ben, and Sandy,
    which one is the girl?
Tim kept pondering the question all day long;
Then, that night, the hugest egg was laid
That ever Parma's vegetables had witnessed.
My cheese came down from the fuel-indoctrinating mountains to witness
For itself the enticing event of pure white docks above the habitable
Tennis shoes, ever tired of renouncing.

Then, suddenly, the sea began to play for assembly
And even the dunce was astonished. Long previously, the white fantastic
    ballroom
Had been imperceptibly vanishing from the cookies' carnival
Of dishwatered kisses, and then she replied The canal.
It was cook's water and old light feeding the empire
Once again, beside the faded bricks. She took a peacock's tail and set sail
Up to the dormitory window, where Peter
Had left the emulsion to savagely rest. Juliet, who had been wintering by
    the phosphate,
Then crushed Olson with a dream. Her purse opens.
In it we see sea monsters of every variety
And this includes the fabulously terrifying sea apples
Which the district attorney of cloud beds was so studiously refurbishing
Above the lacy dormer windows when I cried in bed
About the horror of the flowers and the flies. Jules said: The infection
Will not last past morning; the defeated island
Now brings its crazy promise to the head-rows of the sea. A boat slapped
Against the knee-farmer's tail. It was summer. The glass cloudburst
Had finished by breaking the records of the first clouds—
Of which these islands proudly led the way into the tea shop.

Inside every animal is a beleaguered Shanghai man,
Said Frederick the First of Prussia. We in our modern day
Are fond of the brushwork quotation. We think that protects us from the
    apples.
It was Gabriel d'Annunzio, was it not,
At the time of his tragic love affair with Sarah Bernhardt—
Unless it was with some other great star that he had this affair, Duse?
It was d'Annunzio who said—I have forgot
Whate'er d'Annunzio said. The night is hot.
Come, let's go out into its feverish breeze.
We wandered into a hay station and bar. You had a gin and orange.
I looked at the stable part of the atmosphere disconsolately.
This ambience, I said, 's no *ambiance*—aye, there's a difference, let me tell
    it to you,
Aye, there's a difference to the heart again.
The summer foamed with released past time memories and golden heart-
    attack fundromes
Where the egregious eagles could play at shibboleth and night's pastime
    violin.
The crushing night was sounding

As if the sea were full of air,
And as if some boat came pounding
Along the entire coast looking for a single hair.
A wiry one, I'll warrant; better clues
They make, those wiry ones. He put his shoes
Into the dashboard refrigerator and cleft Yugoslavia
Into the shape of a sloe-eyed button. You must not go there, she said
With a college horse; take along a necktie for his button.
In the winter the clouds gave the heart attack a purse
Of wishes—one of the wisest of these was to play the guitar
With an ikon's shrieking delight. But summer, spring, and fall met at
    once, with great plans for rebellion.
"Oblongs will never be our treat tonight,"
Villa said; but Harry saith,
"Oblongs are going to be our treat tonight."

# The Interpretation of Dreams

I

You are my Sweetheart
Sang the tin can
I was sitting on a truck
As it rolled along
You are my Truck
Sang my Sweetheart
Somehow it was menacing
An ominous song
I hardly knew what to say I went into the truck
It was amazing
That autumn afternoon, when every affection came unsought
As from an unstoppered lute and a glass of Campari
Was downed from a shimmering glass and quickly as if nothing
Could harm the eternal beaver any more. But a policeman of high
   reflection
Suddenly stood up for the traffic crossings' protection
And were we sad, lost in thought at our newfound abortionlessness
In stages, because of a green kerchief stuck in your pocket
As one asks What's the difference between that and a handkerchief? and
Between each stop and its parenthesis? Let's assume we have too much
And pound on the marble table top. It has always gone best that way
Yet you're thinking (I think) "Yet the hand falls off
And the streets of Paris will continue to go every which way.
No, in spite of your palaver
And a summertime gift for describing the rose
You will have to take me into another valley
Where reality is not affliction." Or if you did not think that all at once
Toward that our thoughts have been gathering. Whose omnibus is that
   parked outside the S.S. *Rose*
With a Himalayan flagboy in the window of the car
Scratching his initials A. H., A. H., as the winter evening dies
And turns into a springtime fogbound morning? I was sleeping in the hay
When we awoke. One could just barely make out the sky. A truck raced
   past.
Then I realized where we were. It was potato season. And, Spiff! this
   season was to be our last
Before we dangled before tomatoes, hard red ones and yellow yummy

Tomatoes and huge hard pink ones which were brighter than the nose
Of Snow White in Walt Disney's fiction. I am going into slaveland
To help these tomatoes get free, but they come thumping
After. "Wait for us! Wait! You will see! It is impossible to serve us unless
    we are there!"
And the tomatoes turned into apples. I was wide awake. The cook said,
    "You are my Sweetheart."
And a band played "The Abortion of the Sleeper may be the Swan Song of
    the Sheep-Man's Heart."


2


Into this valley my sweetheart came
The tomatoes were hard as her nose
She was available exactly
Five minutes every afternoon
Then she took Snow White
Into the kidney parlor
She said, "Snow White, be an actress!"
And Snow White implored the yellow movies
To be more reasonable about Al Capp
"He's a swell guy"
We know we know
But he's not purple anymore
A large picture flew through the sky
My Sweetheart put on it
"I am the Capistrani of the Rose"
And William Butler Yeats died
When Auden wrote the poem
About the deftness of the steamship
Plying through the harbor
Is my Sweetheart's nose.


3


Meanwhile Snow White and her boyfriend
Have gone up into the mountains.
It is amazing what they will do for a game of bingo!

No! That is not what they are doing. Look!
They are making love! I didn't know that was allowed in the movies
In this country! But that must be what they are doing!
She is lying beneath him and every time his body rose
I saw her fingerprints gripping the dust like the U.S.S. *Idaho*
In an old story. Do you know the one of the Frightening Fidget?
Well, in this one old Doctor Barnose
Is riding along through Italy on a great white highway
Made of marshmallows, when some greensuited policemen come out
And make him stop to show his passport, which he had had made out of
    clothes
As a modern novelty, but they threw him in the purple prison,
Where like an Italianate tirade of grapejuice something exists to this day
Numbered among the aquanauts who saved this country
From being bombed by the submarines which I purchased you for my
    birthday
In one of my most powerful moods, on the Pomeranian coast.


4


The gasoline must come to a halt, as the great apple shipments have done.

The true Advisor to the lesser party will not permit the Eczema to come
Into the park of Dutiful Silence. This is an Order imposed by Law.

The Marlene Dietrich suitcases are not to be opened
Except by the pink hands of the Prelate in charge of the bombing.
(Cardinal Spellman, I am dreaming of you! I am seeing your plumpness
    insulted by bombs!
And then I am seeing the grass-green acne of the trends.)

In charge of fishes Israel is put; in charge of Packaging, Summer.
(I am sorry, Winslow Homer, that you did not get this job,
And you, yearning seminarians of our Hungarian Pall Mall,
But it is a direct icing I get, and not a "forwarded," from the Divine.)

And now I think it is time to cut out Music.

The musicians are viciously bald. They will not listen to the music
Whether it is good or bad. They say, "Oklahoma has taken the best music.
   And then Snow White. We have nothing left."
They laugh, the musicians, at their own sorrow.
But at least the music has stopped.
I hated the music, it was always resounding in the ears
Like a broken fiddle. I am glad you have imposed on them to stop.
It was of their own free will, like the other decisions
They have made, like which fish to have on Wednesday
And how to catch mackerel without a rod. I am tired now of "not hearing"
   the music
In such a lively way. Can we go down to the harbor?
In the harbor everything was a bad job.
The courts were out of work and the community centers were filled with
   people
Eating pastry-cakes shaped like sheets of music. "All those good pies," I
   said,
"Being wasted like a nuthouse." And I run rampant.
I rock around smashing everything I could find.
They had destroyed my darling and I was going to ruin them as well.
Then struck the clock. It was the time of the oyster and the octopus.
I walked out of the fishstore with a prayer.
The universe was ringing with a song.

Snow White had brought the music back.

The yo-yo capitalists are filled
By the pastry which tyrants heat
On Mediterranean ovens.
You now feel that you will never understand;
But it is about to open, becoming easy
As one may say "Ah!" at the sight of a pink island

Or a tremendous pink apple which is of a different kind
From every other apple one has ever tasted
And as Snow White
Who had an island pedigree in black and white
Came ravished when in colors.

A new hydrofoil has started
To invent the sea. And when the sea comes in
The birthday poem is finished and a nude start begins
On some fantastic island—"Fantastic island?" I'll never question you any
    more.
But sexuality is not all, even though it is beautiful
As Moravian gusts. One also needs a spellbinding heart
And a lethal spelling book, which gives the Seminole report.

"I'm in love with apples,"
The old seminarian says.
But the young Arethusa knows better:
"Alpheus is in love with me."


### 8


Oh American homerun hitter! your balls! your balls!
They are sailing over our trees
And when they land
We feel we pick up a killer
Oh American homerun hitter
Dressed in white tie and tails!

And you smote your guitar
Good cousin Jute with a loud report.
"This is America! This is the Capitalist country
Where witnesses write on the trees
And black meets white
In a catapult, blast, and explosion. It is not Nude Island."

"So what?" said the caterpillar, and
"So what?" whispered the trees. From every direction the "so-whatters"
    came running
To compel him to retain his distance.

The porkchop and the shark said,
"If you come too close to us, we die.
Remember the speech of the living.
And welcome back to Thorax Island."

Then a picture of Snow White completely blocked out the sky.


9

And I was with you again
But we were going in different directions.
We met and started to go in the same direction.
Then once more our paths crossed and we met again
Under the believable blue of a traffic light where we had first met
The village coconut who had forbidden our meetings
But now we meet all the time.
"You go this way and I'll go that,
And when we head back we will meet
And declare our love."

This is the foundation of the emotions.
The sky is our parade ground and our glove.
The fish in the bay are the slaves of their time and not of art
But somehow our emotions can become their emotions.
This is the beginning of Realism. This is the end of the ideal.
This is the degree of front and back.

# Equal to You

Can you imagine the body being
The really body the being the reality
Body being the body if reality
Is what it is it is, not that reality
Doesn't infer the body, still
The body being the bearer of reality
And the barer of the body
The body being reality
That is reality's reality
Hardly on earth ever seen
But from it we have the word *connubial*
Which means
The body bearing the body in reality
And reality being the body
And body-reality being borne.
I am bearing a burden
Which reminded me of you
Bearing away the swell
Of the sea
But can you imagine the body bearing reality
And being reality
That's where we get the
Word *connubial* which is a word for the body's being
Being in reality and being a body
In reality and bearing the burden
Of the body in reality, by being real
And by being the body of the real.

# Faces

The face of the gypsy watching the bird gun firing into the colony of seals;
but it was filled with blanks;
The face of the old knoll watching his hills grow up before him;
The face of the New England fruit juice proprietor watching his whole
supplies being overturned by a herd of wild bulls;
The face of a lemur watching the other primates become more developed;
The face of gold, as the entire world goes on the silver standard, but gold
remains extremely valuable and is the basis for international exchange;
The face of the sky, as the air becomes increasingly filled with smoke and
planes;
The face of the young girl painted as Saint Urbana by Perugino, whose
large silver eyes are focused on the green pomegranate held by a baby
(it is Jesus) in the same painting;
The face of the sea after there has been a storm, and the face of the valley
When the clouds have blown away and it is going to be a pleasant day and
the pencils come out for their picnic;
The face of the clouds;
The faces of the targets when all the arrows are sticking out of them, like
tongues;
The face of insects; the tiny black moustachioed ineptitude of a fly;
The face of the splinters on the orange crate;
The face of the Depression, which shook up America's faith in her
economy so badly;
The face of President Hoover during this event;
The face of Popeye; the face of Agamemnon; the face of Ruth in the
Bible; the face of Georges Simenon;
The face of the hornet; the face of the carnation; of the orchid; the face of
the roots of the elm tree;
The face of the fruit juice stand proprietor in Hawaii—it is black and
lined
With the years and the climate; the face of God in Pinturicchio; the 1920's
face of Gala Eluard;
And the face of Paul Eluard; the face of the birthday party as envisioned
by Pablo Picasso; the map of Ireland
In Barbara's face; the map of Egypt on the wall
Of the Alexander-of-Macedon-looking hotel proprietor's face; the eye's
face; the face of the ear; faces of all the noses;
The face of the snowman; the face of Rome
In being Mistress of Europe (if she was) in the fifteenth century;

The nude in her environment with sketched-in face
Or suggested face; the magic face of the chestnut tree
Blowing in the wind and scattering its teeth; the face of the bachelor's
    button; the face of the east
When, just mounted, Aurora sends forth her streaks
Of amorous potency and blue; and the face of the roost
From which everyone has flown away;
The face of the rushing gopher; the face of the wall
Of the hot, cracking, white clay house in Greece
When the stone hits it; the Russian faucet's face; the face of your loved
    one as depicted on the form
By a "police artist"—she is wanted for entering and breaking
The psalmodizing face of the daybreak sea-green palace to kidnap the face
Of Egypt, Cleopatra's face, carved by a sculptor
With a face like evening's face—blue, quiet, and stirred by a breeze; the
    face of Paris; the beautiful face of the bean
When it has been smashed; the face of the banana
In its bunch, being thrown into the boat, and while sailing through the air
Thinking, "Someone is going to eat me! but, first, a long, solemn
    journey. . . ." A diamond face; the wheel's face
When it has been going downhill for two hours and suddenly realizes it is
    no longer a part of its original wagon—it is now diffuse, or dead, or a
    "spare part," "used," or "free";
The face of the architect who sees his first building crumbling to pieces—
    he has forgotten to put in the beams!
With a sleepy face—awaking in the morning—"This is your building!"
    Moods!
Great Britain's beautiful face during the storm;
William Blake's face; Homer's face; Jack and Jill's faces; Brenda Starr's
    insinuating face;
The wind's face as pictured (actually, carved) on the Tower of the Winds
    in Athens; the new year's face
When it learns it is our last one on earth; and the domed face
Of the cemetery plot in which we lie, finally absorbed and pulled into the
    other faces;
The face of the burning mouse who lived in the chair
When it was manufactured in Sweden, in someone's dream; and the gulf's
    face
When it is full of the Stream; and the egg-like face of the district manager
    of "La Lune."

Notice: the eye is a face. Notice: the wave is a fir tree. Notice:
    impetuously: the nut's face drank from the gala's flutes with precarious
    impunity.
Oh faces like wet summer moods! The face of the champion on the
    mountain
When he is straining to pick up a stone; DNA's toothless face;
The face (I heard this in a story) of the old woman who had not been
    down from the mountains since the nineteenth century
When she was brought down to look at the city—how it astonished her,
    showing in her face
And in the movements of her frail body—she wavered back and forth!
And the sea lion's giant face; the face of the first clouds,
All climbing and responsiveness; the great harvest of the Meuse's face,
Protectiveness, giant, autumnal, and sunny, suggesting strong limbs
    graced by perfect serene contentment;
The Greek face on the jar, so unlimited as to be speechless captions
Of armor and of sleeping love, the beginnings of face
In the infant or really in the embryo deep in womb valley
Where there is nothing to focus on with face, and the faces of the happy
    and satisfied lovers,
One has blonde hair and is a woman, the other has brown hair and is a
    man,
They lie on the beach or the bed of contentment murmuring "Stone's
    face"
And "Burnt reed's face" and all the other faces to each other;
And the breathtaking beauty of the monument-
Al door which the hornets have left unharried, bus face rushing by, this
    sandless evening, oh visage, oh where is that face
Which would have opened these eyes, which, opened, might have shown
    us the truth? the dock's face
When the young boat hits it, it flies apart in merrymaking splinters, fond
    of the boat
And longing for the renewal of its touch; the comic face
Of the drum, when its calfskin is torn during the annual concert
To the royal house of Indonesia; and the cook's face
When he has poisoned the wine. I want to take all these faces
And make them mine. I want hypodermic
Impossibles, nude Bellini, Popeye inside concrete house, with volume
Of bagpipe music concentric, winter, Fra Angelico's face
And the faces he painted, his Virgin, his Musicians; and the face
Of the honeybee when it is wet and dripping
With flowery ooze; the face of the feverfew

Which was growing on the mountain until the shears sliced it; the face of
    the beach
Down which twenty people have been running; the face in the carpet; the
    face of the peach
When it was missed by the bullets; faces of a party of two
Who have been run over in the mountains;
The grapefruit's face, when the season has been hitting it with
    atmospheric drums;
And the beautiful breasts and eyes and face
Of the woman who was shooting coils (electric ones) off the fence at
    Aleppo, where the shoes of Lord Byron
Were claimed to have been found by a woman with an iron face, she had a
    terrible operation
But her interest in Byron's biography has kept her alive; her doctor's face
When he realized the miracle he had performed; Gerard de Nerval's face,
    imagined by Soutine
On a summer morning; the club soda factory's face
And the face of its receptionist, yawning, I am sorry, you cannot see Sir
    Abelard Face; he is dead. There are no more Faces in the world this
    morning. Goodbye. The Cavalcade too is closed."
I had so wanted to go with you to the Cavalcade! It was owned by Sir
    Abelard Face—
An amusement park ride that took you up into the mountains, as if in a
    blizzard.
"Goodbye." O seagreen faces! O endless rough loopabouts of northern
    and also southern seas!
And faces of larger sea units, royally blue; faces of the speak-easy
When its boiler room explodes; O scenic faces of the quiet old women of
    Peru!
Nose face! illegal face! rocket face! and the face of the glue
When it is taken to Fiesole and dropped, actually hurled, down toward
    Florence
But it doesn't get there and is picked up instead on a dark, dry route
By a hen with a clucking face, then dropped again
(Because impossible to use it as food) and on the label of this gluetube the
    lovely face
Of the Italian model, Angelizia, etched in pink and blue
Against a white cloudy background, she became the mistress
Of the owner of the glue factory, now her face lies battered
Upon the Tuscan road, but she is happy, the real Angelizia, as she
    ponders,
Dancing in Tucson, how many times her face is reproduced

And seen around the world; jewelry's faces; faces of firemen; the face of
the bowling pin; the rhubarb's face
When it is growing with abandon; the remarkable face of the street, with
the people in it, each one speaking, there is such a roar;
The hero of comedy's face, when everything is going well,
And the hippopotamus's face, when he finds he has been put in the wrong
zoo, there is no water,
And so he rages, damply, against the summer's bars;
And the chicken's face when the thief has not succeeded in stealing him;
The leader of the orchestra's face when the music flies off as if by magic
(the wind is carrying it) and the beautiful valentine face
With gold hair—it is real, you can touch it—reminding me of you;
Alfred Jarry's face on a winter afternoon, when *Ubu Cocu* has just opened
at the Théâtre des Champs Elysées
And his followers have mounted him on their shoulders, they wind
through the wintry streets with the characteristic abandon
Of open-face sandwiches, and no one is troubled
Except the ocean, whose moon-abiding, satellite face
Speaks to the nuts just once, then speaks no more.
The face of the blue coca-cola when the Acropolis frieze of the
Panathenaea has been defaced by secret marbles
Blown from an overhanging hedgehog's pepsi-cola balloon; December's
face
When January is over and he again feels the cool form behind him in the
parade of months;
The faces of fleas and of firecrackers; the faces of stopwatches; faces of
stock markets, prices going up and down;
The face of the legs, when you are stepping proudly; and the face of
Alaska;
The faces of hammering fools, faces of elephants; faces of discarded
raincoats; bras' faces; aprons' faces; the branchings of the yew;
The face of the Unknown Madonna, and the cork's face
At noon, the orange face, the cocoa's face,
The face of the needle, which is chiefly an eye; and the face of the guru
and of the couturier;
The loom's face, when weavers' hands delay; the face of the crow
When the sky light hits it; and faces with teeth,
Eyes, ears, nose, and cheekbone, faces for cold weather
And steaming faces for hot weather; the face of the owner of the farm
When the camels have ripped it to pieces; the face on the fan, I believe it
is Herodiade; the stick's face
When it is lying in the garden, and the faces of fliers

When they find that they are floating toward the sun;
The faces of Oz, of China, of Brittany; the face of Chang Fu and Brit the
　Chambermaid;
Faces of old Athens and Sparta, faces of Argos, the unserious face of Gus
　the Goose;
Faces of the sunbathers when the clouds split into eighteen hundred
　shapes; the amazed face of the mule;
The faces of ants, as they run all around; the face of Lucas van Leyden;
　the face of Hindemith; the face of Childe Harold;
The face of the ox pulling his cart;
The face of Sinbad the Sailor; of Pontius Pilate; of Jesus; of Nestor;
The faces of Sappho, of Lord Elgin, of Bix Beiderbecke, of Saint
　Valentine, of Daphnis and Chloe, of Hero and Leander;
The face of Hamilcar; the face of Sally Mara; of Sir Thomas More; of
　Miss Fujiyama; and of the Duchess of Falling Out
Of Bed; the face of the earth before it is bitten by the blue
Of morning; and its daily face afterward;
The faces of fifteen Romantics; the faces of stones;
The face of Haussmann, rebuilding Paris in the eighteen fifties; the face
　of Dmitri Mitropoulos; the face of Mr. Bones; Raymond Queneau's
　face;
Marcel Raymond's face; the face of the paper on which the face is drawn
　of the Queen of Sheba
By an artist with a bearded face—last night he had drunk a good deal
But today he is happy, to be creating; and the face of the paper after the
　drawing is on it
Almost entirely concealing its original face; and the face of Modern Art
Which is fascinated by this problem; the face of Calvin Coolidge
And of Gertrude Stein; the underwater tow which brings all these faces
　together
And makes them mine, then distends them and scatters them; the frilly
　blue lace face of Uncle Ho
And the Winged Victory's face, where it lies, so far lost beyond all
　salvation;
And the face of the grass; Alaska's snowy face; the billboard face
　advertising a certain kind of cheese
In Italy; and the fat industrialist's face as he slowly gains recognition
That the heyday of his class is ended; the museum director's face
Who thinks his has come before it has; face of Abelard; and face of Peire
　Vidal; face of the orchid
And of the oyster; the faces of Venice, when everyone is wearing a mask—

Some faces! the End; or rather the Beginning; or really the End. Faces
   taking a fall,
Faces to be discriminated, faces in bathtubs, gorgeous, risky faces totaling
   into the billions,
Unimaginable faces shaped like a hat or a football; clowns' faces; the face
   of Saint Ursula
When she was playing a banjo; the face of Einstein; the face of the East;
   the face of grain; the face on the weathervane;
The face of Liberal London; the Seine's rusty face; the visitor from
   Mexico, mangled by disease;
Bentham's face; and the face of the secret
Which no one can tell, which is continually bursting from these faces—
Noah's face, Kusawara's face, Poussin face, Tiepolo face, frog faces,
   browed faces, angular face, peppy face; the faces of seaweed; the faces of
   seeds.

# The Pleasures of Peace

Another ribald tale of the good times at Madame Lipsky's.
Giorgio Finogle had come in with an imitation of the latest Russian poet,
The one who wrote the great "Complaint About the Peanut Farm" which
    I read to you last year at Mrs. Riley's,
Do you remember? and then of course Giorgio had written this imitation
So he came in with it. . . . Where was I and what was I saying?
The big beer parlor was filled with barmaids and men named Stuart
Who were all trying to buy a big red pitcher of beer for an artiste named
    Alma Stuart
Whom each claimed as his very own because of the similarity in names—
This in essence was Buddy's parody—O Giorgio, you idiot, Marian Stuart
    snapped,
It all has something to do with me! But no, Giorgio replied,
Biting in a melancholy way the edge off a cigar-paper-patterned envelope
In which he had been keeping the Poem for many days
Waiting to show it to his friends. And actually it's not a parody at all,
I just claimed it was, out of embarrassment. It's a poetic present for you
    all,
All of whom I love! Is it capable to love more than one—I wonder! Alma
    cried,
And we went out onto the bicycle-shaped dock where a malicious swarm
    of mosquitoes
Were parlaying after having invaded the old beer parlor.
The men named Stuart were now involved in a fight to the death
But the nearer islands lay fair in the white night light.
Shall we embark toward them? I said, placing my hand upon one
    exceedingly gentle
And fine. A picture of hairnets is being projected. Here
Comes someone with Alma Stuart! Is it real, this night? Or have we a
    gentle fantasy?
The Russian poet appears. He seems to consider it real, all right. He's
Quite angry. Where's the Capitalist fairy that put me down? he squirts
At our nomadic simplicity. "Complaint About the Peanut Farm" is a
    terrific poem. Yes,
In a way, yes. The Hairdresser of Night engulfs them all in foam.

"I love your work, *The Pleasures of Peace*," the Professor said to me next
    day;

"I think it adequately encompasses the hysteria of our era
And puts certain people in their rightful place. Chapeau! Bravo!"
"You don't get it," I said. "I like all this. I called this poem
*Pleasures of Peace* because I'm not sure they will be lasting!
I wanted people to be able to see what these pleasures are
That they may come back to them." "But they are all so hysterical, so—so
    transitory,"
The critic replied. "I mean, how can you—what kind of pleasures are
    these?
They seem more like pains to me—if I may say what I mean."
"Well, I don't know, Professor," I said; "permanent joys
Have so far been denied this hysterical person. Though I confess
Far other joys I've had and will describe in time.
And then too there's the pleasure of *writing* these—perhaps to experience
    is not the same."
The Professor paused, lightly, upon the temple stair.
"I will mention you among the immortals, Ken," he said,
"Because you have the courage of what you believe.
But there I will never mention those sniveling rats
Who only claim to like these things because they're fashionable."
"Professor!" I cried, "My darling! my dream!" And she stripped, and I saw
    there
Creamy female marble, the waist and thighs of which I had always
    dreamed.
"Professor! Loved one! why the disguise?" "It was a test" she said,
"Of which you have now only passed the first portion.
You must write More, and More—"
"And be equally persuasive?" I questioned, but She
Had vanished through the Promontory door.

So now I must devote my days to The Pleasures of Peace—
To my contemporaries I'll leave the Horrors of War,
They can do them better than I—each poet shares only a portion
Of the vast Territory of Rhyme. Here in Peace shall I stake out
My temporal and permanent claim. But such silver as I find
I will give to the Universe—the gold I'll put in other poems.
Thus in time there'll be a mountain range of gold
Of considerable interest. Oh may you come back in time
And in my lifetime to see it, most perfect and most delectable reader!
We poets in our youth begin with fantasies,

But then at least we think they may be realities—
The poems we create in our age
Require your hand upon our shoulder, your eye on our page.


Here are listed all the Pleasures of Peace that there could possibly be.
Among them are the pleasures of Memory (which Delmore Schwartz
    celebrated), the pleasures of autonomy,
The pleasures of agoraphobia and the sudden release
Of the agoraphobic person from the identified marketplace, the pleasures
    of roving over you
And rolling over the beach, of being in a complicated car, of sleeping,
Of drawing ropes with you, of planning a deranged comic strip, of shifting
    knees
At the accelerator pump, of blasphemy, of cobra settlement in a
    dilapidated skin country
Without clops, and therefore every pleasure is also included; which, after
    these—


Oh Norman Robinson, the airplane, the village, the batteries,
All this I remember, the Cheese-o-Drome, the phallic whips, the
    cucumbers,
The ginger from Australia, the tiny whorehouses no bigger than a
    phallus's door,
The evenings without any cucumbers, the phallus's people,
The old men trailing blue lassos from door to door,
Who are they all, anyway? I was supposed to be on my way to Boston
To go to college or get elected to the Legislature
And now I'm here with a lot of cowboys who talk spiritual Dutch! Let
Me out of here! The lumberyard smelled of the sweet calla lilies
The courtyard was fragrant with thyme. I released your hand
And walked into the Mexicana Valley, where my father was first a cowboy.
I take a genuine interest in the people of this country
Yes sir I think you might even call me Coleman the Dutch but now the
    night sky fills with fairies
It is all that modern stuff beginning to happen again, well, let it—


We robots tell the truth about old Gabby
But when the shirtfront scuffs we yell for Labby
It is a scientific stunt
Which Moonlight has brought you from Australia
Sit it down on this chair shaped like a pirate

When you have come three times I will give you a silverware hazelnut
With which you can escape from time
For this I'm calling in all the poets who take dope
To help me out, here they come
Oh is there room in the universe for such as we?
They say, but though we cannot make our Time
Stand still, yet we'll him silver like a Dime.
Inversions yet! and not even sexual ones!
O Labrador, you are the sexual Pennsylvania of our times!

Chapter Thirty Seven.
On the Planisphere everyone was having a nut
When suddenly my Lulu appeared.
She was a big broad about six feet seven
And she had a red stone in her ear
Which was stringent in its beauty.
I demanded at once the removal of people from the lobby
So we could begin to down ABC tablets and start to feel funny
But Mordecai La Schlomp our Leader replied that we did not need any
That a person could feel good without any artificial means.
Oh the Pleasures of Peace are infinite and they cannot be counted—
One single piece of pink mint chewing gum contains more pleasures
Than the whole rude gallery of war! And the moon passes by
In an otherwise undistinguished lesson on the geography of this age
Which has had fifty-seven good lovers and ninety-six wars. By Giorgio
    Finogle.

It turns out that we're competing for the Peace Award,
Giorgio Finogle and I. We go into the hair parlor, the barber—
We get to talking about war and about peace.
The barber feels that we are really good people at heart
Even though his own views turn out to be conservative.
"I've read Finogle's piece, the part of it that was in *Smut*," he
Says, "and I liked it. Yours, Koch, I haven't yet seen,
But Alyne and Francie told me that you were the better poet."
"I don't know," I said. "Giorgio is pretty good." And Giorgio comes back
    from the bathroom
Now, with a grin on his face. "I've got an idea for my
Pleasures of Peace," he says, "I'm going to make it include
Each person in the universe discussing their own bag—
Translation, their main interest, and what they want to be—"

"You'll never finish it, Giorgio," I said. "At least I'll
Get started," he replied, and he ran out of the barbershop.

In the quiet night we take turns riding horseback and falling asleep.
Your breasts are more beautiful than a gold mine.
I think I'll become a professional man.
The reason we are up-to-date is we're some kind of freaks.
I don't know what to tell the old man
But he is concerned with two kinds of phenomena and I am interested in
     neither. What *are* you interested in?
Being some kind of freaks, I think. Let's go to Transylvania.
I don't understand your buddy all the time. Who?
The one with HANDLEBAR written across his head.
He's a good guy, he just doesn't see the difference between a man and a
     bike. If I love you
It's because you belong to and have a sublime tolerance
For such people. Yes, but in later life, I mean—
It is Present Life we've got to keep up on the screen,
Isn't it. Well yes, she said, but—
I am very happy that you are interested in it. The French poodle stopped
     being Irish entirely
And we are all out of the other breeds.
The society woman paused, daintily, upon the hotel stair.
No, I must have a poodle, said she; not an Irish setter
Would satisfy me in my mad passion for the poodle breeds!
As usual, returning to the bed
I find that you are inside it and sound asleep. I smile happily and look at
     your head.
It is regular-size and has beautiful blonde hair all around it.
Some is lying across the pillow. I touch it with my feet
Then leap out the window into the public square,
And I tune my guitar.
"O Mistress Mine, where are you roving?" That's my tune! roars Finogle,
     and he
Comes raging out of the *Beefsteak*—I was going to put that in MY
     Pleasures of Peace.
Oh normal comportment! even you too I shall include in the Pleasures of
     Peace,
And you, relative humidity five hundred and sixty-two degrees!
But what of you, poor sad glorious aqueduct
Of boorish ashes made by cigarettes smoked at the Cupcake
Award—And Sue Ellen Musgrove steps on one of my feet. "Hello!"

She says. "You're that famous COKE, aren't you,
That no one can drink? When are you going to give us your famous Iliad
That everyone's been talking of, I mean your Pleasures of Peace!"

Life changes as the universe changes, but the universe changes
More slowly, as bedevilments increase.
Sunlight comes through a clot for example
Which Zoo Man has thrown on the floor. It is the Night of the Painted
    Pajamas
And the Liberals are weeping for peace. The Conservatives are raging for
    it.
The Independents are staging a parade. And we are completely naked
Walking through the bedroom for peace. I have this friend who had
    myopia
So he always had to get very close to people
And girls thought he was trying to make out—
Why didn't he get glasses?—He was a Pacifist! The Moon shall
    overcome!

Outside in the bar yard the Grecians are screaming for peace
And the Alsatians, the Albanians, the Alesians, the Rubans, the Aleutians,
And the Iranians, all, all are screaming for peace.
They shall win it, their peace, because I am going to help them!
And he leaped out the window for peace!
Headline: GIORGIO FINOGLE,
NOTED POET, LAST NIGHT LEAPED OUT THE WINDOW
    FOR PEACE.
ASIDE FROM HEAD INJURIES HIS CONDITION IS REPORTED
    NORMAL.
But Giorgio never was normal! Oh the horrors of peace,
I mean of peace-fighting! But Giorgio is all right,
He is still completely himself. "I am going to throw this hospital
Bed out the window for peace," when we see him, he says.
And, "Well, I guess your poem will be getting way ahead of mine now," he
    says
Sadly, ripping up an envelope for peace and weakly holding out his hand
For my girl, Ellen, to stroke it; "I will no longer be the most famous poet
For peace. You will, and you know it." "But you jumped out the
Window, Finogle," I said, "and your deed shall live longer
In men's imaginations than any verse." But he looked at the sky
Through the window's beautiful eye and he said, "Kenneth, I have not
    written one word

Of my Poem for Peace for three weeks. I've struck a snarl
And that's why (I believe) I jumped out the
Window—pure poetic frustration. Now tell them all that, how
They'll despise me, oh sob sob—" "Giorgio," I said, trying to calm him
　　down but laughing
So hard I could barely digest the dinner of imagination
In which your breasts were featured as on a Popeye card
When winter has lighted the lanterns and the falls are asleep
Waiting for next day's shards, "Giorgio," I said, "the pleasures—"
But hysteria transported us all.

When I awoke you were in a star-shaped muffin, I was in a loaf of bread
Shaped like a camera, and Giorgio was still in his hospital bed
But a huge baker loomed over us. One false moof and I die you! he said
In a murderous throaty voice and I believe in the yellow leaves, the
Orange, the red leaves of autumn, the tan leaves, and the promoted ones
Of green, of green and blue. Sometimes walking through an ordinary
　　garden
You will see a bird, and the overcoat will fall from your
Shoulders, slightly, exposing one beautiful curve
On which sunbeams alighting forget to speak a single word
To their parent sun and are thus cut off
Without a heating unit, but need none being on your breast
Which I have re-christened "Loaves" for the beginning of this year
In which I hope the guns won't fire any more, the baker sang
To his baker lady, and then he had totally disappeared.
It looks as though everyone were going to be on our side!

And the flowers came out, and they were on our side,
Even the yellow little ones that grow beside your door
And the huge orange ones were bending to one side
As we walked past them, I looked into your blue eyes
And I said, "If we come out of this door
Any more, let it be to enter only this nervous paradise
Of peaceful living conditions, and if Giorgio is roped down
Let them untie him, so he can throw his hospital bed out the door
For all we need besides peace, which is considerable, but first we need
　　that—"

Daredevil, Julian and Maddalo, and John L. Lewis
Are running down the stairways for peace, they are gathering the ice
And throwing it in buckets, they are raising purple parasols for peace

And on top of these old sunlight sings her song, "New lights, old lights
again, blue lights for peace,
Red lights for the low, insulted parasol, and a few crutches thrown around
for peace"—
Oh contentment is the key
To continuing exploration of the nations and their feet;
Therefore, andiamo—the footfall is waiting in the car
And peaceful are the markets and the sneaks;
Peaceful are the Garfinkle ping-pong balls
And peaceful are the blooms beneath the sea
Peaceful are the unreserved airplane loops and the popularly guided blips
Also the Robert Herrick stone sings a peaceful song
And the banana factory is getting hip, and the pigs' Easter party too is
beginning to join in a general celebration
And the women and men of old Peru and young Haifa and ancient Japan
and beautiful young rippling Lake Tahoe
And hairy old Boston and young Freeport and young Santo Domingo and
old father Candelabra the Chieftain of Hoboes
Are rolling around the parapets for peace, and now the matadors are
throwing in
Huge blops of canvas and the postgraduates are filling in
As grocery dates at peanut dances and the sunlight is filling in
Every human world canvas with huge and luminous pleasure gobs of
peace—
And the Tintorettos are looking very purple for peace
And the oyster campus is beginning its peaceful song—

Oh let it be concluded, including the medals!
Peace will come thrusting out of the sky
Tomorrow morning, to bomb us into quietude.
For a while we can bid goodbye
To the frenesies of this poem, The Pleasures of Peace.
When there is peace we will not need anything but bread
Stars and plaster with which to begin.
Roaming from one beard to another we shall take the tin
From the mines and give it to roaring Fidel Castro.
Where Mao Tse Tung lies buried in ocean fields of sleeping cars
Our Lorcaesque decisions will clonk him out
And resurrect him to the rosebuddy sky
Of early evening. And the whip-shaped generals of Hanoi
Shall be taken in overcoats to visit the sky
And the earth will be gasping for joy!

"A wonder!" "A rout!" "No need now for any further poems!" "A Banzai
   for peace!" "He can speak to us all!"
And "Great, man!" "Impressive!" "Something new for you, Ken!"
   "Astounding!" "A real
Epic!" "The worst poem I have ever read!" "Abominably tasteless!" "Too
   funny!" "Dead, man!
A cop out! a real white man's poem! a folderol of honky blank
   spitzenburger smugglerout Caucasian gyp
Of phony bourgeois peace poetry, a total shrig!" "Terrific!" "I will expect
   you at six!"
"A lovely starry catalogue for peace!" "Is it Shakespeare or Byron who
   breathes
In the lines of his poem?" "You have given us the Pleasures of Peace,
Now where is the real thing?" "Koch has studied his history!" "Bold!"
   "Stunning!" "It touches us like leaves
Sparkling in April—but is that all there is
To his peace plea?" Well, you be the one
To conclude it, if you think it needs more—I want to end it,
I want to see real Peace again! Oh peace bams!
I need your assistance—and peace drams, distilling through the world!
   peace lamps, be shining! and peace lambs, rumble up the shore!
O Goddess, sweet Muse, I'm stopping—now show us where you are!


And the big boats come sailing into the harbor for peace
And the little apes are running around the jungle for peace
And the day (that is, the star of day, the sun) is shining for peace
Somewhere a moustachioed student is puzzling over the works of
   Raymond Roussel for peace
And the Mediterranean peach trees are fast asleep for peace
With their pink arms akimbo and the blue plums of Switzerland for peace
And the monkeys are climbing for coconuts and peace
The Hawaiian palm
And serpents are writhing for peace—those are snakes—
And the Alps, Mount Vesuvius, all the really big important mountains
Are rising for peace, and they're filled with rocks—surely it won't be long;
And Leonardo da Vinci's *Last Supper* is moving across the monastery wall
A few micrometers for peace, and Paolo Uccello's red horses
Are turning a little redder for peace, and the Anglo-Saxon dining hall
Begins glowing like crazy, and Beowulf, Robert E. Lee, Sir Barbarossa,
   and Baron Jeep
Are sleeping on the railways for peace and darting around the harbor

236

And leaping into the sailboats and the sailboats will go on
And underneath the sailboats the sea will go on and we will go on
And the birds will go on and the snappy words will go on
And the tea sky and the sloped marine sky
And the hustle of beans will go on and the unserious canoe
It will all be going on in connection with you, peace, and my poem, like a
    Cadillac of wampum
Unredeemed and flying madly, will go exploding through
New cities sweet inflated, planispheres, ingenious hair, a camera smashing
Badinage, cerebral stands of atmospheres, unequaled, dreamed of
Empeacements, candled piers, fumisteries, emphatic moods,
    terrestialism's
Crackle, love's flat, sun's sweets, oh Peace, to you.

# THE ART OF LOVE

# The Circus

I remember when I wrote The Circus
I was living in Paris, or rather we were living in Paris
Janice, Frank was alive, the Whitney Museum
Was still on 8th Street, or was it still something else?
Fernand Léger lived in our building
Well it wasn't really our building it was the building we lived in
Next to a Grand Guignol troupe who made a lot of noise
So that one day I yelled through a hole in the wall
Of our apartment I don't know why there was a hole there
Shut up! And the voice came back to me saying something
I don't know what. Once I saw Léger walk out of the building
I think. Stanley Kunitz came to dinner. I wrote The Circus
In two tries, the first getting most of the first stanza;
That fall I also wrote an opera libretto called Louisa or Matilda.
Jean-Claude came to dinner. He said (about "cocktail sauce")
It should be good on something but not on these (oysters).
By that time I think I had already written The Circus.
Part of the inspiration came while walking to the post office one night
And I wrote a big segment of The Circus
When I came back, having been annoyed to have to go
I forget what I went there about
You were back in the apartment what a dump actually we liked it
I think with your hair and your writing and the pans
Moving strummingly about the kitchen and I wrote The Circus
It was a summer night no it was an autumn one summer when
I remember it but actually no autumn that black dusk toward the post
    office
And I wrote many other poems then but The Circus was the best
Maybe not by far the best Geography was also wonderful
And the Airplane Betty poems (inspired by you) but The Circus was the
    best.

Sometimes I feel I actually am the person
Who did this, who wrote that, including that poem The Circus
But sometimes on the other hand I don't.
There are so many factors engaging our attention!
At every moment the happiness of others, the health of those we know
    and our own!
And the millions upon millions of people we don't know and their well-
    being to think about

So it seems strange I found time to write The Circus
And even spent two evenings on it, and that I have also the time
To remember that I did it, and remember you and me then, and write this
    poem about it
At the beginning of The Circus
The Circus girls are rushing through the night
In the circus wagons and tulips and other flowers will be picked
A long time from now this poem wants to get off on its own
Someplace like a painting not held to a depiction of composing The
    Circus.

Noel Lee was in Paris then but usually out of it
In Germany or Denmark giving a concert
As part of an endless activity
Which was either his career or his happiness or a combination of both
Or neither I remember his dark eyes looking he was nervous
With me perhaps because of our days at Harvard.

It is understandable enough to be nervous with anybody!

How softly and easily one feels when alone
Love of one's friends when one is commanding the time and space
    syndrome
If that's the right word which I doubt but together how come one is so
    nervous?
One is not always but what was I then and what am I now attempting to
    create
If create is the right word
Out of this combination of experience and aloneness
And who are you telling me it is or is not a poem (not you)? Go back with
    me though
To those nights I was writing The Circus.
Do you like that poem? have you read it? It is in my book Thank You
Which Grove just reprinted. I wonder how long I am going to live
And what the rest will be like I mean the rest of my life.

John Cage said to me the other night How old are you? and I told him
    forty-six
(Since then I've become forty-seven) he said

Oh that's a great age I remember.
John Cage once told me he didn't charge much for his mushroom
    identification course (at the New School)
Because he didn't want to make a profit from nature

He was ahead of his time I was behind my time we were both in time
Brilliant go to the head of the class and "time is a river"
It doesn't seem like a river to me it seems like an unformed plan
Days go by and still nothing is decided about
What to do until you know it never will be and then you say "time"
But you really don't care much about it any more
Time means something when you have the major part of yours ahead of
    you
As I did in Aix-en-Provence that was three years before I wrote The
    Circus
That year I wrote Bricks and The Great Atlantic Rainway
I felt time surround me like a blanket endless and soft
I could go to sleep endlessly and wake up and still be in it
But I treasured secretly the part of me that was individually changing
Like Noel Lee I was interested in my career
And still am but now it is like a town I don't want to leave
Not a tower I am climbing opposed by ferocious enemies

I never mentioned my friends in my poems at the time I wrote The
    Circus
Although they meant almost more than anything to me
Of this now for some time I've felt an attenuation
So I'm mentioning them maybe this will bring them back to me
Not them perhaps but what I felt about them
John Ashbery Jane Freilicher Larry Rivers Frank O'Hara
Their names alone bring tears to my eyes
As seeing Polly did last night
It is beautiful at any time but the paradox is leaving it
In order to feel it when you've come back the sun has declined
And the people are merrier or else they've gone home altogether
And you are left alone well you put up with that your sureness is like the
    sun
While you have it but when you don't its lack's a black and icy night. I
    came home

And wrote The Circus that night, Janice. I didn't come and speak to you
And put my arm around you and ask you if you'd like to take a walk
Or go to the Cirque Medrano though that's what I wrote poems about
And am writing about that now, and now I'm alone

And this is not as good a poem as The Circus
And I wonder if any good will come of either of them all the same.

# The Magic of Numbers

### *The Magic of Numbers—1*

How strange it was to hear the furniture being moved around in the
   apartment upstairs!
I was twenty-six, and you were twenty-two.

### *The Magic of Numbers—2*

You asked me if I wanted to run, but I said no and walked on.
I was nineteen, and you were seven.

### *The Magic of Numbers—3*

Yes, but does X really like us?
We were both twenty-seven.

### *The Magic of Numbers—4*

You look like Jerry Lewis (1950).

### *The Magic of Numbers—5*

Grandfather and grandmother want you to go over to their house for
   dinner.
They were sixty-nine, and I was two and a half.

*The Magic of Numbers — 6*

One day when I was twenty-nine years old I met you and nothing
   happened.

*The Magic of Numbers — 7*

No, of course it wasn't I who came to the library!
Brown eyes, flushed cheeks, brown hair. I was twenty-nine, and you were
   sixteen.

*The Magic of Numbers — 8*

After we made love one night in Rockport I went outside and kissed the
   road
I felt so carried away. I was twenty-three, and you were nineteen.

*The Magic of Numbers — 9*

I was twenty-nine, and so were you. We had a very passionate time.
Everything I read turned into a story about you and me, and everything I
   did was turned into a poem.

# Alive for an Instant

I have a bird in my head and a pig in my stomach
And a flower in my genitals and a tiger in my genitals
And a lion in my genitals and I am after you but I have a song in my heart
And my song is a dove
I have a man in my hands I have a woman in my shoes
I have a landmark decision in my reason
I have a death rattle in my nose I have summer in my brain water
This is the matter with me and the hammer of my mother and father
Who created me with everything
But I lack calm I lack rose
Though I do not lack extreme delicacy of rose petal
Who is it that I wish to astonish?
In the birdcall I found a reminder of you
But it was thin and brittle and gone in an instant
Has nature set out to be a great entertainer?
Obviously not A great reproducer? A great Nothing?
Well I will leave that up to you
I have a knocking woodpecker in my heart and I think I have three souls
One for love one for poetry and one for acting out my insane self
Not insane but boring but perpendicular but untrue but true
The three rarely sing together take my hand it's active
The active ingredient in it is a touch
I am Lord Byron I am Percy Shelley I am Ariosto
I eat the bacon I went down the slide I have a thunderstorm in my inside I
    will never hate you
But how can this maelstrom be appealing? do you like menageries? my
    god
Most people want a man! So here I am
I have a pheasant in my reminders I have a goshawk in my clouds
Whatever is it which has led all these animals to you?
A resurrection? or maybe an insurrection? an inspiration?
I have a baby in my landscape and I have a wild rat in my secrets from you.

# Some General Instructions

Do not bake bread in an oven that is not made of stone
Or you risk having imperfect bread. Byron wrote,
"The greatest pleasure in life is drinking hock
And soda water the morning after, when one has
A hangover," or words to that effect. It is a
Pleasure, for me, of the past. I do not drink so much
Any more. And when I do, I am not in sufficiently good
Shape to enjoy the hock and seltzer in the morning.
I am envious of this pleasure as I think of it. Do not
You be envious. In fact I cannot tell envy
From wish and desire and sharing imperfectly
What others have got and not got. But *envy* is a good word
To use, as *hate* is, and *lust*, because they make their point
In the worst and most direct way, so that as a
Result one is able to deal with them and go on one's way.
I read *Don Juan* twenty years ago, and six years later
I wrote a poem in emulation of it. I began
Searching for another stanza but gave in
To the ottava rima after a while, after I'd tried
Some practice stanzas in it; it worked so well
It was too late to stop, it seemed to me. Do not
Be in too much of a hurry to emulate what
You admire. Sometimes it may take a number of years
Before you are ready, but there it is, building
Inside you, a constructing egg. Low-slung
Buildings are sometimes dangerous to walk in and
Out of. A building should be at least one foot and a half
Above one's height, so that if one leaps
In surprise or joy or fear, one's head will not be injured.
Very high ceilings such as those in Gothic
Churches are excellent for giving a spiritual feeling.
Low roofs make one feel like a mole in general. But
Smallish rooms can be cozy. Many tiny people
In a little room make an amusing sight. Large
Persons, both male and female, are best seen out of doors.
Ships sided against a canal's side may be touched and
Patted, but sleeping animals should not be, for
They may bite, in anger and surprise. Of all animals
The duck is seventeenth lowliest, the eagle not as high

On the list as one would imagine, rating
Only ninety-fifth. The elephant is either two or four
Depending on the author of the list, and the tiger
Is seven. The lion is three or six. Blue is the
Favorite color of many people because the sky
Is blue and the sea is blue and many people's eyes
Are blue, but blue is not popular in those countries
Where it is the color of mold. In Spain blue
Symbolizes cowardice. In America it symbolizes "Americanness."
The racial mixture in North America should
Not be misunderstood. The English came here first,
And the Irish and the Germans and the Dutch. There were
Some French here also. The Russians, the Jews, and
The Blacks came afterwards. The women are only coming now
To a new kind of prominence in America, where Liberation
Is their byword. Giraffes, which people ordinarily
Associate with Africa, can be seen in many urban zoos
All over the world. They are an adaptable animal,
As Greek culture was an adaptable culture. Rome
Spread it all over the world. You should know,
Before it did, Alexander spread it as well. Read
As many books as you can without reading interfering
With your time for living. Boxing was formerly illegal
In England, and also, I believe, in America. If
You feel a law is unjust, you may work to change it.
It is not true, as many people say, that
That is just the way things are. Or, Those are the rules,
Immutably. The rules can be changed, although
It may be a slow process. When decorating a window, you
Should try to catch the eye of the passer-by, then
Hold it; he or she should become constantly more
Absorbed in what is being seen. Stuffed animal toys should be
Fluffy and a pleasure to hold in the hands. They
Should not be too resistant, nor should they be made
With any poisonous materials. Be careful not to set fire
To a friend's house. When covering over
A gas stove with paper or inflammable plastic
So you can paint the kitchen without injuring the stove,
Be sure there is no pilot light, or that it is out.
Do not take pills too quickly when you think you have a cold
Or other minor ailment, but wait and see if it
Goes away by itself, as many processes do

Which are really part of something else, not
What we suspected. Raphael's art is no longer as popular
As it was fifty years ago, but an aura
Still hangs about it, partly from its former renown.
The numbers seven and eleven are important to remember in dice
As are the expressions "hard eight," "Little Joe," and "fever,"
Which means *five*. Girls in short skirts when they
Kneel to play dice are beautiful, and even if they
Are not very rich or good rollers, may be
Pleasant as a part of the game. Saint Ursula
And her eleven thousand virgins has
Recently been discovered to be a printer's mistake;
There were only eleven virgins, not eleven thousand.
This makes it necessary to append a brief explanation
When speaking of Apollinaire's parody *Les
Onze Mille Verges*, which means eleven thousand
Male sexual organs—or sticks, for beating. It is a pornographic book.
Sexual information should be obtained while one is young
Enough to enjoy it. To learn of cunnilingus at fifty
Argues a wasted life. One may be tempted to
Rush out into the streets of Hong Kong or
Wherever one is and try to do too much all in one day.
Birds should never be chased out of a nature sanctuary
And shot. Do not believe the beauty of people's faces
Is a sure indication of virtue. The days of
Allegory are over. The Days of Irony are here.
Irony and Deception. But do not harden your heart. Remain
Kind and flexible. Travel a lot. By all means
Go to Greece. Meet persons of various social
Orders. Morocco should be visited by foot,
Siberia by plane. Do not be put off by
Thinking of mortality. You live long enough. There
Would, if you lived longer, never be any new
People. Enjoy the new people you see. Put your hand out
And touch that girl's arm. If you are
Able to, have children. When taking pills, be sure
You know what they are. Avoid cholesterol. In conversation
Be understanding and witty, in order that you may give
Comfort and excitement at the same time. This is the high road to
  popularity
And social success, but it is also good
For your soul and for your sense of yourself. Be supportive of others

At the expense of your wit, not otherwise. No
Joke is worth hurting someone deeply. Avoid contagious diseases.
If you do not have money, you must probably earn some
But do it in a way that is pleasant and does
Not take too much time. Painting ridiculous pictures
Is one good way, and giving lectures about yourself is another.
I once had the idea of importing tropical birds
From Africa to America, but the test cage of birds
All died on the ship, so I was unable to become
Rich that way. Another scheme I had was
To translate some songs from French into English, but
No one wanted to sing them. Living outside Florence
In February, March, and April was an excellent idea
For me, and may be for you, although I recently revisited
The place where I lived, and it is now more "built up";
Still, a little bit further out, it is not, and the fruit trees
There seem the most beautiful in the world. Every day
A new flower would appear in the garden, or every other day,
And I was able to put all this in what I wrote. I let
The weather and the landscape be narrative in me. To make money
By writing, though, was difficult. So I taught
English in a university in spite of my fear that
I knew nothing. Do not let your fear of ignorance keep you
From teaching, if that would be good for you, nor
Should you let your need for success interfere with what you love,
In fact, to do. Things have a way of working out
Which is nonsensical, and one should try to see
How that process works. If you can understand chance,
You will be lucky, for luck is what chance is about
To become, in a human context, either
Good luck or bad. You should visit places that
Have a lot of savor for you. You should be glad
To be alive. You must try to be as good as you can.
I do not know what virtue is in an absolute way,
But in the particular it is excellence which does not harm
The material but ennobles and refines it. So, honesty
Ennobles the heart and harms not the person or the coins
He remembers to give back. So, courage ennobles the heart
And the bearer's body; and tenderness refines the touch.
The problem of being good and also doing what one wishes
Is not as difficult as it seems. It is, however,
Best to get embarked early on one's dearest desires.

Be attentive to your dreams. They are usually about sex,
But they deal with other things as well in an indirect fashion
And contain information that you should have.
You should also read poetry. Do not eat too many bananas.
In the springtime, plant. In the autumn, harvest.
In the summer and winter, exercise. Do not put
Your finger inside a clam shell or
It may be snapped off by the living clam. Do not wear a shirt
More than two times without sending it to the laundry.
Be a bee fancier only if you have a face net. Avoid flies,
Hornets, and wasps. Clasp other people's hands firmly
When you are introduced to them. Say "I am glad to meet you!"
Be able to make a mouth and cheeks like a fish. It
Is entertaining. Speaking in accents
Can also entertain people. But do not think
Mainly of being entertaining. Think of your death.
Think of the death of the fish you just imitated. Be artistic, and be
    unfamiliar.
Think of the blue sky, how artists have
Imitated it. Think of your secretest thoughts,
How poets have imitated them. Think of what you feel
Secretly, and how music has imitated that. Make a moue.
Get faucets for every water outlet in your
House. You may like to spend some summers on
An island. Buy woolen material in Scotland and have
The cloth cut in London, lapels made in France.
Become religious when you are tired of everything
Else. As a little old man or woman, die
In a fine and original spirit that is yours alone.
When you are dead, waste, and make room for the future.
Do not make tea from water which is already boiling.
Use the water just as it starts to boil. Otherwise
It will not successfully "draw" the tea, or
The tea will not successfully "draw" it. Byron
Wrote that no man under thirty should ever see
An ugly woman, suggesting desire should be so strong
It affected the princeliest of senses; and Schopenhauer
Suggested the elimination of the human species
As the way to escape from the Will, which he saw as a monstrous
Demon-like force which destroys us. When
Pleasure is mild, you should enjoy it, and
When it is violent, permit it, as far as

You can, to enjoy you. Pain should be
Dealt with as efficiently as possible. To "cure" a dead octopus
You hold it by one leg and bang it against a rock.
This makes a noise heard all around the harbor,
But it is necessary, for otherwise the meat would be too tough.
Fowl are best plucked by humans, but machines
Are more humanitarian, since extended chicken
Plucking is an unpleasant job. Do not eat unwashed beets
Or rare pork, nor should you gobble uncooked dough.
Fruits, vegetables, and cheese make an excellent diet.
You should understand some science. Electricity
Is fascinating. Do not be defeated by the
Feeling that there is too much for you to know. That
Is a myth of the oppressor. You are
Capable of understanding life. And it is yours alone
And only this time. Someone who excites you
Should be told so, and loved, if you can, but no one
Should be able to shake you so much that you wish to
Give up. The sensations you feel are caused by outside
Phenomena and inside impulses. Whatever you
Experience is both "a person out there" and a dream
As well as unwashed electrons. It is your task to see this through
To a conclusion that makes sense to all concerned
And that reflects credit on this poem, your species, and yourself.
Now go. You cannot come back until these lessons are learned
And you can show that you have learned them for yourself.

# The Art of Poetry

To write a poem, perfect physical condition
Is desirable but not necessary. Keats wrote
In poor health, as did D. H. Lawrence. A combination
Of disease and old age is an impediment to writing, but
Neither is, alone, unless there is arteriosclerosis—that is,
Hardening of the arteries—but that we shall count as a disease
Accompanying old age and therefore a negative condition.
Mental health is certainly not a necessity for the
Creation of poetic beauty, but a degree of it
Would seem to be, except in rare cases. Schizophrenic poetry
Tends to be loose, disjointed, uncritical of itself, in some ways
Like what is best in our modern practice of the poetic art
But unlike it in others, in its lack of concern
For intensity and nuance. A few great poems
By poets supposed to be "mad" are of course known to us all,
Such as those of Christopher Smart, but I wonder how crazy they were,
These poets who wrote such contraptions of exigent art?
As for Blake's being "crazy," that seems to me very unlikely.

But what about Wordsworth? Not crazy, I mean, but what about his later
    work, boring
To the point of inanity, almost, and the destructive "corrections" he made
To his *Prelude*, as it nosed along, through the shallows of art?
He was really terrible after he wrote the "Ode:
Intimations of Immortality from Recollections of Early Childhood," for
    the most part,
Or so it seems to me. Walt Whitman's "corrections," too, of the *Leaves of
    Grass*,
And especially "Song of Myself," are almost always terrible.

Is there some way to ride to old age and to fame and acceptance
And pride in oneself and the knowledge society approves one
Without getting lousier and lousier and depleted of talent? Yes,
Yeats shows it could be. And Sophocles wrote poetry until he was a
    hundred and one,
Or a hundred, anyway, and drank wine and danced all night,
But he was an Ancient Greek and so may not help us here. On
The other hand, he may. There is, it would seem, a sense
In which one must grow and develop, and yet stay young—
Not peroxide, not stupid, not transplanting hair to look peppy,

But young in one's heart. And for this it is a good idea to have some
Friends who write as well as you do, who know what you are doing,
And know when you are doing something wrong.
They should have qualities that you can never have,
To keep you continually striving up an impossible hill.
These friends should supply such competition as will make you, at times,
    very uncomfortable.
And you should take care of your physical body as well
As of your poetic heart, since consecutive hours of advanced
    concentration
Will be precious to your writing and may not be possible
If you are exhausted and ill. Sometimes an abnormal or sick state
Will be inspiring, and one can allow oneself a certain number,
But they should not be the rule. Drinking alcohol is all right
If not in excess, and I would doubt that it would be beneficial
During composition itself. As for marijuana, there are those who
Claim to be able to write well under its influence
But I have yet to see the first evidence for such claims.
Stronger drugs are ludicrously inappropriate, since they destroy judgment
And taste, and make one either like or dislike everything one does,
Or else turn life into a dream. One does not write well in one's sleep.

As for following fashionable literary movements,
It is almost irresistible, and for a while I can see no harm in it,
But the sooner you find your own style the better off you will be.
Then all "movements" fit into it. You have an "exercycle" of your own.
Trying out all kinds of styles and imitating poets you like
And incorporating anything valuable you may find there,
These are sound procedures, and in fact I think even essential
To the perfection of an original style which is yours alone.
An original style may not last more than four years,
Or even three or even two, sometimes on rare occasions one,
And then you must find another. It is conceivable even that a style
For a very exigent poet would be for one work only,
After which it would be exhausted, limping, unable to sustain any wrong
    or right.
By "exigent" I mean extremely careful, wanting each poem to be a
    conclusion
Of everything he senses, feels, and knows.
The exigent poet has his satisfactions, which are relatively special,
But that is not the only kind of poet you can be. There is a pleasure in
    being Venus,

In sending love to everyone, in being Zeus,
In sending thunder to everyone, in being Apollo
And every day sending out light. It is a pleasure to write continually
And well, and that is a special poetic dream
Which you may have or you may not. Not all writers have it.
Browning once wrote a poem every day of one year
And found it "didn't work out well." But who knows?
He went on for a year—something must have been working out.
And why only one poem a day? Why not several? Why not one every
    hour for eight to ten hours a day?
There seems no reason not to try it if you have the inclination.

Some poets like "saving up" for poems, others like to spend incessantly
    what they have.
In spending, of course, you get more, there is a "bottomless pocket"
Principle involved, since your feelings are changing every instant
And the language has millions of words, and the number of combinations
    is infinite.
True, one may feel, perhaps Puritanically, that
One person can only have so much to say, and, besides, ten thousand
    poems per annum
Per person would flood the earth and perhaps eventually the universe,
And one would not want so many poems—so there is a "quota system"
Secretly, or not so secretly, at work. "If I can write one good poem a year,
I am grateful," the noted Poet says, or "six" or "three." Well, maybe for
    that Poet,
But for you, fellow paddler, and for me, perhaps not. Besides, I think
    poems
Are esthetecologically harmless and psychodegradable
And never would they choke the spirits of the world. For a poem only
    affects us
And "exists," really, if it is worth it, and there can't be too many of those.
Writing constantly, in any case, is the poetic dream
Diametrically opposed to the "ultimate distillation"
Dream, which is that of the exigent poet. Just how good a poem should be
Before one releases it, either into one's own work or then into the purview
    of others,
May be decided by applying the following rules: ask 1) Is it astonishing?
Am I pleased each time I read it? Does it say something I was unaware of
Before I sat down to write it? and 2) Do I stand up from it a better man
Or a wiser, or both? or can the two not be separated? 3) Is it really by me
Or have I stolen it from somewhere else? (This sometimes happens,

Though it is comparatively rare.) 4) Does it reveal something about me
I never want anyone to know? 5) Is it sufficiently "modern"?
(More about this a little later) 6) Is it in my own "voice"?
Along with, of course, the more obvious questions, such as
7) Is there any unwanted awkwardness, cheap effects, asking illegitimately
  for attention,
Show-offiness, cuteness, pseudo-profundity, old hat checks,
Unassimilated dream fragments, or other "literary," "kiss-me-I'm-
  poetical" junk?
Is my poem free of this? 8) Does it move smoothly and swiftly
From excitement to dream and then come flooding reason
With purity and soundness and joy? 9) Is this the kind of poem
I would envy in another if he could write? 10)
Would I be happy to go to Heaven with this pinned on to my
Angelic jacket as an entrance show? Oh, would I? And if you can answer
  to all these Yes
Except for the 4th one, to which the answer should be No,
Then you can release it, at least for the time being.
I would look at it again, though, perhaps in two hours, then after one or
  two weeks,
And then a month later, at which time you can probably be sure.

To look at a poem again of course causes anxiety
In many cases, but that pain a writer must learn to endure,
For without it he will be like a chicken which never knows what it is doing
And goes feathering and fluttering through life. When one finds the poem
Inadequate, then one must revise, and this can be very hard going
Indeed. For the original "inspiration" is not there. Some poets never
  master the
Art of doing this, and remain "minor" or almost nothing at all.
Such have my sympathy but not my praise. My sympathy because
Such work is difficult, and most persons accomplish nothing whatsoever
In the course of their lives; at least these poets are writing
"First versions," but they can never win the praise
Of a discerning reader until they take hard-hearted Revision to bed
And win her to their cause and create through her "second-time-around"
  poems
Or even "third-time-around" ones. There are several ways to gain
The favors of this lady. One is unstinting labor, but be careful
You do not ruin what is already there by unfeeling rewriting
That makes it more "logical" but cuts out its heart.
Sometimes neglecting a poem for several weeks is best,

As if you had forgotten you wrote it, and changing it then
As swiftly as you can—in that way, you will avoid at least dry
    "re-detailing"
Which is fatal to any art. Sometimes the confidence you have from a
    successful poem
Can help you to find for another one the changes you want.
Actually, a night's sleep and a new day filled with confidence are very
    desirable,
And, once you get used to the ordinary pains that go with revising,
You may grow to like it very much. It gives one the strange feeling
That one is "working on" something, as an engineer does, or a pilot
When something goes wrong with the plane; whereas the inspired first
    version of a poem
Is more like simply a lightning flash to the heart.
Revising gives one the feeling of being a builder. And if it brings pain?
    Well,
It sometimes does, and women have pain giving birth to children
Yet often wish to do so again, and perhaps the grizzly bear has pain
Burrowing down into the ground to sleep all winter. In writing
The pain is relatively minor. We need not speak of it again
Except in the case of the fear that one has "lost one's talent,"
Which I will go into immediately. This fear
Is a perfectly logical fear for poets to have,
And all of them, from time to time, have it. It is very rare
For what one does best and that on which one's happiness depends
To so large an extent, to be itself dependent on factors
Seemingly beyond one's control. For whence cometh Inspiration?
Will she stay in her Bower of Bliss or come to me this evening?
Have I gotten too old for her kisses? Will she like that boy there rather
    than me?
Am I a dried-up old hog? Is this then the end of it? Haven't I
Lost that sweet easy knack I had last week,
Last month, last year, last decade, which pleased everyone
And especially pleased me? I no longer can feel the warmth of it—
Oh, I have indeed lost it! Etcetera. And when you write a new poem
You like, you forget this anguish, and so on till your death,
Which you'll be remembered beyond, not for "keeping your talent,"
But for what you wrote, in spite of your worries and fears.

The truth is, I think, that one does not lose one's talent,
Although one can misplace it—in attempts to remain in the past,
In profitless ventures intended to please those whom

Could one see them clearly one would not wish to please,
In opera librettos, or even in one's life
Somewhere. But you can almost always find it, perhaps in trying new
    forms
Or not in form at all but in the (seeming) lack of it—
Write "stream of consciousness." Or, differently again, do some
    translations.
Renounce repeating the successes of the years before. Seek
A success of a type undreamed of. Write a poetic fishing manual. Try an
    Art of Love.
Whatever, be on the lookout for what you feared you had lost,
The talent you misplaced. The only ways really to lose it
Are serious damage to the brain and being so attracted
To something else (such as money, sex, repairing expensive engines)
That you forget it completely. In that case, how care that it is lost?
In spite of the truth of all this, however, I am aware
That fear of lost talent is a natural part of a poet's existence.
So be prepared for it, and do not let it get you down.

Just how much experience a poet should have
To be sure he has enough to be sure he is an adequate knower
And feeler and thinker of experience as it exists in our time
Is a tough one to answer, and the only sure rule I can think of
Is experience as much as you can and write as much as you can.
These two can be contradictory. A great many experiences are worthless
At least as far as poetry is concerned. Whereas the least promising,
Seemingly, will throw a whole epic in one's lap. However, that is Sarajevo
And not cause. Probably. I do not know what to tell you
That would apply to all cases. I would suggest travel
And learning at least one other language (five or six
Could be a distraction). As for sexuality and other
Sensual pleasures, you must work that out for yourself.
You should know the world, men, women, space, wind, islands,
    governments,
The history of art, news of the lost continents, plants, evenings,
Mornings, days. But you must also have time to write.
You need environments for your poems and also people,
But you also need life, you need to care about these things
And these persons, and that is the difficulty, that
What you will find best to write about cannot be experienced
Merely as "material." There are some arts one picks up
Of "living sideways," and forwards and backwards at the same time,

But they often do not work—or do, to one's disadvantage:
You feel, "I did not experience that. That cow did
More than I. Or that 'Blue Man' without a thought in the world
Beyond existing. He is the one who really exists.
That is true poetry. I am nothing." I suggest waiting a few hours
Before coming to such a rash decision and going off
Riding on a camel yourself. For you cannot escape your mind
And your strange interest in writing poetry, which will make you,
Necessarily, an experiencer and un-experiencer
Of life, at the same time, but you should realize that what you do
Is immensely valuable, and difficult, too, in a way riding a camel is not,
Though that is valuable too—you two will amaze each other,
The Blue Man and you, and that is also a part of life
Which you must catch in your poem. As for how much one's poetry
Should "reflect one's experience," I do not think it can avoid
Doing that. The naïve version of such a concern
Of course is stupid, but if you feel the need to "confront"
Something, try it, and see how it goes. To "really find your emotions,"
Write, and keep working at it. Success in the literary world
Is mostly irrelevant but may please you. It is good to have a friend
To help you past the monsters on the way. Becoming famous will not hurt
    you
Unless you are foolishly overcaptivated and forget
That this too is merely a part of your "experience." For those who make
    poets famous
In general know nothing about poetry. Remember your obligation is to
    write,
And, in writing, to be serious without being solemn, fresh without being
    cold,
To be inclusive without being asinine, particular
Without being picky, feminine without being effeminate,
Masculine without being brutish, human while keeping all the animal
    graces
You had inside the womb, and beast-like without being inhuman.
Let your language be delectable always, and fresh and true.
Don't be conceited. Let your compassion guide you
And your excitement. And always bring your endeavors to their end.


One thing a poem needs is to be complete
In itself and not need others to complement it.
Therefore this poem about writing should be complete
With information about everything concerned in the act

Of creating a poem. A work also should not be too long.
Each line should give a gathered new sensation
Of "Oh, now I know that, and want to go on!"
"Measure," which decides how long a poem should be,
Is difficult, because possible elaboration is endless,
As endless as the desire to write, so the decision to end
A poem is generally arbitrary yet must be made
Except in the following two cases: when one embarks on an epic
Confident that it will last all one's life,
Or when one deliberately continues it past hope of concluding—
Edmund Spenser and Ezra Pound seem examples
Of one of these cases or the other. And no one knows how
*The Faerie Queene* continued (if it did, as one writer said,
The last parts destroyed in the sacking of Spenser's house
By the crazed but justified Irish, or was it by his servants?).
It may be that Spenser never went beyond Book Six
In any serious way, because the thought of ending was unpleasant,
Yet his plan for the book, if he wrote on, would oblige him to end it. This
   unlike Pound
Who had no set determined place to cease. Coming to a stop
And giving determined form is easiest in drama,
It may be, or in short songs, like "We'll Go
No More a-Roving," one of Byron's most
Touching poems, an absolute success, the best
Short one, I believe, that Byron wrote. In all these
Cases, then, except for "lifetime" poems, there is a point one reaches
When one knows that one must come to an end,
And that is the point that must be reached. To reach it, however,
One may have to cut out much of what one has written along the way,
For the end does not necessarily come of itself
But must be coaxed forth from the material, like a blossom.

Anyone who would like to write an epic poem
May wish to have a plot in mind, or at least a mood—the
Minimum requirement is a form. Sometimes a stanza,
Like Spenser's, or Ariosto's ottava rima, will set the poem going
Downhill and uphill and all around experience
And the world in the maddest way imaginable. Enough,
In this case, to begin, and to let oneself be carried
By the wind of eight (or, in the case of Spenser, nine) loud rhymes.
Sometimes blank verse will tempt the amateur
Of endless writing; sometimes a couplet; sometimes "free verse."

"Skeltonics" are hard to sustain over an extended period
As are, in English, and in Greek for all I know, "Sapphics."
The epic has a clear advantage over any sort of lyric
Poem in being there when you go back to it to continue. The
Lyric is fleeting, usually caught in one
Breath or not at all (though see what has been said before
About revision—it can be done). The epic one is writing, however,
Like a great sheep dog is always there
Wagging and waiting to welcome one into the corner
To be petted and sent forth to fetch a narrative bone.
Oh writing an epic! what a pleasure you are
And what an agony! But the pleasure is greater than the agony,
And the achievement is the sweetest thing of all. Men raise the problem,
"How can one write an epic in the modern world?" One can answer,
"Look around you—tell me how one cannot!" Which is more or less what
Juvenal said about Satire, but epic is a form
Our international time-space plan cries out for—or so it seems
To one observer. The lyric is a necessity too,
And those you may write either alone
Or in the interstices of your epic poem, like flowers
Crannied in the Great Wall of China as it sweeps across the earth.
To write only lyrics is to be sad, perhaps,
Or fidgety, or overexcited, too dependent on circumstance—
But there is a way out of that. The lyric must be bent
Into a more operative form, so that
Fragments of being reflect absolutes (see for example the verse of
William Carlos Williams or Frank O'Hara), and you can go on
Without saying it all every time. If you can master the knack of it,
You are a fortunate poet, and a skilled one. You should read
A great deal, and be thinking of writing poetry all the time.
Total absorption in poetry is one of the finest things in existence—
It should not make you feel guilty. Everyone is absorbed in something.
The sailor is absorbed in the sea. Poetry is the mediation of life.
The epic is particularly appropriate to our contemporary world
Because we are so uncertain of everything and also know too much,
A curious and seemingly contradictory condition, which the epic salves
By giving us our knowledge and our grasp, with all our lack of control as
    well.
The lyric adjusts to us like a butterfly, then epically eludes our grasp.
Poetic drama in our time seems impossible but actually exists as

A fabulous possibility just within our reach. To write drama
One must conceive of an answerer to what one says, as I am now
   conceiving of you.

As to whether or not you use rhyme and how "modern" you are
It is something your genius can decide on every morning
When you get out of bed. What a clear day! Good luck at it!
Though meter is probably, and rhyme too, probably, dead
For a while, except in narrative stanzas. You try it out.
The pleasure of the easy inflection between meter and these easy vocable
   lines
Is a pleasure, if you are able to have it, you are unlikely to renounce.
As for "surrealistic" methods and techniques, they have become a
Natural part of writing. Your poetry, if possible, should be extended
Somewhat beyond your experience, while still remaining true to it;
Unconscious material should play a luscious part
In what you write, since without the unconscious part
You know very little; and your plainest statements should be
Even better than plain. A reader should put your work down puzzled,
Distressed, and illuminated, ready to believe
It is curious to be alive. As for your sense of what good you
Do by writing, compared to what good statesmen, doctors,
Flower salesmen, and missionaries do, perhaps you do less
And perhaps more. If you would like to try one of these
Other occupations for a while, try it. I imagine you will find
That poetry does something they do not do, whether it is
More important or not, and if you like poetry, you will like doing that
   yourself.

Poetry need not be an exclusive occupation.
Some think it should, some think it should not. But you should
Have years for poetry, or at least if not years months
At certain points in your life. Weeks, days, and hours may not suffice.
Almost any amount of time suffices to be a "minor poet"
Once you have mastered a certain amount of the craft
For writing a poem, but I do not see the good of minor poetry,
Like going to the Tour d'Argent to get dinner for your dog,
Or "almost" being friends with someone, or hanging around but not
   attending a school,
Or being a nurse's aid for the rest of your life after getting a degree in
   medicine,

What is the point of it? And some may wish to write songs
And use their talent that way. Others may even end up writing ads.
To those of you who are left, when these others have departed,
And you are a strange bunch, I alone address these words.

It is true that good poetry is difficult to write.
Poetry is an escape from anxiety and a source of it as well.
On the whole, it seems to me worthwhile. At the end of a poem
One may be tempted to grow too universal, philosophical, and vague
Or to bring in History, or the Sea, but one should not do that
If one can possibly help it, since it makes
Each thing one writes sound like everything else,
And poetry and life are not like that. Now I have said enough.

# On Beauty

Beauty is sometimes personified
As a beautiful woman, and this personification is satisfying
In that, probably, of all the beautiful things one sees
A beautiful person is the most inspiring, because, in looking at her,
One is swept by desires, as the sails are swept in the bay, and when the
    body is excited
Beauty is more evident, whether one is awake or asleep.
A beautiful person also suggests a way
To be at one with beauty, to be united with it, physically, with more than
    our eyes,
And strange it is, this tactile experience
Of beauty, and the subject of many other works. The first beauty one sees
That one is conscious of as "beauty," what is that? Some say
"The mother's face"—but I do not think
The baby is conscious of anything as "beauty"—perhaps years after
When he looks at Carpaccio's Saint Ursula, he thinks of "mother"
Subconsciously, and that is why he finds her *"bella—*
*Poi anche bellissima,"* as he says in Italian
To the guard or fellow-viewer at his side. The guard smokes a cigarette
Later, on the steps of the palazzo, and he gazes at the blue sky,
And for him that is bellissima. Perhaps the sky reminds him
Of someone's eyes. But why is that, this human reminder,
If that is what accounts for beauty, so enchanting? Like a thigh, the island
    of Kos
Is extremely lovely, as are many other Greek islands—Lemnos,
Poros, and Charybdis. We could sail among them, happy, fortunate
To be in such places, yet tormented by an inner sense
Of anxiety and guilt, beleaguered by a feeling we had torn
Ourselves from what is really important, simply for this
Devious experiencing of "beauty," which may be nothing but a clumsy
    substitute
For seeing our mothers again. But it is not that,
Not a substitute, but something else. There is no going backwards in
Pleasure, as Hemingway wrote, in *Death in the Afternoon*, speaking of
    Manolete
Who changed the art of bullfighting around, and there is
No going backwards, either, in beauty. Mother may still be there,
In dimity or in nakedness even, but once you have seen Lemnos
It is all over for mother, and Samos and Chios and Kos, and
Once you have seen the girls of your own time. Perhaps one's earliest
    experience

Of beauty is a sort of concentrate, with which one begins,
And adds the water of a life of one's own; then
Flavors come, and colors, and flowers (if one's
Mother is Japanese, perhaps), mountains covered with flowers, and clouds
   which are the
Colors of blossoming trees. One cannot go back to a
Nightingale in the hope of getting a "more fundamental
Experience" of it than one has gotten from Keats's poem. This
Schema is not impoverishing but enriching. One does
Not have the Ode instead of the bird, one has them both. And so
With mother (although mother dies), and so with the people
We love, and with the other things of this world. What, in
Fact, is probably the case is that the thigh
And nose and forehead of a person have an interchangeable
Relationship with landscape; we see
The person first: as babies we aren't tourists, and our new-flung eyes
Are not accustomed to looking at mountains, although
Soon we see breasts—and later see the Catskills, the
Berkshires and the Alps. And as we were moved by breasts before
We are moved by mountains now. Does that mean the
World is for us to eat? that our lives are a constant re-
Gression? Or "Plato inside out"? Or might it not mean, as
I have suggested, that we are born to love either or both?

Beautiful, Charybdis, are your arms, and beautiful your hands;
Beautiful in the clear blue water are the swift white-tinted waves;
Beautiful is the "starlight" (is there any light there,
Really? We may come to the question in a while of whether
Beauty is a reflection); beautiful is the copy
Of Michelangelo's David, and the original; beautiful the regatta
Of happy days one receives, and beautiful the haymow
From which the birds have just flown away. If they
Have left some eggs there, let us go and look at them
To see if they are beautiful as well.

If all these things are carry-overs from mother,
Then mother is everywhere, she completes our consciousness
On every side and of every sight we see. We thank you, mother,
If that is so, and we will leave you there at the beginning of it all, with dad.

It is always a possibility that beauty does not exist
In the realest sense, but that is just as true of everything else,

So in a way it does not modify this poem but actually strengthens it
By being a part of the awareness that puts it together.

Beauty suggests endlessness and timelessness, but beauty
Is fleeting in individual instances, though a person's
Or a landscape's beauty may last for quite a long while.
It is worth preserving, by exercise, good diet, and other
Ways of keeping in good health, and in the case of
Landscape, careful gardening, and good, enforceable zoning and
Anti-pollution laws. Even though it may cause desperation
In the abstract, the thought that "beauty is only for a day,"
So to speak, in individual instances it need not. A good
Night's sleep and wake up happy at all that is beautiful now
Is the best remedy. It is just a quality of beauty that
It comes and it goes. We are contented with the ocean's
Being that way, and summer, winter, fall, and
Spring also leave and return. If beauty does not return
In all cases to the same objects, we must simply be alert and
Find it where it has gone. Every good artist knows
This, and every person should know it as well, it being
One thing one can learn from art, and of course as I said
From close study of nature—though art is sometimes easier
To learn from, whether one is viewing it or creating it.
People, of course, are often depressed,
Despite philosophy and art, about the loss of their own
Beauty, and it is a fact that once one has something
To no longer have it is a sorrow, and there is nothing
This poem can do about that. On the other hand,
You participated in it for a while (for twenty or for
Forty years) and that is pretty good. And there it is,
Shining in the world. Your own exterior is, after
All, just a tiny part of that.

Beauty quite naturally seems as if it would be beautiful
No matter how we looked at it, but this is not always true. Take a
    microscope to
Many varieties of beauty and they are gone. A young girl's
Lovely complexion, for example, reveals gigantic pores, hideously, gapingly
Embedded in her, as Gulliver among the Brobdingnagians observed. And
Put some of her golden hair under the microscope: huge,
Portentous, menacing tubes. But since
Our eyes aren't microscopic, who cares? To have an

Operation to make them so would be insane. A certain
Sanity is necessary for life, and even our deepest studies need not
Carry us beyond a certain place, i.e. right here, the place
Where we would get microscopic eyes. Nor is it necessary to
Pluck out the eyes of an animal (a dog, say) and
Transplant them for our own, so we can see
Beauty as a dog sees it, or as a kangaroo or as a rhinoceros.
We do not know if animals see beauty at all, or if
They merely see convenience and sex, a certain useful log here or there a
Loyalty-retaining moving creature. I do not think we need to know,
Physically, in our own bodies. To give up our human eyes,
And indeed our human brain, for those of a horse or lion might
Be fantastic to write a book about, but then we would
Never know anything else. I suggest, instead,
Walking around beautiful objects, if one can, for that
Is sometimes very pleasant and reveals newer and, if
That is possible, even more beautiful views. One's first view
Of the Bay of Baia, for example, may be improved
Sharply by the view from a boat coming into the harbor or
From the Hotel Shamrock on the mountain's peak. First sight of a girl
Is often one of best ones, but later, sighing above her in bed,
She is even more beautiful. And then in a.m. waking you up
With a happy alarm. Who would want microscopic eyes at
Such a moment? or macroscopic ones, for that matter, which would make
Your girl look extremely tiny, almost invisible, like an insect
You might swat, if you weren't careful; and you would feel
Funny, wondering how someone so small
Could make you feel so happy; and it would be so hallucinatory, to
Go to bed with her and hold her in your arms, for unless you had
Macrotactile arm and hand nerves as well, she would
Feel as large as you are, almost, and yet be so small! You
Would think you were stoned on something monstrous. I think
The proportion between eye and nature, then, is, as
Far as beauty goes, the most important proportion of all.

Like your own eyes, it is probably best to accept your own culture
In responding to what is beautiful. To try to transform yourself
To an Ancient Mesopotamian or a Navajo priest
In order to decide on the beauty of a stallion or a
Stone jar could end up being an impediment to actually seeing anything.
  Some
Knowledge is helpful, but you should exercise reason and control.

In general, any sort of artificial aids
To looking at something may be an impediment to beauty
Unless you are so thoroughly accustomed to them that
You do not know they are there. So a telescope,
When looking at the Valley of the Arno for the first time, may not
Give the pleasure you might get from your naked eye,
Even if your eye did not enable you to see things in
So much detail. Eyeglasses can be annoying at first, as
Well, and even such a slight thing as a map, looked at
Too closely, can keep you from enjoying the landscape it explicates.

Naturalness, important in the looking at beauty, is also esteemed
A main characteristic of the beauty of what is seen.
"Naturalness" is difficult to define, though one knows what it is
When one sees it. Greek statues, for example,
Are both more beautiful and more natural-seeming
Than the people in the harbor of Lemnos, or more natural in
A certain way. One says of a certain statue
"How natural it is!" but does not praise Astrovapoulos the butcher
Or Axanthe the waitress in the same way. It may be
It is because it would seem foolish to praise a living
Human creature for being "natural," but we do praise some—usually
   children,
Or famous or prestigious people one would not expect
To behave like everyone else, or great beauties who do not
"Put on airs"—those we'd expect to be stiff, but
Who are not, except in the case of children, but
Them we seem to be comparing to our stiffer selves. Statues,
Which are expected to be rigid, may have a strange appearance of motion
And ease. And in dancers one admires the same contrast
Between rigidity and movement. Where does this leave us
As we look at the ocean, then? It too is both frozen and mobile. Without
   the tides
It would probably be a great mess. And in a girl
Naturalness is real breasts and a warm, attempting smile,
Combined with bone structure and a good complexion. Pimples, however
Natural they may be, are rarely praised as such. Nor are .
Snoring people or the deaf, though both conditions are
Natural. At the opposite, or not quite the opposite, pole from naturalness
Is strangeness, though strange need not be unnatural. Beauty seems a
   combination
Of natural and strange, which is one thing that makes it so complex

To talk about to some people, who want it to be one
Or the other: avant-garde people wishing for it always to
Be strange, "traditionalists" wanting it always to be
Natural—neither really understanding what those words mean
Or how they are related to things, since
The world is naturally strange, i.e. what seems to us natural
Is really bizarre—the composition of a human face, for
Example, or the splendors of the sun. Though strange as
Well as natural, dependent on our culture and on our vision,
Beauty is a good companion, trustworthy and cheerful.
People are right to look for a beautiful mate and to
Put windows where the beauty is outside.

Animals, though natural and strange, I do not usually find beautiful,
Or fish or insects either. I do not know why this is. Many
People feel otherwise. Birds make me think uncomfortably of color
(Except when they whiz past by surprise) and the idea of feathers
I find disturbing. Whatever its cause, a strong feeling of discomfort
Makes hard the perception of beauty. You should not worry
If some people find some things beautiful that you do not
Find so. There is probably something that seems ugly to others
Which gives you the pleasure that beauty brings
Into our lives. Such strong feelings as physical
Discomfort, or deprivation, or a terror of disease or
Death, can make beauty unlikely to get through to you. It may be
That seeing birds in a more natural, everyday way would
Make them seem more beautiful to me. I do not know
Since this has not happened. Birds are something I was told
Were "beautiful" when I was a child. Flowers also were, and
Especially roses. I am still slightly uncomfortable with
Roses. The moon and the stars were also on my parents' and
Teachers' list of what was beautiful. It has been
Hard for me to love them (stars and moon, I mean) but I have,
Despite this early "training," which may be injurious to beauty
In some cases, in others not. In raising your child,
You should share your feeling with him of what is beautiful,
But do not expect a child to respond to it that way.
He or she is likely to respond more like a poet or an artist,
By wanting to "do" something with it—to run
Through it, or eat it or tear it apart. It is in later life perhaps
Precisely the suppression of these feelings, or some of these feelings,
That results in our feeling of beauty, which we are merely to contemplate.

Contemplation seemed to Aristotle the superior mode, to others may
   seem an unnatural mode
Of life. Most people still feel in the presence of beauty that old wish
To do something, whether it is to make love
To the beautiful person, in the case it is a person, or if
It is a landscape or a seemingly billion stars, or a
Light blue scarcely rippling bay, to run through it, get out a
Telescope, or dive in and swim or build a boat or buy a piece of
Property adjoining it. Sometimes it is merely an impulse to
Jump up and down, or to scream, or to call people up on the telephone to
Tell them about what one has seen. In any case, nothing satisfies
The impulse but merely exhausts it. The perception of beauty wears out
After a while, speeded up by activity, and then one is all right again or
Not all right again, depending on how you look at it. Remembered beauty,
On the other hand, if protected properly, can be a source of light and
Heat to one's imagination and one's sense of life, like
The sun shining in on one's shoulder. It is difficult to make
The impression of beauty last as it is difficult to make the pleasure of love-
Making last for days, but it can sometimes happen. The length of time
   one stays with
Something one thinks is beautiful can help it to stay
With one, so going back through the gallery is often a good idea.
In these cases, contemplation itself is a form of activity
The object of beauty incites. But children, told to contemplate
In this way, are likely to dislike what they see
Because they cannot contemplate and thus can do nothing
With it. Beauty, along with seeming strange, natural, and being temporal
And adapted to the size of human eyes and being a concentrate
With time added, must also seem like something of one's own.
Roses and birds belonged to my mother and her friends. I loved
Tulips, daisies, daffodils, and the white
Tiny flowers whose name I don't know which grew in
The woods in back of my house, which was used as a dump (the
Woods, I mean) and which were so small they were useless for the
   decoration of homes.

One reaction beauty sometimes causes, in the absence
Of other responses, is that it makes one cry, perhaps
Because of seeming a possibility of happiness projected
Into the past, as it is, in fact, in space, which one
Can never again reach, because irrevocably behind one. It may be
That there was never any chance of the kind of happiness

Beauty suggests, and thus that our tears are
In vain, but it is hard to imagine what "useful" tears would be
After one is an adult. Crying is crying, and
Blossoming plum and cherry trees may make one cry
A good deal, as may rocky coastlines and Renaissance art.
The tears in such cases are probably caused by the conflict
Beauty sends up of "Too much! There is no way to
Deal with me!" And the presence of beauty may make
Tears easier and seem safer, too, since it seems, also, to warrant and protect.

If none of the actions we take in regard to beauty
Seems completely satisfactory, and if we go on feeling
An impulse to do, to finally do something when we are in its presence, then
It may be either that beauty is a front for something else or that
It has a purpose our minds have not penetrated yet—or both. Many people
Say that it is all a trick of "Nature." "Nature" makes people
Beautiful, so people will make love to each other and the
Human race will go on, which "Nature" apparently desires.
Others, and sometimes some of these same ones, assume there is
A God, a Divine Being, with absolute power, who also wishes
The human race to go on, as well as to remind them
By the beauty of mountains, lakes, and trees (as well as of human features)
Of how bountiful He is, so that they will do His Will. The
Human features are lovely, also, to remind them
Of what God Himself looks like (approximately). I believe
All this is too simple to be correct, but you are free to believe what you will.
Nor can I subscribe to the "Analogy Theory" of beauty,
That beautiful things exist to show us how to behave
To ourselves and to each other. For one thing, the correspondence
Is insufficiently clear—just how that blue sky, for example, can
Help me to do what is right. It is true that clarity and harmony
May be the result of an ethical action, but it is also
True, often, that such actions involve pain and deprivation
Which seem inimical to beauty, and which I cannot see up there at all.

The beauty of many things does seem to show
They are good for us (or good for our descendants), but
What about poison flowers and berries? Treacherous bays? Beautiful.
Wolf women who simply wish to devour us? What about Blake's Tyger?
My own view is that we are in a situation
That is not under our control (or anyone's, for that matter) but
Which we can handle, if we are wise about it, fairly well.

Temper your admiration for beauty with whatever
Else you know of the particular example you are looking at. Do not
Leap into a reflection in a lake, or take up with a bad woman
Because her breasts are beautiful, or commit
Suicide because Botticelli's *Venus* (it is not a real
Situation) reminds you of what your life has not been. These are times to
 let the
"Enchantment" wear off for a while—for it is an
Enchantment, and it will go away. You will feel driven
To act on your feeling immediately, and—
Perhaps you should go ahead and do it, even though you will be destroyed.
Not every man can die for beauty. Perhaps there is some kind of List
On which your name will be recorded. I don't know. I don't know if I
 approve of that.
However, my approval may not be that which you are after.
As a young man myself I felt I would do anything for
Beauty, but actually I was fairly cautious and did
Nothing that seemed likely to result in the destruction of my ability
To stay around and have these ideas and put them into words.
I would go forward one step, and back another, in regard to
Beauty, but beauty of course was mingled with other things. I don't
Propose myself as a model. Far from that. Since I am still the
Same way, I am interested, though, in if how I am
Makes sense to me in the light of these other things I am saying.

One thing I notice I have done which does seem right to me
Is to think about beauty a good deal and see many examples
Of it, which has helped me to have what is called "good taste"
In it, so I am able to enjoy a great many things
That I otherwise could not have. Discriminating taste does not
Decrease the amount of beauty you perceive, but adds to it.
If you notice an opposite effect, you are "improving" in
The wrong way. Go visit a lot of foreign places
Where ordinary things have an extraordinary aspect and thus
Invite you to see them esthetically. Travel with someone
Else, and travel alone. Stand in front of a beautiful object until you
Are just about to feel tired of being there, then stop
And turn away. Vary your experience of what you see.
In variety is refreshment of the senses. A great painting, a
Mountain, and a person are a good combination for one day.
Sometimes, sameness increases beauty, or, rather,
Variety within sameness, as when looking at beautiful twins,

Triplets, or quadruplets, or in climbing a lot of staircases in Genoa,
A city famed for the beautiful structure of its stairways.

The impulse to "do something" about beauty
Can be acted on, as we have seen, by making love or, sometimes,
Even by marrying. Man is capable of improving
The beauty of nature in numerous ways, of which planting
Huge long rows of beautiful flowers is not the least. The
Cannas are nodding, the roses are asleep. And here's a
Tiny or medium-sized bumblebee, no it's a great big one!
And the oleanders are planted, they are standing
Next to the palms. You feel a surge of unaccountable delight. The wind
   moves them. And
Extraordinary cities may also be tucked together by
Human imaginations and hands. And other works of art as well.

Beauty is perceived in a curious way in poems,
Like the ocean seen through a partially knocked-down wall.
In music, beauty is "engaged in," as in sculpture and dance.

"I am beautiful, O mortals, like a dream of stone," says
Beauty, in Baudelaire's sonnet "La Beauté," where Baudelaire, in
Fewer words than I, has set down his ideas on the subject. Essentially he
Sees Beauty as eternal and pure, an enslaver of poets.
Rilke says that we love beauty because it "so serenely
Disdains to destroy us." In making works of art, then,
Is the excitement we feel that of being close to the elements of
Destruction? I do not want any mystery in this poem, so I will
Let that go. Or, rather, I want the mystery to be that it is clear
But says nothing which will satisfy completely but instead stirs to action
   (or contemplation)
As beauty does—that is, I wish it to be beautiful. But why I want that,
Even, I do not entirely know. Well, it would put it in a class of things
That seems the highest, and for one lifetime that should be enough.

Beauty is sometimes spoken of
As if it were a "special occasion," like going to the ballet
If one does that only once a year, or like going to
Church, if one does that only on religious holidays. Ex-
Perienced in this peripheral fashion, beauty cannot be
Sufficiently understood so as to be as valuable
To us as it should be, even if we do not understand it

Completely. Some understanding will rub off from frequent
Contact with it in both physical and intellectual ways,
And this understanding will do us some good. Of course,
It is possible to live without ever having seen mountains
Or the ocean, but it is not possible to live without having seen some
Beauty, and once one has seen something and
Liked it, one wants to have something more to do with
It, even to the point of having it inextricably tangled
Up with one's life, which beauty may be, anyway, whether we
Want it to be or not. It is a pleasure to be on top of things,
Even if only for a moment. Beauty may be an unsatisfiable
Appetite inducer, the clue to an infinite mystery, or a hoax,
Or perhaps a simple luxury for those with enough money and time
To go in pursuit of it, like châteaux vintages. Or it may be the whole works
    (see
Keats). It may simply be a bloom which is followed by
Fruition and not supposed to last and we have perversely arranged things
So in many cases it does, the way we force-feed geese
And pigs, and now we are simply stuck with it, grunting and
Cackling all around us, from which we try to make music.
Or it may be that beauty is an invitation
To a party that doesn't exist (Whitman thinks the party exists).
In any case, you will probably want as much
Of it as you can take with you, because it is, in spite of
All the doubts expressed above, certainly one of the sweetest things
In life. Of course, this is not the end of the subject, but it is
As far as I now can see, which in regard to beauty is
All we have, and one thing it seems to be about.

# The Art of Love

*"What do you know about it?"*

I

To win the love of women one should first discover
What sort of thing is likely to move them, what feelings
They are most delighted with their lives to have; then
One should find these things and cause these feelings. Now
A story illustrates: of course the difficulty
Is how to talk about winning the love
Of women and not also speak of loving—a new
Problem? an old problem? Whatever—it is a something secret
To no one who has finally experienced it. Presbyopic. And so,
Little parks in Paris, proceed, pronounce
On these contributing factors to the "mental psyche
Of an airplane." Renumerate
The forces which gloss our tongues! And then Betty,
The youngest rabbit, ran, startled, out into the driveway,
Fear that Terry will run over her now calmed. Back
To the Alps, back to the love of women, the sunset
Over "four evenly distributed band lots in
Which you held my hand," mysterious companion
With opal eyes and oval face without whom I
Could never have sustained the Frogonian evening—
Wait a minute! if this is to be a manual of love, isn't it
Just about time we began? Well . . . yes. Begin.

Tie your girl's hands behind her back and encourage her
To attempt to get loose. This will make her breasts look
Especially pretty, like the Parthenon at night. Sometimes those
    illuminations
Are very beautiful, though sometimes the words
Are too expected, too French, too banal. Ain't youse a cracker,
Though? And other poems. Or Freemasonry Revisited. Anyway,
Tie her up. In this fashion, she will be like Minnie Mouse, will look
Like starlight over the sensuous Aegean. She will be the greatest thing
    you ever saw.
However, a word of advice, for cold September evenings,

And in spring, summer, winter too, and later in the fall:
Be sure she likes it. Otherwise
You are liable to lose your chances for other kinds of experiments,
Like the Theseion, for example. Or the two-part song. Yes! this
Is Athens, king of the cities, and land of the
Countries of the Fall. Where *atoma* means person, and where was
A lovely epoch once though we however must go on
With contemporary problems in ecstasy. Let's see. Your
Girl's now a little tied up. Her hands stretched behind her at
An angle of about 40 degrees to her back, no, say, seventeen
And Z—— sending his first roses at seventeen (roses also work
As well as hand tying but in a different less fractured
Framework) and she receiving them writing "I have never
Received roses before from a man. Meet me at the fountain
At nine o'clock and I will do anything you want." He was
Panicky! and didn't know what to do. What had he wanted
That now seemed so impossible? he didn't exactly know
How to do it. So he wrote to her that night amid the capitals
Of an arboring civilization, "Fanny I can't come. The maid is shocked. The
Butter factory is in an endzone of private feelings. So
The chocolate wasp stands on the Venetian steps. So
The cloudbursts are weeping, full of feeling
And stones, so the flying boats are loving and the tea
Is full of quotients. So—" That's enough cries Fanny she tears
It up then she reads it again. One breast may be somewhat higher
Than another with the hands tied behind. As Saint Ursula and her Virgins
Had the right attitude but were in the wrong field of fancy,
Not the sexual field, so these erogenous zones come
Forward when we need them if we are lucky and now I will speak
Of the various different virtues of rope, string, and chicken-wire—
If you want her to break loose suddenly in the middle
Of the lovemaking episode when you are inside her and cry yes
Yes throwing her arms and hands around you, then try string. Otherwise
   rope is most practical. As at Ravenna
The mosaics that start from the wall stay on the wall, in
The wall and they are the wall, in a sense, like the tracks in Ohio,
Pennsylvania, and Illinois. Rounding the bend you will see them.
They are hard to tell from the earth. She will kiss you then.

Thank you, parents of loving and passive girls, even a little bit masochistic
   ones

Who like the things this book is recommending. It is to you,
Although they do not know you often and
Even if they did might not consider this, men owe these joys.

To lack a woman, to not have one, and to be longing for one
As the grass grows around the Perrier family home
That is the worst thing in life, but nowhere near the best is to have one
And not know what to do. So we continue these instructions.

The woman's feet may be tied as well as her hands. I'd suggest tying them
Or really the ankles, that's easier, to the legs at the foot of the bed
Or of the pool table if that is what you are making love upon. I
Remember a day in Paris when a man had a dancing bear
And I walked home to Freesia thinking about ape-mongering and death—
    Hold on a minute, there are
White blocks or cubes on the jetty of French poetic-political involvement
Which "Love Does Not Need a Home" will cannily play for you on the
    phonograph
If you are not AC/DC ruining a certain part of the equipment. Her smile
Will be glorious, a sunrise, her feet tied to the legs of the bed.
If her hands are free she can move up and down readily (the
Sit up/lie down movement, near the Boulevard Raspail
And in irregular patterns—for some reason certain details
Keep coming back to undermine their candidacies). What good this will
    be to you
I don't know, but her sitting up and then lying down will (again)
Make her breasts look pretty (Fontainebleau you are my ark,
And Issy you are my loom!) and give tensity to the throat
Muscles and the stomach muscles too! You can simply enjoy that
(The tensing in the abdomen) by putting, lightly, your fingers on it (the
Abdomen) as one voyages on a Sunday to the Flea Market
Not in the hope of really finding anything but of sensing a new light
    panorama of one's needs.
So much for the pleasure in tensing stomach muscles. Of course with the
    girl tied this way
You can hit her up and down if you like to do that
And she will never be able to get up and walk away
Since she can't walk without her feet, and they are tied to the bed.

If you combine tying her hands to the bed and her feet
You can jump on her! She will be all flattened and splayed out.

What a fine way to spend an autumn afternoon, or an April one!
So delicious, you jumping up and down, she lying there, helpless,
  enjoying your every gasp!
You may enter her body at this point of course as well
As the Postal Museum stands only a few meterage yards away.
They have a new stamp there now, of a king with his crown
On backwards, dark red, it is a mistake, and worth five million pounds!
You can come out and go there, away! Dear, stay with me!!
And she pleads with you there as she lies on the bed, attached to the bed
By the cords you have tied with your hands, and attached to you by her
  love
As well, since you are the man who attached her there,
Since you are the knowing lover using information gleaned from this
  volume.
Tying up, bouquets, bouqueting bunch-of-flowers effects. Tie her hands
  and legs
Together, I mean her hands and feet, I mean ankles. There are different
  processes.
Tie the left hand to the left ankle, right hand to right ankle.
Spread out in any position and make love. She will be capable of fewer
  movements
But may bring you a deep-sea joy. Crabs and lobsters must love like that
And they don't stay down at the bottom of the ocean for nothing—
It must be wonderful! In any case you can try it in your mistress's bed
Or in your own course. You can tie left hand to right ankle
And so on. This gives a criss-cross effect
And is good after a quarrel. The breasts in all these cases look
Exceptionally beautiful. If you do not like liking
These breasts so much you may hit them
If she likes that, and ask her to ask you to hit them, which
Should increase your pleasure in mastery particularly if she is all tied up.
"Hit My Tits" could be a motto on the sailboat of your happiness. If you
  don't think
You have gotten your money's worth already
From this book you deserve to turn in an early grave
Surrounded by worm women who assail and hit you
Until there is nothing left of you so hard that they can't eat.
But I am sure this is not your feeling. So, having agreed,
Let us go on. You should buy another book
And give it to your best friend, however, if at this point you do agree with
  me.

I will wait; meanwhile we can both stare at your mistress, where she is all
    tied up.

Well, you can roll her like a wheel, though I doubt she'll approve of it,
Women rarely do, I knew one once, though, who did. For
This of course you use the right hand right ankle left
Hand left ankle arrangement, using splints on both sides of each
Knot so that the limbs will stay in wheel-position. Now that she
Looks like that which makes a chariot roll, roll her! If this hurts her,
Soothe her a little by kissing her all around, saying
"Ah, my lovely wheel, went over a bump, did it?" and so on,
Until she finally is resigned to being your wheel, your dear beloved one
And is eager to be rolled about by you. Small objects placed on the floor
Will give you brief twinges of sadistic energy and speed up your wheeling.
I suggest ending by wheeling her out an opened door
Which you then close and stab yourself to death. This procedure,
    however, is rare.
I was carried away. Forgive me. The next chapters will be much more
    sane.


Nailing a woman to the wall causes too much damage
(Not to the wall but to the woman—you after all want to enjoy her
And love her again and again). You can, however, wrap tape around her
    arms, waist, ankles, and knees
And nail this to the wall. You'll enjoy the pleasure of nailing
And the very thought of it should make her scream. You can fit this tape
On her like tabs, so your girl will be like a paper doll.
And you can try things on her once she is nailed up. You can also
Throw things at her, which is something I very much like to do—
Small rakes, postal scales, aluminum belt buckles, Venetian glass clowns—
As soon as you start to hurt her, you should stop
And kiss her bruises, make much of them, draw a circle around each hit
With a bold felt pen. In this way you can try to hit the same spots over and
    over again
As the little park grows larger the more you look at it
But the flowers are in another story, a lemon-covered volume, stop! The
    knees
Of this girl are now looking very pretty, so go and kiss them
And slip your hands around the back of them and feel what is called
The inside of the knee and tell her you love her.
If she is able to talk she will probably ask you to take her down,
Which you then can do. However, if she wants to stay up there

As blue day changes to night, and is black in the hemispheres, and boats
    go past
And you are still feeling wonderful because of her beautiful eyes
And breasts and legs, leave her there and run up against her
As hard as you can, until the very force of your bumping
Breaks tape from nail or girl from tape or breaks great chunks of wall
So you and she lie tumbled there together
Bruises on her body, plaster on your shoulders, she bloody, she hysterical,
    but joy in both your hearts.
Then pull off the tape if it hasn't come off
And bite her to the bone. If she bites you back, appoint her
"Lover" for a while and let her do all this to you. That is,
If you'd like it. You'll suffer, of course, from being less beautiful than she
And less soft, less inviting to cause pain to. To be a great lover,
However, you must be a great actor, so try, at least once.

Oh the animals moving in the stockyards have no idea of these joys
Nor do the birds flying high in the clouds. Think: tenderness cannot be
    all
Although everyone loves tenderness. Nor violence, which gives the sense
    of life
With its dramas and its actions as it is. Making love must be everything—
A city, not a street; a country, not a city; the universe, the world—
Make yours so, make it even a galaxy, and be conscious and unconscious of
    it all. That is the art of love.


2


Which cannot be begun, however, until you meet somebody
You want to make love to, a subject to be dealt with in these chapters.
So, avanti! Here you are, girl-less, wandering the city's streets
Or deep in the country, pale amid flowers, or staring, perhaps too!,
At barrels of camel dung being shoved down a road in the Middle East
Or on a skyscraper in a great city, ten thousand miles beneath the ocean
    floor,
How do you meet a woman? or, if you like younger women, a girl?
Well, the thing to do is find out where local girls congregate—
This may be at the camel shack, along the shore of the Ashkenazi or the
    Mediterranean
At a beach, or along the side streets or at the school, wherever

It is, go there! You will be happy once you have seen the girls
Or women and your body becomes active, reminding you you must
 succeed
As the earthquake and the volcano remind life they must succeed
And it must succeed. Success is a joy although it is not everything,
Still, in matters of love, there is nothing without it! With no
Success, simply nothing happens. You are a dead person in a field
With mud being heaped on you; without success,
Nothing happens in the field of love. Something
Has to be there, a spark, a firm handclasp, a meaningful look, some hope,
Something, which one only can get in the presence of women
Since if they are not there, how can they give it? But
You do not need to be reminded of this, you are already reading
This strangely eventful and staggering "Art of Love."

Many people get married before they even realize how to meet girls
And so have a wide selection; this may result in infidelity, divorce,
And frustrated feelings; so it is a good idea, whether you are
 contemplating marriage or not,
To learn where to meet, to find the women whom you might love.
In big cities often guidebooks are accurate indications
Of some of the spots to begin your search. Great tourist attractions
Such as the Acropolis, the Bermuda Shorts factory, and St. Peters in
 Rome
Are likely to attract women as well as men, since they too share such
 human feelings
As curiosity, interest, the desire to find "something afar
From the sphere of our sorrow" (as Shelley says), always hoping to find
 this,
Even as men are, in some storied successes of history, business, or art.
So that is a good place to meet them, too, since their souls are likely to be
 open
In a way they are not otherwise: historical beauty is a friend,
Opening and softening the feelings, but no human friend is there,
So you may fill the gap by sharing the openness with her,
And by appreciating the work at hand. Some like to fall down right there
And "made love my first sight of the Acropolis" or
"Bellini's pictures moved me, so—" As the ferry boat
Pursues its course from Brindisi to Corfu and back again
Many young couples were seen steaming on its decks
With happy energy, and among the lime trees in Southern Africa
A thousand hippopotamuses met with glee and frightened everyone away

By their lovemaking, which increased the acidity of the limes
One million per cent. Why should they be having all the fulfilment and
  fun
And you not? My friends, there is no reason. So another kind of place to
  go
In cities is the college restaurants. There young girls congregate speaking
  of their courses
And their boyfriends and their professors. You can pretend to be a poet
Or a professor, and speak to them about starting a little shop
Where no one will come. Their curiosity piqued, they may follow you as
  far as a coffee shop
Where you can go on speaking to them, in private—but that is covered in
The next chapter—"Antic," or "What to Say." Sometimes a department
  store
Will be full of women. You can go as a woman yourself, as a
Cripple who needs their help, or as a regular man shopping for some real
  woman he knows
Who needs their advice. It doesn't matter how you go; what matters
Is getting the woman alone, so you can speak of your desires.
No one can resist this, but first you have to find the one to speak to.
Well, almost no one—but your ratio anyway should be seven to one,
Success over failure. Dangerous intersections in mid-city
Are good places to meet girls and help them across the street.
You can stand there and do this all day, madly dodging the traffic
And with a happy smile you find the one you like and cross her too
With a swift hit on the belly and a large and wicked smile.
She will look at you surprised and you can carry on from there, but at least
  you will be beginning
With her grateful to you, for having steered her across the street.

Life is full of horrors and hormones and so few things are certain,
So many unknown—but the pleasure of coupling with a creature one is
  crazy about
Is something undisputed. So don't be afraid to spend
Hours, even days, weeks, even months, going to places
And trying to find the person who can give you the maximum pleasure in
  life
As the sun hits the top of mountains but often prefers the hills
Where markets glint in the fading light and one's lungs seem filled with
  silver. O horrors of loneliness!
Abandon my spirit while it walks forth through the world and attempts to
  find for people

And tell them where marvelous women can be found. Of course, you want
   a very particular one.
To find her, however, you may have to look at a great many, and try more,
Some in the light, some in the dark. Orgies are sometimes organized for
   people,
You can try that, but I wouldn't, all life is an
Orgy, why limit oneself to a little room, full of (probably)
Mainly people who are emotionally disturbed
As you and I are not. If you could organize an orgy
Of your own, that might, I think, be something else. But
We have strayed from our subject. The Cross of the Seven Winds Hotel
On East Vortex Street, in Albenport, is a good place to meet girls,
It so happens there are always a tremendous number of them there
And no one has ever known why. But you know what custom is (or
   fashion). It's a great place to go.
If you can't find it, take some girl you already have
And like (if you have one) and whip her until she tells you where it is
   (most women know).
If she hasn't replied after ten strokes it's a sign she loves you
So dearly and is so jealous she is willing to undergo pain for you,
Set sail with her for Zhak or Brindisi right away, she is the one to love you
For the rest of your life and you will only need this manual
In its earlier and later parts, not this part, you already have your girl.

Happy the man who has two breasts to crush against his bosom,
A tongue to suck on, a lip to bite, and in fact an entire girl! He knows a
   success
Not known by Mount Aetna or Vesuvius or by any major volcano of the
   world!
He has someone to come into, and stay there, and tremble, and shake
   about, and hold,
And dream about, and come back to, and even discuss party politics with if
   he wants to,
Or poetry, or painting. But where shall you find this bird? On a gondola
   in Venice
The tour guide said, "Look at those buildings" and I felt my chest crushed
   against your
Bosom, and the whole earth went black; when I awoke we were in Brindisi,
You had nailed me to a canoe, you were standing on my stomach, you had
   a rat in your hand
Which you were waving in the summer breeze, and saying "This is from
   the Almanac

Of Living, attention, please pay attention, greeniness and mountains, oh
this is the art of love!"

Uncooperative cities! your hideous buildings block out air and sunlight!
Fumes
Destroy human lungs! Muggers and burglars
Infest your streets! You're horrible! I hate you! (Sometimes.) Where else
are women to be found
And the sweet joys they furnish, the prospect of a life joined to a life
More wonderful than air joined to a fountain—there is nothing like the
art of love!
A plume, a cabana, a canvas, a modern tire, a pampa, a plume, a sailboat
All have meaning as an ocean has tar, in relation to love only. Yes,
That's my secret. What is yours? I mean to say without love everything is
only half in order,
Or two-fifths, or one-third, perhaps for many and I think I am one
Hardly ordered at all, for us, without love, life is a great mess! By order I
mean clarity, I mean joy.
In India the art of love has been studied in great detail
But that was in another age, another time. My book brings it all up to date
And is oriented to the Western World! Though my Chinese edition
May soon be out! Here's just a hint of it: "Think in love,
Don't think in rabbits." But now back to the Western World! And to the
country! And how there to find girls!

Sometimes in the country there may actually be no girls
And one must return disconsolately to the city. However, first one should
have a good and intensive look,
For to fail, and especially in matters of love, is depressing
And depression eats the heart away and makes one less able to love.
Oysters, clams, steak, anything with a high protein content
Is good for one's sexual powers, since semen is all protein;
For the feeling part, self-confidence, joy, and a tender and passionately
loving heart!
How can girls stay away from you? They will have to find you
If you are like that! But what if they do not know you exist?
So—in the country, WALK! circulate, cover as many square inches of the
area as you can
So that female eyes can see you, even if they are hidden behind ramparts
of hay
Or cow barriers, pig barriers, hog barriers, chicken barriers, bull barriers,
Even peering out from between the interstices of a barn. Once they see you

They will love you, if your radiance shines in your face
(For this there are chemical preparations, but naturalness is best)
And they will tentatively come out to meet you. Here, immediate love-
    making is best
Because of lack of places to go, chance of the angry farmer, etcetera,
But this may be dealt with later. In Turkey, in the country,
Sling your girl under a camel, and have her there. You will thrill gently
And greatly as the camel trots down the road toward the mill,
Where you will be thrown amidst the raw grain. You must immediately
    escape
Or you'll be ground to bits! And take the girl off with you
For she may later come to be the one that you will love,
Which you cannot do if she is in a thousand pieces, or even in fifteen
Or three. One man once loved a girl who was in two
But that was a rare occasion and does not affect the more general behavior
That is the subject of this book. So rescue the girl. In any case,
Even if you do not love her later, you will, I feel sure,
Enjoy making love that once after escaping from death.

For meeting girls, then, in the country, the rule is BE SEEN.
In the city, GO WHERE THEY ARE. In Turkey, or any foreign country,
TRAVEL WITH THEIR CUSTOMS OF LIFE, as with the incident of
    the camel.
Having found the woman, however, what can you say?

Or what if she runs past you, fleetingly, at the beginning of night?


3

Of course you must stop her. Say anything: "Hello!" "Good-bye!"
Anything to arrest her attention, so that when her pace is slowed
She will be able to listen to you and be totally entranced by you,
So that later she will be with you, all breasts and fragrance!
And what you say should not merely win over the woman
But add to the zest and to the glory of everything you do.

Sweet is making love out of doors, and making love on walls
Built to surround ancient cities, sweet being close to a girl beneath
    overhead highways

Or in a downtown sunlit hotel, from which afterwards you walk out and
    look at the statues
Of the city, at the main piazza, and the opera dome. And sweet it is if you
    have engraved your name
Or written it or stamped it on your girl's thigh, to walk on mirrored floors
So you can see it. And it is a great pleasure
To have your girl riding on a wagon and you run after her
And catch her and pull her down and make love on the road in the dust.
Sweet the first contact of bodies—and one of the sweetest things in life is
    to talk to someone
Delicious and unavailable and to wholly win her over by what you say!

When you first see a woman you do not know, some time, some autumn,
    Septembery
Day when the leaves are making curtains through which the gargoyles
    peer
At you as you are standing there astonished by that ivory and those hooks
You imagine to be holding all together without which she would be naked
    and in your arms,
As you stand there thinking of that, you may find yourself speechless
From so much excitement! In such situations, one
Thing you can usually rely on is asking for directions—
To someplace, to be sure, which you cannot find unless she goes with you,
And of course you should have some room along the way
To which you can take her. And it is a good idea in most cases also
To ask for directions to places that are likely to excite the
Woman you are asking them of, such as "Where is the Duomo of Ropes?"
    or
"In what museum is the Daumier painting of the girl who is rolling like a
    wheel?"

If you pretend a woman is someone you already know,
An already existing girlfriend, lost love, former student, and so on, that is
    also a good way to
Begin, and you can start in talking at once in a relaxed and
Intimate way, which is a joy in itself. And if you pretend to know a woman,
    you can kiss her
At once, which is always an excellent idea. Not only does doing so
Sometimes bring instant success, but it also prepares the way
For possible future encounters, as does thoughtful praise—

For the well-placed compliment, like an Easter egg, beautiful but hidden,
Can influence a woman, as a kiss can, for years of her life.

In general, you should kiss as many women as you can,
Taking any excuse to do so: pretending you know her, saying
Hello or good-bye to her, seeing her at a parade, at a party, and so on.
In train stations, kiss any pretty girl in sight. A friendly kiss may implant
     in a girl the idea
That she would like to see you again. Then who knows what may happen?

Compliments may be 1) whispered as the girl walks past you
2) stated to her directly, as you move into her path, then bow as she goes
     by you
3) read into a dictaphone and played as woman after woman comes along
4) given when you do not know the woman at all 5) given after one
     minute's acquaintance
6) after two 7) after three. The "striking" compliment, i.e. with which to
Win the one one does not know should not be delayed beyond
     approximately
Three minutes, unless some other potent factor is having an effect—your
Being famous, excessively good-looking, or covered with precious jewels
Or being accompanied by an interesting gigantic animal, i.
E., anything that will make talk easy because of astonishment
Or admiration—but even in these cases you should quickly come to praise
Because it is so moving and love makes it so natural a thing to do.

In regard to content, compliments are of six types, reducible to three
Chief ones, which are Compliments to the Body—including of course the
     face,
The coloration and the movements; Compliments to the Mind—for
Lack of a better term, considered to include the sensibility
As a whole, sensitivity in particular, deep understanding, and
Comprehension of details; and Compliments to Something Else—
     whatever
Doesn't go in One or Two, such as ability to fire clay sculptures, arrange
     flowers,
Or behavior and elegance in general. Under this last could come
Moral or characterological praise, though this might be considered as
     being in Category Two.
The essence of the compliment, of whatever type it is
You give the woman, if it is to give you the maximum
Benefits of her enjoyment and passion for you, and if you are to

Like giving it, as one may like giving the world a poem,
A symphony, or a bridge, is that it be free, a free possession
Of the woman or girl that you give it to, in other words that she
Feels no obligation to respond (though I assure you that she will)
And feels free to wear it entirely on her own. Then she will turn to you
With happy and returning desire. Of all compliments there
Are two kinds: those which show desire, and those which do not. "You
     look Etruscan!"
Is a good example of the compliment without desire
(Apparently) and "You look so delicious I want to bite you! My God, you
     drive me
Crazy!" is an example of the other kind. In the one case the woman is left
     with
A high historic feeling and feeling her beauty is somehow eternal,
That she shares in an eternally beautiful type
Away from the sphere of our sorrow, and thus that her life must somehow
     mean something
And she be an achievement of some marvelous kind (which she is), and the
     other, more
Earthy-seeming compliment makes her feel a happy object of desire,
The source of fervid feeling in others, a sort of springtide or passage of
     time,
Or else a Venus, or else a sunrise, or sunset, the cause of sleepless evenings
     and gasps
(This compliment is not demanding, because it is exaggerated
And humorous in being that, and lets the woman decide).

Everything about love makes people feel in a more intense way,
So it seems natural enough to start right in, with "You are beautiful
As a) Botticelli's Venus, or b) a slice of angelfood cake, I want
To devour you—for my sweet tooth is the ruling tooth of my life!"

Later you can cry to her, when alone with her, "Oh you are the enslaving
     of me,
Dear sweet and irrefutable love!" And when you are dancing with her
Or anywhere in public, you may even wish to praise her
In a secret language which no one else will understand—
"Gah shlooh lye bopdoosh," for example, may mean "Your left leg
Is whiter even than the snow which on Mount Kabanayashi
Tops all Japan with its splendor!" and "Ahm gahm doom bahm ambahm
     glahsh": "I
Would like to tie you to this bannister and

Kill you with my kisses all night!" For if you believe
There is a magic in love, to get to it you will go to any extremes.

And one goes on looking, and talking. And neither the tongue
Nor the eyes wear out, and the streets are filled with beautiful breasts and
  words.

One excellent thing to do once a woman will listen to you
Is to read her poems, and the best of all poems to read is this one,
Accompanied, if you like, by acting out its details. Which now let us
  continue.


4


For there are numerous questions remaining which one must consider
If one is serious about love and determined to learn all its ways.

What is Love's Ideal City? what strange combination
Of Paris and Venice, of Split for the beauty of its inhabitants,
Of Waco for its byways, of Vladivostok for its bars?
What, precisely, is meant by the "love of God"? or the "love of
  humanity"?
How can girls best be conquered in different cities?
What places, or bits of landscape, most speak of love?
How to make your girlfriend into an airplane, or a living kite;
How to convert success in business or art into success in love;
Keeping one's libidinous impulses at a peak all the time;
How to explain, and how to prosper with having two loves, or three, or
  four, or five;
Meeting women, disguised, in museums, and walking with them, naked,
  in the country;
How to speak of love when you do not know the language; how to master
  resentment;
How to cause all the women eating in a given restaurant to fall in love
  with you at the same time;
Greek aphrodisiac foods, how to eat them and how to prepare them;
One secret way to make any woman happy she is with you;
Apollo: woman-chaser, homosexual, or both? Zeus: godlike ways of
  seducing women;

How to judge the accuracy of what you remember about past love;
Building a house ideally suited to love; how to reassure virgins;
How to avoid being interested in the wrong woman; seven sure signs of
  someone you don't want to love;
Three fairly reliable signs of someone you do;
Use of the car—making love under the car; in the car; on the car roof;
Traveling with women; what to do when suddenly you know that the
  whole relationship is no longer right;
How to pump fresh air into the lungs of a drowned girl; the "kiss of
  death"; how to appear totally confident and totally available for love at
  the same time;
Maintaining good looks under exhausting conditions; forty-one things to
  think about in bed;
How to win the love of a girl who is half your age; how to win the love of
  one who is one fifth your age;
Bracelets women like to have slipped onto them; places in which women
  are likely to slip and thus fall into your arms;
The bridge of ships: how to make love there in twenty-five different
  positions
So as to have a happy and rosy complexion later, at the "Captain's Table";
Love in different cultures: how to verify what you are feeling in relation to
  the different civilizations of the world—
Room for doubt: would the Greeks have called this "love"? Do such
  feelings exist in China?
Did they exist in Ming China? and so on. The Birthday of Love—
On what day is Eros's birthday correctly celebrated? Was love born only
  once?
Is there actually a historical date? Presents to give on such a day;
What memorable thing did Spinoza say about love? How to deal with the
  sweethearts of your friends
When they want to go to bed with you; how to make love while asleep;
The Book of Records, and what it says; how to end a quarrel;
How to plan a "day of love"—what food and drink to have by your side,
  what newspapers and books;
How to propose the subject so that your girlfriend will go away with you
On a "voyage to the moon," i.e. lie under the bed while you
Create a great hole in the mattress and springs with your hatchet
And then leap on her, covered with feathers and shiny metal spring
Fragments, screaming, as you at last make love, "We are on the moon!"
  How to dress
Warmly for love in the winter, and coolly in the sun;

Mazes to construct in which you can hide naked women and chase them;
Dreams of love, and how they are to be interpreted;
How "love affairs" usually get started; when to think of marriage; how to
    prevent your girl from marrying someone else;
"Magical feelings"—how to sustain them during a love affair; traveling
    with a doctor
As a way to meet sick girls; traveling with a police officer as a way to meet
    criminal girls;
What is "Zombie-itis"? do many women suffer from it? how can it be
    enjoyed
Without actually dying? where are most adherents to it found?
What ten things must an older man never say to a young woman?
What about loving outdoors? what good can we get there from trees,
    stones, and rivers?
Are there, in fact, any deities or gods of any kind to Love?
And if so, can they be prayed to? Do the prayers do any good?
What can be done to cure the "inability to love"? senseless promiscuity?
    twenty-four-hour-a-day masturbatory desires?
What nine things will immediately give anyone the power to make love?
What three things must usually be forgotten in order to make love?
Ways of leaving your initials on women; other "personalizing insignia";
How to turn your girl into a duck, turkey, or chicken, for fifteen minutes;
What to do when she comes back to herself, so she will not be angry or
    frightened;
How to make love while standing in the sea; cures for "frozen legs";
    Love's icebox;
Love Curses to blight those who interfere with you, and Love Charms to
    win those who resist you;
Traveling while flat on your back; Girls from Sixteen Countries; what to
    do with a Communist or other Iron Curtain Country Girl
So that politics will not come into it, or will make your pleasure even greater;
How to identify yourself, as you make love, with sunlight, trees, and clouds;
What to do during a Sex Emergency: shortage of women, lack of desire,
    absence of space in which to sit or lie down;
How to really love a woman or girl for the rest of your life; what to do if
    she leaves you;
Seventeen tried and tested cures for the agonies of lost love;
Telling a "true" emotion from an in some way "untrue" one;
How to compensate for being too "romantic"; can enjoyed love ever come
    up to romantic expectations?
Ways of locating women who love you in a crowd; giving in totally to love;
How to transform a woman into a "Human Letter"

By covering her with inscriptions, which you then ship to yourself
In another bedroom, unwrap it, read it, and make love;
Making love through a piece of canvas; making love through walls;
What to do when one lover is in a second-floor apartment, the other in
    the first-floor one;
Openings in the ceiling, and how to make them; how to answer the question
"What are you doing up there on the ceiling?" if someone accidentally
    comes home;
Ways to conceal the fact that you have just made love or
Are about to make love; how to explain pink cheeks, sleepiness.
Is love all part of a "Great Plan," and, if so, what is the Plan?
If it is to keep the earth populated, then what is the reason behind that?
Throwing your girl into the ocean and jumping in after her, aphrodisiac
    effects of; genius,
Its advantages and disadvantages in love; political antagonism in love:
She is a Muslim, you are a Republican; or she is a Maoist, and you are for
    improving the system;
How to keep passion alive while beset by anxiety and doubt;
What is the best way to make love in a rocket? what is the second-best way?
How to make sure one's feeling is "genuine"; how to use gags; when to
    wear a hat;
At what moment does drunkenness become an impediment to love?
What is the role of sex in love? Is fidelity normal? Are all women, in one
    sense, the same woman?
How can this best be explained to particular women? Drawing one's
    portrait on a woman's back—
Materials and methods; is growing older detrimental to love?
Use of the aviary; use of the kitchen garden; what are eighteen totally
    unsuspected enemies of love?
Does lack of love "dry people up"? how can one be sure one's love will be
    lasting?
What reasonable substitute, in love's absence, could be found for love?

The best authors to consult about love (aside from the author of this
Volume) are Ovid, Ariosto, Spenser, and Stendhal. Places or bits of
    landscape
Which most speak of love: Piazzale Michelangelo, looking down at the
    Arno, above Florence;
The candy factory in Biarritz, specializing in ruby-red hearts;
Gus's Place, in Indonesia, a small cart-wheel store full of white paper; the
    Rotterdam Harbor on an April evening.
The Ideal City for Love—should be a combination

Of Naples, for its byways and its population and its Bay; Paris
For the temerity and the lovification of its inhabitants;
Rome, for its amazement, not for its traffic; Split, for its absence of the
    Baroque;
Austin, Texas, for having so many pretty girls there; Hangkow, for its evenings.
This ideal city of love will not be as spread out
As London is, or as over-towering as New York, but it will be a city.
    Suburbs are inimical to love,
Imposing the city's restrictions without its stimulation and variety.
The city must include numerous young women. Therefore city planners
Will include as many colleges as they can and encourage
Such professions as will draw young women to the city from outside.

To make your girl into an airplane, ask her to lie down on a large piece of
    canvas
Which you have stretched out and nailed to a thin sheet of aluminum, or,
    if you are economizing, of balsa wood.
When she has lain down, wrap the stuff she is lying on around her
And ask her to stretch out her arms, for these will be the wings
Of the plane (she should be lying on her stomach), with her neck
    stretched taut, her chin
Resting on the canvas (her head should be the "nose" of the plane); her
    legs and feet should be
Close together (tied or strapped, if you like). Now, once she is in airplane
    position,
Wrap the aluminum or balsa-coated canvas more closely around her and
    fasten it at the edges
With staples, glue, or rivets. Carry her to the airport, or to any convenient
    field,
And put her on the ground. Ask her to "take off!" If she does, you have
    lost a good mistress. If not
(And it is much more likely to be "if not"), you will enjoy making love
    there on the field—
You, both pilot and crew, and passengers, and she your loving plane!

Perhaps you would also like to turn your girl into a shoe or into a shoebox
Or a plaster cherry tree or any one of a million other things. A booklet is
    coming out
Specifically and entirely on that, called *The Shop of Love*.

The best way to conquer girls in different cities is to know the mayor or
    ruler of the particular city

And have him introduce you to the women (perhaps while they are under
  the influence of a strong love-making drug).

To revive an old love affair, write the woman concerned, or call her up.
  Suggest converting her into a plane.
If she loves you still, she'll hesitate or say yes. If she says no, propose
  converting her into the summer dawn.

To cause all the women in a given restaurant to wish to make love to you,
Bring in the model of an airplane and stare at it attentively and refuse to eat.

You can tell a woman's character by looking in her shoe, if you have the
  special glasses described in *The Shop of Love.*
Otherwise, the eyes, mouth, and breasts are better indications.
If the breasts are round, she may be foolish; if the eyes are green, she may
  be Jewish;
If the mouth is full, she may be pettish. But everything she is will be for you.

The wrong woman can be identified by the following characteristics:
She eats at least twice as much as you do; her shoes or clothing are
  unbuttoned or untied; she dislikes cold water;
Her face is the shape of a donkey's; she fears evening
For evening draws one closer to bed. She contradicts herself
And is stubborn about each thing she said. She is perpetually unhappy
And would hate you bitterly for changing her condition. Immediately
  leave her! This person is not for you!

Two signs of love-worthiness in a woman are climbing to the roof
Without fear and with a smile on her face; turning around to look at you
  after she turns away from you.

Use of the car is now located in *The Shop of Love.*

When you know the relationship is not right, think of it all again.
Try again the next day. If you still think the same thing, end it.

The kiss of death is currently prohibited by law. Look for it in later
  editions.

To maintain good looks under exhausting conditions, think about an
  eskimo
Riding a white horse through a valley filled with falling other eskimos

So that he always has to be attentive, so that no eskimo falls on his head.
This will give you an alert look, which is half of beauty.

One thing to think about in bed is the full extent of this poem.
Another is the city of Rome. Another is the Byzantine stained-glass
    window showing Jesus as a human wine-press.
Do not think of cancellation of air trips, botched tennis racquets, or
    slightly torn postage stamps.
Think of the seasons. Think of evening. Think of the stone duck
Carved by the cement company in Beirut, to advertise
Their product. Think of October. Do not think of sleep.

To win the love of a girl half your age, add your age and hers together
And divide by two; act as if you were the age represented by that number
And as if she were too; the same with girls one fourth or one fifth your
    age.
This is called "Age Averaging," and will work in all those cases
In which age difference is a problem. Often it is not.

Love between living beings was unknown in Ming China. All passion was
    centered on material things.
This accounts for the vases. In Ancient Greece there was no time for love.
    In Somaliland only little children love each other.

Spinoza's remark was "Love is the idea of happiness attached to an
    external cause."

Friends' sweethearts should be put off until the next day.

To make love while asleep, try reading this book. It has been known to
    cause Somnamoria.

The Book of Records says the record number of times a man made love in
    a twenty-four-hour period was 576 times.
The record number of times a woman made love was 972 times.
The man died, and the woman went to sleep and could not be awakened
    for two years.
She later became the director of a large publishing house and then later in
    life became a nun.

The most persons anyone ever made love to in rapid succession (without a
   pause of any kind) was seventy-one.

Dreams about love should be acted on as quickly as possible
So as to be able to fully enjoy their atmosphere. If you dream about a
   woman, phone her at once and tell her what you have dreamed.

Zombie-itis is love of the living dead. It is comparatively rare.
If a woman likes it, you can probably find other things she likes that you
   will like even more.

Ten things an older man must never say to a younger woman:
1) I'm dying! 2) I can't hear what you're saying! 3) How many fingers are
   you holding up?
4) Listen to my heart. 5) Take my pulse. 6) What's your name?
7) Is it cold in here? 8) Is it hot in here? 9) Are you in here?
10) What wings are those beating at the window?
Not that a man should stress his youth in a dishonest way
But that he should not unduly emphasize his age.

The inability to love is almost incurable. A long sea voyage
Is recommended, in the company of an irresistible woman.

To turn a woman into a duck, etc., hypnotize her and dress her in
   costume.
To make love standing in water, see "Elephant Congress" in the *Kama
   Sutra* (chap. iv).
During a shortage of women, visit numerous places; give public lectures;
   carry this volume.

Lost love is cured only by new love, which it usually makes impossible.
Finding a girl who resembles the lost girl may offer temporary relief.

One test for love is whether at the beginning you are or are not able to
   think about anything else.

To locate unknown-about love for you in a woman in a crowd,
Look intently at everyone you find attractive, then fall to the ground.
She will probably come up to you and show her concern.

Railway Express will not handle human letters, but Bud's Bus and Truck Service will.

Sleepiness may be explained by drugs; pink cheeks, by the allergy that caused you to take them.

Love being part of a Great Plan is an attractive idea
But has never been validated to anyone's complete satisfaction.

Throwing your girl in the ocean makes her feel sexy when she gets out. Genius is not a disadvantage.

Hats should never be worn when making love. All women are not the same woman
Though they sometimes seem so. The aviary is best used on summer nights. There is no
Substitute for or parallel to love, which gives to the body
What religion gives to the soul, and philosophy to the brain,
Then shares it among them all. It is a serious matter. Without it, we seem only half alive.

May good fortune go with you, then, dear reader, and with the women you love.

# THE BURNING MYSTERY
# OF ANNA IN 1951

# Our Hearts

All hearts should beat when Cho Fu's orchestra plays "Love"
And then all feet should start to move in the dance.
The dancing should be very quick and all step lightly.
Everyone should be moving around, all hearts beating—
Tip tap tip tap. The heart is actually beating all the time
And with almost the same intensity. The difference is not in our hearing
Which is also almost always the same. The difference must be really
Then in our consciousness, which they say is variegated.
Black-and-white shoes, red dress, an eye of flame,
A teeth of pearl, a hose of true, a life of seethings. Would
You like to dance? The excitement, it is there all the time.
Is human genius there all the time? With the analogy of dreams,
Which supposedly we have every night, one is tempted
To say, The seething is always there, and with it the possibility for
    great art.

The government is there all the time, or actually the people
Struggle first so the government will be there then so it will not
Be overpowering. When does the art come, and the seething,
And when is the best point for justice, in all these I would like to be living.
The houses come and then the industry and then the people
And the government must control the industry. No smoke in the houses.
And there are people who study this all the time,
Economists, government people, they sit down and walk about
And study these things. And some otherwise indistinguishable boys
And girls become scientists, and complicate these things,
Make them better and worse, and some pale insecure others
Come along and do poems and paintings, and all die
And new ones are born, and there gets to be history and culture
And civilization and the death of civilization and the life of it and in it.

## 3

We, who are born in it, walk around in it, and look at these things
And think of these things. Some things are first and some are second.
No one has yet completely figured out our brain
But some are trying. One of the first things is we try to be "all right,"
To do well and to succeed. Whether this is in all human brains
(We think not) or only in our civilization's, we don't know
For sure, or much care, but we act by it anyway, just as we act
By the morality we happen to be born with (i.e., not eating our
     grandparents
As Herodotus said the Egyptians thought it proper to do).
And in the dim, dazzling adolescent ballrooms we start on our way.
Later, much later perhaps, we try to figure it out—
Or sometimes just start working mechanically on one aspect.
Finding ourselves "in love," we may attach supreme value to that
Or to some crazy religion, finding ourselves in a church at sunset.

## 4

What do you think it is really all explainable by, this
Mystery that has been built up by a natural process
And how much of it do we need? The foot of everyone is advancing
And the knees of everyone should be flexing, legs dancing
And lips moving gaily up over the teeth
For the speaking, and hands driven into the pockets, eyes shining, stub-
bed toes forgotten as we walk down the somewhere else saying God
     Damn
It's good to see you. But what shall we do? The greatest plan
Is participate, aid, and understand. Every dog should be at the foot
Of every man. What evidence this past give us! Examples
With which we impregnate today. But the shirt should fit
Over the chest, the light silk panties over the rear.
The sky is shining. The sun is a basket of wash
Let down for our skin, and germs are all around us like cash.

## 5

In nature is no explanation. In city is no
Explanation. In language is no
Explanation. Explanation is a dog, is a languishing lad
Lanky with lurid binoculars, dilapidated-looking. I am
Sitting and you are standing. We have a knowledge of good and bad.
I am exploding with doubts and with talent. I look everywhere.
I'm always glad when I find something simple.
Breathing is simple, walking is simple, and dancing, sometimes, moving
    one's feet.
A simple way to say that things are simple
Is immensely enjoyable but it is not explanation.
The people should be rushing along. There is in that way no problem
Except there is this problem How to participate aid and understand
Simultaneously. It seems there is too much. Participating in the wall
You forget to understand the tax reform. And aid no one.

## 6

So what is the ecstasy we are allowed to have in this one life
As everybody says that we are getting on with living here?
Should you devote your life to reform? or to understanding your life?
Are different kinds of people born, some for aiding,
Some for participating in, some for understanding life?
Which one are you and how do you know? You are crazy
And don't know it, one person says, and another says, You are asleep.
To myself I seem sane and awake, and I go on.
Maybe a fundamental-type solution, "loss in nature," "mystical religion"
Or "sexual explosiveness" is what we need. But dear civilization—
Who would like to give up theater for climbing up a tree? No one wants
    you to.
Remember where this meditation began (with Cho Fu's orchestra).
It is the problem of living and not being the first one
And yet wanting to do as much as that first one, and, because there is all
    that train behind one, more.

## 7

The people look at all the people they are walking around
One being peaceful or horrid or lonely or bored
Or pleasant and contented the right kind
Of civilization could be good for all these people
And certainly food would be good for the hungry people
And limitations must be placed on the greedy people
And guns must be taken away from the aggressive people
And medicine must be given to the ailing people
And so on and each individual one of the people
Who dreams every night (it is supposed) may be supposed
To have the seething and the golden curiosity. How to organize the thing
So that each of these people
Is happy with it, happy with him, with her, and me
And we also are, and it, and all, with them? That would be the day—
How can it be with everyone feeling he is the main one and the germs
   there every day?

Different civilizations simultaneously existing,
Indian in the throes of one, samurai in the waning of another,
Heck-saying businessman in mine, and little civilizations suggesting
   something
Like farmyard civilization, fishingman and net and boat civilization,
And then back to your own and to my own, all the
Efficiency the good will the weakness and the snobbery
The uncertainty the recovery the rather long life the bursts
Of helpless enthusiasm the sweet reformers in the streets
Today as I just looked out the window and here come the riot police
And the sitting inside and not knowing if I should be outside, in the midst
   of this.
The orchestra plays and everyone is growing up and being
One of who are a various number of beings
Simultaneously dreaming of existing
As the civilizations say they are when we speak.

To be a back, which doesn't break, and to hate what is mysterious
That doesn't need to be, grant me O Athena
Of the roses and the gamma globulin—however, prayer
Is nothing I can ever be serious about (I think).
The answer is elusive and the work about it goes on
A long time and so we want our lives to go on
Among other things in hope to find an answer. Though we know
That the answer of eighty will not be the answer of eighteen.
En route we give titles to things, we further
Complicate our own situation and that of other persons
And we get wiser, sometimes, and kinder, and probably less exciting
(Certainly so), and grow out of our illusions (sometimes) and so
Can look around and say, Oh! So! but usually without the time
Or power to change anything (sometimes—maybe a fraction—if so, it's
      amazing!) then off we go.

# The Simplicity of the Unknown Past

Out the window, the cow out the window
The steel frame out the window, the rusted candlestand;
Out the window the horse, the handle-less pan,
Real things. Inside the window my heart
That only beats for you—a verse of Verlaine.
Inside the window of my heart is a style
And a showplace of onion-like construction.
Inside the window is a picture of a cat
And outside the window is the cat indeed
Jumping up now to the top of the
Roof of the garage; its paws help take it there.
Inside this window is a range
Of things which outside the window are like stars
Arranged but huge in fashion.
Outside the window is a car, is the rusted wheel of a bicycle.
Inside it are words and paints; outside, smooth hair
Of a rabbit, just barely seen. Inside the glass
Of this window is a notebook, with little marks,
They are words. Outside this window is a wall
With little parts—they are stones. Inside this window
Is the start, and outside is the beginning. A heart
Beats. The cat leaps. The room is light, the sun is almost blinding.
Inside this body is a woman, inside whom is a star
Of some kind or other, which is like a uterus; and
Outside the window a farm machine starts.

# Fate

In a room on West Tenth Street in June
Of nineteen fifty-one, Frank O'Hara and I
And Larry Rivers (I actually do not remember
If Larry was there, but he would be there
Later, some winter night, on the stairway
Sitting waiting, "a demented telephone"
As Frank said in an article about him but then
On the stairs unhappy in a youthful manner, much
Happened later), Frank, John Ashbery,
Jane Freilicher and I, and I
Had just come back from Europe for the first time.
I had a bottle of Irish whiskey I had
Bought in Shannon, where the plane stopped
And we drank it and I told
My friends about Europe, they'd never
Been there, how much I'd loved it, I
Was so happy to be there with them, and my
Europe, too, which I had, Greece, Italy, France,
Scandinavia, and England—imagine
Having all that the first time. The walls
Were white in that little apartment, so tiny
The rooms are so small but we all fitted into one
And talked, Frank so sure of his
Talent but didn't say it that way, I
Didn't know it till after he was
Dead just how sure he had been, and John
Unhappy and brilliant and silly and of them all my
First friend, we had met at Harvard they
Tended except Frank to pooh-pooh
What I said about Europe and even
Frank was more interested but ever polite
When sober I couldn't tell it but
Barely tended they tended to be much more
Interested in gossip such as
Who had been sleeping with whom and what
Was selling and going on whereat I
Was a little hurt but used to it my
Expectations from my friendships were
Absurd but that way I got so

Much out of them in fact it wasn't
Causal but the two ways at once I was
Never so happy with anyone
As I was with those friends
At that particular time on that day with
That bottle of Irish whiskey the time
Four in the afternoon or
Three in the afternoon or two or five
I don't know what and why do I think
That my being so happy is so urgent
And important? it seems some kind
Of evidence of the truth as if
I could go back and take it? or do
I just want to hold what
There is of it now? thinking says hold
Something now which is why
Despite me and liking me that
Afternoon who was sleeping with
Whom was best and
My happiness picking up
A glass Frank What was it like Kenny
Ah from my being vulnerable
Only sometimes I can see the vulnerable-
Ness in others I have ever known
Faults with them or on the telephone
The sexual adventures were different
Each person at work autobiography all
The time plowing forward if
There's no question of movement as there
Isn't no doubt of it may I not
I may find this moment minute
Extraordinary? I can do nothing
With it but write about it two
Hundred forty West
Tenth Street, Jane's apartment,
Nineteen fifty-one or fifty-two I
Can never remember yes it was
Later or much earlier
That Larry sat on the stairs
And John said Um hum and hum and hum I
Don't remember the words Frank said Un hun
Jane said An han and Larry if he

Was there said Boobledyboop so always
Said Larry or almost and I said
Aix-en-Provence me new sense of
These that London Firenze Florence
Now Greece and un hun um hum an
Han boop Soon I was at Larry's
And he's proposing we take a
House in Eastham—what? for the
Summer where is that and
Already that afternoon was dissipated
Another begun many more of
Them but that was one
I remember I was in
A special position as if it
Were my birthday but
They were in fact as if my
Birthday or that is to say Who
Cares if he grows older if
He has friends like
These I mean who does not
Care? the celebration is the cause
Of the sorrow and not
The other way around. I also went
To Venice and to Vienna there were
Some people I drove there
With new sunshine Frank says
Let's go out Jane John Frank
And I (Larry was not there, I now
Remember) then mysteriously
Left

# The Burning Mystery of Anna in 1951

### *1. The Burning Mystery of Anna*

"I don't know how to kiss."
Won't you come in?

To have bent her back half across the bed.
To be so bending her.

Not yet having said Won't you come in.
Never yet having said it.

Planning to say, Can we
Would you like to come up to my room?

The bedroom stairway
And then thought about it.

My name is you.
I am not interested him the first place.

I come from Corsica.
The scene is very confusing.

She is dancing and I
Think she is pretty. That's one part of it.


### *2. Why Not?*

It is satisfying to have a nose
Right in the middle of my face.

You asked me the question and I replied
With as much imagination as I could.

Then one foggy morning we met.
We sat in a cold café and compared viruses

Oh, sure, I'd heard of you a thousand times
From E and L and X and A and Y.

What was I trying to hide? Something monstrous?
Is there really anything to hide?

I hate all these guiltmongers. God damn it,
I said to myself one day. I'll let fly!

The story of my existence as I reconstruct it
Now is about one sixth part reconstruction.

Suggested to me by plastic instead of cork
In the bottleneck I said, Well listen, now, well, well, to hell with it! Why
    not?


3. *With Dad*

The fly I cast was red.
Dad said Push it!

We went out in the boat.
Marble-like was the sea.

Down to the sand we went
And to the dock next.

Let's go fishing said Dad.
I pulled on red sweater.

I was sitting on the porch
Peacefully when Dad marched out.

This is one of my experiences
Which I think is fairly typical.

You've asked me to tell you
A little bit about my life.

Hello. How are you? I'm fine,

Thanks. Today there is something new.

### 4. Starting

The oranges subdued the attack
Or rather we endured it.

I am tired of being attacked, she said.
Then the rain fell.

It was a sunny morning.
Sunny sunny sunny sunny sunny.

The night was dark. The dogs
Howled till it got sunny.

The young man is living with the French
Family near the entrance to the trough.

Actual cash value nineteen dollars.
He puts it on but then she takes it off.

What was it I remembered of L. at school?
A keen bursitis lit the window.

Simple simple simple, simply to start,
To be so easy when one is at the start.

### 5. A Critical Point

She: Weren't you curious about our conversation?
I said: I have been watching you all from here.

Then I went up to her and started to speak.
I felt shy but I had to confront the beautiful.

Talking to another stranger, I think a guy
In the distance I saw her, the checked-print-dressed girl I had seen.

Wandering along through the twisting streets of the city
One day as I was, as is my habit.

Perfectly true, but on this day it was different.
You always do the same things every day.

Get up, brush your teeth, eat breakfast, then wander.
I really don't see how you can stand the boredom.

I hope you don't mind if I'm a little critical
I'm afraid that you won't like what I'm going to say.

I had something to say she had never heard.
A bird woke me this morning with the usual.


*6. Two Bicycle Riders*

It is the summer of genius! And also of genes!
You replied, as I gulped over the hill-Alps.

What is the nature of things, I replied,
As we tortured the hill-Alps.

This answers all questions, you described,
As we biked over the hill-Alps.

Then tell me more, I think I squeaked,
As we broke the chains of the hill-Alps.

And so that's the truth, you indicted,
As we tore down the mounts of the hill-Alps.

The mention is cotton to the street
Which in turn encapsules drifted attention.

Finally, with courage mounting, I asked you,
What are we doing on these hill-Alps?

O beautiful person silent and serene
Invited by me to pedal on these mountains.

## 7. *Abstract*

Unavoidable and inescapable.
What is your nature? I said.

Quiet, but how to make them,
Also, grabbing of the spirit?

Admirable, I said.
They presented a problem.

When I first saw them
They felt complete.

Come, said my mind,
I will show them to you.

Where are these new
Unities? I said.

Then something rainbowed
And a new thing promised.

I was living. I said,
I can do all that I wish.


## 8. *What I Was Thinking Of*

The reeds were very sunny. "Yes, he
Lived here—Cézanne," you said.

Retiring from the bicycles and remarking
How painful it was to bike, pleasanter to walk.

Was it the day a man with a moustache, a girl
Anne, three law students and I went?

Come on, let's go for a walk!
Bring not the bicycle.

Je crois qu'il éxagère, says Marguerite.
Then, twoo-twoo, outside hear a bell.

Up to lunch from the wall about which I wrote
The poem "Bricks."

Standing in the sunlight and thinking
Or doing something like that.

First getting up and down the hill
Walking, until I smelled the fields, on two legs.

# The Language of Shadows

Solitude, Presentation, Solitude,
Revery, Perfect Accord, Confidences,
Language of shadows, this is the language we learned
By looking in windows, at backboards and times of day.
The lion weeps in his den for a lady lion,
A lioness, whom, once there, he will rip up in play
And she will give lion cubs to him. Then he, language of jungle,
Will roar. But the language of miracles in store
For the wooden boat smashed just against the harbor's
Pier, where the small mole rushes to his instructress
The mud. Listen! The snail is weeping in another wind.
Far off, an apartment in Athens, a ruins instructor
Is daily with solitude. New nuts are being cracked by the Propylaea
And I can't help remembering our past. Aqua-
Lungs cases drenched in cinnamon, an adagio of feet. Watch
The burros which walk to the beach. It is nothing
In the brightest of noonshine but shadows, a
Language of them. First, he deeply contemplative, waits
She, also, her hand on her face. Then, September,
He kisses her hand. Revery, dreaming of that which may be—
Language, dreaming of how to say it. And
Perfect accord—the feet of old Athenians on this hill
Left footprints but now we can't see them—in perfect accord.

I dreamed about you last night. And I
Dreamed of you. How did you
Know it was I? The story's end, itself
Divided into six partitions, the shadows increase
As the angle of light takes some of its intensity away. The
Painter paints, oh purple is
A shadow to him. Warm day. Sun strikes little building
And a shadow emerges. The dog runs out today
And has a shadow. These shadows don't have shadows. Is it
Polite of me to tell you about the dress?
I love the dress. And you whom I have known there whose names
Were your shadows—as, imprinted on gravestones, they are—
The painter's paintings, the poet's poems (but are these shadows?)—
Solitude, Presentation, Solitude, and roses are,
No doubt of it, opening wide in the two lower corners

Near a diamond in which the initials are "P.F."
And friendship used to be so easy. Two separate pairs of hearts
Both pink, light pink, and below them a crescent moon.
Solitude, Coal Smoke, and Solitude, West, Presentation—
As you walk along your head casts its shadow on your book
And the text, which is something hard, becomes slightly clear.

Light as a means of discovery and not as a theme.
The dog's shadow just escapes the light, and the horse's
Shadow too. It is autobiography, and nothing new—
Everything that's so far happened, caught in a present
Light: Solitude, Presentation, Solitude, Confidences,
Revery, and Perfect Accord. A long time in my life
Passes in a second, a short one spreads out like a ford
Of a river, men and horses crossing it. Everything's extinguished in desire
In fact and action. Solitude is only a word
About which you are nervous. The boat leaves the dock. And
Without discourse. Revery is mine. It is not a race horse. The cake. The
    song.
Teachers start to meddle with the desks. Kites. Nits.
And it feels like the language of light. For after one has been
A baby (Solitude, Window One) and childhood (Presentation,
Window Two), then, with adolescence, Confidences, Revery—and later,
    perhaps, Perfect Accord.

The smell of horse manure is running
Through the field. The grass is helping. The sky is secured
By a shadow's tape, which is a knowledge of the language of feet—
Right, Left, then uphill walking—
You feel amazed to be moving, at each second, in perfect accord.

Weeping, Condolences, and Weeping—
Hesitation, Battle, and Hesitation;
Perfecting the Work, Decision, Formation of Ideas;
Liking, Loving Enormously, and Liking—
Or Solitude, Love Life, and National Acclaim
(Some children are painting a chair)
Solitude, Presentation, Solitude; Insects, Amorousness, A Feud;
Dryness, Inspiration, and Dryness. When roof becomes a gold mine
She sees him, he sees her, they are of one mind, heart, and
Obligation to life. She opens her pocketbook. He relates:

"How much I've wanted to see you when I did."
"How late," she perpetuates, "the happening this arrivals."
And both quite pant. Presentation? And Confidences. Also, Dreams.


Decrepitude, Somnolence, Decay; Ashes, Hip, Ashes.
We should make contact of some kind immediately.
Solitude, Presentation, Kisses, Tears, Laughter, and Fear. She says:
    Acrobatics, Sweetness, Intelligence
And he, Noticing the Lamp Cord, Arranging to Purchase a Fixture, the
    Departure for the Store.
Writing the Letter Arranging to Meet, the Accident,
The Universe of the Vehicle, the Driver, the Burial Mound, What Has
    Been Accomplished—
The sense of a sequence of things is a sense of what wasn't
There at any particular time—the Mattress of the Typewriter,
The Roommate, the Presence in the Store. Or,
Acting in the Play, Knowing about the Auction, Acting in the Play;
Tenderness, Ape Head, Tenderness; Wanting to Go to the Ski Run, a
    Plough, Birdcalls.
In the midst of these actions and wishes, a city: Berlin, Moscow, Rennes.
Dog House, Inversion, Dog House. It is raining in sunlight—shadows:
    Orange, Yellow, Red. Diamond, Sheep, Diamonds.
The dog has a basket of talkative stars, a child is sleeping. There is a
    sequence
Of five arguments: He Will, You Won't, She Can, Who Can't, I Insist.
Rocking, Staying Upstairs All Night, Rocking. Then the darkness is gone.
Another day appears, dying without a doctor. Confidences, Aimlessness,
    Solitude. And the bite of the sheep.
When the light sleeps during the day, then I'm all right; I'm safe for
    another one.
Waiting for the Butterfly, Placing One's Head on a Stone, the Silence of a
    Great Committee.
We have come here to stand. They turned. Language of shadows.
Your vest is contradicted by the shadows of its buttons and its watch. You
    are an unboned man.
A cigarette for skeletons. Now, shadows inside your body are sounds
Like memories—tick tick, drip drop. When October shows its face, it is a
    compendium
Of shadows that seem related to all we are—unless anxiety's best bet is our
    surest nothing.
Solitude, Discovering America, Solitude.

Boiling, Asleep, Boiling. A Baby, Two Successful Men, A Baby.
Confidences, Revery, Dialing a Number, Chrysanthemums, Wildcats,
　　Telephone,
Snow, Perfect Accord, Hello Hello, Solitude, Going to Sleep.
These armatures never end, for after all one needs
Slipping, with no other clothes on, into the Overcoat,
Sleeping with You, Bumping into You on the Beach; and National
　　Acclaim,
Fireworks, Waking up in the Frog's House (the swamp). Swimming,
　　Crying, Swimming.
The horse has a dotlike shadow at his foot when it's noon.


And the rain decks were covered with peapods and
Hogs' backs wore pepsin that light afternoon. It was
The language of the gallows of the leaves, like a wall made of small
White bricks, with an entrance beneath them in
Which walked a mole, with courage of apples, with shadows for seeds.
On the Wall, On the Deck, On the Wall.
Solitude, Excavation, Commandos—things
Happening which only an object could have foreseen.
Typing, Numb Feelings, Typing. No accidents. The Railway Car,
Sophocles, Tingling. Which asylum is raffling off your life?
What hen trades a dock for your ocean? Enamel Slides, Sheaves, Rest.
I could have made love to you. And I with you, too.
Sometimes it works. Solitude, Ecstatic Interlude, Solitude.
A Man, a Baby, a Woman; a Head, a Heart, a Head.
Everything Outside the Window, the Hot Emotions Inside, the Meaning
　　of the Wall.
Comicbook, Dock, Dog. The language of shadows.
Alive, Not Yet Alive, Dead, Possibly Existent but not Known, What
　　Cannot Exist.


If only I could bring this hallway to you directly,
Life mine, without all this static of shadows!
But the lampshade was already on him and was diffusing his light.
His social milieu was a concatenation of shadows. His Mercury and his
　　Mercutio were a dog bite. His
Limps became a lane. These shadows are generous, like wheelbarrows,
They are willing to give us their time, in an all-sun climate.
Everything he does. Everything she does. My heart is stamping in her
　　chest like a thousand butterflies,

Or is it in my own? Linkage of mattress! Choiring uniforms of the lungs
Forever banking on shadows, and no new news but a new re-pasting of
    the light
On pages. We stand up. And day stands up along with us. The lion cub
    roars
For the first time. She, language of mothers, bends down her chorus
Of teeth, they have very small shadows. Speech, Lives, Revery, Solitude,
    and Perfect Accord.

# The Problem of Anxiety

A serious impediment to all endeavors
Of the mind, body, and spirit is anxiety
Which Freud describes as a sort of fidgety return
To infantile helplessness. In those days
(Of infancy) when one could only wriggle,
One did (wriggle) and scream and froth and
Mother came. Now Mother cometh not, although one is
Menaced by terrible things, yet still
The body and mind behave as they did then. One
Becomes cold and hot, one shakes, one gasps and cries
And nerves are tightened all over the body at once.
Anxiety! How terrible you are! Worse even,
In ways, than what brings you on! As if pinned,
Helpless, you writhe there, Reader, and what
Will cure this awful state? Stay with me
And I will try to help you. Perhaps even reading about
Anxiety will make it easier to bear. What causes it.
In contradistinction to its psychogenesis (described
Above) are the following cases: one)
You have come to a point where you must choose
One thing or another, both deep-
Ly important to your life and to your well-
Being, and you have no way to judge—you cannot stand
Even the thought of losing either one. Is it
The presidency of a bank or the love of a girl? A chance
To study with Stravinsky, or an equal chance
To learn the language of the animals? The Maharooshi is in town
For two weeks only, the language of animals man,
And Stravinsky will take you then, too, and only then.
Result? Anxiety! You fall to the floor and shake,
You writhe, you scream, and you cry. The trouble is
That in this state you are likely to lose each
Of your alternatives, so you must work
To get out of it. What if the Trustees came
From the Bank and found you here? and what
If the girl saw how crazy you are? So you must try to choose
The better of the two alternatives. And what if the Maharooshi
Saw you as you are now? Would he think you one
Chosen to speak the language of the animals? And Stravinsky—

"How could this person stand the rigors
Of a week's intensive study with me? No! Cross him out!"
All may be well. If you are president of the bank you
Will have other loves, or at least will have the memory
Of sorrowfully sacrificed love, which can, sometimes,
Seem the best experience in life, even
Though lost, its memory can make you happy. If
On the other hand you give up the presidency
Of the bank and take the girl, how strong you will feel
Having done that for love! There is the chance, of course,
You will feel horrible in either case: with
The girl, that you have given up your chance
For a larger life, with money, with power, and settled for
Something petty, you may even come to hate her some
Day, your darling Sally, the
Worst thing that can occur. And if you opt for the bank
And she goes off with someone else, or dies, or refuses to wait,
How terrible! You may feel such desolation! And
A shot rings out. He is gone! But one
Person still loved him. He didn't know. On
The other hand, the bank may merely be testing you, to
Find out your devotion to human feelings, the
Kind of man they want for their affairs. Or it may be that Sally
Will admire you for what you've done. Maharooshi, or Stravinsky, may be
    impressed
By the moral stamina you have shown, and the psychic, and each
May take you, in spite of his schedule. So
Arise, even if, to do so, you must hold on to a
Chair. You may, once you have decided on one thing
Immediately become aware that this decision is not
A decision that you can stand, so you can change your
Mind, and this time be definitive, having now
Suffered through the reality of it, although
You should be careful that this does not keep
Happening with great rapidity or you will be
Right back where you began. Another cause of
Anxiety is, two) you have a conflict of interest
Between self-advancement and what is according to you
The ethically right thing to do. This may be a
Form of (one) (above), but it is a rather special one
And has caused a great deal of anxiety so I
Will treat it as a separate cause: a vast

Shipment of soap is coming in, and you can make a profit
By not revealing this fact to the stockholders.
They are still bathing with little slivers
Of soap because they think there's a shortage
And the price of the stock goes down and down. Now
You can buy a million shares for fifteen dollars
And, with the shipment in, it goes up, but
You are filled with anxiety! Why shouldn't the
Stockholders know the soap ships are rolling in
To the lathery harbors of this dream
Which is ordinary reality? You cannot give up
The soap money it would make you and cannot
Do a dishonest deed. So you writhe on the floor. Get
Up! At least if you tell them all that the
Soap is coming in, you all can share the money!
If you lie on the floor two days there will be
No money left! The boats will come into the docks
And depart with the Ivory still on them, the
Palmolive, the Camay. And a fortune will be lost.
How pleasant to be down at the harbor, fresh and
Uninvolved with life, not tormented by guilt
And oncoming anxiety over money-making thoughts! To breathe the air
And to see the whitecaps, merely to think of the
Sides of the ships! and to see the blue captain,
To glory in the smokestacks with yellow and red rings!
Is one ever really in such a situation? And
If so, how? and when? Isn't even a small boy plagued by feelings
He cannot deal with? "Do I love her enough? He
Seems quiet. He is getting rather old. As I
Grow stronger. What can I ever do to get rid of such
Terrible feelings?" So, although the fresh air at the docks might
Chase away these feelings for a while, they may come back.
And if urged by your mother, say, to steal your father's
Shaving soap and sell it to the neighbors, they are likely to come back,
Now when you're grown, when this shipment comes in, posing its
     problems,
And at this point or another, anxiety strikes. Have you ever noticed
How involved people are with their parents all
Their lives? It is lucky to have "good parents," who
Don't torment you, divide you, and crush
You into anxiety-form for life! But can any avoid it?
I wonder if any can completely. But completeness

Is not all, or even the main concern we have here.
For life is "relative," just as relatives
Are only a part of life. The Egyptians must have known it
When they made their gods out of cats and horses and
Dogs, that a human being was imperfect. An
Animal, of course, is ridiculously inferior to
Humans, but it can be simplified and fantasized
About, as a human cannot, in the same way. And then animals
Rarely have anxiety attacks. How can
You have a god who has anxiety? Think of Jehovah
In a state of anxiety. "What should I do?" And
Think of Jesus in a similar and think of the Holy Ghost.
Nor is there a record of anxiety attacking the heaven
Of the Ancient Greeks. Apollo did not lie helpless-
Ly suffering while the arrows spat out from the sun
Of their own accord, killing thousands. Nor did
Mediterranean Jupiter rush toward Scamander helplessly
With ragged toga, one clutching hand in his hair.
Zoroaster was never known to stammer, and in fact gods
May be, quite simply, what we humans have imagined
As anxiety-free Beings, those only fit to rule us.
The contrast of their happiness with our (relative)
Lack of it, if we believe in them, need not bother us
Too much since we can resolve these feelings by prayer, by which some
  claim
To have cured their anxiety. Or perhaps it is the answer to prayer—
Which probably comes from the person—like
The answer of this poem, which is "Up!" I would say, "and tell the
Others about the soap. It will be good for your heart."
Three) a cause of anxiety different from these
Two more than these two are from each other is
The general sense of mortality and of impending doom.
The wonder, it seems sometimes, is that anyone at all
Is able to do anything at all, once he knows he
Will die. But the world does seem to go on,
And maybe it is going on mainly because of people with faith
In God and in immortality, for there
Still are some, and when these people are gone
The world will collapse, or it may be because of ignorance,
That "no young man believes he will ever die,"
Or maybe because of a mysterious hang-over from the past
When everyone did believe in some purpose in life

And in continuity, or maybe it is possible to live one's life,
And this is what I think is true, WITH this terrible
Knowledge. But it is there, always, and can cut
Like a knife, one can fall to the floor
With this anxiety, and What for it is cure? For
We will die, there is no doubt about it. We shake
And think What is the point of it after all? But
"Point" does not require "Permanence." There
Is a point in opening the window: to let
In some air; and a point in painting a sign:
So people will know where something is. But what
Is the point of these individual actions if
There is no major point of all? This
I cannot answer, but surely life is better off the floor.
To take a walk with you, how good it is! and
To talk about recoveries from anxieties! to pick
This blossom, it's a purple one, I shall name it
*L'Innocence retrouvée* what does that mean? It's
French. And in these summer days to go with you
To Lo Fung's Restaurant, and to eat the rice! To be
Asleep with you, wake up with you, and strong-
Ly dislike the idea of dying, well that's life! but
At any moment the anxiety over death can strike one. Then
All is despair. Letting responsibilities pile up is another cause of anxiety
And may be dealt with by getting the things done. If
Your arm feels paralyzed, persist. You
Will soon be able to perform the tasks you have
To do, to be free of anxiety, though it may strike again
For a different reason. Five) a cause of
Anxiety is a feeling that one is no good,
And the source of this may be that one is not
In fact good, i.e., you've been doing things you
Don't approve of, or it may come from
Mysterious sources of guilt in early life. Often
It comes from both, this feeling one is no good
And it is hard to deal with, but medical science has many
Successes in curing it, so after you have tried
To act better yourself, I would recommend going
To a doctor and lying down there instead of on your
Floor, which by now must be getting pretty messy
So let us clean it up. Cleaning things up is
Often a good cure for minor anxiety, as is

Straightening things, arranging things, adding things
Up and putting them down, picking them up
And carrying them someplace, doing some laundry,
Cooking a dinner, changing the electric lights, seeding
A garden, and caring for it, looking at the bulbs
Until twilight, then hurriedly calling
Up some friends. The beginning of evening,
The end of the daylight is difficult moment for
Many people, the great and the un-great
Feel anxiety then. Pulling the shades and
Turning the lights on and being ab-
Sorbed in something is a good idea. These
Are minor causes of anxiety, such as the fear
Of no hotel, when one is traveling or,
When one is eating, of certainly becoming sick
Because of something one eats. There is (six)
The fear of failing at something; which can
Cause anxiety of a dangerous kind. It may
Be this is the fear of succeeding, as well. These
Two are not easy to tell apart. In any case
The anxiety is bad because it causes one
To fail, whether one wishes to or not. Some
*Symptoms* of anxiety which I have not
Mentioned yet are stomach-ache, from moderate to
Severe; sometimes attended by diarrhea, sometimes
Not; headache, moderate to severe; rashes on the fingers
And palms of the hand; teeth chattering; stammering;
Temporary blindness; enuresis; vomiting; uncontrolled
Movement of the feet and of the hands; protracted
Head-shakings; neck paralysis; torso paralysis;
Permanent or semi-permanent sexual desire; retching;
Loss of interest in things; loss of appetite; loss
Of desire. It is obvious, no, that it is superior
Not to have these symptoms, yet
Sometimes they may help one, especially
In cases when they seem to be needed to tell one that one
Is not doing things just as one should do, and
Nothing else carries the message. For we can go on
For a long time in the dark. And anxiety means DANGER!
Sometimes it can help us, sometimes not. Of
Course it would be better if we did not let it
Get so far, and if we led better-organized lives

And had had better childhoods and could afford
Psychoanalytic treatment to deal with the
Worst phases of it, but it would be naïve on my part
To think that even all that would make it go away
Permanently, I think—though those things would
Certainly help. While I am writing this poem I am feeling
A tension in my neck and shoulders, a slight
Twinge in my heart and a slight compressed feeling above
My left eye, and that, all of that, I think, is anxiety,
Not taking its revenge because I'm writing
This, for it is always there, setting up its
Flagpoles, its tents, and its guitars. I think it is
Because I am worried about finishing this poem
Which I hoped would cure me of anxiety but does not seem
To be doing so completely, and because I am wondering
Of course if it is any good, and also I am thinking
Of all that I have to do before I pack my suitcase
And leave this room in which I am sitting, for another week
Of teaching, which I am not prepared for (as
Usual, though I've gotten better than I was) and for
Facing various people with whom I have
Uncertain relations, and for seeing my tax consultant
Because the government is auditing my 1972 returns,
And for walking in New York City, and for driving the car in
And parking it, and then going home, and trying to
Get to sleep, and before any of that, cleaning up this mess
Of papers, which are lying all around the studio,
Each pile of them makes me anxious, each is
Something that I should get together and do
Something with instead of writing this poem, but
Isn't this the best thing for me to do of all? Well, my
Headache is worse now and on both sides, still mild though, and I am not
   on the floor.

# In the Morning

In the morning the only thing moving was the garbage on the water.
In the afternoon the fellaheen stormed their tents.
We bought cold cream and lay in the sun.

The birches against the risotto are climbing the arches.
Ah, well, it's a young tree's privilege to climb.
These older torches are scaling the flagons of the night.

Going to parties often meant a welcome
To some new, dear, or old and trusted friend.
Often it meant the chance to make new friendships somewhat in transit.

He felt the new collars and the catalogues
Of old dresses. I'll take this one and this one, said he.
Meanwhile a dark red velvet was staring him in the face.

Baron Haussmann, Claude Debussy, and Sherwood Anderson . . .
Time to get up and go out and feel one's new collar
And the elevator's fresh young smell in the quiet building.

The rats fell, one by one, from the Pontiff's apartment.
It had no political significance. The building was being cleaned.
Music blared, and some of the faithful were touched on the shoulder
    by rats.

We move into the apartments of day. They fold and enwrap us.
The steam rises from their edges. Rat runs past.
Pink clouds of dust jump up. He feels the collar—it's a little cold.

There isn't anything there except what's real.
He walks out feeling his nape. This is sunny weather.
Suddenly the elevator rises to the floor above.

George Bernard Shaw, the Empress of Roumania, Immanuel Kant . . .
He pokes the trees. It's a pleasure to show you these ruins.
This invitation admits one. My son is sleeping.

He wanders in the sense of having only one place to go.
The elevator ambiance is waiting.
Orchids, Impressionism, ice machines, daggers, and bends.

Forms have an attraction to which we gradually yield.
Josephine Baker, Respighi, La Contessa di Alba.
He believed that the city was steel, but it was only the sun. I want to
  see you.

Come over for breakfast. A cow eats a grassblade. Containers.
Our babies will need plenty of milk. He says, I am leaving Paris.
Sohrab and Rustum, Childe Harold's Pilgrimage, the Dybbuk, Titian's
  Assumption.

A swirl of red robes at the throat. Goodbye . . . Are—? Speechless.
The asterisks dust on the paper. Will I see you again?
Boris Pasternak, Abraham Lincoln, Socrates, Orion . . .

I've wanted to ask you one question. She has a baby.
Room full of stars and iridium, eyelids which dazzle.
What can a life be without you? The words didn't say.

I don't want you to be so serious . . .
When he got back, she was already at the door.
Eleanora Duse, Emily Dickinson, Job, Karl Marx, Atalanta. . . .

# The Boiling Water

A serious moment for the water is when it boils
And though one usually regards it merely as a convenience
To have the boiling water available for bath or table
Occasionally there is someone around who understands
The importance of this moment for the water—maybe a saint,
Maybe a poet, maybe a crazy man, or just someone temporarily disturbed
With his mind "floating," in a sense, away from his deepest
Personal concerns to more "unreal" things. A lot of poetry
Can come from perceptions of this kind, as well as a lot of insane
    conversations.
Intense people can sometimes get stuck on topics like these
And keep you far into the night with them. Still, it is true
That the water has just started to boil. How important
For the water! And now I see that the tree is waving in the wind
(I assume it is the wind)—at least, its branches are. In order to see
Hidden meanings, one may have to ignore
The most exciting ones, those that are most directly appealing
And yet it is only these appealing ones that, often, one can trust
To make one's art solid and true, just as it is sexual attraction
One has to trust, often, in love. So the boiling water's seriousness
Is likely to go unobserved until the exact strange moment
(And what a temptation it is to end the poem here
With some secret thrust) when it involuntarily comes into the mind
And then one can write of it. A serious moment for this poem will be
    when it ends,
It will be like the water's boiling, that for which we've waited
Without trying to think of it too much, since "a watched pot never boils,"
And a poem with its ending figured out is difficult to write.

Once the water is boiling, the heater has a choice: to look at it
And let it boil and go on seeing what it does, or to take it off and use the
    water for tea,
Chocolate or coffee or beef consommé. You don't drink the product then
Until the water has ceased to boil, for otherwise
It would burn your tongue. Even hot water is dangerous and has a thorn
Like the rose, or a horn like the baby ram. Modest hot water, and the tree
Blowing in the wind. The connection here is how serious is it for the tree
To have its arms wave (its branches)? How did it ever get such flexibility
In the first place? and who put the boiling potentiality into water?

A tree will not boil, nor will the wind. Think of the dinners
We could have, and the lunches, and the dreams, if only they did.
But that is not to think of what things are really about. For the tree
I don't know how serious it is to be waving, though water's boiling
Is more dramatic, is more like a storm, high tide
And the ship goes down, but it comes back up as coffee, chocolate, or tea.

How many people I have drunk tea or coffee with
And thought about the boiling water hardly at all, just waiting for it to
    boil
So there could be coffee or chocolate or tea. And then what?
The body stimulated, the brain alarmed, grounds in the pot,
The tree, waving, out the window, perhaps with a little more élan
Because we saw it that way, because the water boiled, because we drank
    tea.

The water boils almost every time the same old way
And still it is serious, because it is boiling. That is what,
I think, one should see. From this may come compassion,
Compassion and a knowledge of nature, although most of the time
I know I am not going to think about it. It would be crazy
To give such things precedence over such affairs of one's life
As involve more fundamental satisfactions. But is going to the beach
More fundamental than seeing the water boil? Saving of money,
It's well known, can result from an aesthetic attitude, since a rock
Picked up in the street contains all the shape and hardness of the world.
One sidewalk leads everywhere. You don't have to be in Estapan.

A serious moment for the island is when its trees
Begin to give it shade, and another is when the ocean washes
Big heavy things against its side. One walks around and looks at the island
But not really at it, at what is on it, and one thinks,
It must be serious, even, to be this island, at all, here,
Since it is lying here exposed to the whole sea. All its
Moments might be serious. It is serious, in such windy weather, to be a
    sail
Or an open window, or a feather flying in the street.
Seriousness, how often I have thought of seriousness
And how little I have understood it, except this: serious is urgent
And it has to do with change. You say to the water,
It's not necessary to boil now, and you turn it off. It stops

Fidgeting. And starts to cool. You put your hand in it
And say, The water isn't serious any more. It has the potential,
However—that urgency to give off bubbles, to
Change itself to steam. And the wind,
When it becomes part of a hurricane, blowing up the beach
And the sand dunes can't keep it away.
Fainting is one sign of seriousness, crying is another.
Shuddering all over is another one.

A serious moment for the telephone is when it rings,
And a person answers, it is Angelica, or is it you
And finally, at last, who answer, my wing, my past, my
Angel, my flume, and my de-control, my orange and my good-bye kiss,
My extravagance, and my weight at fifteen years old
And at the height of my intelligence, oh Cordillera two
And sandals one, C'est toi à l'appareil? Is that you at
The telephone, and when it snows, a serious moment for the bus is when
    it snows
For then it has to slow down for sliding, and every moment is a trust.

A serious moment for the fly is when its wings
Are moving, and a serious moment for the duck
Is when it swims, when it first touches water, then spreads
Its smile upon the water, its feet begin to paddle, it is in
And above the water, pushing itself forward, a duck.
And a serious moment for the sky is when, completely blue,
It feels some clouds coming; another when it turns dark.
A serious moment for the match is when it bursts into flame
And is all alone, living, in that instant, that beautiful second for which it
    was made.
So much went into it! The men at the match factory, the mood of
The public, the sand covering the barn
So it was hard to find the phosphorus, and now this flame,
This pink white ecstatic light blue! For the telephone when it rings,
For the wind when it blows, and for the match when it bursts into flame.

Serious, all our life is serious, and we see around us
Seriousness for other things, that touches us and seems as if it might be
    giving clues.
The seriousness of the house when it is being built
And is almost completed, and then the moment when it is completed.

The seriousness of the bee when it stings. We say, He has taken his life,
Merely to sting. Why would he do that? And we feel
We aren't concentrated enough, not pure, not deep
As the buzzing bee. The bee flies into the house
And lights on a chair arm and sits there, waiting for something to be
Other than it is, so he can fly again. He is boiling, waiting. Soon he is
    forgotten
And everyone is speaking again.

Seriousness, everyone speaks of seriousness
Certain he knows or seeking to know what it is. A child is bitten by an
    animal
And that is serious. The doctor has a serious life. He is somewhat, in that,
    like the bee.
And water! water—how it is needed! and it is always going down
Seeking its own level, evaporating, boiling, now changing into ice
And snow, now making up our bodies. We drink the coffee
And somewhere in this moment is the chance
We will never see each other again. It is serious for the tree
To be moving, the flexibility of its moving
Being the sign of its continuing life. And now there are its blossoms
And the fact that it is blossoming again, it is filling up with
Pink and whitish blossoms, it is full of them, the wind blows, it is
Warm, though, so much is happening, it is spring, the people step out
And doors swing in, and billions of insects are born. You call me and tell
    me
You feel that your life is not worth living. I say I will come to see you. I
    put the key in
And the car begins to clatter, and now it starts.

Serious for me that I met you, and serious for you
That you met me, and that we do not know
If we will ever be close to anyone again. Serious the recognition of the
    probability
That we will, although time stretches terribly in between. It is serious not
    to know
And to know and to try to figure things out. One's legs
Cross, foot swings, and a cigarette is blooming, a gray bouquet, and
The water is boiling. Serious the birth (what a phenomenon!) of anything
    and
The movements of the trees, and for the lovers

Everything they do and see. Serious intermittently for consciousness
The sign that something may be happening, always, today,
That is enough. For the germ when it enters or leaves a body. For the fly
    when it lifts its little wings.

# Reflections on Morocco

*Essaouira*

The concept is a country without adequate means of locomotion other than the camels' backs. But camels are not the sole mode of transportation. The French have been here. Morocco, a land of *café ou thé* and a place of conflicting opposites, a sort of Chinatown of the hubristic impulse of the imagination of the contingent. This will not give one an idea. I will begin with Essaouira. How Essaouira became the main subject of this work which was to have been on education and society in the Red Land, i.e. Marrakesh or Morocco.

Essaouira the real name is Mogador thank you very much. No the real name is what the name is now. The astonishing thing about Essaouira: the medina constructed by a French architect captured by the Sultan of or numbered I forget which. The medina (arab city) is all straight lines. The girls' liberal faces there are shaped like valentines. Outside, some little fame related to soup.

Fish soup. The project of long days ahead writing *Essaouira*. Seeing countless movies (all bad) on Morocco to help inspire my Essaouira. Pretending that is a person I love Essaouira. Essaouira Essaouira it is you. Your name is like licorice. I appreciate Mogador too. I just prefer Essaouira. Perhaps because that is the name you have now. And I who have never (never) been thinking of writing a travel book before. How my persistent impulses become unraveled!

The clouds' door opens and Essaouira appears. As I remember it, as it is hearing me now. Then it vanishes and Essaouira appears, a second one, then it vanishes, then comes a third a fourth a third. Now it is going backwards. How I love you Essaouira! Don't completely go away.

I was so hoping but then disease be carried away. No sir they are all out. And how nice to see them, sea urchins, again. Writing, it may be, is what you are like, Essaouira, a delineation and scaramouche of powers. Clouds of thought and feeling, stretched out. And an arbitrary mode. And a sharp left will take you to the sea.

"Why would a nice young person like you ever come to Essaouira?" Have you heard, then, of the Hobos of Mogador? Of the Seven or is it Nine or Eleven Lost Women? I just wanted to stand here and blaze.

The long lines of sage brush and withered grass and tackless ornaments of the seemingly endless but unstructuring desert. The cow who did not have a face. The dawn of selflessness. All this I found on the way to you

Essaouira but in you I discovered La Mer, and La Mère. Both the Mother and the Sea. Historical, astonishing, and moving words.

I never will go with you to Essaouira. People and places. Some people seeming to "fit right in" with evening in Nome or bright afternoons on the Monday luck brokery exchange. But some not in Essaouira. Many not in Essaouira. Many to some might be better than each to be gathering around. A bold lackadaisical strip-mining effect clods hubristic Cataline mumps from low-strength strychnine-oriented buildings. The Frenchman didn't think of that. No Frenchman did! I did. An American did. Though owing something to Rimbaud.

Still I wonder why the French language which has given to English its flexibility in poetry or so it seems to me in and for the past hundred and a little more years why it in itself should be comparatively so limited and unable to spell out in words what it's overturned like a bubbling lexicon? There's no problem here in Essaouira that I can't solve, or at least fathom, but I know (or feel anyway) the French language would be stumping about, in the person of the poet. Ah the French poet. How unlike Essaouira you are. How unlike everything and everybody nothing and nobody is or are! That's one of the great truths from out of the Labyrinth. The Greeks said (of the Cretan buildings) "They just don't make any sense!" And so we have the legend of the Minotaur. What have you given us, Essaouira, of equal mythic humph stature?

And behold and behooey Essaouira answered from the vowel of the Earthatorium, "I have given you my rectangulated medina; in a way the opposite of the labyrinthine palace at Knossos. Reason without disorder. Or within disorder. So you make up the mythings." And so I said "All right" and am here beginning with mouths of praise.

Do you know how absolutely marvelous it is to take the English language into your mouth and turn it out of there like a twisting hurricane of irremediably believably and beautifully alarming words? Well I do and have for many years though sometimes this awareness leads one down into the worst spots of the medina of absolute fear and loneliness and worst of all despair at one's feeling so totally unable to do it. Oh! Muse, Angel of Desperateness, sustain me if I deal with this hard horrible subject for it really makes me feel as weak as an aphid who has just been hit by a glass of water. Her youthful uniform (breasts) betrayed no signs of despair, but next Monday in the arms of "Mogador"—Listen—the brave mocking bird is collapsing his cuckoosong past the musty tri-pad of Scotch inventiveness and I am here without anguish of Mogador in my head but with true perfect anguish as if you began by holding a dead strangled duck and then you became it. Fish soup! It would be nice to be returning to your believable *rivages!* The world moves, but the earth's stone remains unshaken.

A nine o'clock deadline to return to Marrakesh. So we must leave Mogador, uh, Essaouira. It is beginning to rain now but not in Essaouira.

The children are short and tall in Essaouira. Fish and many vegetables being sold from counter and stall. And the big market part where the sheep are. Some stunted fur. A dirty wool promise but we can get it clean later. There are some Arab songs. We live in terror but the surface we keep beautiful and clean, sometimes miraculously so, as here in the formerly called Mogador, a place you should visit during your life.


*Interview with Pierre Sadi-Rab—12/28/72*

PSR

What are your first impressions of Morocco?


K

I thought that would be a good question to ask you. One's "first impressions" being in fact lost amid a "desert of contexts," as John Ashbery once wrote. He said it about a poem, but a poem is in a sense a semi-concrete entanglement of first impressions—or nothing.


PSR

I am glad you have decided to interview me. I am inspired to say some wonderful things.


K

Well, that's the way it usually is when things work out well. The secret is in some kind of exchange and response. You've lived here all your life?


PSR

Yes, except for two student years in Paris.


K

How did you like Paris?


PSR

It was awful.


K

In what way?

**PSR**

Everything. The people, the food, the architecture, the way of life, the way people feel and think. I find the whole French culture appalling.

**K**

I've always liked France very much.

**PSR**

It is easier if one has not been oppressed by it.

**K**

I guess that's so. Didn't you ever get any pleasure from France at all?

**PSR**

My love life there was not bad, but I don't want to talk about that. I thought we were going to talk about education. You're a very odd sort of interviewer.

**K**

There are quite enough of the non-odd kind, I think. As for education, everything is quite obviously connected to it, don't you agree?

**PSR**

My love life in Paris seemed relatively unrelated to education as a matter of fact. Though I did "learn" a few things.

**K**

What?

**PSR**

I said, I believe, earlier, that I didn't want to talk about that.

**K**

An interview that is not completely free is a stunted sort of interview.

**PSR**

Call it whatever you like, I don't want to discuss my love life in Paris.

**K**

Do you feel those are things a man should not talk about with another man?

**P S R**

I certainly wouldn't talk about them with a woman.

**K**

Not under any circumstances?

**P S R**

None.

**K**

How do you feel your education has influenced you in this?

**P S R**

I don't see what my education has to do with it.

**K**

You were educated in a French school here in Morocco, were you not?

**P S R**

Yes. At the Lycée Muhamed Cinq.

**K**

Were your teachers French or Arab?

**P S R**

They were, without exception, except for the lone religious instructor, French.

**K**

Was all the instruction in French?

**P S R**

Yes, except in religion. Actually the religious instructor would tell us about other subjects too, and they were more fascinating to us when he did so, because they were being spoken of in our own, real language. Everything we learned in French seemed ephemeral, not really to touch us.

**K**

The girl, or girls, you loved in Paris, were they French or Arab girls?

**PSR**

I don't see what that has to do with education. I wish you'd in fact try to stick to the subject. I notice that I'm beginning to enjoy talking about it.

**K**

How can a man feel that his love life is unrelated to his education? If love represents and engages the highest feelings—

**PSR**

That may be more a Western idea than one of ours.

**K**

Maybe so. But your literature, both prose and poetry, is almost exclusively erotic in content. Surely that—

**PSR**

Neither love nor literature is anywhere near the top of our pantheon of values. Our highest, most real, and almost exclusive concern is Allah, our God. All other subjects and fields of concern are, compared to that, as dry leaves tumbling down the sides of a mountain.

**K**

And Allah is the mountain?

**PSR**

Yes.

**K**

How many different subjects did you study in each grade of school? I am talking now about school, say, when you were ten eleven twelve thirteen years old?

**PSR**

Every term we had seven subjects.

**K**

And of these religion was always one—but only one?

**PSR**

Yes.

K

Then your education must have seemed to you very wrong, unfair, disoriented, and askew. Since religion was the main topic—

PSR

You're absolutely right. My education seemed to me as poorly balanced, wrong-headed, and superficial as the entire culture of France.

K

Was poetry taught in your school?

PSR

We read poetry every year, either in one term or the other. Not for a whole term however. I would estimate we spent on poetry about one month a year.

K

Did you ever write poetry in school?

PSR

Never.

K

In America a good deal of that is done.

PSR

So I have heard. It is foolish.

K

Why do you say so?

PSR

Writing poetry has nothing to do with being in school. In school one should learn to master one's self and the world and to serve God.

K

Thank you very much.

K

In our last interview you said that writing poetry should not be done in school because the purpose of being in school was to learn to master one's self and the world and to serve God. Do you see no way in which writing poetry, or indeed creating art of any kind, may help one to do those things—to serve God, for example, by writing a great poem in His praise?

PSR

It seems unlikely a little school child would be able to do that.

K

Well, a child at least could make the beginnings of such an attempt. The child could awaken in him or herself feelings that he or she might otherwise not have had.

PSR

Ours is not exactly a religion of "discoveries about God and about our feelings about God" as your Western ones sometimes seem to be. We KNOW about God, know who and what He is, and we love Him. We worship Him, respect Him, and fear Him. I cannot imagine anything that I could "discover" about God. Indeed, perhaps, if I studied the ancient texts with the help of the sagest men of our world for many many years I might attain to some new detail of understanding, as a chemist might discover something new about the nature, say, of water. But, to continue with the analogy of water, it is its coolness, its wetness, and its cleansing properties that will be most important, no matter what else is discovered. And so with God's majesty, mercy, and might. It is hard, besides, to see how a school child, under the best of circumstances, could discover anything new about Him. And certainly nothing that would be to him of proper concern.

K

I was hoping to perhaps introduce the teaching of writing poetry into Moroccan education. I take it you think that would be a foolish thing to do.

PSR

Not foolish but hopeless. How idiotically chauvinistic and imperialistic even the best-intentioned of you Europeans are—

**K**

I am an American.

**PSR**

For me to all intents and purposes the same thing.

**K**

How imperialistic? why chauvinist?

**PSR**

Don't you really see it? You are trying, simply, to "introduce" to us, to our children, in the tenderest phases of their lives, your ruling idea of what the nature of God and experience precisely is—"discovery," "self-expression," and so on and so on. What if an Arab man appeared, as charmingly as you do here, in your country and announced his intention of teaching Fatalism to every American child before he was nine years old?

**K**

But Fatalism—poetry is—

**PSR**

No, my friend. Your country will thrive on poetry, even poetry by children, doubtless, but mine goes forward on other seemingly but not necessarily truly darker paths. You should be more aware of what you are doing.

**K**

Thank you, Pierre Sadi-Rab. You have given me some very interesting things to think about.

*Interview with Solomon El Baid—1/2/73*

**K**

You were going to tell me about the Jewish community in Morocco.

**S**

I can do that. I can speak a little more knowledgeably about the Jewish community in Marrakesh.

K

Would you do that?

S

Yes. There were, up till four years ago, about thirty thousand Jews in Marrakesh. As of now there are about four thousand.

K

Where have they all gone?

S

To Israel. The Jewish people here have been very afraid since the change in government.
(here followed a long section about Jewish political problems in Morocco)

K

What about you and your wife? Have you been tempted to leave?

S

Oh yes, tempted—maybe not tempted but afraid. But we have not left. I do not think we are going to leave.

K

Why not, if you are afraid?

S

Marrakesh is our home. Morocco is our country. We don't want to go anyplace else. . . .


*Interview with Charles N., an American Resident of Marrakesh* — *1/3/73*


K

How long have you lived here?

C

Ten years.

K

What do you think about it?

C

It's the only place in the world now to be. Where else can you be? Spain is finished. Spain used to be possible, but Spain is finished. Mallorca used to be beautiful, now it's completely finished. You can't live in Spain. Maybe in South America, sometime in the future, I don't know. Right now this is the only place.

K

The only place to live?

C

The only place it's even possible. You can't live in Spain now, in France, I can't stand that, America is impossible, I don't know how you can stand to live there. Everybody comes here. Everybody will come here. Then it will be ruined. It will be over. I will go someplace else.

K

What is the mysterious element your conversation seems to be about, i.e., the possible conditions for life. I mean, what is the actual content of the statement that "This is the only place to live"?

C

Just what it says. There is no place else. Look at Spain, look at France, look at America. Here it's amazing. They used to have it—it used to be—in Spain.

K

I don't understand what "it" is.

C

Stop it. You're putting me on. Everybody knows it. You feel it. You only have to come here, you feel it, and, if you care about it that much, you stay.

K

And that is how you stayed?

C

Yes. I came here and felt it. Spain was over. I had been living in Spain.

**K**

How strange we Americans are when you think about it, some of us anyway, with our endless quest for the "secret." It's curious to find it in a place. Is it mainly a question of feeling, of how you feel?

**C**

If you don't understand it—

**K**

I think I do. But it's a thing people usually aren't very specific about. They're mystical. To talk about it in another way might be interesting.

**C**

Americans are always looking for the interesting.

**K**

That's sort of what I was saying about you—living here! . . .

**C**

That's not the same. You, I think, are interested in the "interesting"— it's from living where you do, I don't know, it seems very American— interesting facts, interesting tidbits, interesting data, this and that. And all for what? For nothing. To create more interest for interest for interest and so on ad infinitum, like a billion little fleas each chasing each other all over the place. What is it for? Here that doesn't happen.

**K**

What is there here instead?

**C**

I don't know if I can explain. But it isn't that. There is a kind of centrality to experience. A major tone. Just that.

**K**

It gives you that kind of feeling.

**C**

It is really here, it exists.

K

You receive from living here a main feeling. It makes you "feel proper"—
the way, for someone else, living with his grandparents might.

C

Living with one's grandparents would be limiting.

K

Every situation is. Certainly living here is limiting.

C

But it is right. What is important is here.

K

How can it be here? That doesn't really make any sense.

C

Why not here? Unless you think it is nowhere. Do you think rightness
in fact doesn't exist?

K

I think either it is a feeling that is different and will be in different places
for different persons and it is endless and it is interesting and we could
study that, or, if rightness or whatever causes right feeling or whatever
you want to call it, if this exists, then surely it will not really exist in a
place, though it may be there with the resider to reside, but it will be in a
state of mind, of spirit body and mind the person has attained.

C

But we are not perfect. There are always chinks and cracks. Perhaps I
have that attainment (how do you know?) but also a weakness which
means that I can only find that rightness in this place.

K

I think what you are discussing is still mostly a feeling. I do not think
there is a place. Yes, the place can help—or hurt.

C

Spain used to be the place.

K

I never lived in Spain. I was only there for a visit, in the early years of my marriage, with my wife and then later with my parents.

C

It's not the place. Now this is the place.

K

I wish we could be clearer—but I suppose we can't.

C

It's clear enough.

K

Thank you very much.

C

Good-bye.

K

Good-bye.

Jan. 5th. Ouarzazate, the South. One thing left out of this journal, as the F key is now missing from my typewriter, worse luck, but I can write on it anyway. Don't become panicked the way I used to about every little thing going wrong. I must have been impossible to live with. Inside my problems. Inside my mind. Inside my corporal entity. Inside my subculture. Inside my country. Inside the world. Certain characteristics solid there be fractured here. The man says he can't get the windshield replacement till tomorrow. When it will turn out he does not have one after all. So, endlessly into the future, I'll remain in you, Ouarzazate. What a nice name. Like a drunkard saying What is that? Ouarzazate. Essay on the availability of the light scent of horse manure on a January morning in Zagora where I am going next day. The smell of cigars. Are these really only a repressed sublimating affection for smell of our own excretions? Caramba! It's hard to believe. In my poem "On Beauty" I will write next year I will put that idea to sleep. Or let it rest, in any case. Now if we could open the "Any Case." So many things have been left there! It is so hard to know when, and what, to write. Should one not do it on holidays? on weekends? when other people are around? Is it wrong to be writing this journal? Shouldn't I be up and about? It is hot to be up and about. And I don't know where to be up and about to. Everything in this culture seems too structured for me to

348

be merely and vaguely up and about in it. I guess I could start a school—but at this time of night? And Pierre Sadi-Rab didn't think very much of my ideas. Sans doute il a la raison de son coté. That doesn't sound like completely correct French. Well, onward!

Jan. 6th. In the Western quarter of Ouarzazate we have discovered it, the Any Case. It is full as a bushel basket of clothes. It has dyed-red subject matter. Its daffodils cancel perceptions of a long-drying wall. It seems to be Morocco itself. Lots of children run about it excited. The children in this country—happy, beautiful, excited, a lot of them, as if they had been spared something. Then others who are begging, bruised, aslant, who seem deprived of something momentous. None of them like American children who seem comparatively like lollipop heads. The beauty of the human race as it passes from one age to another. Golden philosophies. Walking past the Any Case, in which so many things have gone on.

\*

Riding my bicycle up the hill to see Jean Johnson. Would living in Arab culture have deprived me of everything? Who, exactly, would I have been? Would that have been "more reality"? The idea of the degree of reality forbids and depresses me. If I shouted "I am I," that would be a case of very pale identity. French writers can go on like this for a long time—the "intimate metaphysics"—"cum deep suffering you will never know it" style. Are they influencing me here in Morocco? I do not suppose I could be influenced tonight by Moroccan (Arab) writers. If I were able to read them, yes. But they seem to be from very long ago—or else to be writing about superficial if "pressing" questions. Is my lack of being "pressed" an example of some sort of horrible exemption from reality? Do I wish to be part of a warm and embosoming culture? And if I do—Now you tell me, at my time in life, how on earth I am ever going to be completely satisfied? The idea is ridiculous. And yet here I am, forever on the hunt . . .

\*

If I could get to Zagora (if that non-arriving man would repair my car) and see the Blue Men, my life would have another chance at fulfillment. The Blue Men. They live in the desert. But what has that to do with me? And merely to see them. I don't want to be one. Perhaps I am not looking for happiness but looking for the most happy-making way to look for it. Like childhood dreams of judging a beauty contest. Miss America! the judge says.

Moslem sex. Moslem girls. Moroccan beauties. Eyes. Eyes look great big over veils. All the face struggling up into the eyes. Veiled faces. What, under the veils, their expressions? Did you know there were people rather unlike you and me? What would you do under a veil? Try one on. Try smiling. Try licking your lips. You would probably not be frowning hideously.

What about this? A whole nation of girls and of women totally unavailable to you. And here you are walking among them, as if everything were perfectly all right. It's actually kind of nightmarish. Fortunately you are running on an electric motor which wakes you and puts you to sleep at regular times.

Seriously. What is one to make of an organization that, like art, involves and engages our most powerful impulses and directs them toward a historically comprehensible but personally unfeelable end, and that is called a country and is this gorgeous place Morocco, which gives impressions while taking away substance because the substance is just incalculably too much for us to bear? And is this true? It sounds too interwoven to be true. I reject it. It's just what I don't like about that kind of French writer I discussed. And now here it is morning. The muezzin is yowling to bust a clavicle. And my windshield appears on the breakfast table. It is Zagora today, on the wings of dawn. Blue Men, watch out. We'll soon be down there where you are.

*Interview with Jean Johnson*

K

Do you remember me, Jean?

J

Why, Kenneth Koch. You haven't changed at all.

K

That's unusual. I haven't seen you for almost fifty years.

J

No, it couldn't be fifty. I'm not even fifty years old now.

K

I guess it was thirty-five. God how I used to love your big tits and your laughing aristocratic airs.

J

I liked your humor, your lean nervousness, and all, but you were such a kid. Others were more grown up. You didn't seem . . .

CHORUS

. . . to want the responsibility of a complete relationship with me.

(As the Chorus says this, Jean gets up and dances. Her dance is a highly stylized and symbolic version of a melancholy waltz. Kenneth watches her, fascinated. Finally, he stands up, takes off his shirt, and rushes toward her, to take her in his arms. But she has vanished.)

CHORUS

That was not the real Jean Johnson you saw but a phantom.

K

And the one I knew as a child?

CHORUS

She was real.

K

What else is real?

CHORUS

Only the movements of this dance.

(The Chorus rises and dances to the same waltz music as before. But Jean Johnson does not appear. Kenneth weeps.)

K

Illusion piled on illusion. Either superficiality of "pressingness" or nothingness. I must find what is in between. And now once again it is dawn. Was this only a dream?

HOTEL WAITER (shouting in Kenneth's ear)
Mr. Koch! Wake up! It's the morning! The man from Marrakesh has come with a new windshield for your car!

That happened yesterday.

Now it has happened again.

Thank you very much. Would you like to be interviewed? How long have you lived here?

All my life.

I think my work on Essaouira may be almost complete.


*More Essaouira*


Not quite yet, though. I see that I have left out so much. And they are, many of these things, the same ones I put in. For example, the blue white rectangular quality of Essaouira. Most people go there and that's that. It's an afternoon, a morning, or a day. But many must go there, too, as I did, a dreamer of the present actuality, as if a street made up of different cobblestones could, for the carriage that went over it, be one huge uneven uncared-for stone. What is Essaouira? I love the name. Or rather I like it. One guidebook says it is a shame to lose its old name Mogador. I can imagine dreary discussions of this, gray wallpapers, snooty-looking people. Palm trees. But I like "Essaouira" better by far. "Mogador" has some obvious charm of an old-fashioned kind that completely puts me off it. Everyone knows how to respond to the word "Mogador." But "Essaouira". . . . The long dusty path there. I've already said that. What did I not say. American poetry at the lesser levels has improved since I began this Essay, though at its higher levels I do not believe one could say that that was the case. Is this a kind of cultural leveling that is frequent in small histories of cultures? Let's walk into Essaouira and find out. You can't find that out in Essaouira. And I doubt you can find it out anywhere. How strange to be among these people whose front is as much as their back indifferent to everything I think and say and do. Yet not wholly indifferent. I always feel they would be surprised by the thoughts I was having because these thoughts would not seem to them significant. I think they, like others, are chiefly practical, but experience shows that once some little adjustment is made this is not necessarily so. Oops! I'm sorry. I almost bumped into that woman. She is wearing a veil as no one here does. As usual I am spending my life doing nothing. If I had never come to Essaouira, would my life be the same? I see the beard twitching, I hear the boredom. Are certain physical movements of our parents' and our own bodies in infancy the determining factors in our lives? The fortress she is that way and the market they are this. If I were at my typewriter describing this, instead of being here ready with the experience. Of course I am now. I would like to know what finally Essaouira

                      you are Essaouira
              obviously palm trees I like your name
You have forgotten about Zagora and Ouarzazate. That's impossible. I just went back to Essaouira because that's where I began. Once the man fixed my windshield I knew I would never go back to Essaouira. It was like the first card dealt. You don't try to draw that again in the same game. Travel, at its utmost reaches, requires a new experience or gamble every time. In experience—you go back to the same girl and after two years of absence if, only if, you find that it is new, an Essaouira


              post-Ouarzazate, after-Zagorian
                                 what's that?


And other travelers to Morocco will relate
              drifting experiences
Wasn't that great, absolutely great
And did you get the shift there?
                          what
                              the shrimp, the shift
    there are some marvelous little ships
                too bad, you missed them
I missed
              SOMETHING!
Ouarzazate thou beautiful breasts of day
      I know *thou* isn't plural, well neither are breasts
    Is the ocean plural? then neither is breasts, are breasts
        Sounding better this way
                Ouarzazate   Zagora down there in the
desert the old old library, with books like a jewel, the terrible roadway, to get there by fuel, better at camelback or horse hoof, to see, among the

divided triangle square at, far from (relatively) Ouarzazate, by Zagora, but distant by bad roads (as Germany is distant from grammar) this

old place

What was I doing exactly in Essaouira in Ouarzazate in Zagora? Say, well, you missed the best thing, the herpes of the mountain/I say to hell with that. At Ouarzazate I believe it was at the hotel upon whose bed I lay breaking my back to see the thin dawn line how easily I write now come out though probably scientifically it was in the window where an automobile flat top bottom lay fatly bulging in the summery Christmas dawn, there was one whom we gave a lift to and he left his shoes in the car in a paper bag and in some bizarre way we mailed them back to him no left them at a car agency with him in some way connected. Did he ever receive the shoes? But that is not in Essaouira.

Let us say, Ouarzazate, here's our lecture, a discussion of place

and of our liking for place
and of the influence of place
in our lives

ENTIRELY IRRESPECTIVE OF WHEN IT HAPPENS<br>AND OF WHO WE ARE

That disappoints sociologists but pleases poets. Philosophers long ago
   dismissed
From the classroom where anyone was listening may now cock an ear
   back-
Wards to see if at this new equality some sea urchins are starting to hiss
What a municipal monument! and I wonder always if my friends (two best
   ones) thought that this
That I always write about but not necessarily always think about most but
   just at certain times of emphasis
(Old-fashioned poetry, you are a dead goat! wherefore I love thee for a sec
   and pick thee up
But then cast thee down again, O goat) I go backwards I wonder
If my friends knew (know) how stupid I am how dirty how shallow
They seem more instinctual, like these, but I am instinctual other
I mean otherwise but now and again I do wonder and now and again I say
   I wonder

UNEXPLAINED INDIVIDUAL FOUND<br>STANDING IN OUARZAZATE

Am I the height and wonder of all civilizations? What the hell is my life getting at? If I conceive it chronologically, it is all some sort of dippy romantic (but slightly comic) tragedy but when I am not obliged to do that (how could I be, fat mountains?), I get to thinking like this, when everything is present, and that's when Essaouira and Ouarzazate are overwhelming and inescapable problems. Either everything has to be satisfied straight on or in backwards-forwards, which at least I began with by coming here first in a plane and then in a car. You whose message delights me! The trouble is you are spread out! No wonder we like big-breasted people. They

> Give the illusion of eternity, the space time infinity
>> that this topic seems to require
> And Essaouira if you—I like better "thou"—art spread
>> out
> Besides, in a mathematical fashion, it is all to the good

And if you give me this feeling more than a larger city it is because if it is too large it is nothing. Sea urchins and the monument. The casbah. And the man puts the windshield on. I was about to say "Man"—Man puts the windshield on. Where have we been since our first houses? And what, aside from that first adjustment, have we been?

> Surely Death will not find us unready for the water
> Certainly if we have been in water already we know death
> Death is heat or air or water
> But where in the shell of Morocco—
> For, if death be the subject, Morocco like every other place is only a
>> shell—
> Can this be placed? Is it all from "displaced need"
> Like the sculptures of ugliness? How much truth can there be in
>> anything or in that?

I want to see the desert
And here it is. And the caravan moves on, the caravan of my thinking I
  might be crazy
No, not crazy, but pitching the wrong thumb, hitchhiking a ride in a
  totally opposite direction
From where I want to go, and I make an adjustment now and go in the
  opposite direction. If I had no money
There would still be a shortage of reality. That shortage is in me. Rather, I
  am the shortage. The shortage had an
Amazing experience in Morocco. Which was also completely ordinary. As it always is. Since no one knows what anything is about. Officially. As a matter of fact I suppose being so abstractly diffused while caring so much in some funny uneven kind of way protects one from the decadence of acting like a cup, ooohooo flopping around in somebody's hand. But so would a lot of other things would. I know there's one too many. Essaouira, farewell! I said that before. If my life means anything, it is that I am always forgetting just what it is that I want. How's that for meaning? I have found

a way to be unsatisfied by everything and always somewhat pleasantly excited. Or painfully excited. What's Zen compared to that? What's Academia's compelling suture? its compiling future? I want to know who has ever found anything as wonderful as being a strain—not the strainer or the strained, but the thing itself, held tight between two eternities (what is that?) like a dog, held on two leashes, by two enraged furies, the eyes of the world, the peacemakers of eternity (that word again, you would think I wanted to die, if you didn't know me better, it is more that in truth I would like to vanish, but into this prose study to live forever here but also be eternally writing, my ideal would be a text that was always writing, but then on the other hand I have never been aware of being interested in that, and I can't imagine actually as I read it over what it means—I have to get out of this sidetrack: I have something important to say), the stones that are never lying in the grass but are always bouncing around. And I'm held between them. They tug me. And I resist. I run and they chase me. They can never stop me from moving and I can never completely get away. What's Dante's Paradise compared to that? You always think I am kidding. I am trying to define happiness by what I've actually got and then go on from there. Afterwards we can have something to eat and drink and re-enter the process, you who seem more comfortable in the process but who are, I imagine, inside, like me, a watcher of Essaouiras. Do I love you for that? I don't know if I love you or have ever loved anything or anyone. I am a desert. Kill me. And now a town. Signed, "Zagora."

### Coda

Morocco, Morocco, the interviews are done
Farewell, Part of the Continuum
Hello, Strangest Days
We appell you Conundrum, the world's greatest word
Your cities—Ouarzazate, Essaouira, Zagora—are like teeth
Part of an enormous jaw, which is You
And the seriousness of a discourse is not in a few details
And the burning soul of a human not available to see in a few frills—
What counts, counts. Childhood is over. Adolescence is over.
The great hunt for death has begun. But you know that isn't it.
O transfer paper of the sun
There's no denying it's painful to leave anything
And in fact so painful do I find leaving
That to hell with it I am going to remain—

Remaining is also a sort of leaving (I am sorry to
Have to say that) so how except by prose can one stay?
I can write about distractions
But I will always come back to you,
Essaouira which moved me so curiously,
Ouarzazate of the broken windshield.

# To Marina

So many convolutions and not enough simplicity!
When I had you to write to it
Was different. The quiet, dry Z
Leaped up to the front of the alphabet.
You sit, stilling your spoons
With one hand; you move them with the other.
Radio says, "God is a postmaster."
You said, Ziss is lawflee. And in the heat
Of writing to you I wrote simply. I thought
These are the best things I shall ever write
And have ever written. I thought of nothing but touching you.
Thought of seeing you and, in a separate thought, of looking at you.
You were concentrated feeling and thought.
You were like the ocean
In which my poems were the swimming. I brought you
Ear rings. You said, These are lawflee. We went
To some beach, where the sand was dirty. Just going in
To the bathing house with you drove me "out of my mind."

It is wise to be witty. The shirt collar's far away.
Men tramp up and down the city on this windy day.
I am feeling a-political as a shell
Brought off some fish. Twenty-one years
Ago I saw you and loved you still.
Still! It wasn't plenty
Of time. Read Anatole France. Bored, a little. Read
Tolstoy, replaced and overcome. You read Stendhal.
I told you to. Where was replacement
Then? I don't know. He shushed us back into ourselves.
I used to understand
The highest excitement. Someone died
And you were distant. I went away
And made you distant. Where are you now? I see the chair
And hang onto it for sustenance. Good God how you kissed me
And I held you. You screamed
And I wasn't bothered by anything. Was nearest you.

And you were so realistic
Preferring the Soviet Bookstore

To my literary dreams.
"You don't like war," you said
After reading a poem
In which I'd simply said I hated war
In a whole list of things. To you
It seemed a position, to me
It was all a flux, especially then.
I was in an
Unexpected situation.
Let's take a walk
I wrote. And I love you as a sheriff
Searches for a walnut. And And so unless
I'm going to see your face
Bien soon, and you said
You must take me away, and
Oh Kenneth
You like everything
To be pleasant. I was burning
Like an arch
Made out of trees.

I'm not sure we ever actually took a walk.
We were so damned nervous. I was heading somewhere. And you had to
    be
At an appointment, or else be found out! Illicit love!
It's not a thing to think of. Nor is it when it's licit!
It is too much! And it wasn't enough. The achievement
I thought I saw possible when I loved you
Was that really achievement? Were you my
Last chance to feel that I had lost my chance?
I grew faint at your voice on the telephone
Electricity and all colors were mine, and the tops of hills
And everything that breathes. That was a feeling. Certain
Artistic careers had not even started. And I
Could have surpassed them. I could have I think put the
Whole world under our feet. You were in the restaurant. It
Was Chinese. We have walked three blocks. Or four blocks. It is New
    York
In nineteen fifty-three. Nothing has as yet happened
That will ever happen and will mean as much to me. You smile, and turn
    your head.

What rocketing there was in my face and in my head
And bombing everywhere in my body
I loved you I knew suddenly
That nothing had meant anything like you
I must have hoped (crazily) that something would
As if thinking you were the person I had become.

My sleep is beginning to be begun. And the sheets were on the bed.
A clock rang a bird's song rattled into my typewriter.
I had been thinking about songs which were very abstract.
Language was the champion. The papers lay piled on my desk
It was really a table. Now, the telephone. Hello, what?
What is my life like now? Engaged, studying and looking around
The library, teaching—I took it rather easy
A little too easy—we went to the ballet
Then dark becomes the light (blinding) of the next eighty days
Orchestra cup became As beautiful as an orchestra or a cup, and
Locked climbs becomes If we were locked, well not quite, rather
Oh penniless could I really die, and I understood everything
Which before was running this way and that in my head
I saw titles, volumes, and suns I felt the hot
Pressure of your hands in that restaurant
To which, along with glasses, plates, lamps, lusters,
Tablecloths, napkins, and all the other junk
You added my life for it was entirely in your hands then—
My life
Yours, My Sister Life of Pasternak's beautiful title
My life without a life, my life in a life, my life impure
And my life pure, life seen as an entity
One death and a variety of days
And only one life.

I wasn't ready
For you.

I understood nothing
Seemingly except my feelings
You were whirling
In your life
I was keeping
Everything in my head
An artist friend's apartment

Five flights up the
Lower East Side nineteen
Fifty-something I don't know
What we made love the first time I
Almost died I had never felt
That way it was like being stamped on in Hell
It was roses of Heaven
My friends seemed turned to me to empty shell

On the railroad train's red velvet back
You put your hand in mine and said
"I told him"
Or was it the time after that?
I said Why did you
Do that you said I thought
It was over. Why? Because you were so
Nervous of my being there it was something I thought

I read
Tolstoy. You said
I don't like the way it turns out (*Anna
Karenina*) I had just liked the strength
Of the feeling you thought
About the end. I wanted
To I don't know what never leave you
Five flights up the June
Street emptied of fans, cups, kites, cops, eats, nights, no
The night was there
And something like air I love you Marina
Eighty-five days
Four thousand three hundred and sixty-
Two minutes all poetry was changed
For me what did I do in exchange
I am selfish, afraid you are
Overwhelmingly parade, back, sunshine, dreams
Later thousands of dreams

You said
You make me feel nawble (noble). I said
Yes. I said
To nothingness, This is all poems. Another one said (later)
That is so American. You were Russian.

You thought of your feelings, one said, not of her,
Not of the real situation. But my feelings were a part,
They were the force of the real situation. Truer to say I thought
Not of the whole situation
For your husband was also a part
And your feelings about your child were a part
And all my other feelings were a part. We
Turned this way and that, up-
Stairs then down
Into the streets.
Did I die because I didn't stay with you?
Or what did I lose of my life? I lost
You. I put you
In everything I wrote.

I used that precious material I put it in forms
Also I wanted to break down the forms
Poetry was a real occupation
To hell with the norms, with what is already written
Twenty-nine in love finds pure expression
Twenty-nine years you my whole life's digression
Not taken and Oh Kenneth
Everything afterwards seemed nowhere near
What I could do then in several minutes—
I wrote,
"I want to look at you all day long
Because you are mine."

I am twenty-nine, pocket flap folded
And I am smiling I am looking out at a world that
I significantly re-created from inside
Out of contradictory actions and emotions. I look like a silly child that
Photograph that year—big glasses, unthought-of clothes,
A suit, slight mess in general, cropped hair. And someone liked me,
Loved me a lot, I think. And someone else had, you had, too. I was
Undrenched by the tears I'd shed later about this whole thing when
I'd telephone you I'd be all nerves, though in fact
All life was a factor and all my nerves were in my head. I feel
Peculiar. Or I feel nothing. I am thinking about this poem. I am thinking
    about your raincoat,
I am worried about the tactfulness,
About the truth of what I say.

I am thinking about my standards for my actions
About what they were
You raised my standards for harmony and for happiness so much
And, too, the sense of a center
Which did amazing things for my taste
But my taste for action? for honesty, for directness in behavior?
I believe I simply never felt that anything could go wrong
This was abject stupidity
I also was careless in how I drove then and in what I ate
And drank it was easier to feel that nothing could go wrong
I had those feelings. I
Did not those things. I was involved in such and such
A situation, artistically and socially. We never spent a night
Together it is the New York of
Aquamarine sunshine and the Loew's Theater's blazing swing of light
In the middle of the day

Let's take a walk
Into the world
Where if our shoes get white
With snow, is it snow, Marina,
Is it snow or light?
Let's take a walk

Every detail is everything in its place (Aristotle). Literature is a cup
And we are the malted. The time is a glass. A June bug comes
And a carpenter spits on a plane, the flowers ruffle ear rings.
I am so dumb-looking. And you are so beautiful.

Sitting in the Hudson Tube
Walking up the fusky street
Always waiting to see you
You the original creation of all my You, you the you
In every poem the hidden one whom I am talking to
Worked at Bamberger's once I went with you to Cerutti's
Bar—on Madison Avenue? I held your hand and you said
Kenneth you are playing with fire. I said
Something witty in reply.
It was the time of the McCarthy trial
Hot sunlight on lunches. You squirted
Red wine into my mouth.
My feelings were like a fire my words became very clear

My psyche or whatever it is that puts together motions and emotions
Was unprepared. There was a good part
And an alarmingly bad part which didn't correspond—
No letters! no seeming connection! your slim pale hand
It actually was, your blondness and your turning-around-to-me look.
   Good-bye Kenneth.

No, Marina, don't go
And what had been before would come after
Not to be mysterious we'd be together make love again
It was the wildest thing I've done
I can hardly remember it
It has gotten by now
So mixed up with losing you
The two almost seem in some way the same. You
Wore something soft—angora? cashmere?
I remember that it was black. You turned around
And on such a spring day which went on and on and on
I actually think I felt that I could keep
The strongest of all feelings contained inside me
Producing endless emotional designs.

With the incomparable feeling of rising and of being like a banner
Twenty seconds worth twenty-five years
With feeling noble extremely mobile and very free
With Taking a Walk With You, West Wind, In Love With You, and
   Yellow Roses
With pleasure I felt my leg muscles and my brain couldn't hold
With the Empire State Building the restaurant your wrist bones with
   Greenwich Avenue
In nineteen fifty-one with heat humidity a dog pissing with neon
With the feeling that at last
My body had something to do and so did my mind

You sit
At the window. You call
Me, across Paris,
Amsterdam, New
York. Kenneth!
My Soviet
Girlhood. My
Spring, summer

And fall. Do you
Know you have
Missed some of them?
Almost all. I am
Waiting and I
Am fading I
Am fainting I'm
In a degrading state
Of inactivity. A ball
Rolls in the gutter. I have
Two hands to
Stop it. I am
A flower I pick
The vendor his
Clothes getting up
Too early and
What is it makes this rose
Into what is more fragrant than what is not?

I am stunned I am feeling tortured
By "A man of words and not a man of deeds"

I was waiting in a taxicab
It was white letters in white paints it was you
Spring comes, summer, then fall
And winter. We really have missed
All of that, whatever else there was
In those years so sanded by our absence.
I never saw you for as long as half a day

You were crying outside the bus station
And I was crying—
I knew that this really was my life—
I kept thinking of how we were crying
Later, when I was speaking, driving, walking,
Looking at doorways and colors, mysterious entrances
Sometimes I'd be pierced as by a needle
Sometimes be feverish as from a word
Books closed and I'd think
I can't read this book, I threw away my life
These held on to their lives. I was
Excited by praise from anyone, startled by criticism, always hating it

Traveling around Europe and being excited
It was all in reference to you
And feeling I was not gradually forgetting
What your temples and cheekbones looked like
And always with this secret

Later I thought
That what I had done was reasonable
It may have been reasonable
I also thought that I saw what had appealed to me
So much about you, the way you responded
To everything your excitement about
Me, I had never seen that. And the fact
That you were Russian, very mysterious, all that I didn't know
About you—and you didn't know
Me, for I was as strange to you as you were to me.
You were like my first trip to France you had
Made no assumptions. I could be
Clearly and passionately and
Nobly (as you'd said) who I was—at the outer limits of my life
Of my life as my life could be
Ideally. But what about the dark part all this lifted
Me out of? Would my bad moods, my uncertainties, my
Distrust of people I was close to, the
Twisty parts of my ambition, my
Envy, all have gone away? And if
They hadn't gone, what? For didn't I need
All the strength you made me feel I had, to deal
With the difficulties of really having you?
Where could we have been? But I saw so many new possibilities
That it made me rather hate reality
Or I think perhaps I already did
I didn't care about the consequences
Because they weren't "poetic" weren't "ideal"

And oh well you said we walk along
Your white dress your blue dress your green
Blouse with sleeves then one without
Sleeves and we are speaking
Of things but not of very much because underneath it
I am raving I am boiling I am afraid
You ask me Kenneth what are you thinking

If I could say
It all then I thought if I could say
Exactly everything and have it still be as beautiful
Billowing over, riding over both our doubts
Some kind of perfection and what did I actually
Say? Marina it's late. Marina
It's early. I love you. Or else, What's this street?
You were the perfection of my life
And I couldn't have you. That is, I didn't.
I couldn't think. I wrote, instead. I would have had
To think hard, to figure everything out
About how I could be with you,
Really, which I couldn't do
In those moments of permanence we had
As we walked along.

We walk through the park in the sun. It is the end.
You phone me. I send you a telegram. It
Is the end. I keep
Thinking about you, grieving about you. It is the end. I write
Poems about you, to you. They
Are no longer simple. No longer
Are you there to see every day or
Every other or every third or fourth warm day
And now it has been twenty-five years
But those feelings kept orchestrating I mean rehearsing
Rehearsing in me and tuning up
While I was doing a thousand other things, the band
Is ready, I am over fifty years old and there's no you—
And no me, either, not as I was then,
When it was the Renaissance
Filtered through my nerves and weakness
Of nineteen fifty-four or fifty-three,
When I had you to write to, when I could see you
And it could change.

# DAYS AND NIGHTS

# In Bed

## MORNINGS IN BED

Are energetic mornings.


## SNOW IN BED

When we got out of bed
It was snowing.


## MEN IN BED

All over Paris
Men are in bed.


## BEAUTIFUL GIRL IN BED

Why I am happy to be here.


## LONG RELATIONSHIP IN BED

The springs and the bedposts
Are ready the minute we come in.


## DOLLS IN BED

With little girls.


## HAMMER AND NAILS IN BED

To make it better
They are making it a better bed
And a bigger bed, firmer and larger
And finer bed. So the hammer and nails in the bed

And the carpenter's finger
And thumb and his eyes and his shoulder.
Bang! Bang! Smap! The hammer and nails in bed.


## SHEEP IN BED

The sheep got into the bed
By mistake.


## BUYING A NEW BED

One of the first things you did
Was buy a new bed.


## WINDOW IN BED

I looked at you
And you looked back.


## MARRIED IN BED

We'll be married in bed.
The preachers, the witnesses, and all our families
Will also be in bed.


## POETRY BED

Whenas in bed
Then, then


## OTHER POETRY BED

Shall I compare you to a summer's bed?
You are more beautiful.

## ORCHIDS IN BED

She placed orchids in the bed
On that dark blue winter morning.

## LYING IN BED

Bed with Spain in it
Bed with Gibraltar in it
Bed of art!

## LOVERS IN BED

Are lovers no more
Than lovers on the street.
(See Picasso's "Pair of Young Mountebanks," FC 533,
Greuze's "Noces," or hear Mozart's "Fleichtscausenmusik," Köchel 427)

## SOME BED

Once
Held
This
All

## GOD IN BED

Christ
Was not
Born
(And did
Not die)
In a bed.

## LÉGER IN BED

Above our apartment
In 1955
Lived Fernand Léger.

## SHOUTING IN BED

We wake up
To the sound of shouts.

## FRIENDS IN BED

Sleep well.

## ANGELIC CEREMONY IN BED

Putting on the sheets.

## MYSTERY OF BED

She takes it for granted
That he will stay up all night long.

## WORKMEN IN BED

With workmen's wives
And workmen's girl friends
And other workmen
And dolls.

## ACAPULCO IN BED

In Mexico, with blue shimmering water,
Acapulco is in bed.

## MY INTOXICATION IN BED

Was not long-lasting.
Was fantastic.

Did not lead me to be very well-mannered.
Wasn't completely romantic.

## BASKETBALL IN BED

The basketball is thrown on the bed.

## EXPENSIVE BED

At the Lutétia 500 francs a night
In the Hôpital St-Antoine 1000 francs a night

## THEATRICAL BED

Exceeded expectations
And received applause.

## SIRENS IN BED

My face is plastered to the window
When the sirens come.

## COURTSHIP IN BED

"Please. Tell me you like me."
"How did you get in this bed?"

## WET DOG IN BED

There is nothing like a wet dog in bed.

## DOG BED

In the dog bed
I cannot sleep.

## ATOMIC BED

Billions of—uncountable—electrons
Compose this bed.

## BEING IN BED

Belongs to everyone
Bed with Spain in it
Bed of art!

## SNOW IN BED (LATER)

When it stopped snowing
We still hadn't gone to bed

## PHILOSOPHY IN BED

(I)
Plato says this bed
Isn't the real one.
What did Plato know
About beds?

(II)
Spinoza constructed a bed
Which was slept in by Alfred North Whitehead.

(XLIV)
You say, "Let's go to bed"
But those words have no meaning.

## SOUTH AMERICA IN BED

Brazil, Argentina, Ecuador, and Peru
Are in bed. The first thing you did
Was to buy a new bed.

## AS WE LAY IN BED

We saw the stars starting to come together
As we lay in bed.

## POLIZIANO IN BED

Angelo Poliziano
Never went to bed
Was it he or Castiglione—
The perfect Renaissance man?

## LUNCH IN BED

It's late! Get up! The roseate fruit trees
Are blushing with the nape of new-frocked day!
Awake! The modern breeze of spring
Is pulsative through nest-caroming branches!

## COWARDS IN BED

Afraid to turn over. Come on. Come on, turn over. Cowards in bed.

## CHOPIN'S ÉTUDES IN BED

Here is the bed
Of Chopin's Études;
Over here is his Préludes' bed,
And here is the bed of his Mazurkas.

## PRÉLUDES IN BED

There are no préludes in bed
Today.

## LET'S GO TO BED

When the tree
Is blossoming. It will be
A long time
Before it is blossoming again.

## STONES IN BED

In the bed are stones
From Egypt and Etruria
And some magazines and a pouch of tobacco.

## BED

I'd wake up every morning
And look out the window across the park.

## WOODEN MECHANICAL FIGURE INDICATING A BED

With a mighty smile
And a mighty gesture
He discloses the bed.

## Y. SICK IN BED

Said, If there is a heaven
I want it to look
Like what is out there.

## MORNINGS IN BED

Are pensive mornings.

## SUICIDE

I was unable to tell you any reason
To get out of bed


## A BLUE AND WHITE BED

Became a yellow and gold one,
Then was green, pale green,
Then violet, then onyx,
Yes onyx, then it was an onyx bed.


## BALCONIES IN BED

When you lean over
When you fall
When you speak


## BEDS IN THE GARDENS OF SPAIN

To the sound of a guitar
When you enter the room.


## POETRY IN BED

Do you remember how this started—
With "Mornings in Bed" and "Snow in Bed"?


## RISPETTO

Good-bye to bed.
The ceiling loses its chance
To see you smile again
In just that way.

## LUXEMBOURG BED

The bed flies past
Like a swing.


## ADVANCE BED

Advance arm. Advance stairs. Advance power.
Advance bed.


## CHILD BED

You had two babies
Before we met.


## ABSTRACT BED

There is paint
On the abstract bed.


## ORCHIDS IN BED

She placed orchids on the bed
On a dark red winter afternoon.


## AT ENDEBED

At Endebed I mett you
You go up on the lift, no, yes
Then we hearing from sounds of guitars
Americans strolling bingo hatrack in the lake.


## ENEMIES IN BED

Enemies sleep in separate beds
But in the same part of the city.

*PRIMAVERA*

He makes up the bed
And follows her home.


*ESTATE*

The bed lies in the room
The way she lies in the bed.


SAWBED

In the bed of the saw
The sawdust is dying.


WINDOWBED

From henna to blue all violet is in bed.


ZEN BED

I can't get to bed.
Show me the bed and I will show you how to get to it.


LARGE SUNDAY BED

Domingo.
Domenica.
Dimanche.


SATURDAY BED

Sabato.

## SNOW IN BED

When we get out of bed
There is no more bed.


## WOMEN IN BED

Everywhere in Paris
Women are in bed.


## MARRIED IN BED

We did not get married
In bed.


## FALSE BED

There are Easter eggs
Red blue yellow and white-pink
In the false bed.


## INVITING SOMEONE FROM BED

Come, let me help you out of bed.
The sun is shining. The window is open. Look!
From the balcony there is the street, which is like a bed.


## THE FUTURE BED

Will be lilac in color
And in the shape of an L or a Z.


## GUITARS IN BED

When we get out of bed
We hear guitars.

## POST-MODERNISM IN BED

Kandinsky, Arp, Valéry, Léger, and Marinetti
Are kicked out of bed.
Then, for a long time, nobody gets back into it.

## THE HOLIDAYS OF BED

Are when no one is there.

## GEORGICS IN BED

Planting wheat and rye and oats—explaining how to do it
And when, what kind of sunlight is needed and how much rain.

## STRANGE BEDFELLOWS

The bear got into bed
With his claws.

## CHAIRMAN BED

There is a little red book
In the bed.

## SHOWER BED

For her engagement they gave her a shower
And for her marriage they went to bed.

## MANTEQUILLA BED

Butter bed, beurre bed, burro bed.

## THESMOPHORIAZUSAE IN BED

Euripides put the Thesmophoriazusae in bed;
Then he also put in bed Elektra, Jason, and Sophocles.
Aristophanes said, Here, let me put you to bed.
No! Euripides screamed. But Aristophanes did
Put Euripides into bed with the Thesmophoriazusae.


## POETRY BED

To have it all at once, and make no decisions.
But that is a decision.


## OLIVE TREE BED

Along the side of the hill
Amid the green and gray trees
There is a place that looks like a bed.


## I AM SORRY I DIDN'T EXPECT TO FIND YOU IN BED

With me I must have misdialed the telephone oh
Wait a minute—damn! I can't extricate
Myself from these sheets yes I'm getting up what
Did you expect after such a long night at the factory
Of unexplained phenomena with your head and shoulders
Beautiful as a telephone directory but please don't talk to me about love
I have an appointment with my head with the dead with a pheasant
With a song I'm nervous good-bye. It was the end of bed.


## STREAM BED

In the stream bed
The snails go to sleep.

## PHILOSOPHY OF BED

A man should be like a woman and a woman should be like an animal
In bed is one theory. Another is that they both should be like beds.


## WE NEVER WENT TO BED

Listen, Kenny, I think it's a great idea! said Maxine
And she helped me sell my book to Chelsea House.
It was spring, with just the slightest hint of white and pink in the
    branches.


## MALLARMÉ'S BED

An angel came, while Mallarmé lay in bed,
When he was a child, and opened its hands
To let white bouquets of perfumed stars snow down.


## PSYCHOANALYTIC CRITICISM IN BED

What are you trying to avoid talking about
When you talk about bed?


## STORM IN BED

It was such a bad storm
That we were hurled out of bed.


## FLEURUS BED

There were flowers on the wallpaper,
There was loss and present excitement,
There was hope for the future, anxiety about the past,
Doubts and hopes about my work, and much to come,
As I lay in my bed on the rue de Fleurus.

## CARTOON BED

The door swings open and the bed comes in
Making a tremendous racket and bumping around.

## OWL IN BED

The owl flew into bed
By mistake.

## DAY BED

When I loved you
Then that whole time
Was like a bed
And that whole year
Was like a day bed.

## DENIED BED

We were not in bed
When summer came.

## LE FORÇAT DU MOULIN À GAZ IN BED

The convict of the gas mill is in bed.

## SNOW IN BED

Vanishing snowflakes, rooftops appearing
And sidewalks and people and cars as we get out of bed.

## DISCOBOLUS IN BED

The discus thrower
Is still in bed.

# The World

Sic transit ego
And sic fugit this poem
I'm through with it
A little yellow-stomached bird
Just leaped on my porch board.
I need to figure out
What is going on.
If bird so happy
And I so unhappy
I'm not in concordance with the world.

Once all contained
In me and around
Waterfall ahead
Whirlpool ahead
Rapids ahead
Poetic fame ahead
Dog ahead dawn ahead
Being less comic ahead
Fortune ahead misfortune ahead
Old age ahead and death ahead
Everything ahead
Inside my heart ahead and in my brain ahead
Meeting her ahead having met you ahead
And ahead even ahead
And within me contained
It bores and depresses me
It excites me
When I finish the day is gone
Everything still ahead
No longer can I believe
For me or a part of me
No one will be surprised

Saying I ought to see
Suffering is simply that
A thing for every day.
Can one person cure me?
Am I sick? I am

Unhappy and I think
I shouldn't be.

Whist! where are you gone, bird?
Departed without a word
Naturally.
Have I won
My freedom to damn myself
To my enemy's exclusive company?
Poetry, my enemy!
Why can't you do everything?
Make me young again.
Give me that hand in my hand.

# Girl and Baby Florist Sidewalk
# Pram Nineteen Seventy Something

Sweeping past the florist's came the baby and the girl
I am the girl! I am the baby!
I am the florist who is filled with mood!
I am the mood. I am the girl who is inside the baby
For it is a baby girl. I am old style of life. I am the new
Everything as well. I am the evening in which you docked your first kiss.
And it came to the baby. And I am the boyhood of the girl
Which she never has. I am the florist's unknown baby
He hasn't had one yet. The florist is in a whirl
So much excitement, section, outside his shop
Or hers. Who is he? Where goes the baby? She
Is immensely going to grow up. How much
Does this rent for? It's more than a penny. It's more
Than a million cents. My dear, it is life itself. Roses?
Chrysanthemums? If you can't buy them I'll give
Them for nothing. Oh no, I can't.
Maybe my baby is allergic to their spores.
So then the girl and her baby go away. Florist stands whistling
Neither inside nor outside thinking about the mountains of Peru.

# With Janice

The leaves were already on the trees, the fruit blossoms
White and not ruined and pink and not ruined and we
Were riding in a boat over the water in which there was a sea
Hiding the meanings of all our salty words. A duck
Or a goose and a boat and a stone and a stone cliff. The
Hardnesses—and, with a little smile—of life. Sitting
Earlier or later and forgotten the words and the bees
At supper they were about in how you almost gestured but stopped
Knowing there were only one or two things, and that the rest
Were merely complications. But one in a trenchcoat said
It's reversible. And, It's as out-of-date as a reversible coat. And
Magna Bear and Minor Orse were sleeping. The soap
Was climbing in its dish but relaxed and came down when cold water
    stopped
Rushing in and the bathroom was flooded. I said, It is not about
Things but with things I'd like to go and, too, Will it last
Or will all become uniform again? Even as she goes
Pottering around the island's peripheries she thinks
Of the obligations. And the sympathies, far stronger than bears.
I was a bush there, a hat on a clothes dummy's head. Receiving letters
Sat down. I avoided being punished. I said,
It's cutting the limbs off a tree but there was no
Tree and I had no saw. I was planning to have infinite egress
While keeping some factory on the surface exceedingly cold. It was
A good source of evening. Sweating, asleep in the after
Noons, later the morning of thumps, unwhittled questions, the freezing
    head. At night
Drinking whiskey, the fishermen were, everyone said, away.
A chrysanthemum though still full of splashes it
Has lost some little of its odor for my nostrils and a girl
In a chalk-pink-and-white dress is handing on the cliff
A glass of emerald water to a pin, or is it a chicken, as you get
Closer you can see it is a mirror made of the brawn
Of water muscles splashing that which has been.
My self, like the connections of an engine—rabbits and the new year—
Having puzzled out something in common, a blue stone duck
As if Homer Hesiod and Shakespeare had never lived at all
And we weren't the deposit. Weinstein puts on his hat
And the women go crazy. Some falter toward the sea. Wein-

Stein come back! But he is leaving. He says Leonard! Good-bye!
So Leonard invites us
To come and to see, where the white water bucket is a dashboard
Of this place to that. You will want to go swimming, and you will want to
    meet
These snobbish absurd Americans who inhabit
The gesso incalcations on the cliff. And we went like a nose
To a neighbor face. Sometimes tilting the grappa
Or in this case the ouzo it spills on my clothes or on yours, the world
    without us, the world outside
As when one of us was sick, which also brought the out world in.
And the art world meanwhile
Was strumming along. Individual struggles
Will long be remembered, of XXX's doing this,
Of YYYY's doing that.
Soap which will start lazily up from those types. Then
We remember to leave and also to stay. Janice said
It may not be hooked on right. Weinstein has been walking
Down a flowery way. Good-bye, nature lovers! he crescendoed.
A locked sail. The bullet of this button isn't right. And the train laughed
And pulled out pulling half of the station with it. The dust
Was indifferent to Americans as to Greeks. What simply was happening
Was beyond the rustication of ideas into the elements but essentially the
    same. Meanwhile, grasses matted,
The leaves winced, ideas one had had in earliest childhood days
Were surprisingly becoming succinct, maybe just before vanishing
Or turning into something you would feel like a belt,
Circling but not in hand. I would find these and set them down
On the sizzling white paper that was slipperier than the knees
That made me feel guilty, and sometimes heavier than the overcoats
    which there we never had
For someone's chest's attention. It was always distraction
But it was also a chair. And a chair is merely a civilized distraction. If
Character wasn't everything, it was something else I didn't
Know less than geography, which is to say, Surprise, Wonder,
Delight. You stood there and the stones
Of Old Greece and our lives, those collegiate stones,
Harvard, Emory, and Marymount, with the blue exegesis of the tide
Against which to fall was a headline—Don't stand.
You give this wish to me—Apollo, in some manner of time, lives on.
    Inside your mind
Things are being washed. Everything was docking

And we went down to see it. Memories of women made exactly the same
Kneeling down in the hot raft of daisies
It also got ragged for my walks. When are we going
To really have the time to have time? I make love to you
Like a rope swinging across a stone wall and you
Are lilacs reflected in a mirror or seen through a window.
Going out. You said I like this one. A pale pink dress
The suds were driving through the water. Moving fairly fast against the
just plain oxygen we ended up looking
A little bit overcome. But I got up
You got up. We went around
Spilling things and putting a few of them on racks.
Those were the important things we never got done
Because they were behind us or
Surpassing us, otherwise unavailable—cherry
Blossoms, clavicles of girls which I can't touch
In the innocuousness, beetles, burring and scampering around a rose
I see is no longer there. Blossoms on the walk we were here, were there
As much as the heat was. I dried my ear at the sink
Then dried the other and quieted my lips and my nose
With a briny dry towel and you slid upon your shoes
And Katherine jumped up, ran around. Soon she will be
Out as usual, down the roadway formally unopened
For my approach, as if not to be drunk
Were a confidence vote from the leaves for the turmoil inside
The ouzo-fed engines of ourselves, when, seated on slabs of wood
As roses on tough ground as eggs were on the morning, deciding to leave,
We oversleep the boat, a shirt, a white shirt gleaming
On the photographic exception of the tide. An airlane of styles.
If it was said, It's hopeless
And you said, The gardens are going over
The edge of the overside sidewalk. Well,
Maybe and maybe not. A foot, I thought (not very intelligently)
In a shoe of newspapers, even ice unstacked about by process—
I loved the texture of your talk, and another woman's
Breast had a texture of a late summer day, while your
Eyes were walking both inside your head and in me, in each of my
    activities
While you both found the cat and he was seated, alive,
Beyond ants, on some anthill pebbles and or gravel. The bar wasn't closed
Or open, it was daylight-surprised. Plate glass was nowhere around.
I looked up. I put on my glasses. There were all these artists

Hot with the prayers of nineteen sixty-one—
Let us be potters, or skunks, but not
Business men! I sat down on a stone
And looked around, my last chance
To never be a doctor, as if it meant something, and a father of four—
In these minutes, of fatal decisions. Decisions! Fatal! Lazy,
Air comes in. What could it have been
To be so exciting? And the Scotch tape jumped into the air
With Leonardo out in a boat, and, miles later, acropoles of bones the dead
Dinosaurs and cities, tied to subjects
All of us present have forgotten—women, failing the Weinstein
Of the season. Rather inform
P.M. while you are re-estimating buttons'
Life by leaving them long-ungone-for in the midst
Of the very short walks we take down the long
Bite narrow street—At night electricity is kissing
The emasculated stars—The new things we had done, in pencil at the side
   of the napkin.
It was hot. Ce qui veut dire we, a cat sitting
On a balcony a plant was wilting. What dialect are you speaking,
You, wearing the loafers of the sea? I couldn't care
For everything simultaneously. A mat was exciting enough. The bath
   came separately
From the dawn. You walk around
Simply looking for strawberries, sun, our baby, oxygen—
"Always not quite unbeginning to be or have been begun."
Leonardo erat other. Iras haec perturbat. Let that be. Another was
Absent in a habit fidget. I was
In a rush. Someone said, hush!
Calm down in this—knife—patterns of things—
Where is the music that's fitting for such an occasion
In those miles of hotel
Corridor followed by Weinstein's weeping at the beach
Girls who followed that for love of him
And why is there not more peaceful melting here
Into the wide wood story of the wall
How I loved those made of stone. And yet poetry has
Messages, interrogations of musics that have been used
In the various islands of acts, staying genuinely still,
And seeing—a piece of life and seeing—
It's a wall inside me
Why dancers were always coming out in a pageant

Wrecking the place animals were in there too
As now, so for music fit?
The pink spot you trotted me out to see with under the sigh which
Something and the great writers were all still alive
Much of the worst had happened, the envelope was still unpeeled.
I am stamping on the path. Alone. Nothing is so essential as this—
Moment. And a red fan wings past—flower? Transatlantic systems
    ourselves
The door unopened, the mail came every day. The grass is soft
Matted, and then there was an enclosure, tar on my leg, on yours
The culture all around us was in fragments, in some chests sure
In others fragments, in some no grasp at all, which I couldn't
Easily perceive, thus making everybody equal,
Almost at least enough to be a rival—perception,
Inspiration—too cloud to care. Voices
I heard on rooftops and cul-de-sacs of meditative sex
Scurried beyond the invisible barrier of you washing
The blouse. Brilliant. In fact, having more meaning
Because of all impulsions. You were
A blue coat—it wasn't
Exactly yours or mine or that place's
But a stinginess of life in packet flying through
Eventually, signing away like papers
A moment of the beach, when the tide dried the invincible
By elbows in comparison to the nude inside—
Look at—it's finished; this rock
Will come with me! Weinstein, walking in his sleep
The first afternoon when I arrived cooling bees they have a hive
Against the cliff, who've kept things in—the art
School, slacks. Normal the Mediterranean
Flows onward and on, boat,
I wore Leonard's jacket and my clothes, then shoes
Meet yours, advancing, so walk about the best
Final of beach, to not notice numbers
Except when they are speaking, as we stopped less
When all this was around.

# Twenty Poems

The diary is open at two o'clock.
Words of love are in it! Words of passion and of love!

2

HEROIC STANDARD

The street winds slowly through the meadow
Where a city once was. Thousands of bluets crawl to cover it
But the street winds on.

3

1958

The violets in the tempest withered, shrunk.
The toilet flushed. The air came liberally in the windows.
Workers went on strike. Somebody else was crazed by somebody else.

4

At the fish market we walked back and forth.
You were thinner. My doctorate was yet unsought.
I had produced "Variations on William Carlos Williams."
The grammar mistakes were everywhere, I thought.
A view was ours past the clinic.
Someone was starting a shop. Another one, this one,
That one, lived in a château. In Italy that's a palace.
I don't like him. We figured out
Everybody running about. Past the streetcar turn-
Around, dark white violets, breakfast, tones
And the roller skates slick on the cement, or tiles.

The personality of the feeding bin
The impersonality of the feed
In the stomachs of the birds a flower
Of hunger and of hunger satisfied. Then cold grips the street
As my hunger grips the flower of your heart. We eat
Dinner. We go to bed. We wake up. Impenetrable and mysterious life!

The dawn woke the hats up in Tuscany.
The flares woke the bats up egotistically.
Drinks are finished and songs put down
On tables and now the pianoforte begins.

He who addresses you
Turns around a hat
Once, he drinks
Glass after glass of something
Wine. He is not dead. He reminds
You of something else.
That's it! The Assumption.

THE SILENCERS

Eyes coveted your elbows;
Ears cupped against your heart.

## 9

ENVIRONMENT

Mist creeps into the environment;
Green is the grass, is the moss, is the whole environment.

## 10

Notices are sent up into the music
Telling the music to be silent
While the notes are being read
But the music which is made of notes
Does not understand
And the snow keeps falling.
The concerto goes on, a pandemonium of sound!

## 11

DISNEY BOHÈME

The stork A-plus Popeye and Olive Oyl sheep
Footsteps sur la neige Debussy
A warm Paris apartment/living with now dead people
Selling books eating idyllically straight from the pan

## 12

ART AND SOCIETY

Formlessness suggested by Debussy's
"Des pas sur la neige"
Copland's repeating the criticism that
Debussy was "bourgeois"
True he wrote in a protected world
No green ate away at his environment
Nor vagrants stormed his windows

None are purple with green rings
In the snow all footsteps are white

### 13

AFTER SOME VERSES BY MORVAEN LE GAÉLIQUE
AND PAUL VERLAINE

Did you call? or was that sound on the telephone
My bad sad beating heart
That only beats for you?
Et puis voici mon corps, not mon coeur,
My body, which is bitten by a barracuda,
And my course, which is straight for you.

### 14

Desire and curiosity
Make me feel I'm indestructible.
My actual fragility
Assails me as I write this poem.
And I put the pen down.

### 15

GORDU WISDOM

An elephant is larger than its master.
The forest is smaller than its trees.

### 16

Words penetrate a poem
As a dog penetrates a court;

Finding the gateway he wants he sees
His master coming toward him and he barks.

### 17

#### TO THE PROSPECT OF TIME

I too remember the summer afternoon
When I was completely happy and alone.

### 18

#### AT NIGHT

Nothing can sleep like irony. You say
One thing and you mean another. Oxygen is matrimony's brother.
When you sleep, you speak alone.

### 19

How many things we are attentive to!
Words spoken in sleep, the dog's paw, the emblem-
Atic significance of everything that is done and seen.
Winter, for example, with its damp sleet and boots.

### 20

Each moment fills him with a desire
For another moment and each incident he makes
As a result of this situation
Leads to another one and another one and another.
So she might be attracted to
Anyone! It frightens him. He says, She is not like me.
Then he loves her no longer,
For one second.

# Days and Nights

*1. The Invention of Poetry*

It came to me that all this time
There had been no real poetry and that it needed to be invented.
Some recommended discovering
What was already there. Others,
Taking a view from further up the hill (remnant
Of old poetry), said just go and start wherever you are.

It was not the kind of line
I wanted so I crossed it out
"Today I don't think I'm very inspired"—
What an existence! How hard to concentrate
On what is the best kind of existence!
What's sure is having only one existence
And its already having a shape.

*Extase de mes vingt ans*—
French girl with pure gold eyes
In which shine internal rhyme and new kinds of stanzas

When I said to F, Why do you write poems?
He said, Look at most of the poems
That have already been written!

All alone writing
And lacking self-confidence
And in another way filled with self-confidence
And in another way devoted to the brick wall
As a flower is when hummed on by a bee

I thought This is the one I am supposed to like best
The totally indifferent one
Who simply loves and identifies himself with something
Or someone and cares not what others think nor of time
The one who identifies himself with a wall.

I didn't think I was crazy
I thought Orpheus chasms trireme hunch coats melody
And then No that isn't good enough

I wrote poems on the edges of the thistles
Which my walking companions couldn't understand
But that's when I was a baby compared to now

"That is so much like you and your poetry."
This puts me in a self-congratulatory mood
Which I want to "feel out," so we sit together and talk
All through the winter afternoon.

I smoked
After writing five or ten lines
To enjoy what I had already written
And to not have to write any more

I stop smoking
Until after lunch
It is morning
It is spring
The day is breaking
Ten—eleven—noon
I am not smoking
I am asleep

Sense of what primitive man is, in cave and with primitive life
Comes over me one bright morning as I lie in bed
Whoosh! to the typewriter. Lunch! And I go down.
What have I lost?
The Coleridge joke, as W would say.

*William Carlos Williams*, I wrote
As the end word of a sestina. And *grass*
*Sleepy*, *hog snout*, *breath*, and *dream*.
I never finished it.

I come down the hill—cloud
I like living on a hill—head

You are so lucky to be alive—jokes
It chimes at every moment—stung

So much of it was beyond me
The winding of the national highway
The fragments of glass in the convent wall
To say nothing of the habits of the bourgeoisie
And all those pleasures, the neat coat,
The bought wine, and the enabling of the pronouncements

For Christ's sake you're missing the whole day
Cried someone and I said Shut up
I want to sleep and what he accomplished in the hours I slept
I do not know and what I accomplished in my sleep
Was absolutely nothing

How much is in the poet and how much in the poem?
You can't get to the one but he gives you the other.
Is he holding back? No, but his experience is like a bubble.
When he gives it to you, it breaks. Those left-over soap dots are the work.

Oh you've done plenty I said when he was feeling despondent
Look at X and L and M. But they don't do anything, he replied.

At the window I could see
What never could be inside me
Since I was twelve: pure being
Without desire for the other, not even for the necktie or the dog

### 2. The Stones of Time

The bathtub is white and full of strips
And stripes of red and blue and green and white
Where the painter has taken a bath! Now comes the poet
Wrapped in a huge white towel, with his head full of imagery.

Try being really attentive to your life
Instead of to your writing for a change once in a while

Sometimes one day one hour one minute oh I've done that
What happened? I got married and was in a good mood

We wrote so much that we thought it couldn't be any good
Till we read it over and then thought how amazing it was!

Athena gave Popeye a Butterfinger filled with stars
Is the kind of poetry Z and I used to stuff in jars

When we took a walk he was afraid
Of the dogs who came in parade
To sniffle at the feet
Of two of the greatest poets of the age.

The stars came out
And I was still writing
My God where's dinner
Here's dinner
My wife! I love you

Do you remember in Paris
When I was thinner
And the sun came through the shutters like a knife

I said to so many people once, "I write poetry."
They said, "Oh, so you are a poet." Or they said,
"What kind of poetry do you write? modern poetry?"
Or "My brother-in-law is a poet also."
Now if I say, "I am the poet Kenneth Koch," they say "I think I've heard
    of you"
Or "I'm sorry but that doesn't ring a bell" or
"Would you please move out of the way? You're blocking my view
Of that enormous piece of meat that they are lowering into the Bay
Of Pigs." What? Or "What kind of poetry do you write?"

"Taste," I said to J and he said
"What else is there?" but he was looking around.

"All the same, she isn't made like that,"
Marguerite said, upon meeting Janice,

To her husband Eddie, and since
Janice was pregnant this had a clear meaning
Like the poetry of Robert Burns.

You must learn to write in form first, said the dumb poet.
After several years of that you can write in free verse.
But of course no verse is really "free," said the dumb poet.
Thank you, I said. It's been great talking to you!

Sweet are the uses of adversity
Became Sweetheart cabooses of diversity
And Sweet art cow papooses at the university
And sea bar Calpurnia flower havens' re-noosed knees

A book came out, and then another book
Which was unlike the first,
Which was unlike the love
And the nightmares and the fisticuffs that inspired it
And the other poets, with their egos and their works,
Which I sometimes read reluctantly and sometimes with great delight
When I was writing so much myself
I wasn't afraid that what they wrote would bother me
And might even give me ideas.

I walked through the spring fountain of spring
Air fountain knowing finally that poetry was everything:
Sleep, silence, darkness, cool white air, and language


*3. The Secret*


Flaming
They seem
To come, sometimes,
Flaming
Despite all the old
Familiar effects
And despite my knowing
That, well, really they're not flaming

And these flaming words
Are sometimes the best ones I write
And sometimes not.

The doctor told X don't write poetry
It will kill you, which is a very late example
Of the idea of the immortal killing the man
(Not since Hector or one of those people practically)
X either wrote or didn't I don't remember—
I was writing (what made me think of it)
And my heart beat so fast
I actually thought I would die.

Our idea is something we talked about, our idea
Our idea is to write poetry that is better than poetry
To be as good as or better than the best old poetry
To evade, avoid all the mistakes of bad modern poets
Our idea is to do something with language
That has never been done before
Obviously—otherwise it wouldn't be creation
We stick to it and now I am a little nostalgic
For our idea, we never speak of it any more, it's been
Absorbed into our work, and even our friendship
Is an old, rather fragile-looking thing.
Maybe poetry took the life out of both of them,
Idea and friendship.

I like the new stuff you're doing
She wrote and then she quoted some lines
And made some funny references to the poems
And he said have you forgotten how to write the other kind of poems
Or, rather, she said it I forget which
I was as inspired as I have ever been
Writing half-conscious and half-unconscious every day
After taking a walk or looking at the garden
Or making love to you (as we used to say)

Unconscious meant "grace"
It meant No matter who I am
I am greater than I am

And this is greater
And this, since I am merely the vessel of it,
May be the truth

Then I read Ariosto
I fell to my knees
And started looking for the pins
I had dropped when I decided to be unconscious

I wanted to fasten everything together
As he did and make an enormous poetry Rose
Which included everything
And which couldn't be composed by the "unconscious"
(At least not by the "unconscious" alone)

This rose became a bandanna, which became a house
Which became infused with all passion, which became a hideaway
Which became yes I would like to have dinner, which became hands
Which became lands, shores, beaches, natives on the stones
Staring and wild beasts in the trees, chasing the hats of
Lost hunters, and all this deserves a tone
That I try to give it by writing as fast as I can
And as steadily, pausing only to eat, sleep, and as we used to say, make love
And take long walks, where I would sometimes encounter a sheep
Which gave me rhyming material and often a flowering fruit tree,
Pear apple cherry blossom thing and see long paths winding
Up hills and then down to somewhere invisible again
Which I would imagine was a town, in which another scene of the poem
    could take place.

### 4. Out and In

City of eternal flowers
And A said Why not make it paternal flowers
And Z said Or sempiternal There were bananas
Lying on the closet shelf by the couch
Forty feet from where your miscarriage began
And we were talking about this nonsense
Which meant so much to us, meant so much to us at the time.

Ponte Vecchio going over the Arno
What an image you are this morning
In the eye of almighty God!
I am the old bridge he said she said
I forget if it was a boy or a girl
A sexless thing in my life
Like sidewalks couches and lunch

Walking around nervously then going in the house
The entire problem is to sit down
And start writing. Solved! Now the problem
Is to get up. Solved! Now the problem
Is to find something equally worthwhile to do. Solved!
Thank you for coming to see me. But
Thank you for living with me. And
Thank you for marrying me. While
Thank you for the arguments and the fights
And the deadly interpellations about the meanings of things!

Your blue eyes are filled with storms
To alter and mildly disarrange an image of someone's, he said it about the
    eyelid
But you are crying. I have a pain in my side.

The idea of Mallarmé
That
Well that it was so
Vital
Poetry, whatever it was
Is inspiring
Is I find even more inspiring
Than his more famous idea
Of absence
And his famous idea
Of an uncertain relationship of the words
In a line to make it memorably *fugace*.

Absence and I were often in my room
Composing. When I came out you and absence were wielding a broom
Which was a task I hadn't thought of in my absence
Finally absence took over

You, me, the broom, my writing, my typewriter,
Florence, the house, Katherine, everything.

Well, I don't know—those were great moments
Sometimes and terrible moments sometimes
And sometimes we went to the opera
And sometime later the automobile squeaked
There is no such thing as an automobile, there is only a Mercedes or a
   Ferrari
Or a Renault Deux Chevaux is that a Citroën
There is What do we care what kind of car but
Often in the sunshine we did. That's
When we were traveling I wasn't writing.

You've got to sit down and write. Solved!
But what I write isn't any good. Unsolved!
Try harder. Solved! No results. Unsolved!
Try taking a walk. Solved! An intelligent, pliable,
Luminous, spurting, quiet, delicate, amiable, slender line
Like someone who really loves me
For one second. What a life! (Solved!) Temporarily.

What do you think I should do
With all these old poems
That I am never going to even look at again
Or think about or revise—Throw them out!
But if I raise my hand to do this I feel like Abraham!
And no sheep's around there to prevent me.
So I take another look.

We asked the bad poet to come and dine
The bad poet said he didn't have time
The good poet came and acted stupid
He went to sleep on the couch
But grandiose inspiration had arrived for him with the wine
Such was the occasion.

Long afternoons, when I'm not too nervous
Or driven, I sit
And talk to the source of my happiness a little bit
Then Baby gets dressed but not in very much it's

Warm out and off we go
For twenty minutes or so and then come back.

Everyone in the neighboring houses
And in the neighboring orchards and fields
Is busily engaged in doing something
(So I imagine) as I sit here and write.


## 5. Days and Nights

A B C D F I J
L M N R Y and Z were the friends I had who wrote poetry
Now A B and C are dead, L N and Y have stopped writing
Z has gotten better than ever and I am in a heavy mood
Wondering how much life and how much writing there should be—
For me, have the two become mostly the same?
Mostly! Thank God for the mostly! Last night with you
I felt by that shaken and uplifted
In a way that no writing could ever do.
The body after all is a mountain and words are a mist—
I love the mist. Heaven help me, I also love you.

When the life leaves the body life will still be in the words
But that will be a little and funny kind of life
Not including you on my lap
And looking at me then shading your beautiful eyes.

Do you want me to keep telling
You things about your
Poem or do you want me to stop? Oh
Tell me. What? I don't think
You should have that phrase "burn up" in the first line.
Why not? I don't know. It
Seems a little unlike the rest.

O wonderful silence of animals
It's among you that I best perhaps could write!
Yet one needs readers. Also other people to talk to
To be friends with and to love. To go about with. And

This takes time. And people make noise,
Talking, and playing the piano, and always running around.

Night falls on my desk. It's an unusual situation.
Usually I have stopped work by now. But this time I'm in the midst of a
    thrilling evasion,
Something I promised I wouldn't do—sneaking in a short poem
In the midst of my long one. Meanwhile you're patient, and the veal's
    cold.

Fresh spring evening breezes over the plates
We finish eating from and then go out.
Personal life is everything personal life is nothing
Sometimes—click—one just feels isolated from personal life
Of course it's not public life I'm comparing it to, that's nonsense vanity—
So what's personal life? the old mom-dad-replay joke or
Sex electricity's unlasting phenomenon? That's right. And on
This spring evening it seems sensational. Long may it be lasting!

It helps me to be writing it helps me to breathe
It helps me to say anything it gives me
I'm afraid more than I give it

I certainly have lost something
My writing makes me aware of it
It isn't life and it isn't youth
I'm still young enough and alive
It's what I wrote in my poems
That I've lost, the way Katherine would walk
As far as the tree line, and how the fruit tree blossoms
Would seem to poke their way into the window
Although they were a long way outside

Yes sex is a great thing I admire it
Sex is like poetry it makes you aware of hands feet arms and legs
And your beating heart
I have never been inspired by sex, always by love
And so we talk about "sex" while thinking a little about poetry

There are very few poems
Compared to all the thought
And the activity and the sleeping and the falling in love

And out of love and the friendships
And all the talk and the doubts and the excitement
And the reputations and the philosophies
And the opinions about everything and the sensitivity
And the being alone a lot and having to be with others
A lot and the going to bed a lot and getting up a lot and seeing
Things all the time in relation to poetry
And so on and thinking about oneself
In this somewhat peculiar way

Well, producing a lot, that's not what
Being a poet is about, said N.
But trying to do so is certainly one of the somethings
It is about, though the products I must say are most numinous—
Wisps of smoke! while novels and paintings clouds go belching over the
    way!

Poetry, however, lives forever.
Words—how strange. It must be that in language
There is less competition
Than there is in regular life, where there are always
Beautiful persons being born and growing to adulthood
And ready to love. If great poems were as easy to create as people—
I mean if the capacity to do so were as widespread—
Since there's nothing easy about going through a pregnancy—
I suppose we could just forget about immortality. Maybe we can!

Z said It isn't poetry
And R said It's the greatest thing I ever read
And Y said I'm sick. I want to get up
Out of bed. Then we can talk about poetry
And L said There is some wine
With lunch, if you want some
And N (the bad poet) said
Listen to this. And J said I'm tired and
M said Why don't you go to sleep. We laughed
And the afternoon-evening ended
At the house in bella Firenze.

# Cherche-Midi

The boxes
Are attractive there
An animal eats its hay
Now there's a car rental station
Where I used to stand gulping the air
And thinking Fresh paint!
Unpasteurized milk!
The essence is in the small glass on the shelf
The sense is in the line of the nose
And the dark eyes staring
A minuet steps out of your clothes

Inside you a foetus roamed
Above us a pigeon homed
The sun set like a dark star

Uncouth modern church bells
Park bench glistering so
I did it and didn't. The painted leg is gone
Moved down the hall. The quiet stairs are empty.

The problem is
That often, in the morning
It is not yet light
And daily life is gone.
The city is there
And the castle is there, with the stucco
Paintings, and the girl is there
With her painted leg—
If only you—
But already you
And so we seek the impossible

I.e. we look for something hard
To accomplish and in
Its experience we sense an end,
That is, an achievement, and
When I met you on the stairs
You said Ho ho ho you

Weren't part of the problem
I was hastening (hurrying)
Up there so I could write!
Write something, anything,
Can you understand that
Or are you always just
Going up and down the stairs with
That painted white platter on your head?
What a picture
You'd make! Botticelli, Giorgione,
The works. A major endeavor
To collate stucco with wit
And I am frothing
(Figuratively) at the mouth
By now with my verbal
Unstemmingness and the non finire
Of the god-knows-what-is-
Here-and-there-now style.
I was
Singing in the shower one fall day
Mood opened the kitchen
Stripes came out
You're on the stairs
And dead are the moments musicaux
Of the sea, where
My shoe is, about a foot and a half
From the painting. But I am
Thinking about you there
While I am here
When noon starts.

Can you, can I
Be satisfied by the masses of time
We're always looking for desire
Like a dime
It's what counts
Your foot mounts
The stair
And walks are everywhere

Walking later
Or sleeping on the floor

This is a pleasure and a confusion
As a camel makes a white vexed swirl
Of the desert sands

The sun is shining
The sum is divine and you are out
I am in; my paper is fine
It proceeds (forward) exceeds (backward)
Until everything is at the same time
False and true
To the invisible
Not giving way
To minor crises of anger and rage
And staying on the boat
Sometimes
Wandering from one hemorrhage
To another of the interview
Often ready to be inquired
Of by some passing desire "Where are you?
And exactly what are you, too?
And in what state of steam is your flesh?"

Strings like stories shine
And past the window flakes of paper
Testimony to live valentine
A gracious start then hand to the chest in pain

And, looking out that window,
I see the boxed window clasped again
By what this series of moments is and is not.

When it shines and is hot, it is cold somewhere, Commander.
This envelope, filled with what is not,
Will soon hold a letter.
Inside the letter will be a heart.
I must sit down and write.
Fortune, what does it mean I "must" write?
I think it means nothing.
It is light sorrow experiencing some fleshy tang.
People are hammering murdering plates

To run up and down stairs with, as if
The result were the cause of the bout
With this day of walking in and out
Whether whirled in rage
Or in a sudden wish to be loving or
Conquer something we sit down, brainily,
Breathing, there seem to be only
Two themes (perhaps four or three)
Which engross us really, the
Theme of what I am doing here and
That one of how is this for you

In summer the abstract words
Accompany me to the interview
And till the rickety clickety train
Went slumping past
Accordions I couldn't be sure exactly
What to say "J'ai guéri ta
Petite amie," the doctor said
Galleries are open or closed.
The Dôme is old and sad.
Perhaps it was a mark on an army
Perhaps the broken arm was seriously bleeding

Perhaps I'll stand up
And perhaps you'll come with me
Where Sunday mornings spell
Anxious commerce to our breathing

She is also your daughter
And the smiling inside
The window, that will never be again

And no one wants it to be
Its sad quality is like a color taken from a shelf
Or maybe it isn't. In black and white it is a daylight
Scene. The water flows past
The place where once he or she was.
A mop is flapping against the door
And the street is alone with history.

They eat dinner and close the door
We go out and come in

Related to putting everything off
Related to the gaga mess of sensation
And thought, related to your relations
And to the baggage
Related to death, yours and mine
And everyone else's, the harm that's done,
To heartbeat and to paralysis
Each morning in the sun
Getting (up) out, glad to be alive
Now we have an elevator (ride)
Into the ravenous day
Ravingly beautiful and egregious

As M. said of D.B.
If you can't change it in
The middle—not at all
Family with too much money
Birds with too many wings

I throw the football
And wait for you to sit down
Then you were gone and generous again
And sleep was escaping me
My head knocked otherwise
You came down the stair

Oh tell me what is this history,
Pure, of the foot? Of the curious lance?
Of the apartment vacated by a footfall? Who is that
Sitting in my chair? My self. My son,
August, July, June. He who was never
Born, the mad one, the one crazy over women
And drugs, the one who never saw
Or would know what to do with
A spatula, a losing streak, or a pump, phantom.

Another time it seems
A long time to be new.

And E. said I knew she wasn't, because
She wasn't pretty enough.
I am having trouble
With this time scission. Bump bump.

The roses wear Mercurochrome on their labels
Because they spit at me with thorns.
And S. said, That's very sexy (about a stanza).
I thought, Oh well, happy, thump. It was something Christmas
For Thanksgiving, death's-heads for the New Year.
If one was sad, another was plunging into the soul
Of things, wherefrom cometh the truth.

My notepaper suggests to me
A revelation
Weren't those surrealist streetcars leaving their traces
On my cobblestoned mind in a way that I had immediately to erase
So you could see them better? Pregnant, and happy, and lost.
As if the whole world were contained within you
You are lost in the one outside, like balls and bats.

Only it is quite a lot
To be trying at any one time
The rent was—bang! My
God! I hope you didn't fall down
But it was only the
Typewriter of the sun
Getting too close to the window
As usual unmarked
By anything except the bars
They leave on unmarked windows—in the courtyard
Sunlight

Sleeping on the floor, O Sunday
Mornings of unless-
We-get-it-right!
The sea brought leaves together
And here's a plant—
Now there's an ant
Making its way along that window line
And all is done.

Youthful happiness is done,
With those aesthetic decisions
Earliest muse makes.
You walked out on the hard
Earth surface hard as cement
It was between Christmas and Lent
All our money was spent

You are on the stairs
Carrying a plate
The ant needs a mate
Needs a mate to do what with?
Sometimes it seems
That one place
And another is enough.
But then the truth starts
Don't want to die don't want to lose
What dying constantly renews
One small round era of the eye

In other days, in other lives
The sense of this one?

Astonished giants spark the ocean's side
Alone there for fifty years

When you were at the interview
These monuments are minutes because they are alive
A seagull flies toward them, that is my mind, then goes away
You had to figure out which one was me
And try to be nice to it. Hello there!

Like a hammer that's been covered with hay
Like breath, like breasts
Like clams opening and closing themselves
Like always looking for what you always never knew
Could be in taking off your shoes when you were alive
And writing, though it never became less blue
Or more so than one morning in Paris
When I was looking out the window
That moment had no importance at all

Such diffidence!
It's made of lead.

It mixes adventure with self-protection
We dressed up to go to the plays
Japanese drama which is so far from my intention
Seemingly legs
Legs in the morning and legs at night
As if all the between times of day
Were not spent I say
With this frenetic happiness true
To whatever arises in you

They walk and are running
A pretty girl made them run over borders
Of cement until where she had given orders
She could be expected and when not there
Was replaced by the loneliness recreation
Of what I could not expect, just air and
Expectation outside there, still walking around a lot
With thinking I am nothing but
Repository of these sensations
Which yet are not what I'm about
To say to the stairs
A moving theme, and the reflection
Of the bourgeois tractor going past.

The problem in the morning
Is knowing this and that
And what is the day supposed to do with that?

I establish five things in the interview
Our apartment is like a hat
The elevator goes up and down
Now there are only stairs

Stark white lights over sleephood—
To compose
To veritably verily veritably compose

In B flat
In you, English Language, like a storm

Tossing against the wall
So suddenly! restlessly! and when awake
I was shooting the rent gap
By writing
But not crap
The good English language of the walls
Oh the sidewalks they are simply the bugs' walls
Sideways in action

We expect to live seventy years
Even eighty, ninety, or more
Pour quoi faire? On the stroke
Of eight o'clock to say It's here
The dinner is served in the alcove! while expediting
I am waiting
I walk around
While the hammer hits
With a pie-plate sound
(Come to the interview!)
On whitest sidewalks
(And try that trill again)
Inside me is something that is cold
And starry and outside
Are you, restoration and score
I'll take this necklace yes
And bracelet bone
Good morning, streets
Red is a diamond
Red is more than a color
As the Communist poets say, though
I don't mean it that way
This crocus morning.

Go in. Gratifying.
Nothing happens. Can I speak
To the person I am supposed to interview?
"I'm not at home"—
Like people on the rivers
Dreaming of the strong breasts and the happiness of scissors

When I look at the window
Just beyond it, there, across the street

This is how they live it, one foot
On the floor, then, head on the table, then
Other foot high
On the stairs

Street under plate and the sound
Of all that has gone on
In the evening, morning, to sit down
Passing it off as eternity, when really—

The roof shows
How the rain feels

Good morning, spendthrift
Or is that only a butterfly
I wouldn't mind
I wood end mine ud
Together we're free as a cow
When I write two legs are displaced

I am up at eight thirty
And ringing a doorbell at ten
Can you see me? We agreed

Oh I know but—that baby's smile again
And the woman at the window
Out on the balcony she steps
Hair blows in the wind
Cutting the earth in two
With a memory: daily life—silent—and the sun
That is falling today

# The Green Step

The green step was near the two girls, five-year-olds, in white rather stiff dresses cut out of lace the way valentines sometimes used to be, and they gesticulated toward it, little fingers pointing this way and that. A bird landed twenty feet away from it. The green step was cold and alone. This step had green carpeting on it which had once been mold, a sort of wet tough tissue of mashed-down grass, stems and leaves—"step mulch." At some time this had changed to a carpet. This carpet was much the same color as the mold of green, though less cold to touch, and with a different smell, not dank and brackish but slightly musty, with a suggestion of chalk or of glue. Underneath this covering, the step was gray-white stone. The step led to the front door of a house. It also led to a small auditorium's stage. It led, once, to a place where a throne began. It led to a place where there is a statue surrounded—on all sides, at a distance of five feet—by columns. The statue is of Diana, the goddess of the chase and of the moon. The white columns around this goddess who so affected the inside and the outside of the woods are not much like trees, although they are tall, straight up, and sometimes cold, and one could hide behind them, hide behind one of them if one were small and slim enough. And this, one of the little girls once did. That was before the step led to a concert stage or into a house. The place with the columns seemed, though no one knew why, to have been the first place to which the step went.

Standing on the step one felt between one place and another. Those who went to see the statue of Diana, those who went to the concert or into the house, had never met the man who made the step. The step was originally a random step in the woods. It led a wild life, not wild in itself but lying amidst nature, and being part of it, in random arrangements. A very long time ago the arrangement had been changed by an earthquake; more recently, by a man. That was the man who made the step. He took pleasure in finding the stone, in carrying it away with him. The next day he made the step. The bird flew some distance away.

That was only one time the step was made. At other times it was changed and became different steps. What happened to the step at one time or another did not very much affect the main characteristic, for most of those who used it or even those who saw it, of the step. Its main quality was that it was solid, it could be relied on, it would take you from one place to the next. Oh, people had fallen off the step, but that was never due to any fault of the step. They fell because they were ill, suddenly, or because they had drunk too much alcohol, or even, sometimes, because they were pushed. Not everyone who came up on the step was welcome at all times to whoever happened to be at the top of the step, or rather where the step led to. However the step is not very high, and no one has been seriously hurt from falling when he was standing on it.

The step had no consciousness of the change in its existence from being amidst wild nature to being a part of something that an animate and mobile species had turned into an object which served one of its manifold purposes. The step had, in fact, no consciousness of a world at all. Children would look at the step, sometimes, and think it felt something, but there is no evidence that it did. The step was there, and one day someone stepped on it who killed the bird.

The house the step leads to is a large house with bedrooms upstairs, and a large living room and dining room downstairs and a modern kitchen. It was built a long time ago but the family who own it live somewhere else and the house is rented to a father, a mother, and a son. The son is a hunter. The father spends his days placing cards in a long rectangular cardboard box. The mother goes into different rooms of the house and her clothing almost always has pleats. The member of the family who spends the most time on the step is the son. He will stand there leaning and looking out at the life of man and nature beyond the house. A domestic servant will sometimes stand there, too, replacing the boy.

The stone that forms the basis of the step, under the green carpeting, is slightly veined with grayish white in a way that suggests distances. The lines move outward and suggest a beyond that no one in the story is able to get to. The stone is thought to be made up of rapidly moving electrons, though this is not part of the common experience of anyone who sees it.

The step in the concert hall is the step that goes to the house and that goes to the throne. The throne is made of majolica, silver, and amber. No one is sitting on the throne. No one is playing in the concert hall. The house is rotting, empty, and is being destroyed. The sound of bulldozers, the noise of drilling things fills the street. There is dust everywhere around, making one passer-by think "I would like to get out of all this; I'll go to a concert." The man with a blue hat says, "It is foolish to waste this step." The step is taken to, and sold for a very small sum to the man who arranges performances in the concert hall. Before, leading to the stage, he had only a rotting wooden step. It's a strange thing to buy, he thinks, a step, but yes, I guess I can use it. Now there is an irregular noise—tuning up of instruments. When the concert is over, the people go out into the street. In the air, for a moment, are their comments on what they have heard.

Now night invests the street, and the step leads to a throne. High above the buildings and the trees, azure, blood- and sulphur-colored formations move about the sky. On her head appear three stars for a crown. Her feet, like clouds, are white. Thundering over the universe, the rainstorm washes this away. Washes her away.

When someone speaks of the step, which had once been part of the house, another says that then there was no green carpet on the step. That would only have been when the step was inside a building. Now in the concert hall, yes, there is green carpeting covering the step, but not before. It is even possible to argue, lightly, as to whether or not it is the same step.

Ideally the step would be part of the procurement of some sort of final fulfillment for everyone, and perhaps it is. The woman knows she will have to sell the piano. She sits down to play it, and once again the child starts to cry. The old man looks at the step and remembers the bird. Every day, for a week, as a child, he had seen it. The concert hall seems to become for him a sort of temple with yellow and white mists beyond, and green and vermilion stripes among its columns, and where one who is a statue, in a final wash of violets and whites, leans over to him and plants a stony kiss on his trembling face. Ah! he screams aloud and everyone turns to look at him. They do not see what is the matter. He walks in the woods. Every day is like a light kiss given by the country, by its air, by its sun, by its trees. There still seems to be no reason to think of a king or a god. Feet tread on the step and the trigger is released. Birds fly in a dance of blood-splatters all over the wall—a painting much later than Cézanne. In the morning the step is nothing and no one in anyone's thoughts. Contracts are made at the Bourse and on the real estate tables. Flies buzz hopelessly against the windows. Men in shirtsleeves, in billows of cigarette smoke, say, "We must take the first step." A dog jumps up, its paws against a little girl's white dress. Her mother is miles away, in a car. The old man is here. A servant comes down the step and picks the child up.

The blue, fluffy bird lands on a gray stone and looks around him. Who knows if he hears the white-blue brook that is going by? He certainly hears, smells or feels something, because, perched on this stone, he dips his beak once, twice, three times in the bubbly stream. This brook starts in the mountains—well, really they are just tall hills, which, in back of the houses, rise toward the once-supposed geographical location of heaven, which is now thought either to be a myth, or, if it does represent something really existing, then to be something that can be found in our own bodies, thoughts, and hearts. About the brook, sitting on the ground, was a rather varied group of people: a young girl from India, in a sari, with a spot of blue paint or some kind of cosmetic, on her forehead, named Shara; a boy from the United States, with a great mop of hair; a young Frenchman whose heart was even now beating only faintly, and who, unbeknownst to himself and everyone else there, would soon be dead; and a French girl, about seventeen, with a rather wide forehead, blue eyes, and a dreamy smile. Her name was Hélène. The men's names were not as important as the girls' names. They had not yet come, for anyone there, to represent high states of abstraction for things beautiful and loved.

The bird, suddenly aware of the people, flies off. The French girl looks at the bird. "How beautiful it is!" "Comme il est beau!" The young French-man's gravestone is five miles away, two miles from the nearest point of the brook. The Indian girl pushes her sari lightly and holds it against the wind. She is like someone, the young American thinks, whom I have seen, read about, in a story. There is an aureole on her hair, caused by the light reflecting from the brook.

As a child he thought of this brook. It was not where he lived. André stands up suddenly and feels dizzy. Out of his pocket he picks an *image d'épinale*. "Here," he says to the American girl, she was now there, legs of her coming up over the path and the stones, "take this because you're so pretty." "Prends donc cela parce que tu es si belle." Si jolie. For her, this man had an important name: André. André de la Fiscourt. The brook ran past very quickly, and it was not clear to anyone there why it seemed to make them feel so much.

Inside it are a great many small stones. Some of these stay in place for a while and then are moved. Shara picked up a little stone, looking at it. Midwinter, February, and a rather warm day. There was a chill in the air, all the same. There is blood on your face. That's from my razor. He wipes it off. A few miles away Cézanne is painting. The snow melts in the hills and the rain falls down. André gave a purple flower to Dorothy. In the morning, after the storm, there are flowers on the ground. Prends donc cela parce que tu es si belle. The brook runs by. If she were not the American girl he would love her. He loves her because she is. He was terribly excited by her. When the brook is dry, it is the bed of the brook. Ants struggle through it, carrying things which, for their tiny bodies, are enormous. When the paintings are carried into the museum, the brook remains. Sometimes it seems like nothing. I read it and thought about you. The old man's heart is steady. How senseless that André should die. They look at each other.

In the mountains—the hills—the way things happen to the brook are the way things happen in memory. Down here it is something else. André caught his arm with his other hand as he tripped, off balance. Dorothy said Good morning. Tiny particles of liquid constantly evaporate from the stream. This made, sometimes, a haze. The dog ran up to the group. The bird flew away.

The old man didn't see all this. He went away from the brook. He is a living repository of memories. He is Spanish music, never far from the popular echoes of the guitar. He is the novel in which someone is dead. He is another book of poetry.

When she stepped so close to him, his heart fell down. It seemed to. He went looking for it someplace on the ground. She was there, too. He knew what this was about. Music gives a faint reflection, but, unlike the brook, which is content to let everything pass, it uses whatever it has to construct something else. Allons à la maison, let's go to my house. It is right there on top of the hill. It is a very small hill, in fact. And so they go up to it. The brook flows down, in another direction.

### 3. The Stone

Sun on the stone. Blond hair beside it. When she gets up, there is sun. He clears the path. The dog runs after the bird. It waits for hours, days, months. Adultery was unheard of at that time. On the path there is a stone. This can be anyone. No harm comes to it. I was lying there, she says, and suddenly I got this idea. Wanted to see you, that's all. The bird flew high, and away. There is a distance of several hundred yards between the terrace with flowers and the stone.

He had some ideas as he took the walk that went past the stone. He is at the telephone. Didn't come to the concert. He is a child compared to the stone. It shows almost no symptoms of change. Some slight flaking, some depetrification is taking place. The old man wept. When the weather changed only slightly, sky grew darker, and bird fell down. It was, near the rock face, moist and humid, but no man or woman was close by. The bird fell into a deserted place. She says I wonder. She had gotten up a long time before.

The stone is a boundary. It may be a headstone when someone dies. It may be split into various pieces and used in many ways. The girl walked to the desk of the hotel. The stone pointed the way to where the ruins could be seen. It is not itself a ruin in the strictest sense of anything. The plain old stone. His hand on hers was hot. Blood coursing through his veins. I can't go with you, she said. His hand is against the stone. "Why?"

The birds flew over the stone and the clouds flew over the traces of the birds. Above the clouds, at night, there was the silverware of paradise. That is when the stone begins to increase. It has been stable for what seems like eternity. Like everything and everyone else it is the remains of an astonishing original event. The dog is panting—hot. "I—I don't know myself." Later, this changed.

I'm not jealous of anybody, the young man said. That morning the old man woke. He said, Will you see him? I have not seen him for a long time. I am a little jealous. The young woman, the old man, and the young man were all from the same country. The bird flew above it. Shooting white fuzzballs exacerbate the morning summer air. When it is blue tonight—the stone cools. The stone is hot. The young woman brings something small, a package. It is far from the stone. I am not jealous of anybody. There is the stone, the land, and the bird. People made a fuss around it. The girl is wearing white, which goes very well with her blond hair. She holds up one arm in her excitement, in such a way that the wind touches her sleeve and twists it around. Then the chanting begins. A young fly stopped buzzing, long before. To see her tonight. The shadows were tough as though drinking the stone. Stars spit on it.

The stone can easily be imagined to have been there since the beginning, thrown by volcanic force. I hoped you could spend the night. The breath is steady, then flurried and a little sharp. Two hearts pounding. It stays that way for what seems a very long and a very short time. There is fast breathing. She called him gaily over the balustrade. Next month. This year. He walks back and forth. The young woman cries. For some it is a central location.

The dog ran over a path, which was a path of leaves. To one side of the path, about thirty yards from where the dog began, there was a stone. Briefly in the depth images of his eyes, and in the more mysterious images of his olfactory sense, rode the sight and the smell of the stone. And then it was forgotten, completely blank. The old man moves from behind a chaise longue on which the dog has been sitting, chases him off it, and goes out the door. The dog does not follow. He is so restless. Booming. The construction, still, is over there, unmenacing to the stone. The old man said it was a most unusual Sunday. Usually they were sitting in the restaurant, but today those familiar habits are disturbed.

She takes off her coat and her blouse and her skirt. The weather is warm. The stone sits still. It depends on how old she is. The world revolves. Now it is silent. No one, within human memory, had ever effectively moved it.

## 4. The Train

This car cannot be backed up once the others around it start moving. The fir-treed landscape skims away. Books fly this way and that. *The Lace Boxes. A Voyage to the Lands Beyond the Seas. The Indifference of Night and of Sky and of Water.* So it moves, as if destined. Listen, it is half past eleven.

The silver train shines. It descends toward the ocean and runs alongside it. A woman is in a shaded garden, where a white-coated waiter is serving her champagne and she says, "He may have missed the train." She says this to herself. White lace. You see this on her. In the distance, though, you can see the train, its silvery shining.

Jean-Claude walked toward the coast this afternoon with Nina and Henriette and they all three see the train. The train sees nothing, thinks nothing, and does not have to. Fueling, to it, is a necessity. The man enters the compartment—he is twenty-three. Anne is there—a baby.

The phone rang and she went into the house. The room was filled with sunlight. Outside, the house cast a dark, cool shadow. Inside the train there is hurtling and sunlight, shadows and drastic combinations of noises and light. It has been moving for hundreds of miles. The clouds cover the sun but the darkness at this moment might come, also, from the train. Inside there, tables are firmly attached. In the house they move the furniture. The fluffy bird lands. And, at the noise of the train, flies away.

The train wreck causes consternation for miles around. Some people were injured, but not killed. It was not the old man. The sun goes around in the sky. It makes a perfect circle. Not quite. The train goes past.

The woman knew that if she got on the train where she lived, it was capable of taking her elsewhere. The train stayed in the station for a little while. It could be boarded by anyone who had a ticket for it. Once inside it, the places you could go and the directions you could go in were restricted. This was not, though it could seem like, a penalty imposed on you in exchange for the fact that the train was going so rapidly from place to place itself, outside.

When he came to see her, she had written to him. She writes about trains for a school composition. The waiter pours the champagne. The students rush out of their compartments onto the station platform, but he does not appear. Ah, yes, there he is now—Father Desportes! My child! she says, and her little girl runs into the garden. So much human happiness, or the possibility of happiness, in every place to which the train goes.

The little girl isn't on the train. There is another one. She is wearing a white lace dress and is so small she has to be helped up the step that leads to the compartment in which she and her father and her mother are sitting. Or are going to sit. The train moves. It makes a whistling noise. The story of the wheels and the track is writing itself across the country. There is heat between these two, which the tracks lose and the wheels retain. The people inside the train are swallowed by distance. The distance is swallowed by the train. The glasses clink against each other. Is this movement from outside or in? She stands, then sits back down. They were gone, and she was there.

Tremendous pieces of metal soar through the air and then are pounded and soldered together. Almost incredibly, the form of a locomotive appears. She stands up, her face and her white lace dress, too, entirely in shadow. He missed the train. He is there, now, almost at the garden door. After several buckets of champagne, the men smoked long cigars. The train pulled into the station. The train was almost invisible. The train disappeared.

The train went heroically backwards and forwards on its path. Sometimes it hurtled the startled professionals sideways. A baby cried. A mother laughed. A dog barked. The train doesn't last, in its present shape, as long as the stone. It is scrap metal. Some of this is used in new trains, which run along. The train brings the man to the woman. They cry, and hold each other in their arms. A child screams. She laughs. She runs down the hill. At last she does get on it and it goes away.

### 5. The Book

The book was *The Poems of Guillaume Apollinaire*, translated into English. Then the book was *Alcools*. It has a white paper cover that is slightly smoother and heavier than the pages inside. Each page has a number, and the pages are stuck together. One has to use a knife, or something like it— a sharp postcard will do—to get them apart.

There is a public garden on the postcard, which is lying between two pages of the book *Alcools*, in French, by Apollinaire. When the pages have all been cut, the postcard is put away. The book was sewn and pasted together someplace outside Paris. After it was printed and bound, it was sold. Someone read it who wished to become a saint. Someone read it who said "God damn it!" Someone read it who liked to tear things apart.

The book went everywhere. Though it spoke, it was blind, deaf, mindless, and dumb. It got damp and took a long time to dry off. A baby touches it. Don't! Years later the baby reads the book, but in translation. Then at last the white original is hers. Sitting in the café, smiles. She goes inside.

The city in which she reads the book is the subject of much that is said in the book, but when she raises her eyes she sees the two things, text and city, are very little the same, in fact are totally unlike. An ant walks on the page and is more like the letters on the page. The margin of the page is more like the empty white sky.

The words in the book speak of the city. Her heart beats in her chest. The words do not beat. They are stationary. Apollinaire, sitting in the cafe on the Place de X, writes the first lines down. Before the book is published these lines may change, or may entirely disappear. He is wearing a white shirt with a loose collar and a blue-gray foulard tied around his neck. He is the writer and she is the woman. Another one is the father, who is also the man. Also, he, the father, writes. Using the back of the book as a table, he writes, "Guillaume Apollinaire." The girl smiles and picks up the unsigned book. The signed book lies on the table. The book is signed. It is unsigned. *Alcools* contains thirty-eight poems. His father had never seen this book, nor his father before him. Nor had the father and grandfather of the woman. Some of these people lived before the poems were written. The book was not published.

Apollinaire was not born. Now he is in existence. The girl picks up the book and opens it at random. "Annie," "Cortège," "La Chanson du mal aimé." The words lie flat on the page. Not quite completely flat but almost. It reappears, in fresh white new stiff clothes, new covers and paper. When it is worn, they decide whether or not to replace it. The book falls on a step and is immediately picked up.

André gives the book to Dorothy. She is unable to read it. The young woman sits in the café. The weather is gray, and even at a short distance things become dim. The old man smiles at her. The rain is falling. She stands up. She wipes some water off the book. He is now a rather young man. May I help you into the taxi. Thank you. Their housemaids clean away the plates and the glasses. A horn sounds. Smoke comes out of the chimney. Apollinaire is born. The mother is nervous. Have you read this book?

The book is printed by a large firm. The roof of the building does not slant. Inside there is the noise of printing presses. *Alcools* emerges from these machines. This book lies on a table. This book is in a young girl's hand. Another book is by Éluard, another by Max Jacob.

The man and the young woman embrace. She says "I can't" and then "I can." The book doesn't move. In the café the book is with someone else. It is autumn. He goes past. Apollinaire writes "Cortège." Children run out of a graveyard and dance. Colors are spread out across windows. A garden filled with roses and a villa which is like a rose. All this is in the book. In the restaurant. The smoke and the service and the smiles and the clutching of hands. Nothing can separate us now. He loved her, but she was unable to love him back. "I don't know why."

From the book ideas fall like snowflakes over foreheads at the cafés bent over the problems of creating a modern classic. The classic forms instantly. Like a newspaper. Coffee is steaming in the cups. He pays for the book and leaves the store.

Where are you going. The book flies into her bag. I am late. Smell of cinnamon. When will you call me. It is held together by tightly sewn threads, and it lies on the table. Apollinaire's experience is inside the book, in a strange form: printed letters—capital and small ones—commas, periods, dashes, spaces. On top of each poem are letters slightly larger than those inside it. Tomorrow, the young woman laughed—and she tossed back her hair. Later he picks it up and begins to read.

### 6. The Music

When the woman heard the music, it was not for the first time. Nor was this the first woman, nor was it the first woman who ever heard the music. The letter arrives with the tickets. We must get dressed up! The white gloves, the shoes, and the sidewalks will carry us. There were five men, or four men and one woman. White neckties hit white shirts, while to either side a neat curving line of black velvet descends. The violin starts, and then there is the sound of a piano. One man and one woman went into the hotel. Today we have a special performance—of Mozart's Quartet for Strings and Piano, Köchel listing 493.

This is the day that Dorothy goes to the concert. André goes. The musicians perform. They do not wear white gloves. Their music is on the page. It is by them picked or strung or brushed or blown into their instruments, and it leaps out, at each second, totally changed.

From far away there is nothing. When you are close to the building, some faint sounds are hearable from inside. Insects are singing. The concert has been planned for months, was organized last year. The music is by Mozart.

She invited them to go with her to the concert. The old bent woman in black clothing walked past the concert. The concert was at nine o'clock. Another is at three. Music was played in the hall. The old man at the concert did not know the old woman who was walking by. She was a new character in the story, and she lived in the mountains. The music slipped out of the instruments and glided away. The men who play the instruments went after it, with their fingers and their mouths, and brought it back. At the hotel, across the street, it is very quiet, and the man and woman look at each other. The music was by Mozart, his Quartet for Strings and Piano, Köchel 493.

An old woman in a lace dress leans forward to tap on the wood of the piano with her fan. November, seventeen sixty-two. Mozart is very young. He wears white knickers with a gold-colored belt. His wrists touched by sleeves, his head tossed back, he sits at the piano.

Two hundred concertgoers are in this auditorium. One of them is a man who was once attacked by a bear in a city zoo. His shoulder still shows scars where the animal's claws dug into him. He was forced to stay in the hospital for a long time. An undertaker is also at the concert. And Shara is there. And one hundred and ninety-seven others. Many "society" ladies are among them. Some of them love music. For others the concert hall is a fashionable place to go. Their dogs are at home, rambling through the furniture. The maid chases one of them off a settee. No, Boxer, you mustn't! The sea decorates its eyelids with piers and stars as the fantastic night in Istanbul breaks through the historical webbing, as a story is broken through by its writing, and as the music is broken through by the fact that it is a concert at which there are two hundred people and the sound of the instruments is of fibre and wood. Something takes the shape of an animal, is about to attack him, draws a valentine in the little girl's mind. How does she happen to be at the concert? Her father is there. Some woman is introducing herself as her mother. What did you say they were going to play? I don't know. The music cannot get through to the Turkish Ambassador. The girl has to relax very hard to make the Mozart decorate the valentine in the way she thinks she wants it to. Some things are too sweet to be named. The future seems there in her consciousness. When she lives, it is the present all the time. He was sitting in a middle row and she near the front. At first they don't see each other. Later they do.

When you were going to the concert, you got all dressed up. White satin blouse, black silk skirt, alligator handbag, and off you go. She powders her nose. The music begins. The violins go very far, then the viola comes, the bass, and then the piano. It is like a brook, rippling. It moves around. The woman is at home. He is at the concert. The bird does not see him. The apricot tree is in blossom. Her cheekbone appears. The man lies down next to his dog. Waking up, the woman was surprised by the music. The young man felt overwhelmed by it.

Dorothy loved music. She loved it more than anything else except André. There are several white limed statues on the hill. The old man did not come to this concert. Shara did, however. She had never gone back to India, as it was originally planned that she would. Nor did the American boy marry her. The concert was scheduled to begin at two o'clock. There were many people who were unable to attend.

The mother sings to the baby. Her song has one quality of the music. She doesn't believe it is exactly that which she wants. There is a definite pleasure in this, but in the Mozart there is more. She has to find someone to stay with the children. Her mother comes in. She had loved the old man as much as life, as breath. The music begins. The music begins again. At each moment she was able again to listen the music was beginning. She would have to learn to listen to music better. He would have to learn to live without her. He would have to learn to live with her. The composer has his work. The people are scattered about. They were both smiling, too. The incredibly sweet sounds of the violins stopped. The little girl—where is her valentine? Perhaps, her mother says, you left it on the train. The old woman wasn't looking—she walked right into the path of a car. Father Desportes ran over to the garden where the citizens were waiting for the mayor to speak. Come quickly! he cried. The concert is going to begin. Ideally, the music would have shown all these people how to live, taught them a harmony they could master in their own lives. Its elements, however, were so different from the elements of their lives—even its terms— *andante*, *stretto*, *largo*, and the rest—that it was impossible for it to do that. It seemed to some to suggest a paradise they couldn't have. This was only, of course, if it was viewed as leading to something other than itself.

### 7. *The Woman and the Man*

In the room there is a chair, a mirror, a window, and a bed. The woman takes off her blouse and the man approaches her. Many years before, the sun shone through the trees and the brook ran across the pasture. The woman is someone he has never seen.

When they placed their hands on each other's bodies, it seemed strange to think of anything else. They were not always doing that. Since, however, it gave more pleasure than anything else they did, they never could decide how often to do it, when to do it and when not.

The man was the conductor of the orchestra at a concert and the man who killed the bird. The woman was the young woman who had loved the old man. The statue of Diana was the model of the form of the woman, and the statue of Apollo the model of the form of the man. When the old man saw these statues, he cried. He had never learned how to accept such a thing. The old man is the man and the young woman is the woman. The Mayan woman is the woman. The Mayan man is the man. The sun shines on the dead shoulder of the man. The shoulder regains life and it moves. The wall is neither the woman nor the man, but with grass and with insects, and the wind in it, it is alive. The life in the wall dies down and the weather turns cold. The woman screams. The man shouts, and the boat comes in toward the dock.

The man places his hand on the woman's shoulder. The street runs backward from where you are. Eventually you do not care what anyone thinks. If it is a street, it is there for you to walk on. The woman takes the man's arm and they go away.

The man wakes up first. The woman saw the bird. When she went back to sleep, the man was gone. The man was Apollo. The woman was made of stone. Apollo said, "If you are stone, then stone shall be my stair." He placed his arms around the woman. The stone became a step. The woman places her hand on the man's shoulder. He too is made of stone.

They are flesh and blood, warm-hearted and humorous. They laugh. The man takes the woman's hand. He takes her hand and they go walking. They walk a very long way. They walk past the place where the piano was. They walk past the stone. The dog saw the man before the bird did who flew away. Apollo took out his gun and aimed it at the sky.

The stone that went into making the statues for a long time resisted the hands of the sculptor. But she does not resist him, nor he her. They, however, make nothing of each other. It is as individuals that they exist, for anyone else. Whatever André said to Dorothy (he could not remember it now) it was certainly about their being the woman and the man. It was not about their being the statues. The old man writes in a journal. The sun streaked yellow over the hills, and the window of the car was open through which she poked her head. Listen, do you want to come to the concert. André looked at the brook. The child who had played with the stone will never see him again. When he came home she had changed into a yellow dress and shoes. He was a statue and she leaned against him. When the woman and the man came out, there was a baby, who didn't know what to do. Later on, they thought, although they said nothing, that the baby would know, just as they did now. The baby would know how to be big and not to be a statue.

André is the man and Hélène is the woman. It is Dorothy. Hello. She leans against him. She is made of velvet. He is a greeting card, white and red and gold. There is a gilded glimmering all about them. On the other side of the card are some words. "Congratulations on Your Marriage." In the comic strip the man looks a long way away and in the next square you see the woman is coming. In the film the woman and the man embrace. Embarrassed, he turned away. She raises the window, and there are words: "Bonne fête."

Together, they like to speak. "You make me very happy." "What did I ever do when I was alone?" "Who are you, really?" "What did life mean without you?" "What time are you coming?" "How would you like my hair?" "My sleeves?" "My boots?" "Give me a little time." "All right, I'm ready." "So it's really you!" The old man saw the statues and cried.

She carries a shopping bag, he a parcel. Inside the parcel is something that can be cut into ribbons. Inside her shopping bag is the marble head of a Cupid. This bag is too heavy. The music plays, and she puts it down. He picks it up. She is gone. The parcel is blue, green, and white ribbons. The shopping bag rustles. The head of Cupid flies out. But it is not that. It is the bird. So it seems. Apollo fires the gun and the man falls. When he gets up again, with sunlight shining in his eyes, the woman is gone. Instead of the man there is the woman. Instead of the bird there is stone.

You must come to the concert. Oh, I will. The statues of Diana and Apollo stand in the field. This is a park. Before it is a park, it is nothing, wild nature. Before that, it is molten lava and gas.

Dawn finds the woman and the man together and wrings her hands. Too late! Lascivious behavior! You should be up! The man gets up. The woman gets up. Together they go back to bed. The slate roof of a low building edges out over the poured concrete of the sidewalk in a recently rebuilt part of the city. They pay tribute to each other with a cup of coffee. The woman dresses. The man dresses the woman. She undresses the man, finding that he is Apollo. He is made of water, air, and stone. She is made, seemingly, of lilacs, anise, and sea foam. The man is not Aphrodite, the man is Zeus. The woman is Aphrodite. The bedroom is the ocean. The window is Botticelli.

The man is Apollo. At the sound of the music they become more themselves. The old man signals to the dog that it is time to run out. Let me show you this book. Too sweet to be named. The city seems "lazy." The country stretches out. They are gods. Out of what is simple something complex has been made. When they touch each other, they are unconscious of where they are. He is the man and she is the woman. He is the young Frenchman and she is the American girl. This takes place in the city. When she touches him, she finds he is made of stone. No god fired the rifle. She takes his arm.


## 8. This Story

The characters are the old man, who is in fact two or three different persons, and the young man, who the old man once was, and another young man, and a few others, such as André, and the young man who is the son of the family in the house with the step and who may be the one who killed the bird. There is the father, the man who loved the woman with the piano, and there is the man on the train, who loved the woman in white lace. The women are Shara, Dorothy, and Hélène, the woman in white lace, and the young woman who read the book, and the woman in The Woman and the Man. Among the other actors are Diana, Apollo, the dog, the bird, Guillaume Apollinaire, and Paul Cézanne. A girl is hanging up the laundry. I am writing. It is a year, nineteen seventy-eight. A month, March. A time of day, afternoon, or it is the late part of morning. It is a light, dark. Or rather dark white light. The old man yawns, and the young woman puts on a dress that is very clean, just washed and ironed an instant ago, and in that same instant it didn't quite yet exist. Now it does and may always exist. This is like the music of Mozart, like the effect it has. The girl runs out of the house. Now the old man feels dead.

He revives at the concert, though, the very next day. It is five o'clock in the afternoon. When the old man meets her at the train she is carrying a light yellow umbrella. These are very strong feelings. Still, as in the Mozart, they are together.

There is the story of how the story was written. It was inspired by a concert of music by Mozart, specifically by his Quartet for Strings and Piano, Köchel 493. The concert hall was in Rome. In the hall, leading up to the place where the orchestra sat and played, was a green step. He had never seen this before. The music created something else in him, in his imagination. The rest of life was not blocked out, but the music made him see and feel green fields and the freshness of everything, people and stones. By repetition, by melody, by recurring sounds which in a way made no point outside themselves, he came, almost instantly, to a vision of nature, a vision of life as being enough in itself, fresh, exacting, firm as a stone, unambiguous, unexaggerated, recurring, and free. It is a version perhaps, the simplest he had ever seen, of paradise.

Sitting at the typewriter, light coming in windows, blood going through the arteries and the veins—the past delighting in itself was far in the distance—melodies become opaque—a man, seemingly a waiter, in a slightly soiled white suit, approaches him with a tray. Signore, would you like your tray? The old man dies. He is born again, in a fortnight. The light changes. The weather changes. The dog's fur changes, but later in the cycle of warm and cold. This palace dates from the sixteenth century. It was constructed then. The tin can outside the window, the cloth-bound books inside.

Inside him Provence is illuminated, and the Boulevard Raspail, what is the name of that huge hotel? And the rue du Cherche-Midi. However—he shuts down the typewriter with a bang. Where is my dinner? Where, for God's sake, is my lunch? Who really owns the Vatican? What is going on outside?

In the Mozart concert the notes went high above the green step, circled, and came down. They gave an impression of continuing and of being connected not only to one another but also to everything else. Will there ever be enough time? Time to do all that is suggested? In ordinary life, no. And to make it into something else is to go beyond.

The story is written and is rewritten and it blows about. It furnishes an apartment. Its oddness is apparent. There is a part about a house in the country, near Aix, with a lawn sloping, and a driveway, a stairway, and a garden. The cork was in a bottle of white wine in a restaurant, on a hill, with terraces, and there the woman in white lace was sitting and waiting for a man. One table was in Paris in a café, almost identical with the table on which the young woman puts down the book, and the table to which the waiter walked, and the other was a table on a hillside near Aix-en-Provence where someone is selling (was selling) little things to eat. "The Pain" became "The Pleasure and the Pain." Its quality changes, and finally it sleeps. The author is the old man, the young man, the young woman, Shara, the green step, the ocean, the city, and the girl. He is all the women. He is the men. He is the statues eternally in union as in disunion. He is the sheets of paper floating above the room. I sit down to write. The woman reads the story. She knows that the author is the old man when he was somewhat younger. He, too, is unable to finish anything. Instead he begins to write about what he has already written. He hears the Mozart. These are very strong feelings to have been suggested by a green step, by a concert, by anything. The laundress hangs things up to dry. Whatever this cost, it is worth it. After a while, of course, it ends up only as part of a book.

The story takes place in Aix-en-Provence, a large part of it. The other largest part takes place in Paris. A small part, the larger part of this last part, takes place in Rome. The reality of objects and sensations in one place combines with psychological availability in another. Recent happiness and present unhappiness mix and unmix and mix. Traffic. Women are a great part for the old man but not everything. If only he had read more books. The young woman hands him the book by Guillaume Apollinaire. "You will learn nothing from this one but about some feelings in your life. It's a reflection of, more than part of, the substance of human wisdom." When the bird was shot, the young woman's piano struck a chord and the shining train went past. The stone remained where it was and is, it could hardly have imagined what was thought and written. The brook darted onwards, and André smiled. Already it was a slightly chilly day. The green step was free of encumbrances. Now there is a shoe's bottom on it and now not, as the concert group begins to play. Is everything included? Shall I take you as far as the bus? The man and the woman are saying good-bye. They have the characteristic of movement, which is the supreme utilization of time.

# ONE TRAIN

# One Train May Hide Another

*(sign at a railroad crossing in Kenya)*

In a poem, one line may hide another line,
As at a crossing, one train may hide another train.
That is, if you are waiting to cross
The tracks, wait to do it for one moment at
Least after the first train is gone. And so when you read
Wait until you have read the next line—
Then it is safe to go on reading.
In a family one sister may conceal another,
So, when you are courting, it's best to have them all in view
Otherwise in coming to find one you may love another.
One father or one brother may hide the man,
If you are a woman, whom you have been waiting to love.
So always standing in front of something the other
As words stand in front of objects, feelings, and ideas.
One wish may hide another. And one person's reputation may hide
The reputation of another. One dog may conceal another
On a lawn, so if you escape the first one you're not necessarily safe;
One lilac may hide another and then a lot of lilacs and on the Appia Antica
    one tomb
May hide a number of other tombs. In love, one reproach may hide
    another,
One small complaint may hide a great one.
One injustice may hide another—one colonial may hide another,
One blaring red uniform another, and another, a whole column. One bath
    may hide another bath
As when, after bathing, one walks out into the rain.
One idea may hide another: Life is simple
Hide Life is incredibly complex, as in the prose of Gertrude Stein
One sentence hides another and is another as well. And in the laboratory
One invention may hide another invention,
One evening may hide another, one shadow, a nest of shadows.
One dark red, or one blue, or one purple—this is a painting
By someone after Matisse. One waits at the tracks until they pass,
These hidden doubles or, sometimes, likenesses. One identical twin
May hide the other. And there may be even more in there! The
    obstetrician
Gazes at the Valley of the Var. We used to live there, my wife and I, but

One life hid another life. And now she is gone and I am here.
A vivacious mother hides a gawky daughter. The daughter hides
Her own vivacious daughter in turn. They are in
A railway station and the daughter is holding a bag
Bigger than her mother's bag and successfully hides it.
In offering to pick up the daughter's bag one finds oneself confronted by
    the mother's
And has to carry that one, too. So one hitchhiker
May deliberately hide another and one cup of coffee
Another, too, until one is over-excited. One love may hide another love or
    the same love
As when "I love you" suddenly rings false and one discovers
The better love lingering behind, as when "I'm full of doubts"
Hides "I'm certain about something and it is that"
And one dream may hide another as is well known, always, too. In the
    Garden of Eden
Adam and Eve may hide the real Adam and Eve.
Jerusalem may hide another Jerusalem.
When you come to something, stop to let it pass
So you can see what else is there. At home, no matter where,
Internal tracks pose dangers, too: one memory
Certainly hides another, that being what memory is all about,
The eternal reverse succession of contemplated entities. Reading *A
    Sentimental Journey* look around
When you have finished, for *Tristram Shandy*, to see
If it is standing there, it should be, stronger
And more profound and theretofore hidden as Santa Maria Maggiore
May be hidden by similar churches inside Rome. One sidewalk
May hide another, as when you're asleep there, and
One song hide another song; a pounding upstairs
Hide the beating of drums. One friend may hide another, you sit at the
    foot of a tree
With one and when you get up to leave there is another
Whom you'd have preferred to talk to all along. One teacher,
One doctor, one ecstasy, one illness, one woman, one man
May hide another. Pause to let the first one pass.
You think, Now it is safe to cross and you are hit by the next one. It can be
    important
To have waited at least a moment to see what was already there.

# Passing Time in Skansen

I went dancing in Stockholm at a public dancing place
Out-of-doors. It was a beautiful summer evening,
Summer as it could only come in Sweden in nineteen-fifty.
You had to be young to go there.
Or maybe you could be old. But I didn't even see old people then.
Humanity was divided into male and female, American and other,
    students and nonstudents, etcetera.
The only thing that I could say in Swedish
Was "Yog talar endast svenska"
Which meant I speak only Swedish, whereas I thought it meant
I DON'T speak Swedish.
So the young ladies, delighted, talked to me very fast
At which I smiled and understood nothing,
Though sometimes I would repeat
Yog talar endast svenska.
The evening ended, my part of it did, when they started to do folk dances.
I didn't even know how to look at them, though I tried to for a while.
It was still light out though it was after eleven p.m.
I got on some kind of streetcar that eventually stopped near my hotel.

# Energy in Sweden

Those were the days
When there was so much energy in and around me
I could take it off and put it back on, like clothes
That one has bought only for a ski trip
But then finds that one is using every day
Because every day is like a ski trip—
I think that's how I was at twenty-three.

Seeing those six young women in a boat I was on a ski trip.
They said, We are all from Minneapolis. This was in Stockholm.
The melding of American and Swedish-American female looks was a ski
    trip
Although I had no particular reason at that time to put all my energy on
Yet there it was, I had it, the way a giant has the hegemony of his nerves
In case he needs it, or the way a fisherman has all his poles and lines and
    lures, and a scholar all his books
The way a water heater has all its gas
Whether it is being used or not, I had all that energy.
Really, are you all from Minneapolis? I said, almost bursting with force.
And yes, one of them, about the second prettiest, replied. We are here for
    several days.

I thought about this moment from time to time
For eight or ten years. It seemed to me I should have done something at
    the time,
To have used all that energy. Lovemaking is one way to use it and writing
    is another.
Both maybe are overestimated, because the relation is so clear.
But that is probably human destiny and I'm not going to go against it
    here.
Sometimes there are the persons and not the energy, sometimes the
    energy and not the persons.
When the gods give both, a man shouldn't complain.

# A New Guide

*What is needed is a guide to all situations and places . . .*
LE VICOMTE DE CYRILLAC


*Vous voyez cette ligne télégraphique au fond de la vallée
et dont le tracé rectiligne carpe la forêt sur la montagne
d'en face/Tous les poteaux en sont de fer . . .*
BLAISE CENDRARS, *Feuilles de Route*

I

Look at this Champagne factory
It is in Epernay
From it comes dry white wine with innumerable bubbles
(It is made in a series of fifteen gabled white buildings—sheds)
Borges writes that mirrors and fornication are "abominable"
Because they increase the amount of reality
This champagne factory transforms reality rather than simply
     increasing it
Without it Epernay champagne wouldn't exist.

2

Look at this wolf
He is lighter than a car
But heavier than a baby carriage.
He is highly effective.
Each wolf manifestation is done entirely in the classic manner of a wolf.
He stands completely still.
He is not "too busy to talk to you,"
Not "in conference" or "on the phone."
Some day there may not be any more wolves.
Civilization has not been moving in a way that is favorable to them.
Meanwhile, there is this one.

## 3

Look at this opera.
People are moving without plan.
They are badly directed.
But how they can sing!
One can tell from the faces of the audience how marvelously they sing.
That man there's face is like a burst of diamonds.
That very slim woman has fallen in a faint.
Four nights ago at this opera house a man died.
The opera stopped four young men came with a stretcher to carry him
    out.
I was told that when he was in the lobby a doctor pronounced him dead.
Look at the audience now. They are full of life.

## 4

Look at this camel.
A man unused to camels is trying to mount it.
The camel's driver motions for the camel to kneel down
On its front knees, which it does.
The man mounts it. The camel gallops away.
To qualify for his position the man must demonstrate his ability to ride a
    camel. He has failed.
Maybe he will be given another chance—if it is decided that this was a
    defective camel.
The worst thing that can happen is that he will be out of a job. He will not
    be shot.
The camel crouches down now in the sand,
Quiet, able, and at ease, with nothing about it defective.
If the camel were found to be defective, it would be shot.
That much of the old way still goes on.

## 5

The purple architecture runs all around the top of the Buddhist temple
    and then it is graduated into sculptured green, yellow, and pink strips.

Look at the young monk in a yellow and orange silk gown—he begins a
   prayerful journey up the four hundred and fifty steps.
Red blue white and purple sculptured kings and demons and Buddhas
   look down at him as he climbs and then look level at him but never look
   up at him
For they are near the top and their heads aren't constructed so that they
   are able to bend.


6


Look at this orange.
It was "made" by that orange tree over there.
That orange tree seems to be smiling
As it waves a little bit, just the slightest little bit, in this Andalusian wind.
If it waved much more it might start to lose its oranges.
It would.


7


Look at this arch.
It is part of a building more than seven hundred years old.
Every day from the time he was eighteen, probably, the man who made it
   worked in stone.
Sometimes he had a day off—the stone would be in his mind.
He would find in his mind ideas for patterns, lines, and angels.
Now those ideas are gone.
We have a different art.
But for what we believe most we don't have art at all.


8


The woman is covered by a sheet and the man has on a white mask.
The man takes out the woman's heart
And puts in another. He bends down to listen—
The new heart is beating! He asks for the wound to be closed.

He takes off his mask and goes into another room.
The woman stays in this room. She has a good chance of staying alive.


## 9

Look at this old tower in Lisbon that is now a museum for Portuguese
   blue tiles called Azulejos.
On each tile is a patterning of blue lines,
Thick ones and thin ones curving and straight but more curved ones than
   straight ones
And on most of them a picture and on some of them, actually on a good
   many of them, words.
One tells the story of Orpheus
On this one is a young woman
Holding a cane she points to an allegorical landscape—
A river, a bridge, and sheep. Underneath the image is written
WHATEVER PROSPERS, PROSPERS BEST IN ITS OWN PLACE.
This other tile (there are, it is said, eighty
Thousand of them, one cannot describe them all)
Shows a large blue-and-white-scaled fish. Underneath it, it says
In dark blue letters, in Latin, PISCIS NUNQUAM DORMET: THE
   FISH (OR THIS FISH) NEVER SLEEPS.


## 10

You see this actor, on this stage, he is rehearsing his role in a play
Shakespeare's *A Winter's Tale*. He wears jeans and a frayed white shirt.
It is not yet dress rehearsal. He is rehearsing the part of Florizel. He is
   speaking
In unrhymed decasyllabic verse. Over here to his left is a young woman,
   Perdita.
She too is casually dressed—shirt and jeans.
Her brown hair is tied behind her head in a knot.

Look at this Greece.
It is hardly the same as ancient Greece at all
Not even the old buildings:
Look at this man walking with this woman
In a public park in Athens, in possession of happy lust.
Their faces can't have been the same in the fifth century BC.
Nothing can have been.

## 12

Look at this woman.
It has taken the human race millions of years for anyone to get to be the
    way she is:
An old woman in a red dress sitting looking at television.
Look at her hands.
They are a little dry but she is healthy.
She is eighty-two years old.
On the television screen is pictured a ship. There is a close-up of the deck,
    where
A little boy is playing with a dog. The woman laughs.

Look at the clouds.
They may be what I look at most of all
Without seeing anything.
It may be that many other things are the same way
But with clouds it's obvious.

The motorboat runs through the sky reflected in the river.
Look at the long trail of clouds behind.

Look at this celebration.
The people are festive, wearing masks.
There is a great variety of masks—dog mask, horse mask, mermaid mask,
    mask of a giant egg—
Many people are drinking despite the mask.
To get the drink to their lips they tilt the mask.
The masks, tilted upwards, look like hats.


15

*Callé de los Espasmos*

This is Spasms Street, named for a symptom of a fever one can get from
    mosquitoes at the very end of this street, where it becomes a path, near
    the mountain and surrounded by jungle, and leads to a waterfall and
    also sometimes to this fever.
Few people contract the disease and few know why the street is named
    Spasms Street. It is identified now and then by signposts: Calle de los
    Espasmos. The house this woman lives in is a kilometre from here, the
    zone is not dangerous.


16

Look at this bannister.
People put their hands on it as they went down.
Many many many many hands. Many many many many times.
It became known as the "Bannister of Ladies' Hands." It was said one
    could feel the smoothness of their hands when one touched it oneself.
Actually what one felt was the smoothness of the marble
That had been worn down by so many touching hands.
Look at the sign that is on it now: The Bannister of Ladies' Hands. To
    Preserve This Monument Each Person Is Requested To Touch It Only
    Once.
Look at the young boy there touching it twice, then a third time.
What if a guard catches him.

The fear is that if the bannister is touched too much it may completely
     wear away—the illusion of touching the soft hands of women in low-cut
     red dresses, going down to their friends and lovers, will exist no more.
The sensation will have vanished from the world.


17

Look at this beautiful road
On which horses have trodden
Centuries ago. Then it was a dirt road.
Now it is a stone road
Covered with tar.
The horses' prints are no longer visible.
Nothing is visible. Yes,
Now a motorcycle and a car go past.


18

Look at my friend.
He is saying to me Did you know that I am sixty-three?
He has a beautiful wrinkled face but in which the face has an almost
     complete mastery over the wrinkles. The wrinkling process is still held
     in abeyance by the face.
You're looking pretty good to me, I say.
He smiles.
Some day his face will be totally invaded by wrinkles like the pond in the
     Luxembourg Gardens on a windy fall day.
Even then, though, the main features of his face that I like will be visible.


19

This Egyptian temple is five thousand years old.
Look at the lion and look at the baboon. Both are in sphinx shape.
Look at the pattern of the notes on this sheet of music.
Look at this well-known beauty now seventy years old. She says

It's fine up till seventy when you can still be sexually appealing. But after
    that—
Look at the harbingers of tempest—or of spring?—birds,
Birds are like thoughts that the sky had after it had made its decision
About what to do, and today they are flying violently.
Look at this cloth
Spread out on the roof, beginning to show drops of rain.
Look at the green iris of this Peruvian flamingo's eye.
Look at the gravel on this path. Look at this old man's unevenly knitted
    grey sleeve.


20


Look at this woman.
The man she is with can't believe she has any connection to him.
She doesn't. She turns the corner.
But he walks after her.
After a few hundred feet he has the courage to say Hello.
You are very beautiful. May I walk with you a little ways.
She nods her head, smiling. She doesn't understand him because he is not
    speaking Spanish,
The only language she understands.
The man says, in English, I have just arrived in Barcelona.
She smiles, not understanding a word, except "Barcelona"
Two women and three men go by, speaking Catalan.

# Io

Look at this lovely river maid, who bears the name of Io—
Her youthful beauty caused in Jove such ache that "Me, oh! my, oh!"
He cried, "she must be mine!" and when he had the maid deluded
And had some happiness with her, she as a cow concluded.*

*Behind, above, below all modern manners of invention,
Ovid resides, and to the sides, sublime beyond dissension—
Finnegans Wake is wide awake, and Proust so widely ranges;
Stendhal's a wall where roses fall and Blake is full of dangers;
Byron is great, Williams of late, and Shakespeare for the ages;
But what is life, and what is fate, without Ovidian changes?
No place to go, no one to be, stuck in romance's muddle—
There's no escape! There is one, though—you change into a puddle!
Or to a stone that stops lamenting at the puddle's edge
Or to the grass beneath your lady lying on a ledge.
Why be enslaved to human form when there are countless others?
Why be the dull amalgams of our fathers and our mothers?
Is not that eagle soaring there, is not that goldfish bubbling,
Is not that perfume in the air that is so subtly troubling,
Are not all these, are not these bees, so bossy and so buzzing,
A part of us, a gift to us, and close as any cousins?
If I so choose I can amend my speech to make it doglike—
I bark; I grunt to be a pig; I croak and I am froglike;
I raise my arms and spread them out and feel I am a maple;
I touch the floor upon all fours and have become a table.
And when—it happens most in love—I lose my whole identity,
I still am something—clearly, though, I am a different entity.
Without this change what is one but a sort of vegetation
That, once it's planted, grows and shows the rose of expectation,
Then withers and is scissored off and thrown into the barrow?
What if, most fragrant, pinkest, best, one changed into an arrow?
What if, when sitting longing for a life-preserving call,
In tears, you were transformed into a mighty waterfall?
Then could you tolerate the vacant spaces of the night,
Or if you were an olive tree, or shark about to bite.
In fact, we are so changed by love that what we recognize
When looking in a mirror is a pitiable disguise.
We are transformed! It is a horror, and it is a glory.
With racing heart and strafing nerves we make the inventory,

It happened this way. Jove one morning as he walked along,
Singing a sort of thissy thatsy gay Olympian song,
Beheld a female, Io—and her beauty made him shiver—
Come running from her father's banks (her father was a river,
Inachus, a Thessalian one, who flowed through Tempe Valley—
So many lovely girls have river dads originally!
Rivers who are immortal but must flow against the odds
Being no match, in case of crisis, for the greater gods,
Such as, in this case, Jupiter, who strolling by their waters
May bring great harm because of love intended to their daughters—
And yet, and yet, you'll see when you are finished with this story
They suffer, yes, but often end up consummate with glory—
Io, I'll tell you in advance, was in this category)—
In any case, the King of Gods (as if gods needed rulers—
It's a conception both profound and worthy of pre-schoolers),
The King of Gods espying her, in her bodacious tresses,
Desired for to fuck with her beside the watercresses,
"Where we'll be cool," he said, "and you'll be safe as you are stunning—
I shall protect you—"
                      But she had already started running
And ran through Lerna Marsh and ran through Lincie's budding woods
Till Jove, impatient, brought a fog upon these neighborhoods,
A thick and foggy mist, in which the girl had trouble seeing,
And being lost was to her cost one with Eternal Being—
Which is to say, Jove had his way and pressed himself inside her
And for that portion of the day felt happy as a glider.
      However, Juno, jealous Juno, zealous brunette, looking
At so dark mist on such fair day, demanded what was cooking,
For there was not a river or a marsh or swamp around
That could be sending up such foggy substance from the ground.
Husband! she cried, and went around to all Olympian places
Searching for him but found him not among the bearded faces.
"Well, I suppose, what else, God knows, he's at his usual capers,
Getting a girl with the assistance of substantial vapors.
We'll put a stop to that!" she said. And, "Mists, be on your way!"
And suddenly above the god it was translucent day.
But Jupiter had seen in time what Juno was about

---

*But never see it quite so clearly as in Ovid's story—*
*The clouds, the woods, streams, beasts, and birds, all life's surrounding creatures,*
*Are what we shall be, were, and are, and bear our loving features.*

And by the time she got to earth there was a kind of snout,
Well not snout really but a bovine heightened kind of nose
On Io's face and from her flattened head two horns arose;
Her arms had turned to legs—so she was well-equipped to walk
Close to the ground—her mouth could graze, and gape, but could not
    talk.
She still was white and pretty though she was a heifer now.
Juno admired her grudgingly. "Where did you find this cow?"
She questioned. "From what herd is she?" And Jupiter replied,
"She sprouted up here from the ground." But Juno knew he lied.
"Darling, she's such a lovely one, I'd like her for a gift."
"Er, well, my dear—"
                    Jove felt some fear. And he had little shrift—
He didn't want to give his sweetheart to his nagging wife,
But also didn't want her nagging at him all his life,
Which was eternal. And it seemed so small a thing to ask—
A cow!—"Of course, all right," he said, his face a pleasant mask,
Although inside he didn't like at all what he was doing.
    The goddess, having got the former Girl, who now was mooing,
Needed to figure out a way to keep her precious prize
Away from Jupiter. And then she thought of Argus' eyes!
One hundred eyes adorned the head of Argus. When he slept
He closed but two (I do not know what happened when he wept)—
In any case, for guardian of a woman or a cow,
No one could watch as Argus could, and his is Io now.
"Let her go out by day," said Juno, "let her roam around,
But when the night comes, fasten her with willows to the ground."
Argus agreed, whose sight was such that Io he discerned
When facing her or to the side or when his back was turned.
She fed on leaves and bitter plants and muddy water drank
And oft at night to rocky ground in restless sleep she sank.
She wanted to stretch out her arms to him in supplication
But had no arms to stretch, and in no way by conversation
Could she excite his pity, but could only moo, and seem
The more a cow.
                One day she walked beside her father's stream.
The sun was bright, the air was still, there scarcely was a zephyr—
It made the heart expand even though the heart was in a heifer.
Then, bending down her head, she looked and saw her face reflected:
What gaping jaws, what horrid horns were to her self connected!
She started back in awful fear and bolted here and there;
Her sister naiads petted her to soothe her, unaware

Of course that she was Io. (How she wanted to be one
Of the Inachus girls again, handmaidens of the sun
And wood and way and water, but those days, it seemed, were done!)
Now she was with her sisters, but she walked on hoofy feet;
Was with her father, but was dumb. He brought her grass to eat.
He, miserable, aflood with grief, had searched with no success
For Io everywhere, and did not know and could not guess
Whether she was among the Shades or if she still drew breath—
Since she was nowhere, he feared for her something worse than death.
Distracted now he feeds the pretty cow, who licks his hand.
Weeping, she longs to find some way to make him understand,
And with her hoof she traces her name IO in the sand.
(How fortunate that she was not named Thesmophoriazusa
Or Melancholy Myrtle, or Somatacalapoosa—
For by the time she wrote it out her strength would have been wasted,
Inachus have gone elsewhere, or the rising tide erased it.)
At once her father understood. "Oh woe is me!" he cried
"You are a cow, who were my dear, my darling, and my pride!
I hoped that you would marry soon as other maidens do
And I would have a son-in-law, and have grandchildren, too,
But now I see that it must be a bull who marries you!"
He wept. She wept. He held her close, her horns and all, and said,
"What pain it is to know your pain! I wish that I were dead!
No help to you is to be had, and all to me is futile—
Alas the Gate of Death is closed and I am an immortal!"
Now as her father made lament, Argus with eyes like stars
Removed her from those latitudes and past the Eastern bars
To where she grazed in other pastures; and he found a seat
Atop a mountain where his view of Io was complete.

     Jupiter now had had enough. He didn't want the heifer
Because of Juno's jealousy so horribly to suffer.
He summoned Mercury and said "O nephew of the Pleiade,
Great messenger, enchanter, go, and rescue me my Naiad!"
Whereat the god took up his magic cap and wingèd shoes
And sleep-producing wand—he didn't travel without those—
And came to earth. Pretending he's a goatherd, he advances
Where Argus is, upon a syrinx playing songs and dances.
Argus was smitten by that music. "Come and sit with me.
There's grass for goats and shade for us," he said to Mercury.

     The god agreed, and sat and played sweet notes till Argus dozed
But also stayed awake, since only half his eyes were closed—
Some of those open still kept watch, and others paid attention

To the strange reed-pipe Mercury played, which was a new invention.
When Argus asked about it, Mercury left off playing lyrics
And told him how the pipe was born: of Pan's pursuit of Syrinx,
A wood nymph, fair and much pursued, whose wish it was to be
Diana-like, a huntress, and of perfect chastity—
And when she was attired like her, and when she held her bow,
Whether or not she was Diana it was hard to know.
Many mistook her for the goddess. When she walked one morning
On the cool slopes, and in such guise, the god Pan saw her coming
And felt for her, divinely fair, his godly spirits soaring
And went to her and said to her, "O Maiden, thou art—" Snoring!
Not Syrinx, no, but Argus, of whom the star-studded cranium
Was veiled by eyelids like the undersides of a geranium.
Could this be true? It was. So the remainder of the tale
Argus was destined not to hear—how Pan pursued the pale
And trembling hamadryad till she came to Ladon's banks
And begged to be transformed—she was, to reeds; she murmured, Thanks
Just at the moment racing Pan caught up to her and found
He held no nymph but what best grows on moist and sandy ground,
A bunch of hollow reeds. He sighed. To lose his girl was odious
But what those reeds made of his sigh was haunting and melodious.
Touched by the wonder of the reeds, enchanted by their tone,
Pan said, "In playing, thus, on thee, my dear, we shall be one."
The instrument of reeds forthwith retained the name of Syrinx.
Mercury meanwhile separated Argus at the larynx,
Swiping him with his curving sword, once he had made it certain,
Using his wand, each eyeball slept behind its lidded curtain.
Bounding and bouncing down the rocks, the head of Argus flies,
One single darkness in what used to be a hundred eyes.
Juno, at seeing Argus wasted and herself upstaged,
Was—how could Jove not know she would be?—totally enraged.
First, she took Argus' eyes and placed them in the peacock's tail
Where they would always shine. Then, something sharper than a nail
She set in Io's hide, a terror-causing wasp-like goad
To torture her like fury as she ran down every road
She came to, mad with pain, forgetful even of her shape,
Wishing above all other things that stinging to escape—
Poor Io, tortured out of Greece, to race through alien dust,
Her only crime for a short time to have aroused the lust
Of one who saw her not, as she ran, stumbling in her pain,
On four short legs, until she came upon the waving grain
Of the Nile Delta, then the Nile, that cuts the land in two,

And there she stopped, Great Nile, for having got as far as You,
She could no more. Upon your shore, she lifted up her face
To stars where she thought Jove might be, commanding from that place,
And by her moos and mournful moans, on bent and knobby knees,
From suffering unendurable did beg forthwith surcease.
Jove heard her then. And pleaded, with his arm about his wife,
That she permit him to give Io back her former life.
"Fear not," he said, "she'll be a source of grief to you no more!"
"Swear!" Juno said. And by the deadly Stygian pools he swore.

    Juno relents. And Io starts to be herself again,
Her former self that brought delight to gods as well as men.
Her mouth and eyes decrease in size, her gaping jaw deducted,
Rough hair and hide are altered, and her horns are deconstructed.
Ten fingernails appear where were two hooves, and she has hands
And shoulders, and a waist, and, now, upon two legs she stands—
She who had altered from a naiad to a bestial form
Becomes a queenly girl again, too royal for the farm,
And is completely Io (of the cow she keeps the white
And nothing more), but, standing so, she feels a sort of fright,
A fear of speaking—what if she should moo?—but has no choice
And speaks—in words! and owns once more her interrupted voice.

Now she is worshipped as a goddess, with the greatest honor,
After she gives birth to a son perhaps begot upon her
That summer day when, graceful, gay, she ran up from the river
Her father was, and stirred the lust of Jove the Thunder-Giver.

# A Time Zone

*On y loue des chambres en latin Cubicula locanda*
*Je m'en souviens j'y ai passé trois jours et autant à Gouda*
APOLLINAIRE, *Zone*

A light from the ceiling is swinging outside on Forty-second Street traffic
    is zinging
Collaborating on The Construction of Boston is interesting
To construct the city of Boston Tinguely is putting up a big wall
Of gray sandstone bricks he is dressed in a French ball
Gown he puts the wall up during the performance
His costume is due to art and not to mental disturbance
Now the wall ten feet high is starting to tremble
People seated in the first rows run back for shelter
However the bricks stand firm Niki de St. Phalle dressed as Napoleon
Shoots at a Venus full of paint with a miniature (but real) cannon
Rauschenberg's rain machine's stuck it gives too much moisture
People look very happy to have gotten out of the theater
People ask that it be put on again but it can't be done
Tinguely with his hand bleeding says Boston can be constructed only
    once
And that is the end of that
Next day the Maidman Theatre stage is flat
I like the random absurdity of this performance
Done only once with nineteen-sixty-two-and-art romance
I meet Niki four years earlier in France in the spring
Five years before that I am with Janice and Katherine
In Greece two thousand years ago everything came crashing
We stand and try to imagine it from what is still standing
Years before this in Paris it's the boulevard Montparnasse
Larry Rivers is here he is living with a family that includes a dwarf
We are talking I have a "Fulbright" with us is Nell Blaine
I am pulled in one direction by Sweden in another by Spain
The idea of staying in Europe jolts me gives a convincing jerk
It's New York though where most of my friends are and the "new work"
Today with Frank O'Hara a lunch connection
The Museum of Modern Art is showing its Arp collection
Frank comes out of the doorway in his necktie and his coat
It is a day on which it would be good to vote

Autumn a crisp Republicanism is in the air tie and coat
Soon to be trounced by the Democrats personified as a slung-over-the-
     shoulder coat
Fascism in the form of a bank
Gives way to a shining restaurant that opens its doors with a clank
However before being taken into this odoriferous coffer
A little hard-as-a-hat poem to the day we offer
"Sky/woof woof!/harp"
This is repeated ten times
Each word is one line so the whole poem is thirty lines
It's a poem composed in a moment
On the sidewalk about fifteen blocks from the Alice in Wonderland
     Monument
Sky woof woof! harp is published in *Semicolon*
Later than this in this John Myers publication
O'Hara meanwhile is bending above his shirt
His mind being and putting mine on being on International Alert
There's no self-praise in his gossip
Which in fact isn't gossip but like an artistic air-trip
To all the greatest monuments of America and Europe
Relayed in a mild excited wide open-eyed smiling conversational style
Larry he says and Larry again after a while
He is crazy about Larry these two have a relationship
That is breaking the world's record for loquaciousness
I first meet Larry on Third Avenue
The El goes past and it throws into my apartment rust dust soot and
     what-have-you
Larry has a way of putting himself all out in front of himself
And stumbling through it and looking good while seemingly making fun
     of himself
This is my friend Larry Rivers says Jane Freilicher
She lives upstairs Larry is a sometime visitor
He is dedicated at this moment entirely to drawing
Abstract split-splot and flops and spots he finds a blur and boring
Give me a glass of pencil that hath been
Steeped a long time in Delacroix and Ingres nor does he neglect Rubens
He is drawing up a storm in his studio working hard
A little bit earlier he and Jane and others are bouleversés by Bonnard
Bonnard show at the Modern Museum
I meet these people too late to go and see them
I am of New York not a native

I'm from Cincinnati which is to this place's nominative like a remote
   dative
In 1948 from college I come here and finally settle
The city is hot and bright and noisy like a giant boiling kettle
My first connection to it aside from touristy is sexual
A girl met here or there at first nothing serious or contextual
That is earlier now I'm here to live on street subway and bus
I find people exciting unrecognizable and of unknown-to-me social class
Finally they start to come into focus
For a while it's like being at a play I may have the wrong tickets
On West Tenth Street now I am firmly settled in New York
I am a poet je suis poète but I'm not doing very much work
I'm in love with a beautiful girl named Robin
Her father has a hand-weaving factory he gives me a job winding bobbins
It is a one-floor loft in the garment district on Thirty-first Street
Pat Hoey visits someone next door on snow-white feet
Pat and I like to go to the ballet at the City Center
I get "Balanchined" as in a wine-press all Jacques d'Amboise has to do is
   enter
My poetry is somewhat stuck
It's taking me a little while to be able to write in New York
My painter friends help and what I am reading in the library
It is not the contemporary antics this happens later of John Ashbery
This shy and skinny poet comes down to visit me from "school"
When he and Jane Freilicher meet it's as if they'd both been thrown into a
   swimming pool
Afloat with ironies jokes sensitivities perceptions and sweet swift
   sophistications
Like the orchids of Xochimilco a tourist attraction for the nations
Jane is filled with excitement and one hundred percent ironic
This conversation is joy is speed is infinite gin and tonic
It is modernism in the lyrical laconic
Our relationship's platonic
With what intelligence linked to what beauty linked to what grassy gusty
   lurch across the canvas
Jane and her paintings I realize once again happiness
Huh? is possibly going to be available after long absence
Here today in a gray raincoat she appears
The style is laughter the subject may be a cause for tears
Larry has some of the qualities of a stand-up comic
He says of John Myers John Myers he always calls him that

John Myers never John John Myers says he isn't fat
Well doesn't have a fat EAR but look at his stomach
And oft at a party back his head he throws
And plays the piano singing a song he made up "My Nose"
His nose bothers and is thus conquered by Larry Rivers
He's doing a Bonnardesque painting it's so good it gives me "recognition"
    shivers
It's a room filled with women with somewhat beautiful fishlike graces
Mostly orangey-yellow they have sexy and sleepy looks on their faces the
    thick
Oil paint makes it look as if you'd stick
To it if you got next to it it also looks very spacious
Now Larry is sitting and smiling he is copying an Ingres
His hand is shaky his lines are as straight as coat hangers
Why don't you I say rather dumbly put something witty in your work
No Kenneth I can't he says prancing around like a funny Turk
Charcoal in one hand and making a little gesture with the other
One Sunday I go with him to the Bronx to visit his sister and his mother
Here I am with Larry's sister and his mother
Sitting in the kitchen above us is a motto
Joannie is blonde her brunette friend is warm and flushed as a risotto
I rather fancy her and Larry's mother fancies it stupid
To have invited this girl at the same time as me so interrupting the arrow
    of Cupid
Posing for Rivers his mother-in-law Berdie before a screen
Posing for her son-in-law this woman full and generous as the double
    issue of a magazine
The French *Vogue* for example or the *Ladies Home Journal*
Frank thinks her marvelous he finds the sublime in her diurnal
Larry is making a leafy tree out of metal
Here is his Jewish version of Courbet's painting of a funeral
Jane loves Matisse and is a fan of Baudelaire
In these paintings she is working on a secret of yellow blue and pink air
She and Larry make a big painting together
Larry with an unmeditated slash Jane with the perpetuity of a feather
That in a breeze is trying to pull itself together
I'm looking at the finished product it's rather de Kooningesque
Being de-Kooning-like some way is practically of being a New York
    painter the test
Here today though is not a de Kooning but one of Jane's it's luscious big
    and feminine
I am inspired by these painters

They make me want to paint myself on an amateur basis
Without losing my poetic status
Jane is demonstrating to me the pleasures of using charcoal
I am copying a Delacroix of a black woman called I think The Slave Girl
Erasing makes a lovely mess
It looks like depth and looks like distance
Ink at the opposite end of materials is deliberate and daring
No chance to erase it and oil pastels like wildflowers in a clearing
My Aesthetic I only paint for a few years is rather elementary
Get something that looks good looks real looks surprising looks from this
    century
I am sitting at a little table downstairs in the Third Avenue apartment
I like buying slabs of masonite and all kinds of equipment
At the Metropolitan on a big wall is a great big Rubens
Of a king and some nobles on horses bigger than cabins
I am walking through the European Collection
With Larry and Jane they're giving it a professional inspection
On drawing paper I'm doing some Seurat-like dotting
I like this even love it but I know it's going to come to nothing
It is invigorating to stand in this studio
John Ashbery comes to visit he is listening to Bob and Ray on our radio
It is a small old-fashioned console attacked by salt water
John finds them wheezingly amusing all over the house sounds his
    raucous laughter
He and I "go back" to Harvard College
Now he is sitting at his typewriter in Greenwich Village
He's just finished a poem and he's happy as after a good repast
He is certain this feeling won't last
John is predictably and pleasantly gloom-filled
I've just driven to New York from some place north of Bloomfield
I'm an hour and a half late
This enables John to finish his poem as I with mixed feelings find out
"The Picture of Little J. A. in a Prospect of Flowers"
He made good use of this couple of wasted hours
Dick gives Genevieve a swift punch in the pajamas
It's a vault over W. C. Williams and a bypass of Dylan Thomas
He is still sitting at his little portable
Being because of my poem-causing lateness exceptionally cordial
We are both fans of the old Mystery Plays
We also find each other mysterious in certain ways
This mystery becomes greater as more time passes
Then finally the mystery itself passes

We're at Harvard together
We walk along talking about poetry in the autumn weather
He is not writing much this year but he likes to collaborate
So do I we do a set of sestinas at a speedy rate
Six sestinas each about an animal with one concluding one called The
    Bestiary
There is also a three-page poem in which all the lines rhyme with the title
    The Cassowary
Next we do a poetic compendium called The New York Times
September Eighth Nineteen Fifty-One both with and without rhymes
Our poems are like tracks setting out
We have little idea where we're going or what it's about
I enjoy these compositional duets
Accompanied by drinking coffee and joking on Charles and Perry Streets
We tell each other names of writers in great secret
Secret but absolutely no one else cares so why keep it
We're writing a deliberately bad work called The Reconstruction of
    Colonial Williamsburg
In a feeble attempt to win a contest the style is the Kenyon Review absurd
Larry and Jane propose to me renting a house in East Hampton
We go sizzling out of the city with the rapidity of a flu symptom
No this is actually a year later my memory missed it
I now go to California to be a "teaching assistant"
This year goes by I meet the girl who is later my wife Janice
I love to kiss her and to talk to her very often it's talking about my friends
I also talk a lot about "Europe" and France
She's a little deflating and tells me that to be a great poet
I have to do something she tells me but I forget exactly what
I think have for all my poems some sort of system
I am shaken but still feel secure in my avant-garde wisdom
East Hampton glaringest of Hamptons Hampton of sea shine of de
    Kooning and of leaves
Frank's visiting we're composing a poem he tugs at his sleeves
It is a Nina we are composing it is a Nina Sestina
For Nina Castelli's birthday her adorable sixteenth one
This year this month this week in fact Frank writes "Hatred"
A stunning tour-de-poem on an unending roll of paper
It makes going on forever seem attractive
Writing in the manner of O'Hara means being extremely active
Twenty people are over then thirty now about forty
Zip Frank sits down in the midst and types out a poem it doesn't even
    seem arty

I try it out with little success
It's one of those things the originator can do best
"Hatred" is full of a thundering array of vocables
From it straight through to the Odes Frank's talent is implacable
Now here he is holding out to me a package
Of Picayunes he taps one on his kneebone-covering khakis
Finally we have a poem for Castelli's daughter
Moonlight dissolve next day we're visiting Anne and Fairfield Porter
Fairfield is in his studio a mighty man
Posing like fluttering then settling sea birds around him Jerry Katie
      Elizabeth and Anne
He has opinions that do not waver
On his canvases he creates a bright and wholesome fever
Flowers like little pockets of yellow and pink pigment
Are aspiring up to a tree or a wall or a house like a sunlight shipment
At a John Cage concert there is hardly a sound
It's the paradise of music lost and music found
I find it pure and great as if a great big flash of light were going off
      underground
Satie and Webern are hitting me in the head and so finally with the
      Cantos is Ezra Pound
Frank and I are writing very long poems
Long is really the operative word for these poems
His is called Second Avenue mine When the Sun Tries to Go On
I don't know where I got the title
I'm working on it every afternoon the words seem to me arriving like
      stampeding cattle
It's not at all clear but for the first time in my life the words seem
      completely accurate
If I write for three hours I allow myself a cigarette
I'm smoking it's a little too much I'm not sure I can get through it alone
Frank and I read each other segments of these long works daily on the
      phone
Janice finds it funny now that I've dropped this bunch of pages
That I can't get them back in the right order well I do but it's by stages
It is April I have a job at the Hunter College Library
I come down to the Cedar on a bus hoping to see O'Hara and Ashbery
Astonishingly on the bus I don't know why it's the only occasion
I write a poem Where Am I Kenneth? It's on some torn-out notebook
      pages
The Cedar and the Five Spot each is a usable place

A celebrated comment Interviewer What do you think of space? De
    Kooning Fuck space!
In any case Frank is there he says he likes Where Am I Kenneth?
I carry this news home pleasantly and the poem it mentions her to Janice
John's poem Europe is full of avant-garde ardor
I am thinking it's making an order out of a great disorder
I wonder at what stage in life does this get harder
The Cedar Bar one hardly thinks of it is what may be called a scene
However one closed to the public since no one goes there to be seen
It is a meeting place for the briefest romances
And here is Norman Bluhm at the bar saying Who cares about those
    nances?
And here he is shoving and here is de Kooning and there is a beer
Being flug at someone Arnold Weinstein or me through the smoke-talky
    atmosphere
Of this corner booth
Voici Guston and Mitchell and Smith and here on top of everything is
    Ruth
Kligman being bedazzling without stop
She writes a poem with the line At the bar you've got to be on top
Meanwhile tonight Boris Pasternak
Is awarded the Nobel Prize and is forced to give it back
Frank O'Hara is angry there seems both a flash and a blur in his eyes
Kenneth we've got to do something about Pasternak and the Nobel Prize
What? well we ought to let him know
That we support him Off flies a cable into the perpetual snow
Dear Boris Pasternak We completely support you and we also love your
    early work
Signed puzzlingly for him in the morning's glare if he ever receives it
    Frank O'Hara and Kenneth Koch
Staging George Washington Crossing the Delaware
Alex Katz comes up looking like a pear
He has some white plywood boards with him he says where
Shall I put this stuff and a big bare
Wall is the side of their emplacement No chair
For Alex painting and cutting And now they're there
The seven soldiers one cherry tree one Delaware crossing boat
Hey hey Ken cries Alex I've done it
I've made you a set for George Washington Crossing the Delaware
The British and American armies face each other on wooden feet
I write this play in our apartment on Commerce Street
I am working in the early afternoon and stay up late

Dawn is peeling oranges on top of the skyscrapers
On the stage a wall goes up and then it's taken down
And under the Mirabeau Bridge flows the Seine
Today Larry and Frank are putting together "Stones"
It's a series of lithographs
Larry puts down blotches violently they look like the grapes of wrath
Frank is smoking and looking his best ideas come in transit
I walk the nine blocks to the studio he says Come in
New York today is white dirty and loud like a snow-clogged engine
Huge men in undershirts scream at each other in trucks near Second
    Avenue and Tenth Street
De Kooning's landscapey woman is full of double-exposure perfections
Bob Goodnough is making some small flat red corrections
Jane is concentrating she's frowning she has a look of happy distress
She's painting her own portrait in a long-sleeved dark pink dress
I'm excited I'm writing at my typewriter it doesn't make too much sense

# The First Step

*A journey of ten thousand li begins with the first step.*

In the country of the middle
The person in the middle is king
No one walking on the outskirts
No sprechstimme singing in Beijing

Splash of water at the end of the ship
Flash of sky at the end of the plane
Dash of suit at the end of the man
Clash of music going away

There is no moulding
There is no "souk"
There is no pounding and no landing
Nothing but Chinese absence soup

A journey of five hundred limits
Begins with the first one met
After the first, one knows that this is not
The "real" journey and yet and yet

No Africa, no rest of Asia, no Europe no sweet continent
No Italy no England no Portugal no Spain
And Spain exists outside the scientific revolution
As Sicily exists outside it, no Brazil, no Cuba, only China

One sensuous life and three parks
Two kinds of government eighteen minority nationalities
One woman two women a man three
A long corral of roofs a boat an evening

The new dawn rises
With the first ray of the sun
Why are you going away?
From the born smoke rises

The first whisper of departure starts in his nostrils
It starts there though it comes from far away
His life today is like a stereopticon
He sees more than at any other time

No chamber orchestra to say when you have arrived there
No religious chorus to say when you have gotten there
No French horn section to say when at last you are there
Only a beat de-tuck-tucking of a single heart

Seventeen intellectuals on a train
The train is not going nowhere
Inside it as it is going somewhere
The intellectuals' minds are moving around

Panda on a stamp
Hing Chow post office
Panda on a stage
Beijing Zoo

"Call Amalgamated Chinoiseries and get me the manager!
Give me a bowl of the share-holding poundings of the sea!
Let them be like flowrets on my army bandage!
I want to never leave the hinges of this diamond sleep!"

So much depends upon
The room temperature
Hitches up skirt. He lifts
Phonograph needle. Day fleets down.

The basket of laundry starts on Huang Yin Street
It moves through the crowded city with a bustle of napkins
Finally it arrives at the large hotel
There it is undone like a flapping of wings

I have never
Seen such streets
Such had never
Sight of me

Man woman baby bicycle basket
Truck crossroad vanishing composite northern

Great Wall resolute slow
Table rock needle tire sting .

With song of self pity denigrated by taste
Soaring apathetic and night-canoey
Walking along streets that seem going to waste
Outside Paris and in Shanghai and Huan-Shi City

If only you had come
When the need was highest
Romantic hooey
But some drenched train

Green moss scabs the sides of trees
Wisteria-reaches clutch the wood railing of the porch
A diet is proposed: Don't eat.
The point of life is discussed: Sleep together.

The walls of this farmhouse
Are made of stone
Everyone thinks
To live a long time

In the post office
No postage meter
No automatic box to give stamps
No special delivery and no federal express

Showers fall down
He is unhappy
Out comes the sun
Shakes off and smiles

He speaks crop language
To farm analysts
Beside the white
Un-analyzed chickens

Skeletons in Salvadorean pits
Black needles of Hong Kong

Ships burning like coats eagles like aprons
Gas the good air of paradise turned to stench

At the poultry market
The sun shines. A chicken jumps up
At the sea-bait market
A snail jumps up

These pink Chinese characters, San She Dan Chen Pills!
Two birds with blue back-feathers
Lean over a spray of blossoms white and pink
Take them for your health Signature baseball
Followed by the author's explanation

Post office has stamps yellow color green blue orange red brown
Many picture panda embrace follow plus leaders ruling men
Lick of stamp to other side come glue and postal paste fellow
Bringing a lamp to mailbox show by light how get them in

No stopping those officials on the way to the airport
No reasoning with them to about-face
No saying Better to stop and have a good time
Good time for them is this not our good time

He was sorry to be so angry
He was sorry to be so nervous
He was sorry to be so absent
He was sorry to be so stunned

No soft breast
No soft bottom
No soft sleeper
No one on the train

After a mile
No more music
After five miles
No more news

While she was there
While he is here

Pink buds blossom
In the People's Park

The baby is not a soft sleeper but a hard sleeper
The train from Kunming to Shanghai the baby runs on alone

How amazing to see so many hundreds
Of international celebrities at once!
They are all in a picture on a poster
They stand pasted to a billboard—lucky ones

The automobile holds still
Inside is Official
The automobile moves
The Official sits back and smiles

Only canal with muddy boat
Purple what-have-you
First mate smiling
Second or third face smiling

Perimeter of lake
People very busy
Only one loony-seeming man
Stands and screams before Authorities

Moment to hush those talkies
Very strange man
Feminine police mood filling cabinet
Very very strange man

In head no thought
On heart no scar
In mouth no word
Dead so far

The Shanghai skyscrapers shine like fire of dragons
The Huangpu River Bridge is like a palace woman's hairpin
The People's Park is like a jungle without trees or animals
The people crowded on the boat are like boxes in a store

No fish on menu
No meat on menu
No vegetable on menu
No rice no tea

The young day ruins itself for democracy
The blue river stabs itself into trees

No Beijing Opera
No King with red face
No King with white face
No Queen with whitish-blue face

Ivy falling forward
Over gray great wall
Men seeming lacking in compassion
Driving a human pile-driver twenty miles long

She wakes up goes to market
A fine white hen flies to the floor
She tries to pick it up
But she does not have enough yuan

The soft sleeper leaves the city at dawn
The hard sleeper leaves at the same time
One sleeper is attached to the other sleeper
Rolling quietly they are the same train

Today in the dimness
Nine persons eating Dim Sum
Tonight in the darkness
Ninety-seven persons eating shark

No pigs standing in front of the grocery store
No wagon of cow manure stopped in the middle of the major road
No huge advertisements for doctors in the center of the square
No women tugging their husbands through canal pits thick with mud

No burning face from suddenly-fired sexual excitement
No teacher with white hand turning away embarrassed and pleased

No warrior with grim expression keeping watch
No herbalist no pencils no camera salesman nothing four hundred city
    blocks

No banners signalling reprieve from someone's dying
No reverse funeral body up others beneath
No birth changing baby gives birth to mother
Everything happens reply to question long ago set

In the room she sits and sews
Seventeen seventy seven
In the boat he so painfully rows
Nine hundred and ten

This farm man's forcefulness begins in childhood
It rides through adolescence and into manhood
There gathering into a personal and/or social clump
It dazzling leaps forward and achieves nothing or something

No back of the basement
No Egyptian tile replacement
No oaken stuff
Only an under-ample yuan disbursement

The schoolteacher stands
Waving his hand sideways
The car backs in
That brings the Official to his school

No boat no pyramid in this part of town
No float no cinnamon in this part of town
No coast guard in this part of town
No École des beaux arts in this part of town

No fat women
No fat crowds
No fat safety police
No fat fowls

Engine
Sea gull

Fold up
Flash

Amoeba serena
Cows ilk
Uncomprehending
Sample of speech: "Whiff"

What do you write about? "Four Modernizations
Modernization of agriculture, of education,
Of industry, of science" The poets' explanation
"We write about the Four Modernizations"

Eternally weather of spring
Sixty-seven degrees temperature sing

No room on airplane Shanghai Kunming
No room on airplane Queylin Hanshu
No soft sleeper
Only hard sleeper journey five days

Suddenly wakes up man room
Bed rumpled dirty several newspaper
Table cup little dishes tea leaves
Meiyou What do you want

Dancers on stage in the theatre
Cow at the end of a rope
In the field
Gray dog sitting by a wall

Nothing moving in lifeboat
No one walking in corridor
Only in main salon lobby
Magician describe take handkerchief

Suddenly losing interest
Suddenly losing narrow
Suddenly losing valley
Suddenly losing train

No snow on the gate to the Forbidden City
No snow on the Hall of Felicitous Harmony
No snow on the Pathway of Endless Peace
No sun there either

Empty empty
Quiet quiet
Thousand thousand
Sleep and stand

The panda in the Beijing Zoo
Is a minority nationality
The panda in the American zoo
Is overseas Chinese

In and out in and out of traffic goes the car
Drops of rain fall on the Huangpu River
Someone bends forward with anxiety
Another bends back with the machine

When the car comes back
The back seat is empty
When the car sets out
Its seat contains one

Bed is absent
Breast is absent
Bend is absent
Bet is absent

No Western prescriptions
No Vicks VapoRub and no Anacin
No Empirin no Kotex no Trojan rubbers
Only jars of deer horn ground to powder

"Into my brain pattern noxious Occident
Stoop is restful in rain battering uncopying Orient
A glad dry, a roomy husk, pretensions
But later a soothing cry, abrasions, summing up."

Light on water
What is this?

Little boat with light
What light is this?

A man on the boat
A line in the water
A line around the park
Of bushes and trees

# Poems by Ships at Sea

*It was not known that ships at sea wrote poetry. Now it is known. Captain Henry Dreyfus has recorded some of these Pacific and Atlantic songs, most of them composed by large, cargo-bearing vessels of the Dutch, British, Portuguese and French lines. One poem, the last, is by an American ship.*

BEARING CARGO

*By the SS Van Djik of the Dutch and Homburg Line*

Bearing cargo, heavy cargo over the plain
Level friction of the water, I sometimes see
A delicate ship waving to me from the distance
And I go more swiftly, as if to carry my weight to her knees.
Alas, she vanishes
Before I become acquainted with the night
Of the first day out—
But, on the second, she is there again!

*Atlantic Ocean, near Cape Verde, September 1919*

AUTUMN LEAVES

*By the HMS Mother of God of the British Catholic or "Lesser" Navy*

In autumn the leaves fall
From the maples the oaks the birches
But not on me
For I go far from them
As if I were unburdened,
Suddenly, of all that is heavy in existence,
All that is tainted and painted
All that is dead and all that bears (even fading) life.
Such is my journey—without seasons I sail toward you,
Final Harbour, who are the mother of life.

*Location unknown, 1920s*

## BOXERS

*By the SS Oporto, Portuguese Line*

Boxers sometimes try to stabilize
The energy of their feet and their haunches
Standing on my waving decks exchanging punches
One topples. Knockout! Yet
He wasn't so hard hit. No it was I
Making a swerve or knocking back a wave
Unwitting. He gets up and tries to pit
His strength against a human force and mine.
I'll try, but can't do much, to let him win.

*South Atlantic, off the coast near Swakopmuna (Walvis Bay), 1949*


## BRAGAN

*By the RFSS Messieurs-Dames, French Merchant Export Lines*

Way over the expanding water
There is an island, called "Bragan"
Which means "alone one" in Javanese.
This island is alone in the middle of the sea
As a woman may be alone
In the middle of a crowd or when she is with no one
And as a man may be
Anywhere, in a mass of persons, alone,
Or with others, when he is not with this woman,
And as I, the *Messieurs-Dames*, am alone—
And as she will be home to me,
This island, this woman, this Bragan.

*Indian Ocean, 11/24/1926*

# AMERICAN FOAM

*By the USS United States, United States Navy*

You can talk about the Banda's crazy waters
Where mermaids splash around and kiss and comb
You can yak about the Andaman and Flores
But there's nothing like American foam.

You can say I wish that I were in the Tasman
Or that the Laptev froze me to a stone
But I will tell you, lads, that there is nothing
As soothing and as cooling as the foam

That slaps my keel when I am in Penobscot
Or Tampa Bay, or, when I'm heading home,
The West Atlantic and the East Pacific
Or Puget Sound, or Norton, close to Nome.

There's nothing like the feel of U.S. water
It's straight and sharp and clear and it alone
Can make a ship feel she is Ocean's daughter
Carried upon her parent's shoulders home.

*(probably) Tasman Sea, 1930s*

# Talking to Patrizia

Patrizia doesn't want to
Talk about love she
Says she just
Wants to make
Love but she talks
About it almost endlessly to me.

It is horrible it
Is the worst thing in life
Says Patrizia
Nothing
Not death not sickness
Is as bad as love

I am always
In love I am always
Suffering from love
Says Patrizia. Now
I am used to it
But I am suffering all the same

Do you know what I did to her
Once?—speaking
Of her girlfriend—I kicked her out
I literally kicked her she was down on the floor and I
Gave her the colpi di piedi the
Kicks of my foot. She slided out.

She did this
To me promised to go on a trip
I am all waiting prepared
Suitcases and tickets
She comes and says her other friend finds out she
Can't go she guessed about it. I KICKED her out

Oh we are still together
Sometimes. But love is horrible. I thought
You might be the best
Person to talk to Patrizia since you

Love women and are a woman
Yourself. You may be right Patrizia

Said. But this woman who abandons
You I think you should
Disappear. Though maybe with this woman
Disappearing won't work.
I think not disappear.
It's too bad I don't know her

If I knew her if I could see her
Just for ten minutes—I'm afraid
If you saw her you might take
Her away from me. Patrizia
Laughs. No it hasn't happened to me
Thank God to like such young women yet

Why? When you are my
Age—still young—she
Is thirty . . . nine? you are close enough
To people very young to
Know how horrible they are
And you don't love them

You don't want to have anything
To do with them! Oh
Uh huh, I said putting
My hands down on the table and then off
Look at you excuse me but I have to laugh
At you sitting in this horrible

Restaurant at one o'clock
In the morning in a
City you don't want to be
In and why? For this woman.
It is horrible I know but
Also funny

I know I said. Listen I have
An idea. Do you know her address? You know where
She lives? You should go there
Go and hide there

Outside her house
In the bushes

Then when she comes out
You jump out
You confront her. You will see
If there is love
In her eyes or not. It can't
Be hidden. You will know It can't be mistaken

This works This has always worked
For me. It won't work for me. I can't
Go and hide there It is true
Patrizia says when there is love everything
Works when there isn't nothing does. Love
Is a god These Freudian things I don't believe at all

This god you have to do what
He wants you to you are
Angry but all you really want
Is to get her back. Then—revenge! If
This woman did something like this to me
I would simply dislike her in fact

I would hate her You may want to consider
Patrizia said that this woman is
Doing this test to you. No, I
Said. I know she's not. I know something. I feel
A hundred years old. Yet
You don't look so bad, Patrizia said.

Find another woman. I can't. I
Know Patrizia said. But one always thinks it
Is a good idea. But
If you can't you can't. I
Can't even eat
This food Patrizia I said.

I'm sorry I said Patrizia to be so
Boring I can't stop talking Forgive
Me. It doesn't bore me at all
Patrizia says It's my favorite subject

It isn't every day one sees somebody
In such a state you can help him by talking to stay alive

You know, Patrizia says if she
Does this thing to you now
She will do it again
And again so you'd better be ready
Maybe you can get the advantage
By saying she is right you

Don't love her Good bye You leave
However if you want her
You should go into the bushes
And surprise her when they see you
It always makes a difference
I can't go hide there Patrizia

That's insane. I went but not
Hiding and not confronting.
Patrizia: What did she say? I said
The same things. Patrizia said
Did you see love in her eyes? I said
No. I didn't. I saw

Something else. In Florence it's rainy
Her (relatively) short hair and
Her eyes along the Arno
The last time I'll ever see her again
As the one I am seeing again
When seeing again still has some meaning.

It's finished Patrizia's saying
For now but don't worry
I think you will get her back
But it will be too late. Oh Patrizia I
Let my back and head fall against
The chair Late isn't anything!

# At the Opera

Ah do you remember
                    the voice of Gianni Poggi
                                    in Firenze
"in tuo splendor' "
                the clear light
                        and easy division
of the Italian language
                  "aurora" so it sounds like
                                Bobby Burns
it's another sign
                Katherine is two—
                        not quite—grand opera
and you still alive
                "lucevan le stelle"
                      and Gozzanno
in the morning
                the true pink light
                      and Gatto, the cat
who walked to our doorstep
                      from higher
                            on the hill
I think, that led
                someplace (Fiesole?)—
                              "led" che splendore, "led"
and we, we were
            led
                Gianni Poggi was led
He was leading
                but not the orchestra
                      led
to his death
              alla sua morte
                    che orror'
but not
        a real one
                he
was still alive
              when we left
                    the theatre and came home.

# No One Else

I could never have had anything
Quite as radical as all this
Was by reason of having known it
Was very soon to go away
As that movie went away from the little theatre
Crossed by our liberal eyes

The other glass by the beam
Orphaning the house with its bulbs
Its way-walks like tusks
And the cut-up scenes
That straightened the glasses
The steam that shows is knowing everything
Is the fax to a fax of itself

At daytime water came unsyphoned
Spoofing our house
I wore a net necktie a button
Or trees with a breeze for a mouth
But nothing could prevent it
As nothing north or south

A bagpipe failed you like Elijah
Women came forth
Reading and tacking fishnets to a port
An old woman rode in a hansom
Beer was an invidious sport

Idiot agreement—and summer tide
These seemed like works to be taught
One kept walking
"Yours to tour but mine to seek from birth"
Cadillacs wrecked
Forgotten and evenings
Boat-flat similar and signed: "No one else."

# L'art d'être grand-père

We like the reticent muscle of these days
Enduring what we have to in order to kiss a lot;
Now the art of being a grandfather sits up on my days
With the look of someone hot
"I'll grab you where the matter's at with praise,"
It says, "and take whatever grade you've got
To give to yourself for what you've done to days
During and up till now your lifetime spot."
I said I didn't deserve another's praise;
Saying I thought my achievements might be rot.
"Maybe," my art said, starting to peel off stays,
"But who you are is like to what is what
And when you've risen as you best can raise
Yourself, the day is here and you are not, but that is not"—
And here it stopped, my art—"the end of praise."
"Which, rather?" I demanded, and was shot,
Shot by I know not what, but other days
Must fall as they are falling and are not.
The lifetime of each person is a phase
That paves the ways but never saves the lot—
That is for others' days and waves to spot.

To be alive at all is to amaze
Someone who, looking around, might see a lot
But not a single person; then he prays
That you won't hurt him. You say, "Of course not,"
For you are full of civilizing ways
And don't destroy even when your temper's hot
Though sometimes younger years caught in a maze
Would do their goddamned damnedest to get out
And hit out in all ways
But now concede what pays
The child is on the way—what's that about
It isn't like the mention in a phrase
Of Christ or Colin Clout
It's more like rays

You have to hear this shout
Bareness is coming out

Into a very corridor of praise
Switching about
Until we can adorn it with bouquets
Because of all the ways of turning out
Pleasure to meet the measure of our days
A year, I thought, could be made up of Mays
But what of Guinevere and Lancelot?
They are in a time syndrome like the clays
Infinite Sculpture throws into the pot
And must go later, as I kiss these days
I kiss, they go, they leave us like a shot
Not even clear to us what they're about
Except that what they are about they're not
But something else which, gone a little ways
May turn around and tell us we have got
Something but they can't help us. Oh the ways
We ran each which way trying to work it out
And run each which way trying to work it out,
For grandfather's is not the end of days—
Whoever's sitting in this burning spot
Deserves to figure out
The matchstick and the kindling of these days
When forward steam is not. But still is not.

A reminiscent peacock bunch of plays
I wrote when I was feeling pretty hot
Could persuade nobody to mend his ways
Or become a heroic astronaut
They bent the status quo into a maze
And sent the verse lines jabbering like jays
Across the fragments, kissing in a daze
And I was sad and happy with my lot
I struck at foul confusion with a mace
Of interlocking ways of looking out
Making the wind my messenger of face
But now great sorrow for those aching years, they're gone like mace
Swift evanescence for a mugger's face
And mired in mud is every Camelot
I ever did imagine, not a trace
Is there as I pull in the vacant lot
By vacant lot of thee, old Samothrace,
And think about the art d'être grand-père.

How musically there
A trumpet sounds or slot machine or car
And dims my lifeboat with ten waves of care,
But never separate, knowing you are there,
Which to the best intents of time we are, you are.

Hurrah in praise
Of what is said will still be staying there
The sculptures of infinity's last days
Which cannot be imagined and cannot
Exist in any but imagined ways
And so is our existence on this spot
What splendid days
Anointed, glassed out, pinned, expressive days,
Impressive days, days which to figure out
Which bring the baby like a tiger out
Of his befriending den to give a shout
To mend the cataclysmic trend of days
So human fears know what they are about:
Never to know again the painter's art
And never more the Chevrolet shall start
With who inside it, you inside or out—
This is the very palliative of art
To make you a conundrum on the spot
Which you can burn but never make it blaze
A dream comes stammering out
But only is a dream and that is that
The art of being grand-père finds me out
In searching me through catacombs of rays
To make me stay and state what it's about
To have so rugby-like a field of praise.
Matters to matters, time is in its phase
I fold the rug but I the rug am not
To go through distance and the first of days.
Some man comparing princes being shot
Came up with an unmemorable phrase
Which every king's original forgot
But I'll remember it one of these days
When baby has decreed it shall come out
Making the spinning earth its messenger
Of all that it's about.

# On Aesthetics

## AESTHETICS OF TAKING A WALK

You
Put
One
Foot
In
Front
Of
The
Other.

## AESTHETICS OF THE LITTLE HOUSE

The little house in Italy
Looks good in ports.

## AESTHETICS OF BEING A BIRD

Eat brusquely
With a half-closed mouth;
When another speaks, glance up
But don't respond.
After you have eaten
Take off
And sing
Portuguese songs—a fado, if you please!

## AESTHETICS OF VICTOR HUGO

Place the Poet in the valleys
Place the Poet in the hills
Let the hills and the valleys
Know that the Poet is there.

## AESTHETICS OF THE MAN IN THE MOON

To be the man in the moon
You have to be sunny.


## AESTHETICS OF CREATING LIGHT

Put one hand
Next to a light-switch
With the other hand
Feeling for the wall.


## AESTHETICS OF FAMILY PICNIC

Take a basket
Of food and drink
And two children
(Aged five and three),
With your husband, the painter,
As close as you can get
To the sea.


## AESTHETICS OF OBITUARY

To avoid the clichés
Of the obituary writers,
Die in obscurity.
A fine bed in a light-filled room
Someone who adores you is at your side
And vowed to silence.


## AESTHETICS OF STANDING UP

Keep one foot
On the floor
At the same time keeping
The other foot firmly at its side.
Then stand.

## AESTHETICS OF HARSHNESS TO A HORSE

You should never be harsh
To a horse. A horse is always doing
Its best. Otherwise it is a bad horse
And harshness has no effect.


## AESTHETICS OF CLIMBING STAIRS

With a carpet in the middle
With friends,
With the certainty of love

O friends
O certainty of love!


## AESTHETICS OF PAUL VALÉRY

Better a single line that I have worked on
Than a whole epic dictated by the Muse!
Better to walk, even lost, in my own direction—and find the way.
If not . . . not count the day.


## AESTHETICS OF BEING A SAILBOAT

Go this way and that
Have a reflection
Be upside down


## AESTHETICS OF BABY

Seat yourself on the floor
Bend your trunk forward
Head outstretched with hands reaching
And crawl.

## AESTHETICS OF AVANT-GARDE THEATRE

Make the stage an actor
Make an actor the stage.


## AESTHETICS OF BEING WITH CHILD

You have the kid
Within what hid
That once did serve
Some lesser curve

So shall the wit
Of having it
Be inly lit
By white by light of day.


## AESTHETICS OF FRIENDSHIP

A world without friendship
Is a world without forms.


## AESTHETICS OF OTHER LANGUAGES

A young woman without a word
Of English to her vocabulary
Sang like a bird
To a Huguenot student in the moss of February.


## AESTHETICS OF GENEROSITY

Give love as a gift
But use your brain.


## AESTHETICS OF WAKING UP

Close one eye
After the other.

Whisper "Good-bye!"
To the Unconscious.


## AESTHETICS OF BEING ELEPHANTS

When the elephants came to town
The dry cleaning establishments came with them.


## AESTHETICS OF BEING THE YOUNGEST OF FOUR SISTERS

Take a day off
While your sisters are working
Work on a day
When your sisters are taking off
Be bright in the kitchen
Be sullen in the pantry
When they listen to music, cough
When they go to their lovers, be sultry
There is no solution
To being the youngest sister
The hottest summer day
To you is the most wintry
Take your shirt off
And read a while.


## AESTHETICS OF BEARS

To be a bear, be active
In the bear world—
Fur, limbs, and claws.
Rampage. Stay. Mate.
Give birth to another bear.


## AESTHETICS OF PEARLS

Pearls on a necklace
Are not anything

Compared to pearls
In a late fourth-century Greek frieze.


AESTHETICS OF AIR

Serafina said E bello avere
Nell'appartamento un po
Di natura meaning the window
That let in the sky


AESTHETICS OF VERLAINE AND RIMBAUD

De la musique avant toute chose—Happiness
From which no one gets away.


AESTHETICS OF OTHER WOMEN

They are general and ephemeral;
Your quarrels are engraved in stone.


AESTHETICS OF CLOUDS

Sometimes be red
As Lipstick Number Two;
At others pink
As Corinne on the brink
Of loving you, and saying so,
And also sometimes white
As news at night.


AESTHETICS OF GREEK NIGHT

In the Greek night
The statues
Of Athena and of Apollo
Are no longer white
But painted

In many colors
As they used to be
Two thousand years ago.


## AESTHETICS OF BEING GEESE

It is always rush hour
When you are honking.


## AESTHETICS OF CREATING TIME

To create time
Relinquish space—that is, the place
Where the time used to be.


## AESTHETICS OF ECHO

| Echo was | Us |
| A nymph who lived in | Din |
| Every cliff. | If |


## AESTHETICS OF CIVILIZATION

Every dog has the whiff of civilization.
A priest plays ball in the street
With some schoolboys. The overworked chambermaid
Smiles like a duchess.
Even a beggar is addressed as Monsieur or Madame.


## AESTHETICS OF PLATO

There has to be something better
Than what we see. Otherwise, we'd see it.

## AESTHETICS OF BEING A BASEBALL

Go as fast as you can
In whatever direction.

## AESTHETICS OF CÉZANNE

To have painted
the apples
that were in
the orchard
so red
and so gold.

## AESTHETICS OF LOVING AN AZTEC

Be careful of your heart
Or the Aztec will rip it out.

## AESTHETICS OF SMALL THEATRE

Don't bring a horse
Into a small theatre
But, if you must,
Put it on stage.

## AESTHETICS OF SURREALISM

To find the impossible
With breasts.

## AESTHETICS OF ROUGH ART

Smash smudge and erase
So that the true lovely face
Will emerge or maybe will not
But at least you've given it a shot
Somehow characteristic of the age.

## AESTHETICS OF MULTIPLICITY OF AESTHETICS
## (IN BOTTICELLI'S BIRTH OF VENUS)

In The Birth of Venus, these are some
Of the aesthetics to consider: the aesthetics of shape,
Of line, of color, of contrast, of shadow, of sea clouds, of sky,
Of filmy drapery, of cherubs, of angels, of sunlight,
Of waves, of water, of posture, of hair, of hairdo,
Of wind, of breeze, of puffed cheeks, of the marvelous,
Of realism, of mythology, of paganism, of antiquity, of seeing,
Of allegory, of perfection, of the "exact moment," of sea shells,
Of shoulders, of eyes, of gazing, of breasts, of waists, of feet—
For each of these one has an ideal conception
Whether conscious or unconscious, and when one sees
The Birth of Venus one is moved by, and may think about, these things.

## AESTHETICS OF FEET

To move together
Even when apart.

## AESTHETICS OF AFTER THE OPERA

When the singing has stopped
The silence of the singing begins
If you are the opera.

## AESTHETICS OF DANTE

Invite your best friends
To go out with you in a boat
That's magic and can go anywhere
And sail and talk, and talk and sail,
Until you find Beatrice
Like an endangered species
With luminous antlers
Rising through the Medieval dark.

## AESTHETICS OF CAVALCANTI GRIEVING FOR LOST LOVE

Be like a dead person, who seems to those
Who see him a man
Made of branches or stone
Who is able to walk only as a result of cunning
And who has in his heart a wound
Which is, since he is dead,
A visible sign.


## AESTHETICS OF CREATING SOMETHING

This doesn't just happen:
It happens to you.


## AESTHETICS OF CHINESE OPERA

The Chinese Opera was dealing with what a brain
Has to deal with only part of the time: the excesses and fantasies of kings.


## AESTHETICS OF NOAH'S ARK

Every animal needs a mate
Under Ark conditions; its bar is a dark, dull place.


## AESTHETICS OF RONSARD

Try to meet
A girl of fourteen
Cassandre Salviati
At Blois
Then never see
Her again
Now write
And write and write
Until you become
An old intellectual bum
Philosopher, esthetician,
Leader of a school,

Monsieur Ronsard
Doctor of the Pléiade.


## AESTHETICS OF PAUL KLEE

Little bits of freedom
Imprisoned by light blue sound
Is, it may be, an "oversensitive" way
Of thinking about Paul Klee
For whom smallness relayed a message
To the German-Swiss mountains around.


## AESTHETICS OF LORCA

Federico García Lorca stands alone
Luna, typewriter, plantain tree, and dust
The moon is watching him. It is watching over him.


## AESTHETICS OF BEING IN HAITI

Don't take off
With a Zombie
On a barge
In the heavy rain.


## AESTHETICS OF THE NOVEL

Put one plot
Inside another.


## AESTHETICS OF HILL TOWN

Put the cathedral
Or the church
That has the "scheming

Look of an ex-cathedral"
Ronald Firbank's phrase
On top of this hill.


## AESTHETICS OF FEELING FINE

Feel fine
Then go away.


## AESTHETICS OF DIFFERENCE

What a difference
When the words
Come tangled
In contradictions!


## AESTHETICS OF BEING A BOX

Look forward to always containing
What is contained
Whether it is dry
Or raining. Then one morning early
Someone may come by
(This has been known to happen)
Who will take
Your top off! and they will say
Thus, thus! was this result obtained.


## AESTHETICS OF OPERA

Don't sing an aria
To someone who can't
Sing one back.

## AESTHETICS OF LE GRAND MALENTENDU

Don't be mistaken
About being mistaken—
The Divinities are mistaken time after time

## AESTHETICS OF UNION MAN

"You either are a Union man
Or a thug for J. H. Blair"
"I'm working for the Union"

## AESTHETICS OF ARISTOTLE

They recognize each other, the one
Who has killed their father, and the other
The one who has killed his son. And she—that woman,
The wife of both—is their sister. They
Are brothers. After twenty years
Unknown to each other, they meet—they
Recognize each other. It is
The Recognition Scene, the
Core of Aristotle's theory
Of the purgative effect of tragedy—he says we feel
The purgative shock effects most
In watching the Recognition Scene.

## AESTHETICS OF RIGHT

Right is the aesthetic form
Of good and wrong is the aesthetic form
Of bad. In which case Aesthetics
Is a form (or branch) of Ethics
Which is neither good nor bad.

## AESTHETICS OF BEING A ROAD
(Hommage à Rilke)

It is long since you were a lane.
Now you leave off being a street
And don't become a highway yet.
You are cautious
But cautiously exploring what it might be
To be wider than you were before
And go further, and be less familiar with trees.


## AESTHETICS OF BEING A MOUSE

Look at the floor.
Look up.
Look at the wall.


## AESTHETICS OF POETRY AND PROSE

Chekhov told Bunin
Not to begin writing
Until he felt as cold as ice.
Keats wrote to Shelley
"I am a fever of myself!"


## AESTHETICS OF UNANIMITY

The waves come all at once
When you are a sailboat
And the wind
As when you used to be a tree.


## AESTHETICS OF FICTION

Don't write stories
That have no plot
And have no characters
And have no style.

## AESTHETICS OF INTEGRITY

For every star in the sky
Someone is holding his ground.

## AESTHETICS OF EARLY ON

Oh the glove in the fish bowl
Oh the flyers in the sink

## AESTHETICS OF HONFLEUR

Put one ship
Next to another
—Honfleur

## AESTHETICS OF INSTRUCTION

Do this, do that! is not instruction;
Instruction is a plausible bond
Between one patented enterprise and another.
A song instructs us to be singing;
A house, to live like women and men.

## AESTHETICS OF ARIOSTO

Meanwhile someone is going
Another way.

## AESTHETICS OF BRANCH

To hang over and to stretch out
To bear leaves
And flowers and fruit—
And still be branching.

## AESTHETICS OF ROBERT MUSIL

Musil saw that life
Was without meaning
While at the same time seeing
That Rilke had perfected
Or even that he had discovered
The lyric poem in German.
Before that, it had been nothing
Since the Middle Ages.

Aesthetically one must say
That inside a meaningless whole
Significant particulars exist.
Kicking, passing the ball
And rushing may fill us with life
In even a one-sided game
That is ended by freezing rain.

## AESTHETICS OF MOSS

Moss covers
Unwilling things
The way old poetry covers
Unwilling subjects:
The death of kings,
Women lost, spring
Arrives, you take
A flower and place it
In your hair or lie
Beside it in the moss.

## AESTHETICS OF SAYING GOODBYE TO A FRIEND

Walk him to the place
Where he can get a taxi
And say good-bye.
If he is wearing
An overcoat
Place one hand

On his shoulder—or if he is not.
Shake hands, embrace
Your friend and say good-bye.
Soon the sky
Will cover him
With only a plane between.


## AESTHETICS OF COMEDY ASLEEP

Don't wake the clown
Or he may knock you down.


## AESTHETICS OF CERTAIN THINGS

Certain people for certain things.
Certain women for certain things.
Certain men for certain things.
Certain occasions for certain things.
Certain lives for certain things.


## AESTHETICS OF SILENCE

Silence is not everything.
It is half of everything
Like a house.


## AESTHETICS OF THE MAIN PART OF LIFE

The late early and the entire middle
Are the main part of life. Be as kind
As you can in this part, and get done
What it seems to you has to be done.
If you find time for it, have a good time.

## AESTHETICS OF PLAZA

Christ comes down from the cross
Into a plaza.


## AESTHETICS OF OUTDOOR OPERA

Sing as loud
As you can
At the outdoor opera—
It will never
Be loud
Enough.


## AESTHETICS OF PENISES

Rising and falling like swans
On Greek vases
Suggesting the connection
To life, that Greek men had,
And satyrs and gods.


## AESTHETICS OF CANNON

Being near a cannon
When it was firing
Was as exciting
Stendhal said
As writing
What no one had ever said.


## AESTHETICS OF LATE

Light falls on the fountains
When they are off.

## AESTHETICS OF THE NUDE

To be a nude
Take off your clothes
And stand
Five or ten feet away
From a painter of nudes.

## AESTHETICS OF JAZZ

Play
One
Note
After
Another
On
The
First
Day
Of
The
First
Year
Of
The
First
Century
Of
Jazz.

## AESTHETICS OF THE AESTHETICIAN

What is the aesthetician
But a mule hitched to the times?

## AESTHETICS OF TALLEYRAND

"No one has any idea
Of the sweetness of life

Who wasn't alive
Before seventeen eighty-nine."


## AESTHETICS OF LOUIS KAHN

"The sun never knew
How wonderful it was
Until it fell on the wall
Of a building."


## AESTHETICS OF BEAUTY AND DEATH

When one sees a beautiful woman
One can assume that somewhere
(Stendhal says) there is a happy man;
On the other hand,
When one sees a gloomy funeral
One can assume that somewhere
There is a woman or a man
Wondering if going on living is worthwhile.
Put the two together: beautiful woman and gloomy funeral
And what do you get? The death
Of Cleopatra and her obsequies.


## AESTHETICS OF SUFFERING

Suffering comes to people as war comes to countries
And issues are clarified. Others are completely lost.


## AESTHETICS OF BEING GLORIOUS

To be glorious, take off your wings
Before you fly.

## AESTHETICS OF STONE

The gods take stone
And turn it into men and women;
Men and women take gods
And turn them into stone.


## AESTHETICS OF PASSING BY *(After Reverdy)*

One shadow—
      Enough!
Is passing by

# STRAITS

# The Human Sacrament

Is nothing new sacred? The book, the sky,
The women on the blue and red screen
Painted in Japan about five hundred years ago. Someone
Has tipped the screen over. I'll set it back up
Putting all the emotion in the thing felt at the thing done. A mirror can be
  clearer
Than a dog, but a small dog can run. Sacred
Is perhaps the relation that caused
My daughter to be born. Yet is she sacred?
She is a woman with someone's arm
Around her shoulders. She is of this world
The way that pipe is, that goes from the well to the house,
And the way the grass is that at this season leaps about up and under it,
And as the cigarette is that the gardener throws in the grass.
Has it a sacred flame? The pipe going to the house. Later, who knows?
The sacred is the sacrament. And it is what
We wanted once to be—
Give me some more coffee,
Some more milk, some more bread, some more breakfast!
Is nothing new sacred? The screen is standing up.
My daughter and her baby come for tea. The baby comes for milk.
They're here in time.

# Straits

*To Viktor Shklovsky (and containing some of his sentences)*

It is easy to be cruel in love: one merely has not to love.

Mayakowsky entered the Revolution as he would his own home. He went
    right in and began opening windows. How serious is it

That something final be accomplished before it is too late?

One entered the earth. One started flinging up diamonds.

They are valuable because they are few not because they are old.

Sitting with Harry in Venice in Loredana's living room

It was easy to be amusing about France. One merely had not to be present

There but in Venice instead. And all that the other guests said to me

How inaccurate or accurate or part of some meaningful or unmeaningful
    or cruel or stupid or worthwhile or happy and life-and-love-giving life
    they seem and related to literature

"A house is at the opera" "Likely it won't be on time," "Town's bridges"
    "I love,"

Wrote Mayakowsky. It was time to disappear into a group of three

And not either be one or a twosome for all eternity.

In this way one could avoid love. Civilization has reached a certain point.

When it had reached a lesser point was the time of one's father

Who seemed a greater point by filling the horizon. Water slopped on the
    walks.

The women wear high-heeled shoes and talk about Christ. "They say he
    is sure to come back." "When?" "I don't know!"

It has never been any man's total destiny to be a father. To this, God may
    be the only exception.

But when God was a man he was a Son.

Many race to be first. Giselle doesn't move. The road passes through oak
    trees. Some trees are pink when in bloom.

New strategies for naval warfare have been worked out

That show that most maneuvers are irrelevant. The most important thing
    is the first engagement.

Gide entered the stables as he would his own home. He went right in and
    began opening gates. It was like a billiards room—with six tables.

A bird may fly through a window directly into a cage.

Bankers are people without a homeland. They live in apartments that look
    like oriental bath houses.

They collect china and occasionally say something witty. We are pleased
  when they come to visit us. The days pass away like a shower.
They are accompanied by actresses, who say, "The world is a gentle
  place."
I will never marry. Oh but you must marry. It's the only way to bear a
  legitimate son.
An illegitimate son is fine with me. I don't want to marry. It is easy to lie
  down on the stones.
The knife craves a throat. The hangman's noose is giddier than a razor.
She goes away. When he comes back to meet her the curtains are yellow.
They are folded, in pleats. You say to me "It is all over." It is all over at
  home.
As soon as you say "It is not all over" it is no longer all over at home.
We had to hoist a sail into a new wind. The movie star and the novelist
Are dead still not knowing anything, the scientist who improved our lives
And the German shepherd also who brought us delight for years.
Windows are broken and some have been boarded over. It is easy to be a
  glazier to the young
Harder to be a plasterer to the old. Not only the strong but the weak leave
  a legacy. They show life is not gone
When half gone. The man with the broken leg in the swimming pool is an
  encouraging sight. It is Andy.
Andy is it really safe for you to be swimming alone today? Yes, he replies. I
  am looking for a strait,
A way from this pool into the sea. If he cannot have everything, he will
  have something.
The birds also found it possible to make an adjustment. They took fresh
  views of the clouds.
One flew over here, one flew under there. An orchestra conductor raised
  his glove
To throw it to a woman in the first row. The city was sunny because no
  smoke rose from the chimneys.
Unchallenged, everyone remained alive. Once the boat started moving,
  some did not.
He saw the old way of life as a bunker that had to be stormed.
Do you remember the idea "Revolution"? planning for and waiting for
  the revolution?
A painter took over Venice's outdoor cafés as his own private particular
  province.
This was true for three and a half months even though his paintings were
  not very good

By objective standards. For a while he had a certain panache.

The world lives through long periods of drudgery so it can enjoy one splendid space.

The great, dutiful buildings had no tendency to fall down. But one bomb or one rocket

Could change their sunny adolescence. What building cares if it is knocked down?

The facade longs for a bombshell, the infrastructure for an air raid.

It was daylight in the apartment. I usually visited there in the evening.

Magellan sailed along the shore of America, looking for straits.

He sailed into the wide estuaries of rivers, but there he found that it was fresh water.

Fresh water meant no straits. Straits would be filled with salt water. But there were bays.

Magellan solved his problem of circling America but he didn't return home alive. He went in and began testing estuaries.

At noon he was on a coastline looking for a channel to another ocean. Vales of rocks. But there are bays. They are panoramas.

Magellan had to hoist a new sail. Once it was hoisted he had to find a briny path.

The wind roars like a madman. Magellan goes to sleep. When he wakes up it is the Pacific.

Birds stand on the deck. They are Indians.

One does not die of love unrequited but of ceasing to love. Chaliapin sings. The audience sits down.

The Zairians sold the machinery from the Belgian coppermines. No more copper could be pulled from the earth.

Belgians had to be called back. Their cruelty was equaled only by their mining expertise. They were nasty colonialists but good miners.

The sun shines on the rolling water and also on the marble tiles. The penguins were replaced by Indians.

We are looking for a shortcut.

The tree doesn't exist in a metaphysical world. The roots crave water, the trunk is ready for an axe.

At that time I was a Futurist.

Mark Twain loved his double, Huck Finn. He loved him more than himself.

He never did renounce him. When Hyperion wakes up the world is already full of sun.

Nonetheless it doesn't seem true what a Swiss banker said to me in Haute Savoie one evening: "Banking is just like poetry."

There were painted red tiles. Here and there were interspersed some blue
ones. A few were green or white.
The sky was old by then: the morning and evening papers were
interchangeable.
One gives money for a work by Velasquez—not to pay Velasquez for the
time he spent painting the work
But to pay the countless others who couldn't do it—to cover their costs.
We have to find straits but instead we find intelligence.
Why did you hurt your leg? Freud asks his son.
The moon rises over the inland ocean even on revolutionary holidays.
In love, as in art, we pay for failures. We thank one individual for the
success of humanity.
Freud's son didn't know what to say to his father. Other people's troubles
are easy to bear.
Neither the bankers nor the women they went out with were interested in
marriage. They thought it the ruin of love.
Mayakowsky was sure of himself as long as he was in action.
Unable to break out of his style of painting, Velasquez painted five
hundred canvases.
Eventually his stylistic problem was solved—by another painter.
The actor started speaking words as if they were his own
And not those of Shakespeare or of de Montherlant or of Chaliapin.
Looking up at the hilly shore, he saw the fires made by Indians.
He supposed a name for the peninsula: Tierra del Fuego.
But what if it were not a peninsula? The birds might then be presumed to
go further away.
They were used to seeing it only in the afternoon.
"With these you can start a new life." She gave him her jewels.
Conversation is one thing in the South and another in the North.
In the North one keeps moving.
In China, they risked banishment or prison if they talked. This then was
changed but not completely changed.
The opening up of freedom takes place in steps:
First one speaks of the ocean, then of the boats, then of the people on the
boats, lastly of their ideas.
The fishstore man praises the young woman's smile and her clothing.
What munitions makers do is to diversify. There are annuals.
Magellan sent an Indian boy to pick some before they had faded; when he
came back,
Magellan had decided. "We'll call it Tierra del Fuego."
The sun rose high over the fourth or fifth inland ocean he had seen. At
home in Europe he had been a shy student,

Thought lazy and not very good with girls. When he set off, however,
Flags from every nation and of every color adorned the flagpoles
And the tallest masts of the highest ships of the world. And Magellan went
As Mayakowsky went, and as Mark Twain and Cicero went, into the
future. He stood on a promontory.
Bankers predicted flax was on the rise and, with it, maize and broccoli.
It's not true that all predictions are false. But it is true that those who
make them don't know if they are or not.
Pushkin and Lermontov and Gogol waited on the bookshelf for
Mayakowsky—
If people were on the moon, they could have seen, for one second, a new
world.
Then just as suddenly Mayakowsky re-became a book; his covers were like
penguins.
The hot vibrations of his poetry flamed and calmed down. They
wandered around the apartments
Looking for girls who spoke their own language. Some were fond of
saying,
You don't really need to know more than a few words, maybe not even
that.
Ponce de Leon noticing his graying beard in the mirror
Said, "I know what I have to find!" He set off, but he never found the
Fountain of Youth.
Poniatowsky once found something he thought resembled it: a railroad
station.
He was fascinated by the choice of different directions. But he aged
anyway. By then Ponce de Leon was gone.
He imagines a woman who is like a strait, into a cold happiness, which is
like a sea.
Cranes looking down see only fragments, gay Twombly-like interrupted
scrambles.
Thenceforth we didn't write our work in regular lines
But in staffs, like music. Satie came out and sat at the mendicant's door.
Gandhi said, "I didn't know I had a door! Now I need no longer be
wandering!"
They were waiting for a foot; and, after the foot, a leg; and then a staff.
Life brims with music when a country is founded
Or merges with another, or is diversified, like the Dionne Quintuplets.
Cicero gave his best speeches
When he was a drunk, and Horace wrote his finest poems. There were no
brothels: property tax had gone up.

Zeus was not a god but a projection of human consciousness. We live in
the consequences
Of what we imagine persons like Gandhi have done.
The portholes looked like windows of a shop in which they were selling
the ocean—
How much do you want for this? how much for that?
Eskimos are amazed at the size of the apartments. They think that they
must be places to keep the dogs.
They are uninterested in politics but fascinated by the apartments.
No casino was opened because no one was rich—
One night's losses could ruin a person for the rest of his or her life.
For Poniatowsky, gambling was displaced to love—also for everyone he
knew.
Bankers invested heavily in Magellan's voyage and their money was never
paid back.
They invested in something that might pay off centuries in the future.
Magellan returned dead although he had circled South America.
One banker's girlfriend walked in freezing weather all the way from
another district
To see Mayakowsky. But he was never at home. She installed herself in his
apartment.
Her banker came there looking for her; she met him at the door.
She said, "There is no going backward in a revolution. A revolution is like
a devaluation of currency.
It is what it is and it happens when it happens." He said "You will never
win the love of Mayakowsky."
She said that that however was what she wanted.
The idea of installing a phone booth to some seemed central.
People wished to communicate. The sight of a phone booth was like a
whiff of salt air, from the sea.
The plan of having a Doge as governor was quickly abandoned—it was
impractical
From every point of view. The china belonged to an admiral. Forty-five
years ago he had gone to school
With Yesenin's father. He had padded shoulders, like a football player; he
was sturdy but short.
We came to see him to ask help for an artistic project; he was amiable but
unresponsive.
In a civilization one has to be Mark Twain or André Eglevsky or, at the
limit, Lord Byron.
Shakespeare looked in a mirror. It was much more bracing to open a
window:

There one could see only what one was not. Prospero found Ferdinand as
   a husband for Miranda.
Once Shakespeare had written the play the subject was dead.
I had seen the apartment only in the afternoon or early evening.
Once I had done that, it was easier to see what had to be done.
Music didn't sound to Orpheus as it did to Rilke. Orpheus took it for
   granted
As a natural thing and an accompaniment to words. Parliament was
   convened.
"When were you here last?" Napoleon whispered to his horse.
When his horse didn't reply, Napoleon smiled, and rode him into battle.
   When his horse died, he wept.
I didn't know you were living near this pool! "Oh, I don't," said Andy; "to
   swim here I come a long way
Past shops and market stalls—I am looking for a strait." But there is none
   in this pool, Andy. Humanity is astonished
By the successes it contains and tends to celebrate the failures
Until a new explanation comes to light.
Mayakowsky imagined he saw a wolf in the long Moscow night
But actually he committed suicide. The deed was signed but no one had
   looked at the property.
The sun went into the west opening up portholes. These were stars
At which you could buy the Ascension.
Books were a scarcity. A man would fold up a newspaper and read it as a
   book. The ice lasted
Until spring. The orchestra was conducted
By a former slave but everyone was free when Chaliapin sang. During the
   Cold War
Forgetfulness was almost a necessity, it was difficult to live without it.
I made friends with a member of the Russian embassy. I asked him if he
   was an attaché or the ambassador.
The Russian only nodded grimly and walked into the canal.
The newspapers next day reported Mayakowsky's death
As an accident. The Apollos had an "archaic smile"—one theory was that
   there existed a happiness
At that time in that place that never existed anyplace else.
Wallace Stevens thought to find it in Florida, taking the boat
Across the Gulf to Havana, where he would find compliant young women.
   This was the source of many of his poems.
El Greco lived in Seville but wasn't a Spaniard

But a Greek. As was the case with Christ, his name designated what, not
  who, he was.
There was a phone booth about every half mile. Magellan had an address
  book
With nothing in it. He had burned all his past relationships. He might not
  have recognized Chaliapin
As a great singer. But he was going to the South Pole
Whether anyone wanted him to or not. The "archaic smile" is attributed
  by others,
Like Disney's use of four-fingered gloves, to the relative easiness of
  making things that way, a smile is easier to draw
Than a ruminative or prescient expression. A proletarian navy
Seemed a contradiction, like ordinary eyes with an avant-garde nose.
One had to be a "Lombardi" to work on the church. He wanted to detain
  autumn.
It was departing. It took the drapes down from the trees,
Threw everything on the floor, started packing.
Autumn was holding its gun to the head of the willows.
The streetcar tracks brought syphilis to the door. Tall and sometimes
  blissful
She was running around his apartment dressed in fabric.
At the end of the month, when the rent came due, she got on a bus
And went to the Vatican. The linden's leaves dried. A notice came again
For the rent. Convicted intellectuals were confined to a room and allowed
  only one book per month.
The captain changed into a dinner jacket. On holidays, the villagers would
  choose up sides and fight.
Walt Whitman wrote, There was never any more perfection than there is
  now.
When he looked out the window he saw the sun.
Poetry burned on tables. Whitman wrote flattering reviews of himself. A
  German scholar
Who up till that time had been a fervent admirer, changed, when he found
  this out,
And became a ferocious detractor. He confused what Whitman was with
  what Whitman wrote.
If Giselle lay down, the people danced over her. She has on a vest of aqua.
But there are bays. Andy is carving his way through one of them, hand
  over hand.
The Doge acknowledged that trade was bad. He went back in and began
  opening up trade routes.

Later he was deposed, an old man who was too fond of young women. But no one else could be found at his level.

Venice remained ungoverned for forty years. It could thank one of its leaders for the success of its trade routes.

When the rat came out from behind the curtain it seemed no longer a rat

But it was—it just happened that the sunlight had disguised it as a ball of yarn.

It was easy to be a signer of the Constitution. One merely had to be there.

Youth gave power to some people, and money gave power to others.

Some spent their youth devising theories, others on experiencing sex

With as many persons as possible. Only a small minority were fascinated by estuaries.

Music was defined by Tchaikowsky as "disappearing youth." When he wrote music, it stopped disappearing.

The ocean is a source of elegies and a popular location for casinos.

There wasn't money for people to spend on taking taxis. The taxi drivers didn't blame them.

They felt, correctly, that they were stuck in a proletarian society

With providing an aristocratic mode of transportation. They took their plight with some humor.

Occasionally a banker took a cab and spent a lot of money. He was paying not for the ride he got

But for the availability of the service. What if the revolution were like a taxi

And couldn't be afforded? We say that life is beautiful

Not only to pay a compliment to something in which we are already included

But to separate inside and outside, if only for a moment.

Shklovsky said, "I speak in a voice grown hoarse from silence and pamphlets."

It didn't pay him to be wrong about the Soviet State and it didn't pay him to be right.

He said, "Spring was creeping under coats and over bosoms," and "Quiet and fat, I ran around in a shiny black jacket."

With style, he opposed the state. "Death is not the worst of all sorrows," said the Italian

Who came to fix Shklovsky's clock. This clock was stuck at quarter after eleven.

Elsa didn't call back. He spoke of the factory.

No one was supposed to comment on the failings of Soviet industry.

Putilov has an area of fifty square miles and a population of thirty-five thousand.

Most of these people work in the plant. The plant makes a tremendous
  amount of noise but produces very little.
The machines are out-of-date and not well taken care of. Thus the clatter.
Mayakowsky opened windows. Shklovsky wrote,
"Noise is work for an orchestra, but not for the Putilov plant."
He spent a number of years in exile. "It is supposed to be turning out
  products."

# Vous Êtes Plus Beaux que Vous ne Pensiez

I

Botticelli lived
In a little house
In Florence
Italy
He went out
And painted Aphrodite
Standing on some air
Above a shell
On some waves
And he felt happy
He
Went into a café
And cried
I'll buy
Everybody a drink
And for me
A punt e mes
Celebrities thronged
To look at his painting
Never had anyone seen
So beautiful a painted girl
The real girl he painted
The model
For Aphrodite sits
With her chin in her hand
Her hand on her wrist
Her elbow
On a table
And she cries,
"When I was
Naked I was believed,
Will be, and am."

## 2

Sappho lived
In a little house
Made out of stone
On the island
In Greece of Lesbos
And she lived
To love other women
She loved girls
She went out
And was tortured by loving someone
And then was
Tortured by
Loving someone else
She wrote great
Poems
About these loves
Poems so great
That they actually seem
Like torture themselves
Torture to know
So much sweetness
Can be given
And can be taken away.

## 3

George Gordon Lord Byron lived
In a little house
In England
He came out
Full of fire
And wild
Creative spirits
He got himself in trouble all the time
He made love to his sister
He was a devil to his wife
And she to him!
Byron was making love

Part of the time
In ottava rima,
And part of the time
Really
Teresa Guiccioli lived
In a big palace
In Venice
And Byron made love to her
Time after time after time.


## 4


Saint Francis of Assisi lived
In a little house
Full of fine
And expensive things
His father
Was a billionaire
(SIR Francis of Assisi)
And his mother was a lady
Most high and rare
Baby Francis stayed there
And then he went out
He found God
He saw God
He gave all
His clothes away
Which made
His father mad
Very mad
Saint Francis gave
To poor
People and to animals
Everything he had
Now he has a big church
Built to him in Assisi
His father has nothing
Not even
A mound of earth
With his name

SIR
FRANCIS OF ASSISI
Above it
Carved on a stone.


                    5


Borges lived
In a little house
In Buenos Aires.
He came out
And wrote
Stories, and
When he was blind
Was director
Of the National Library
La Biblioteca Nacional.
No one at the library
Knew he was a famous man.
They were amazed
At the elegant women
Who came to pick him up—
Like a book!—
At the Library day's end!


                    6


Vladimir Mayakowsky lived
In a little house
In Russia
He came out
And painted pictures
And wrote poems:
"To the Eiffel Tower"
"To My Passport"
"At the Top of My Lungs"
"A Cloud in Trousers"—
Before he died—

Was it suicide
Or was he murdered
By the Secret Police—
Crowds of fifty thousand gathered
To hear him read his lines.

7

Maya Plisetskaya lived
In a little house
In Russia
There was snow
All around
And often
For weeks at a time
Maya Plisetskaya's feet
Didn't touch the ground
The way, afterwards,
They never seemed to touch
The stage
She said The age
When you begin
To understand dance
Is the same
As that at which
You start to lose
Your elevation.

8

Ludwig Wittgenstein lived
In a little house
In Vienna
He came out
And went to live
In another house
In England
He kept coming out

And going back in
He wrote philosophy
Books that showed
We do not know how we know
What we mean
By words like Out and In.
He was revered like a god
For showing this
And he acted like a god
In mid-career
He completely changed his mind.


## 9

Frank O'Hara lived
In a little house
In Grafton, Massachusetts
Sister and brother
Beside him.
He took out
Toilet articles from his house
And he took out
Candles and books
And he took out
Music and pictures and stones
And to himself he said
Now you are out
Of the house Do something
Great! He came
To New York
He wrote "Second Avenue," "Biotherm"
And "Hatred."
He played the piano
He woke up
In a construction site
At five a.m., amazed.

Jean Dubuffet lived
In a little house
In the south of France
He came out
And made paintings
He went back in
And made some more
Soon Jean Dubuffet had
A hundred and five score
He also did sculptures,
And paintings
That were like sculptures
And even some sculptures
That were like
Paintings Such
Is our modern world
And among the things
He did
Was a series
Of portraits
Of his artist and writer
Friends A large series
Entitled You Look
Better Than You Thought You
Did Vous Êtes
Plus Beaux que
Vous ne Pensiez.

# Study of Time

One bird deserves another. One white and orange tabletop.
One twenty-five-year-old deserves another
Twenty-five-year-old. One harlequin deserves another harlequin. One
    rich cocktail of flames deserves another
And one extravagant boast: I am the Obvious. My hunch is me.
One brain deserves a brain that has been hatched in the tropics
One broken heart a heart that has been differently broken.
It seems to me time to get something done. But if I get in the car
I am forty-five years old and you are nineteen. We are
Not going anywhere. The car won't start. And if I get out
I am sixty years old. I look around but don't see you there.
I expect it's a good presumption that you are coming back,
But hurry. If I go into the drugstore
I am thirty-three. The boy behind the counter
Is not a girl, but we discuss national politics anyway.
That fucking Nixon. Or That damned unholy war! If I read a magazine
At the stand, on the other side of the drugstore,
I am twenty-five, and you, dressed with some hoop-la, come in.
I am sixteen when I am lying on the floor, with you beside me
Reading a newspaper. One stone man
Deserves one stone woman, and one glad day of being alone
And in good health. If at seventy
I get up and close the door,
I am fourteen and you are twenty. I'll put on
My blue shirt. My white tie, I'm twenty, twenty-one. Now we are eighty.
One five o'clock sunny day
Deserves another. We are both fifty-four. You pick up the bar that holds
    the door
And hit it as hard as you can at twenty. The floor deserves the floor
Of heaven that is a ceiling as we see it. One coldly affected group
Deserves another. We both very much enjoy engaging in sports.
You fall down, I pick you up. I am eight
You are sixty-six. Today is your birthday. You stand opening a cantaloupe.
    You say, Let's
Try another! You are sitting in the car,

You are twenty-three, I am forty-four and singing a Spanish song.
If she is nine years old, then I am fifty.
The birthdays come and go talking of Prospero. Good-bye, house!
Do you remember when we used to live in you
And be forty-eight years old? One age deserves another. One time
    deserves another time.

# Currency

In the Fifties Western Europe was the place
That had just been through a war. The currencies were wobbly.
A run-down American student could live like Wallace Stevens
Among the moguls of Hartford. This was helpful for poetry
If bad for a lot else. Not many French apartments had bathrooms,
Almost none refrigerators. One went to the public baths and looked out
The already steamed-up windows at the city.
I sat around a lot in Montparnasse
Cafés—you know them, the Select, the Dôme, and
The Rotonde. The Rotonde those days stayed open
All night. The old-fashioned French coffee machine was steaming.
It gave off an awful and awfully exciting smell.
The Surrealists were aging, like the paper of their books
*Le paysan de Paris* and *Les malheurs des immortels*
Above—up there—the river is winding. The museum is full of busts
Its large paintings are like days.
A friend was foreign and far away.
Everyone understands these things but no one is looking.
The fire escapes are in New York with everyone else.
Important here is to get my foot on the street
Before the car gets there. From the asphalt gas and steam not going up.
However, there is a book store on the rue de Rennes.
Its French books are very cheap.
A book costs hardly more than a postcard in the United States.
This situation is temporary. Meanwhile I am becoming well-read
In modern French poetry. I also read *La chanson de Roland* translated into
    Modern French
And Virgil's *Eclogues* and his *Georgics* translated into French.
They seem to make more sense to me than in English.
I find it in the air as well as in Max Jacob,
In Jouve and in de Montherlant. Surrealism is bouquet to these arrogated
    French tables.
Who thinks about those things.
I am away from ghostly and boasting New York.
In the bookstore I meet Henri Michaux. The kind man who owns the
    bookstore introduces me to him
He thinks we may both like it
I more than Henri Michaux. I like it.
I am nervous I am some kind of phantom.

No don't buy the Larousse buy this a truly serious dictionary a man under
    the sidewalk in his papery dusty crowded store says to me
But I am not that scholarly American
I am learning from Paris's streets to lead a life without consequence
But isn't that a life of consequence?
It is not very often that I get around to love-making
Not in this first early year.
Sexual passion and excitement are more interesting to me when I am
    older.
They interested me every year.
I am not studying this but Je t'aime and je vais jouir
I'm learning French phrases but I feel mystified and off to the side
I notice her long thin arms she wants to be an airline stewardess
If I held on long enough I'd be perhaps somewhat "French"
I want to be famous amidst the prose of everyday existence
In fact this year I don't care about fame
I have never cared about it I just want to be delighted and I'm envious
I want to be part of that enormous cake over there
That is a monument being wheeled down les Champs Elysées
I am daft about Paris's white sidewalks
Everything I have read and done since then
Is not more real. I wrote I completely forget what.
One friend said this version (#2) is "more abstract" than this (1st) one. I
    said Thank you.
Michaux was pleasant with me, and witty.
Invisible the monstrous sufferer of his poetry
Whereas my overexcited feeling is all too evident.
I am twenty-five years old and in good health sleeping
I'm sitting in a smoky restaurant
Thanksgiving Day Sixth Arrondissement I was not eating turkey
Or cranberry sauce but some petits suisses
These are very petits but are they suisses in what ways are they suisses
The conversation's booming around me
I feel lost in this breaking ocean of French happiness-inducing culinary
    indulgence
These fat bourgeois I am a thin bourgeois only because I am twenty-five
Giacometti is sitting drinking at the Dôme. He is with his followers.
I have a bicycle. I try but I can't hear one word that Giacometti says.
How long ago is it that I started to "dream in French"? Two months.
I want to be something else. I keep listening.
Life isn't infinite.
Now it may seem infinite but it isn't infinite.

Minor ailments don't interfere with my struggle to become French.
I will never become French.
I like too much being American. Also partly French.
Jean Cocteau equals Juan Gris. They even have, almost, the same name.
Birds ce sont les oiseaux.
Here I am in Paris being miserably lonely. All the same.
All the same even Amadis de Gaul knew when it was time to go home.
When he had conquered his enemies.
I have not yet conquered France.
By the time I get close to it I think death may have conquered me.
My first "moment" on French soil which is the soil of Normandy
The ship the Degrasse lands and I put down my foot
On some sparsely grown grass mud that leads up to the platform where
    the train
Is that will be taking me to Paris
To Montparnasse its beds are its streets
Its pillows the cafés. I am streetless in the Hôtel de Fleurus
Then I came down from there.
My mail is at American Express.
I have a friend who will not be my friend for very long.
And many, unknown, I have yet to meet.
What will it matter? It matters that I am not alone.
It matters that someone agrees
And that there are walls like energy.
I am unaware of a lot that has gone on here—the herding of the Jews
Into railroad cars, to Belsen.
I read Max Jacob "La rue Ravignan" in
Le cornet à dés with its conclusion "c'est toi, Dostoievski"
In the road I pick up leaves in the street I pick up books
Max Jacob who had long ago proofread the last page of his *The Central
    Laboratory*
Is dead, killed by the Nazis.
Now Larry like a clown down the street
It's extremely late and Nell we three meet
And drink coffee
It tastes like dirt or metal, hot and steaming, like the whole world that's
    coming to be,
The coffee of our lives, the strong and bitter café de nos vies.
The yellow and pink lines come marching down the boulevard
    Montparnasse
We can pay for the coffee so we have the dawn.

# My Olivetti Speaks

Birds don't sing, they explain. Only human beings sing.

If half the poets in the world stopped writing, there would still be the same amount of poetry.

If ninety-nine percent of the poets in the world stopped writing poetry, there would still be the same amount of poetry. Going beyond ninety-nine percent might limit production.

The very existence of poetry should make us laugh. What is that all about? What is it for?

Oxford and Cambridge, two great English universities, are based on poetry. If poetry vanished, they would fall down.

Olive likes poetry but Popeye doesn't. Popeye says, "Swee'pea is poetry for me." Popeye is making a familiar mistake. Human beings and poems are entirely different things. But, claims Popeye, Swee'pea is not a human being. He am a cartoon. It may be that Swee'pea is a poem but he is not exactly written. He is a calligramme without words. It is quite possible to like such kinds of poems but I prefer the others, the regular ones, written out.

In the old days a good place to publish a poem was the *Partisan Review*. Heady—among those thick, heavy pages—one felt ranked by the rankers, a part of the move, a part of the proof—toward what? of what? To find out, you had to read countless *Partisan Review*s. Then you would see what it was. You could be as serious as Delmore Schwartz, as serious as anyone who ever lived. He consistently turned down my poems. I loved that magazine. It weighed an intellectual ton. What would a poem of mine have been doing inside it anyway? How could it have fitted into that heavy and amazing vision of contemporary life?

Sex is to poetry as sex is to everything else. It forgives it, but it also forgets it even while it is planning it.

"I don't like it but I know it is a great poem." I feel the same way about you.

"Poetry is making a comeback." But why is it always bad poetry, or a false idea about poetry, that is making a comeback? I don't think good poetry has ever made a comeback, or ever will. That's one reason it's necessary to keep on writing it.

A dog barks in rhyme but the rhyme is never planned by the dog. This is not a value judgment in any way but it may be an introduction to the consideration of the aesthetic pleasures of being and not being a dog.

Rhyme was very good. Then rhyme was very bad. Then it was forbidden. Then, leader of a rebellion, it came back. Now it has grown old and mellowed, no longer smokes cigars, is less militant, seems sinking into acceptance of parliamentary democracy (to a degree!), and a poet can use it or not, pretty much as he or she chooses. However, anyone who uses it has to be careful, extra-careful, he doesn't get shot. No old-fashioned communism, if you please! Use it and get out. Use it and run. Probably more quickly than anything else, rhyme can show how self-uninformed you are.

On the island of rhymesters, anyone who is any good is king. It's a rare talent. Statues of Byron, Ariosto, Petrarch, and Herrick on the coast are misleading. In the interior, there are no statues at all.

A short life and one hundred good poems. A long life and two good poems. No one has ever had to make this choice.

Here is someone talking about poetry. The only people who listen are those who don't know anything about poetry and those who do.

Shakespeare was the last great poet of the Middle Ages. Keats was the first great poet of Modern Times. Each poet alive now is both desirous of, and afraid of, being the last.

"I bring fresh showers for thirsting flowers." Poetry sometimes seems part of an enormous game of Fill in the Blanks. Let every emotion, idea, sensation be covered (filled in) and may none escape. When we have totally completed this board, when all is color, line, and shading, no blank spaces at all, we may, then, see what this great solved jigsaw puzzle means. (I already have one idea: the refreshment of childhood grossly modified by social and historical change.) The Last Judgment is nothing compared to what then we shall see! Otherwise (if there is no puzzle of this sort) why is Shelley disguising himself as a cloud? Wouldn't that be a waste of time?

The awakening of sexual feelings in a hedgehog is a poetic subject possibly not yet covered. This doesn't imply, however, that we should concentrate our efforts on covering it, though someone may, and if he is as good a poet as Ronsard, and has a thriving tradition behind him, he may do it well.

The last century was full of music, as this one has been full of painting. Poetry, complexly amused, has been content to take second place in both.

Byron was so unlikely ever to write a sonnet that people in his time used to say, when they were skeptical about a thing, "Oh, sure, like Byron's sonnet!" A seemingly impossible windfall, any staggeringly unlikely event was called a "Byron's sonnet." When someone proposed removing all the Carpaccio paintings from Venice, the witty Doge Meduno Rabanatti is reported to have said, "Certainly! as soon as we get Byron's sonnet in exchange." Byron, according to one story, hearing of this conversation, immediately sat down and wrote a sonnet, which—since he loved the Carpaccios and wanted them to stay—he then just as immediately tore up.

Nostalgia for old poetry is like nostalgia for Ancient Egypt—one is hardly lamenting one's own youth. Imagine an Egyptian youth and that he speaks to you. Who is that lovely young woman by his side? No one you have ever hurt with your fear or your false promises, that's sure. Dissolution may not be so bad, if only it didn't need to be preceded by death, as it isn't in poetry.

A glass breaks when someone sings a high note, and when someone makes a great breakthrough in a poem there is a stranger in the mirror.

To read a poem we sit down; to look at a painting we stand up. Art is always saying hello and poetry is always saying good-bye. It says, Your dreams are leaving town, and not even Byron can prevent it, nor any other Lord.

To look at a painting we stand up because of our voracity. We don't want anyone else getting it before us, not the slightest part. We are quickly satisfied, however, given how strong this voracity is. We soon move away. Reading a poem we don't mind interruptions. That poem will be there when we come back. Still, we don't want someone reading over our shoulder.

I will live in that little house with you and write poetry! This statement, taken in isolation from all others, and from all the rest of reality, is wonderful and touching to think about.

Yes! I will write too! Already the situation is less "ideal." This means two quiet places and two typewriters. And as for the house—

Five great poets writing about five different things constitute a Renaissance. Five great poets writing about the same thing constitute a "school" (une école).

A mermaid who recites poetry is a lost mermaid.

A curious thing about the wind is that one can't tell if its music is ever the same, because one never hears the beginning.

Write poetry as if you were in love. If you are always in love you will not always write the same poem, but if you are never in love, you may.

The relation of emotion to poetry is like that of squirrels to a tree. You don't live in what you never have to leave.

"The most modern person in Europe is you Pope Pius the Tenth," Apollinaire wrote in 1913. Being modern was equivalent to being surprising—for about twenty years (1908–1928).

To be ahead of everything and still to be behind in love—a predicament poets may imagine they are in.

That person in the corner has published poems!—A marvel for youth.

My brother-in-law here is a poet.—Leap out the door! Though the brother-in-law may be a much better poet than that person in the corner. Or they may be the same one.

This poem is worth more than these emeralds and diamonds. How can that possibly be? there is no monetary value to a poem. To this one there is: I set the price myself.

I know for sure that I am not a calligramme. When I look at my arms or my hands or my legs, there are no comments, they aren't formed by letters of words. From birth to death I remain unexplained—at least in that manner.

The first poem one writes is usually not the worst. It is not like one's first kiss or one's first time driving a car but more like one's first success.

Ice is like prose; fire is like poetry. But neither melts nor goes out. Ideally (or unideally, some would say) they generally ignore each other's existence.

Rhyme is like a ball that bounces not in the same place but at least in another place where it can bounce.

Poets who write every day also write every year, which is the important thing for poetry.

The poet is the unacknowledged impersonator of the greatest unborn actors of his time.

The Romantic movement left, when it departed, a tremendous gap in poetry which could be filled by criticism and by literary theory but which would be better left alone.

Rome inspired architects and sculptors and painters; the Lake Country inspired poets. Milton inspired Keats. Perugino taught Raphael. Blake gave ideas to Yeats. Sciascia read *Chroniques italiennes* once every year. Byron learned something from Pope. Even the most unsentimental person is glad to see his home country again.

A tapestry is not like a lot of little poems woven together but like one big poem being taken apart.

Starting off as an Irish poet, one has a temperamental and geographical advantage. Starting off as a French poet, one incites an overwhelming curiosity as to what can be done. Starting off as an American poet, one begins to develop a kind of self-consciousness that may quickly lead to genius or to nothing.

Would that he had blotted a thousand! "Perfection" is wonderful in poetry but Shakespeare is good enough—one reads on!

There are three Testaments and one is illegible.

The iris is a flower that is past meridian, a ghost come bearing you a villanelle.

What is the matter with having a subject? Wittgenstein says, "There are no subjects in the world; a subject is a limitation of the world." In fact our subject is all around us like a mail-order winter that we carelessly sent in a request for when it seemed it would always be spring.

Eve was the first animal. Therefore she could not have been Eve, and Adam could not have written poetry. Adam could not write poetry unless there was a human Eve. Thousands of years later, there was: Eve de Montmorency. But she didn't encourage the production of poetry. She said I'll kill anyone who writes me a poem. I like life to be real! Inspired, all the same, a few poets began writing "free verse" (and it was pretty good) which she was unable to recognize as poetry. Meanwhile, back in the Garden of Eden, Eve woke up. She was a fox no more, but a woman, and a ravishing one! Adam saw her and became terribly excited. Without willing to or wishing to at all (for who could know the consequences?) he fell to one knee before her, held out his hands and recited: Roses are red, violets are blue. Yes, what's the rest? Eve said. I don't know, Adam said. I'm not yet fully a poet. That's as far as I've got. So far so good, Eve said, and she loved him with a new ardency that night. From their union were born Abel and Cain, who represented two dissenting schools of criticism: Abel, the "inspirational," let-yourself-go, just SAY it, let it all hang out, or blossom! Lyrical School; Cain, the party of more rigorously crafted delight, a sylvan Valéry: l'inspiration n'est pour rien—le travail, en poésie, est tout! They fought and killed each other many times, while Eve brought forth more children in sorrow, and Adam, his body aching, tilled the land.

Once I taught polar bears to write poetry. After class each week (it was once a week) I came home to bed. The work was extremely tiring. The bears tried to maul me and for months refused to write a single word. If refused is the right term to use for creatures who had no idea what I was doing and what I wanted them to do. One day, however, it was in early April, when the snow had begun to melt and the cities were full of bright visions on windowglass, the bears grew quieter and I believed that I had begun to get through to them. One female bear came up to me and placed her left paw on top of my head. Her mouth was open and her very red tongue was hanging out. I realized that she, and the other bears, must be thirsty, so I procured for them several barrels of water. They drank thirstily and looked up at me from time to time gratefully but even then they wrote no poems. They never did write a word. Still I don't think this teaching was a waste of time, and I'm planning on continuing it in the future if I find I have the necessary strength. For hard and exhausting it is to attempt something one knows it is impossible to do—but what if one day these bears actually started to write? I think we would all put down our Stefan George and our Yeats and pay attention! What wonders might be disclosed! what dreams of bears!

Reading is done in the immediate past, writing in the immediate future.

The world never tires of bad poetry, and for this reason we have come to this garden, which is in another world.

I don't think one can avoid irrationality when one is young if one is planning to enjoy it when one is old. For this reason a poet's life may be called "precarious."

Similarity of sound is similarity of adventure. If you believe that, you are a musician.

Poetry, which is written while no one is looking, is meant to be looked at for all time.

# Ballade

### EN L'AN SOIXANTE-ONZIÈME DE MON AGE

We who have ten years to live, approximately,
Are having a good talk at this party.
Ten years of good health, if we're lucky—
O foot on the moving stair!

### EN L'AN QUARANTE-HUITIÈME DE MON AGE

Whoever wants to make love to all of them
Women I mean—whoever wants to see all the shows—
Flower, dramas, dog—come forward now
And eat this cheese and see if it will make you want more.

### EN L'AN CINQUIÈME DE MON AGE

It's okay, pillaging
And loving mud. Knowing my tranquility
Is hard due to constant desire
For education, I steam through a winter's young fires.

### EN L'AN QUINZIÈME DE MON AGE

Girl with ruffles in your hair
And tussles in your dress
And flamingos for bouche
And gladiolas for clasps gosh we're idiots.

### EN L'AN VINGT-DEUXIÈME DE MON AGE

I watch this fuel
Burning down
And think I'm an expert
On zooming life.

## EN L'AN TRENTE-HUITIÈME DE MON AGE

A book comes out. And then another. I'm gratified
Like a house robber. I am planning another side-
Ways book and then another. I go abroad and
Write a play, called "Husband Blubber."


## EN L'AN DIX-HUITIÈME DE MON AGE

Oh eighteenth year! Truly you are like a jewelry box.
You open and shut with a pam! I know it's over.
Everything is over. The ballgame. My friendship. My romance.
Before my next birthday it seems as though twenty years pass.


## EN L'AN SOIXANTE-DEUXIÈME DE MON AGE

Lying on the operating table
I wrote a letter to myself in code
And, while the morphine was wearing off,
I had a strange vision of Goldilocks.


## EN L'AN SOIXANTE-QUATRIÈME DE MON AGE

I lost you, flowers. I lost you, lovely V,
Neckline of straw and flowers, I lost your key. I lost my key.
It could have been everything that I lost
If I had died this year.


## EN L'AN SOIXANTE-TREIZIÈME DE MON AGE

I am polite to women and puppies
And cross with cads. I have a lot of years and decades in me
And they divide me like Sunday ads.
It's the Big Sale of the Week, when I can speak in song.

## EN L'AN ONZIÈME DE MON AGE

Occurring and curving and curving and occurring
The dynamic street on which I live
Is blending graciously this evening with another street
On which two whom I play football with live.

## EN L'AN QUATORZIÈME DE MON AGE

I much prefer the arrondissement
To this terrible year.
My dog becomes hysterical.
I come home to opened doors.

## EN L'AN TRENTE-SIXIÈME DE MON AGE

My daughter is five years old.
Can you imagine, five?
For five years she has been growing
She has been roving, she has been improving, she has been alive.

## EN L'AN VINGT-HUITIÈME DE MON AGE

Give me some more poetry and I'll get you some more whiskey
I can drink all night and I can sleep well all morning
I am typing out more poems than there are paintings by Wassily
    Kandinsky
And, as you know, that's quite a lot.

## EN L'AN SIXIÈME DE MON AGE

If I pause on my way past the statue of Abraham Lincoln
That sits in front of our school
It is to easily pick up a snowball
And when I throw it to try to nick you on the ear.

## EN L'AN CINQUANTE-SEPTIÈME DE MON AGE

The worst things that happened
Did not happen before
But happen this year
Like the crack of a gun.


## EN L'AN TRENTIÈSME DE MON AGE

I'm writing like François Villon but not really.
There's no doom in it. I'm not being tried for my life.
I have a thousand years in which to write
A wonderful seamlessness has just come up in my poetry.

# Artificial Intelligence

### GETTING BACK ON LAND

The arms of those armchairs resemble the legs
Of young women who have just come over
From the coast of America in a tramp steamer;
They sing happily of the long days of their voyage
And they are glad to see the armchairs again, which remind them of their
    legs.


### VIDA BREVE

Nothing else matters, only the clam with the little william nose
And the clive bracelet, and the george scene and the tom acorn;
Here, eat him, now here, eat him; and then smile.


### WAHEGO

Aren't you afraid of being a few
Paces behind the Lead Runner
When he reaches the Last Place of Rest?


### FROTH

Coppers in the ocean, millions of them, dropped there
By tourists, men and women, who believed
They could do it and make a wish
To be Red masters.


### PASSAGE

A boat comes by, captain smiling, lady on his arm
Tatooed there by Plush the Pirate; I wish I were here with you
Written on the paper beneath his pen. Boat goes by with a frown.

## MATTERS

At eight o'clock the torn apron was willing
To depart with her lover, the cleaning;
But at the stroke of nine exactly
He was already tired of her and had gone to the hearing
Of sunshine and beautiful ways.

## FRAGMENT

Moon in the mirror, are you the same as the one outside
Or are you a different moon, filled with artifice and pride?
Are you like that lady, who . . .

## CHIAROSCURO

Other Romes, other moons, other umbrellas.
And streetcleaners, patching up the Forum,
Gaze at us with another sense of space.

## THE FLOWERS OF EVIL

Lay on the table
I picked it up
As well as I was able
And grappled with an eagle
Who is my Savior.
Savior mine,
Let me read this book,
I said.
OK said he,
And I read it
While he flew around.
My brain is burning
O eagle, I cried.
Do not fear
I shall be at your side
To quiet your yearning
My Savior replied.

An anthology of Magical poetry
Lay on the table in the rookery
I opened it and began to charm
Began to charm the birds away:

"Robin redbreast and sparrow
Bluefinch of waist that is narrow
Joyous kingfisher, catbird so black
All fly away, and never come back!"

Then from the nuttery
Came a voice so softly
That I could scarcely hear it.
So I drew near it.

It said, "Scaly fish,
Porcupines who never adorn my dish,
Finned carp, and nasal porpoise
Abandon pour toujours my habeas corpus!"


## LA DIMINUZIONE DALLA MAMMA

La mia mamma
Nel tempo in cui ero bambino
Fu una donna
Molto grande e molto bella
Allora che ora
E minuscola
Come una cosa
Che si vedrebbe dalla finestra
Di un palazzo, verso la sera,
Come di quest'altezza
Potrebbe sembrare un dente
Di una sconosciuta
Nell'aria bruna di Firenze.

## SOLEMN

Les jeunes gens jouent des Checkers
Pendant que leurs grandpapas regardent—d'assez loin.
Their grandfathers are in Mexico City;
One of them is dead, and the other lies very ill
In the Clinica de Los Altos Man.
The boy stares at his checkers, and the other cries "Move!"

## FRAGMENT

They wandered in the scorched and gloomy summer
As far as Franklin's beach. Tod stood amazed
At all the huts which dotted now the water.
"Why there is a development here," he muttered,
"Where there before was only beach and sky!"
A large bird fluttered over them, which caught
The first rays of the setting sun, grew pink,
And vanished. Tod took Ellen's hand and smiled:
"So like the bird, so like our good old beach,"
He said . . .

## MORRO ROCK

No more sandals made from fibrous particles of lunch
Dropped on the equally fibrous cheerleader. Uhuh, Henry Hudson!

## SCHWEITZERREICH

Geneva. A bird call. Someone's name.
Geneva. The flowers. The flower. The Geneva.

## VAGABONDS

Vagabonds! that's what we are—vagabonds!
Early in the morning we pack up and change our clothes
Into little strips of cloud
And march forth into the blue universe.

While lingering pennies chime in black pools
We lunch on paralyzing blood-slugs
And drink hog-water.
We are happy at centrifugal force.
We would fly away if we did not like earth so much;
We roll in dung like a scarf of good cheer.
Sometimes meadows consisting wholly of stones
Offer us couches for our revolting amours;
But then, at other times, at the beginning of evening
We stand and watch, enchanted, some human fiesta.


MATEEYANAH

Not like a child but like a wild blackbird
She descended the stairs from her tree.


OFFER

Morning may find us whiter, perhaps surprised
By the clanging streetcar.


NINETEEN THIRTY SIX

Paint the house, painter!
Hit the sidewalk, cement!


LITTLE-KNOWN HISTORICAL FACT

Charlemagne, don't be so unhappy! You gadabout, rain!
The old French king kept sitting sideways
On top of his throne; then he fell off.
"It's raining," said Charlemagne. "Look! La pioggia!"
Charlemagne was an Italian.

## THE RUE QUENTIN-BAUCHART IN 1951

It was horsemeat!
Yes, I did.
Did you like it?
Thanks for the lunch.
Okay.
Okay?
No, I have to be going.
Would you like something else?
Did you?
No I else.
Good-bye.


## TRIESTE E UNA DONNA

Vagabond silence, music of my tears,
And the whole world of yesterday
Chugging like a train, into Trieste.


## GREAT BEAUTY

It's like being received in the arms of a great beauty
When she throws aside her cloak and has nothing on underneath
Except that being received in the arms of a great beauty is better
But I love this fog.

# Commosso

Perhaps at the end of the mountains that isn't a woman
But a literary place with tables
Where one can be with friends. But Milan is angry
It is throwing out these terrifying bolts of storm
That sound like a dog who is coming from a far-off country
To meet the master he is going to bite before anything happens
To separate these two and keep them apart
When the storm is over and, settling down again,
Milan seems merely helpful, a source of cash and tourists
Or else annoying, ruining with cash and tourists
Everything it touches and that touches it but not this storm
That shows the end of the mountains where lie love,
Friendship, and work, if only I can find them
With the help of these extravagant flashes and the rain
That spends its wild excitement on the water.

# The True Story of the Mule

Enjoying everyone
It meets
Like a sunrise
Over distant façades.

# Ulla

I followed the young woman—Ulla, was that her name?
Down the hallway—what a strange destiny it is
To be so beautiful! I followed
And that was all I was doing—following. It was not a Civil War
Thank goodness! not even something I had to work on
And as some would follow a matador and others a thrilling soprano
I walked on after this Ulla down the hall
To a light and airy room. She said, This is your chamber.
You will stay here tonight, and, then, tomorrow morning
We will change you to another one, which is a little bit more comfortable
    than this.
I'm perfectly happy with this room, I said. I thought,
Today I've seen Ulla. Is that enough? But, well,
Yes, now, could you show me the other
Where tomorrow I may be lodging. The rooms are national.
Ulla is one part of what is real. She says, yes,
Please follow me. On the walls are designs of roses and of fleurs-de-lys.

# The Promenade of the Ghostly Subtitles

It was the time of the promenade of the ghostly subtitles
No one could prevent their walking forth
Everywhere you looked you would see *A Girl's Story* or
*Vignettes of the Andalusian Forest* or something of that sort,
While the real titles, slumbering in ignorance of this,
The great, heavy, burdensome, entitled titles,
The big, even gigantic refreshing and obvious titles,
The gorgeous titles, the fine titles, the magnificent ones,
*Home for the Holidays, Anna Karenina, War and Peace, David Copperfield,*
*The Red and the Black, Father Goriot, Barchester Towers, Emma, Hamlet, Julius*
   *Caesar, Death on the Installment Plan, Wozzeck,*
Lay dead to the world in castles, chateaus and villas
All round the earth, while the subtitles sauntered forth
As if they were titles, showing the world their value
Which once the titles awoke they would never have.

# The Seasons

*To James Thomson*

### I  *SPRING*

Now pizza units open up, and froth
Steams forth on beers in many a frolic bar
New-opened-up by April. People find
White sheets and envelopes that blow through streets
And pick them up to read them but to find
That it is SPRING and all is vain to read.
Lovers, of course, avuncular old men,
And primrose-cheeked domestics pushing strollers
Meet smiling then pursue their golden ways
Down sunlight-sparkled vales of plain cement.
The red transforms to green. 'Tis silence all,
And pleasing expectation. Herds and flocks
Drop the dry sprig, and mute-imploring eye
The falling verdure. Boys and girls exclaim
In wonder at the new-arriving tides
Of energy's full swell. Up springs the bark
Of Peppy who's been left, tied by a string
Of stout white cord to a tough lamppost gnarled
With many a dolloped spackle of green paint
Implanted in the sidewalk like an oak
That outward further spreads its soft regret
That it is not spring always. To such post
Is Peppy tied while that into the shop
For a new lacy bra his mistress bides
And looks at stockings also. Peppy's yell
Is springtime's herald, all its mighty morn
Is welcomed by his yapping; and some birds
On nearby roofs take up his rough exclaim
And parcel it in sweets of various kinds.
What passing fellow with his shirt undone
One or two buttons down a whistle on
His lips looks round and pities Peppy there
But does not when he sees that beauty leave

The shop door open half behind and dog
Now straining at what improvised as leash
Could much serve to un-breath him did not she,
One package under her left arm, another
Tucked in with it, release him from the post
And let him jump upon her like the leaves
That West Wind blows in autumn's coming days.
Flushed by the spirit of the genial year
And by the smile of Bob who at her side
Now asks her if some package he can take
To make her task the easier, she says yes,
For she has need of help, the knot once tied
So quickly now resists but with two hands
Free for this enterprise she does it well.
Thank you she says and asks her bundles back.
Bob, teasing won't return them, then he does.
She smiles, relieved. He dares and asks her out
What of some coffee in O'Toole's Garage
The place right on the corner there? Okay!
Do they let dogs in? Yes I think they do
And Peppy jumps, to emphasize his thought
That where Louise goes he goes with her now
And would not stay imprisoned any more
To yap at the green budding all around.
This once agreed, the two walk slowly down
The emerald-studded street, green lights on green.
Bob's feet feel easy moving in their shoes
And on the virgin's cheek a fresher bloom
Than ever was before is now perceived.
Her lips blush deeper sweets; she breathes of youth;
The shining moisture swells into her eyes
In brighter flow; her wishing bosom heaves
With palpitations wild; kind tumults seize
Her veins, and all her yielding soul is love.
Bob doesn't know this as he chats away
Telling this girl of his accomplishments
In selling carburetors which she loves
To hear about because that magic tinge
Of fresh beginning that was clear just now
In Peppy's bark roves scintillant in her.
What kinds of carburetors, used or new?

She asks him and he takes her trembling hand
To lead her, Peppy held by t'other one,
His leash, into the midst of the Garage
A fashionable place to sit this spring
And drink non-alcoholic drinks and say
Inane things to your loved one while the light
Comes smashing through the glass in images
That never are forgotten being those
Associate with such dear starts of love.
Now Peppy barks, and barks. The waitress says
He'll have to go outside. So all three leave
Go somewhere else and never do find out
Why Peppy barked. Enough to say perhaps
He's worried for Louise. "Ah, then, ye fair,
Be greatly cautious of your sliding hearts,"
Perhaps he barked, not saying, for even spring
Cannot give power of words to canine kind,
And barking so may have felt the frustration
All lesser creatures feel when close to us
Yet taking in our power, energy
Which once they've felt they scarce can live without;
So we perhaps with spring are in this state.
In any case, Louise now bares her arm
To look at a small smutch on it was made
By Peppy's jump and Bob's heart skips two beats.
Rattled he laughs. She smiles. Now in the Park
Where woodbines flaunt and roses shed a couch
Peppy lies down, and our two humans sit
And contemplate the splendor of the season
Though scarce aware of other things. Bob says,
"Louise, now pepper plants begin to leaf
And, next, to bud, beside the canopy
O'erhanging Mrs. Olson's Fudge Bazar—
I'd like to walk you someday on that street
And" then he smiled and then he turned away
He'd seen a robin fluttering in retreat
From a crouched cat who stood the oak beside
To which the bird had fluttered. Peppy, tense
At visioning the feline, strained his leash
Till it was almost bursting. With a tug
Bob pulls him back and with the pup in tow

And Robin Redbreast safe within his tree,
Resumes—"And oh so many other places,
There are so many places we can go
While April spackles sap in every smudgeon
And banner of surcease." He glanced around
Then pulled the young girl to him without sound,
Her blue-blouse-clad back clasped his hands around
And felt like his her heart begin to pound.
He kissed her. At that moment Peppy dulled
For a few moments by the episode
That separates him from the cat and bird
Now leaps again to life and yaps aloud
At what is happening to his mistress. Harm?
No harm yet, Peppy: she is happily
Embraced by one she finds good all around.
And Peppy quiets. Then there is no sound
Save for the gentle murmurs made by love
When two draw back from kiss and gaze around
Amazed at where they are and what they've found.
Leaves, even as they sit there, come to shape
On many a slender branch; and, low, the worm
Inventive, cramps for space in paths well hidden
From yellow-shaded beak with tints of rose
In clacking quest for quell of appetite.
Now Bob stands up, he gives Louise his hand
And bids her to observe the vernal scene
Before they amble further. "Fairest One!
Look! Thespius ropes Coniglia with his bars
And Leonine protects the rule of three.
New shirts are worn, no stockings, and new shoes
New blouses blossom. Air creeps past its post
And stations coolness on a breast or thigh
That hitherto was covered or if numb
From other gesture not so simply spanned.
Long legs are looming past, and biscuits dance
In popping ovens for the furious taste
Of casual strollers in the urban glare
Of April sunlight like an opened cave
In which the diamonds of Hesperides
Are cast in all their gleaming. To decide
To not walk thither on a day like this
Is to be pent in prison like a rug

Rolled up and in the warehouse. Let us drive
Or walk or leap with such impulsive aim
That we bounce high on this day's trampoline!"


## II  *SUMMER*

So do they prosper, and so do we look
To the next season now, whose mighty sun
Unbolts the doors and steams the swimming pools.
From brightening fields of ether fair disclosed
Child of the Sun, refulgent SUMMER comes
Colossal with its shining envelope
Of white hydrangeas flush to nature's green
Defenses unencumbered. Roses mount
Erupt in fragrant blossom pinkest white
And reddish hue and then are seen no more
Till early autumn taps them with a spout
Of latter-springing laughter. Lavender,
Sansevieria, scabiosa prim
As other evening light in bloodied mode
And portulaca hovering next to him,
Godetia grandiflora, morning glory,
Ajuga, azeratum, columbine—
All these and more come crowding, none to stay
Yet powered each with the capacity
To flower and stay flowered if but for
What moments they enchant us. Rabbits bound
Less than they did in spring but still there are
Enough to fill the gardens with the bites
Unauthorized that bring the gardener down
To knees to note his basil and his thyme
In an imperfect state, which have been bit
By some young rodent's teeth who then away
Into the meadows lush with clover leaps
Then burrows in the ground, where it is cool
Within the bosom of the panting earth—
Hot outside, inside cool, creative earth!
That, by the summer mothered, gestures forth
Such produce as imprinted on our tongues
Descends into our muscles, skin, and bones
And redesigns our essence, in accord

With that First Contract by which growing things
Give nurture to us that we here remain
In body and in soul to see once more
The seasons' lazy susan whirl around.
And what in country brings the flower and fruit
In town brings on the people. End of dark—
Roused by the clock, the quick-clad city youth
Leaves the apartment-fold in which he dwells
To journey through the summer-morning-sweet
Unending avenues that Gotham gives
To those who wake in summer soon and glad.
Till when arrived at office where the sun
Blinds through the windows harming not with heat
As insulation and conditioned air
Make their own spring of summer, he may smile
At rosy-fingered thoughts, that on his desk
The contract for a Coliseum lies
That will transform him to a billionaire.
Be quiet, quiet my heart! He breathes and stands
A moment with heart shaking. Then he tends
Slow, downward, to his chair. Is it too much
To hope of summer morning that one be
Transformed to such a person? It may be
Only a dream that lingered in his thoughts
That waking should have transferred. He's a clerk
And has more modest duties to perform
Than those that populate his fantasies.
And fifty floors below him the young bum
Who long has taken alcohol for wife
Stands in a daze, one hand extended. But
A grey-garbed kindly Quaker woman there
Gives him the hand of friendship, not a coin,
And may convince him, in the dulcet air
Of summer morn to try to take a cure.
And it is so. He follows her. Good luck!
Though hard it is to give addiction up,
It's kindness and concern that give best chance
Not prison and dour drubbing. On this block
Performs the hot dog man his ritual task
Of feeding those who wander through the streets,
Or haste, they run, for they'll be late for jobs
And had not time to pour the foamy cream

Into their blazing coffee. No, they leapt
Almost unclothed outside and ran to catch
The seven-twenty or six-forty-five
To way downtown Manhattan then to run
To their old building but can scarce resist
The summer fragrance of the hot dog stand.
Here hot dogs sizzle at the curb, there flash
From windows rays of sunlight that bedazzle
The eyes of those who buy them and begin
To take a bite before the change is given
For the five dollar bill they have extended
To the frankfurter salesman, smiling man
In workaday blue apron with two hands
That rapidly can shuffle sauerkraut
Between two halves of bun and with his spoon
Or ladle slap the mustard on, present
The finished hot dogs to the waiting friends
Ere they were conscious he had yet begun.
So they begin to nibble, to resist
Is vain, for the aroma brings them in
And heat to heat doth drive the splanging tongue
To ever more endeavour through the kraut
And then, cold Doctor Pepper there beside
Clamped in one's other hand, one takes a swallow
And feels emparadised, with golden birds
Incumbent of their wingspans all around.
Yet pent-up in the city in the worst
Of suffocating summer, Man take care!
Or else survive not to the season's end!
For these bright times can sudden darkness bring—
Heart surgeons reap a harvest: people drop
In doorways and on driveways, stop in cars
And never start again, run to the pump
But do not reach it, fail to find the way
To serve the tennis ball but find instead
They are face-down on the court. Unhappy game!
It may be Jane who grieves for Albert then
His lifetime ended by a strike of sun.
But no, now he recovers and stands up
Though weak and dazed, his hand upon the net—
Oh they will stop to drink in swift delight
Some haughty iced tea of the afternoon

And till Al's heartbeat's normal once again
Not stir one inch from such beatitude
As death makes known when breath to life returns.
Many, when city streets become so hot
As to resemble radiated halls
And every moment's like some blanket that
Comes stifling down to make the chance to breathe
Unusual without a choke of pain,
Look at the weather and decide it's wise
To pack the trunks and towels and seek the beach
Where Oceanus like a freezy coin
Of green-blue gold and silver brings to play
Upon hot legs and faces sprigs of wind
That make the heart a placid occupant
Of the o'erheated body that it was.
Bronzed boys and girls stride slimly down the sands
And dash into the surf as if themselves
They were cool sticks of summer like the trees
That hide themselves in mass of foliagery—
Now these are hid in foam and off they swim
And clash about and touch each other's arms
And shoulders; now hand on a waist is placed
And one drawn to another in a scene
Of mermaid/merman swift frivolity
Unchaperoned by any but the waves.
On shore, they pile up castles in the sand,
Build campfires, and sing songs till the shy moon
Comes plunging upward into the dim sky
Of night when all regain their shady homes.
Some older persons too come to the beach
And 'neath umbrellas watch the thunderous waves,
Admiring youth in what they see and feel
And read, forgetful of the sun-stung streets
They left to voyage here. Or it may be
One falls in love with a brown-shouldered girl
With whom one later may abridge the time
Of being in the sun by seeking shade
Of arm and shoulder or the ascending knee
That brings the leg with it and sometimes all
Of the loved body making a young tent
To give such cool with such solicitude
The whole life breathes with it and is engaged;

So far no such event, but each may dream
In summer of such unprepared elans
That mix the dark and light by varied means.
Too hot, just hot enough, in shade, ablaze—
All those who love such changes and do read
These sun-flocked pages standing near the rock
On which the lichen of distress looks out
Will know a scene of power. For as the bee
Full of his quizzing and his upscale sum
Of sun-delighting symmetries does one
And then another flip-up off to green
From green, so shall one message from the sun
Be weight enough to tip the scales of dreams
And make them in accord with where they beckon
And toward which they resume their silent strains.


III  *AUTUMN*

But now hear AUTUMN bellow from the trees
And send to us the first announcing drops
Of harvest rain. Busses wait at their stops
A little longer in the cooling breeze
As more each day get onto them and off.
Oh time delighting, to be back in school!
Back with the bright cool bodies of the girls
And the bold sturdy bodies of the boys
Who are the same age and who were last year
The same age also but are older grown
And larger and of more connecting heft!
To fly into the classroom like a wave
Of idiot excitement and be quelled
One brief hour only by the teacher's drawl
Who teaches us a little though we find
Truth more gigantic in the sexual mind
That steers us through the corridors with bump
Occasional, deliberate of some one
We wish to hug or battle with, toward lunch
Appalling in the cafeteria dim
Then in the mind proud Mathematics sports
Till once again at three o'clock one finds
The world delicious as a lemon rind

In a martini, serve it to us straight
This tactile joy of autumn, when the skin
Of arbors reddens, flushed with bliss of change.

Now wheat crops come to harvest; blooming late
Chrysanthemums adorn the garden's edge
Autumn affects the gutters; through the streets
A rush of water comes, for it has rained
And rained and rained, I think it rained all night.
And moody earth, true to the prophesies
Of spring and summer shows its treasures forth
Of pumpkins and potatoes, and the proud
Zucchini and the squash and melon huge—
Portentous products whose gay husks conceal
Inside such tastes as to the earth re-wed
Our selves, divorced by being, yet to which,
Less soon than these, yet soon, our husks return.
And, in cemented city, apples shine
In outdoor markets, moist inside bright skins,
All ready to be taken with a smile
And bitten with anticipated twinge
Most redolent of autumn on the tongue.
Bob Blentz comes by and buys one which he bites
As Microsoft goes plunging down which bites
The young investor; nights like summer nights
Yield to some somewhat colder ones, and tents
Are taken down and folded. Ducks and geese
Whizz overhead to Carolinas, quit
Of cooling air which soon into deep freeze
Would place them, not to be revived next year.
And the World Series closes like a fist
On all that has been baseball. One home run
In such a game may justify the life
On one fall day of that autumnal man
Who bats the ball out of the park then runs
With hands extense above his capless dome
Fist clenching and unclenching, in his eyes
Catching the solar dazzle. At his name
Swell baseball-crazy hearts which find in this
Cool season summer pastime's apogee
And thrill to that which now must be forgot
Until next spring, swift fallen like the leaves.

566

Tuned in, though far from Stadium or Shea,
Miss Lisbeth in her Austin drives along
East Twenty-First Street marvelling at fall
And so does Mr. Peterson the grump
Of Twenty-Ninth and Broadway who ascends
A stairway in his antiquated home
Once the apartment of a billionaire
But now a place divided into ten
Apartments each one smaller than the next
Through which however now an autumn breeze
Blows rapid breaths delighting one and all.
And Hugo now a new apartment finds
For Sarah. They for weeks have scanned the ads
For someplace in a neighborhood she'll like
While autumn dusts the windows with its leaves
And now at last have found one. He believes
It's better for them that they live apart
A while; it's a mistake. But now they smile
At every detail of the place, and light
A fire in the fireplace and, content
For what shall be short time, find in a kiss
What seems an answer even to the pain
Such short-lived bliss must cause. From poultry shelves
Gobblers are grabbed and gutted for the clones
Of passionate pilgrims whom digestion greets
Traditionally on one cold clean day
While cranberries are roughed from swamp and pond
Until one might esteem that cool Cape Cod
Had lost the blush of youth but to grow pale
For pleasures of the feasting multitudes.
Then harmless sweet potatoes, too, are set
Upon the coals to please and warm our jaws;
Amidst the strip-tease oaks and birches here.
Yet still there's time to travel! Fall is kind
To whoso has fond wish to reinvent
This earth's imagined confines. Sweet it is,
Cool-clad in hopes, to take one's wallet out
And buy the tickets that in fair exchange
Get one an airplane seat, which, sinking down
Onto a field near Venice, jolts and bumps
And then grows still, as one goes out to see
This treeless town of autumn at its best,

Where the Casino like an emerald shines
Atop the silver-circling Grand Canal—
Or northward makes its landing: I have stood
In the Place Saint Sulpice and wished to die
I was so full of happiness, one hour
When autumn brushed the stemless stones with gems
Of intellectual brilliance, like desire
For what we have but dare not call our own.
And then return with winter drawing near—
Fall, thou ambiguous season, who begin
With the red cast-off sun-scorched skin of summer
And end with winter's pallor, hear oh hear
My chant to thee, harbinger of rebirth
Of school and love and work, and scene of death
That in thy colors stuns us dim with joy
Till hap we feel the wild cold-warm confusion
Confucius once when rapt in Glade of Ho
Felt stumbling on a rattler and being bid
By conscience to step back, not harm the thing,
But human instinct urging him to fear
Did pound it with a stone—then, quick, aghast,
Through autumn's cool bamboo that halled his home
Turbulent fled and wrote his *Analects*
A source of wisdom for all time to come.
'Tis Autumn brings such changes most, its dark
Mortality that sparks ascending life—
Leaves flushed by color look like cardinals,
And cardinals like energetic leaves—
Together cardinals in red leaves do make
A red embrasure that the wind does shake—
And brings revival where was almost not
The hope of something living—work by dead.
Chagall adorns the Modern, Henry Moore
Is spread out all along Park Avenue;
De Kooning has at last come into focus
For multitudes who, standing in the Met
Before his sitting Women, feel the crazed
Delight of stout Balboa, termed Cortez
By dreamy Keats, when once in Darien
He stared at the Pacific, all alone
In speculation, circled by his men.

All this the human soul absorbent makes
Contiguous to its essence, and looks out
At the confounding city whipped by breeze
And, breathing in what life is breathing there,
Becomes a thing autumnal of its own.


IV  *WINTER*

If the west wind is Autumn's, what is that
Which WINTER gives to speed the skates along?
To freeze the engine while the snowball fights
Erupt on guttered streets and garbage trucks
Pick up the snow and let the garbage stay
A while in plastic bags for rats to seek
Out every night impenetrable not
To those sharp teeth? Oh, from what Arctic bulge
Of everlasting winter slicked by spring
And summer with its meltingness re-formed
Into another shape as fearsome and
Relentless as its former, does there come
A messenger with one would say a hope
To pry conversion from the temperate zones
Convincing them with killing blasts of air
That sempiternal winter would be best
For everything there living? Spring has marked
The one end of this season as has fall
The other, yet, ignoring these, it comes
As it would stay forever. Flying force,
Go back to that sad cemeteried zone
In which you prosper, being there the king,
Unwanted here where soft erupts the rose,
The pear tree blossoms, and the children walk
To playgrounds through the heaps of autumn leaves,
With warm and cool, to each appointed each
A guardian and a limiting effect
Caught in the mild democracy of days.
Return, return thy spite! And yet it stays,
And while it stays brings railings to which stick
The hands, and chill that makes the limbs to shake
To point of death sometimes although we try

To shelter those who lack the force to place
Warmth's wall between its bristling and their lives.
Unknowing its harsh powers some lucky young
May find it pleasure purely, and indeed
May all who have the means to keep them warm
For in contrast is pleasure—the swift sting
Of wind is bound by a fur-coat embrace
In a light-wingèd mix of joy and pain
And few would banish winter from their midst
Could they quell its excess. Amantha slips
Her formal on that shows her shoulders smooth
And white as all that snow. Warm paradox
Of dressing up in winter to be bare
Beneath the glowering chandeliers of heaven
Two instants to the car! And she goes down
The stairs into her waiting date's hired car
And is whisked off to Princeton for a ball
While gentle flakelets flutter in the sky.
Now bold Arcturus weaves for the event
A sudden dreadful thunder that portends
A storm to bring New Jersey to its knees.
Amantha's scared. But Tom says "Oh there, there!
There's nothing to be scared about, I'm here—"
And puts his hand upon her shoulder, which
Brings both a soft delight. "Oh you are mine."
"Yes, I am yours if we get through this storm,"
Amantha says; and they get through the storm.
Princeton is radiant. Red and dark blue lights
Shine through the sleepless snow that hides each ledge
And every dancer feels upon his head
A little of that wildness and that cold.
This leads to some lovemaking in the cars
And to long mornings after spent in bed
With pleasant hangovers and gilded arms
From sunlight that comes through the frosted pane.
There on the pillow rests the golden head
Of captivant Amantha whom beside
Restless the cat of Tom sends forth in glee
His tiny claws to test the mattress out
And tears the sheet a little. Oh that's nothing!
Cries Tom who, just awaked from a sweet dream
Of carnivals' inflexible parades

With snow explosions scared by colored lights,
Can only smile at everything there is
Within him and around him. "Fair Amanth!"
He calls the girl, and she to him replies
"Inevitable Tom, my winter's love!"
Then out again, but careful! Tom descries
Pure purple winter lunging through the skies
And whistles to Amantha, "Let's go home!"
This boreal light has angels of its own
That in no milder season hearts can find.

So some being hastened to a matinee
Of *L'Elisir d'Amore* ride through snow
On taxi's spattering rims to hear the soul
Of Pavarotti melted into song
Swirling among the shoulders bare and proud
Of radiant women who are gathered here
To see the opera and be seen themselves
As lovelier still—but cannot be to those
Like Bob and Humphrey standing at the bar
Poor standees stand at to await the thrill
Of some high tone globescent with the heat
Of universal energy, at which
To cheer, ev'n weep, as if that note were home,
Unknown, unseen, for many a forlorn year
And now made present through a door of song!
Or NORMA sings, or TOSCA, and in waves
Of bright effluent heat comes the applause
Of all who here from brittlest winter's day
Have sought a costly refuge. Wreathed in furs,
Others find naught so bracing as a zoo.
These fanciers most delight in the white bears
Who name the polar region as their home,
Which beasts give courage to the urban throng
Who see them lope, with fascinated eye,
From one height to another in their pen
Constructed to resemble something like
A cold place they might live in but do not.

And, see great trains run like demented creatures
From one place to another finding stations
To house them on their way! Enormous things

Like bridges aqueducts and factories sting
The brittle air with sharpness like its own.
And by the frost refined the whiter snow
Is crusted hard and sounding to the tread
Of early salesman as he nervous seeks
His office door, hopes for a killing, but
So taken with that unanimity
Of white all but forgets his chance and walks
This way and that to see the little caves
And craters deep created by his tread.
Elsewhere the snowplow wanders, with its task
Of clearing ways where stocked with antifreeze
Much frailer vehicles may journey take.
Here Celia's father mystified by storm
That piles a sum of snow before him on
The road now blocked impossible, with joy
And tense relief, a plow's proboscal heave
Considers, grateful for its aptitudes.
The plow has many errands, many streets
And lawns and driveways and industrial parks
And fairgrounds swift with lights in summer now
Bedredged with blue of snowglow, which it owes
And must incite to clearance on this day.
Don Muff the snowplow driver heaves a ton
Of white from place to place and would be known
As a great sculptor if the thing were done
With an aesthete's attention but is not
Alas yet glad the rows of random piles
Do make the hearts of Alex and Cecile
Who sidle mittened through it, giving yells
To show each other which they roam behind.

And then what pleasure when first hint appears
That Winter's reign is over! It had seemed
It would be cold forever but not so.
Friends come with frost upon their cuffs but smiles
Upon their faces that betoken some
Small mutual understanding with the time
That all may soon be well. It's March the first
And we can't tell each morning if we should
Dress for the cold or not. Today we will,
For Boreas only coughs, not dying gasps.

572

Yet days grow longer and the chilled romance
Of lipstick-smearing seeming endless nights
Veered to the side lies haplessly enditched
Encroached upon by crocus. And how strange
That Winter will be battered down by Spring,
Which like a babe on Goliathic rocks
Melts them with his attentions, kissing stone
And turning it to roseleaf, basil, sun.
He takes the Old Man's house, his hearth, his wife
And finally deprives him of his being,
This childlike innocent who seemed a son
Of gentler nature but whose bite is stronger
Than winter's teeth e'er muster, ending knocked
Across the way by primaveral fist.
But yet not yet—still, with the bitter wind,
A gasp of dying that is no less fierce
Than at its midmost raving cuts the tape
Of morning to let peep the frozen day.

Sing louder, bird hibernal, if you please!
I shall not quail at your more vatic strains
But be content to have perceived so far
Into the whites of these four seasons' eyes,
Perceived young lovers in them touched by sun
Or in the snow in parks and on the roads
And to have known the anguish and the change
Of bitter disparition and the bite
Of what seems not to come but then perhaps
Does come, or then does not, or not renews,
And to have felt the blood in changing flow
That seasons bring, and the light grace of flesh
In cold or warmer weather, to have known
The change that does not change, in being change
Itself, the clime in which we most must run
And so find Thomson's reasons and our own
To go on living at their latitudes
And in the range of how they most appear.

# Songs from the Plays

*Around the hero, everything becomes a tragedy.*
*Around God, everything becomes what? a world?*
NIETZSCHE

*Around songs, everything becomes a play.*
SHAKESPEARE

## BRING BACK THE BEDS

Bring back the beds
And the hotels
And the sheets
All the pillows
Red of flowers
Out the windows
In a contract
An option
To do
Again what we
Did do
How often?
Make love
—Two hundred times?

*Summer Vacation*


## LET THE OBI FALL

Let the obi fall
Energy is all
Don Juan of Kyoto!

Women of the night
Standing left and right
Don Juan of Kyoto!

Peace is a ball
That rolls through space
And holds up time

With energy!
Obi! Obi!
Let it fall!

*Don Juan of Kyoto*


## THIS DANCING MAN WAS ONCE THE POPE

This dancing man was once the Pope
The leader of all Christians

His dancing partner, she
Was President of Israel.
These others, gathered round,
Were nothing quite so grand.
"Pius!" they cry, "With Golda
Please dance another round!"
He is a dancing man
And she a dancing woman. That is all
We know of them
And all we need to know.

*Easter in the Vatican*


WHEN I WAS A YOUNG WOMAN

When I was a young woman
Before I came to Israel
I never dreamed that I
Would spread beneath the sky
Patriotic motions
Patriotic notions
Patriot emotions
Country-serving words!

It is hot in Haifa
And it is hot in Tel Aviv
I would be a dancer
Before my senses leave
My mortal, grand persona
And either go to sleep
Or join some other soldier
Some other mighty Golda! Oh I weep
That it may chance again!

*Easter in the Vatican*


YOUR GENIUS MADE ME SHIVER

Your genius made me shiver
It seemed to me
That you were greater than I

Could ever be
Your genius made me shiver.

Pure genius makes us shiver
We who want to be
Torn out of history
And raised up to be
Intellectual heroes.

How easily you do
What I must work to do
Long and long hours
How quickly you renew
Your much-spent powers.

Your genius makes to shiver
All those who have forever
Longed, longed for the caress
Of glory and the Muses
Who, all, know now that they shall have it less

Than you shall have it, ever—
Illumined, and onrushing like a river.

*Brothers and Friends*

## LET US PRAISE THE ELEPHANT

Let us praise the elephant
Oooh hooo bando!
The elephant is severe and great
Ohh hah bando lai go shi
Manageable elephant
Hoo tai yan!
Unmanageable tree—
O bajyo!
He will tear it down
We will make a town—
Ban do he mai ho shi!
A town of broken branches
Wooden city!

The elephant brings it down—
Man gai no chi!

*Under the Savanna's Blue Sky*


## AFRICA PAESE NOTTURNO

Africa paese notturno
You turn out the light
And we are in Africa
Africa the country of night
Africa the city of night
Africa the village of night
Africa my Africa

But, ah! turn it back on
And Africa is gone!
In the lights of the coming dawn
And in the haze of noon
Africa paese diurno—
One continent gone, one returns
With one ray of light
Africa my Africa

*Under the Savanna's Blue Sky*


## HOW IN HER PIROGUE SHE GLIDES

How in her pirogue she glides
Like a flower seen from all sides!
She the universe divides
Into sunshine, rain, and snow.

Wonder when she will decide
To get out and from which side
Then all eyes shall she divide
By the way she means to go

But not yet. Like lily still
Upon the Congo's moving hill
She floats, and makes men's hearts to ride,
Like boats, themselves, upon the running tide.

*Edward and Christine*

## DRIVING ALONG

Driving along
His pregnant wife is in
The other seat the
Baby sings a song:
"I want to be born" etc.
"I want to be born" etc.
"I want to be born" etc.
"Tonight"
"Unto this planet."

*New Faces of Forty Years Past*


## MEDITERRANEAN SUNS

Mediterranean suns!
Shine on, in, and around
To light up our sterns and our prows
And to keep us out of trouble
By showing us the waves
That loop around our boat!
It's made of wood
And linen. Come down
From Antibes, come down
From Nice, from Cannes
Come down into my boat.
The Mediterranean sun
Is shining on the boat.
Won't you come, too,
From the fresh air
Of these resorts?
Just climb down.

*New Faces of Forty Years Past*


## THEY SAY PRINCE HAMLET'S FOUND A SOUTHERN ISLAND

They say Prince Hamlet's found a Southern island
Where he lies happy on the baking sand
A lovely girl beside him and his hand
Upon her waist and is completely silent;
When interviewed, he sighs, and makes a grand

Gesture toward the troubled Northern places.
I know them not, he cries, and love them less.
Then he is once more lost in loveliness.

They say King Lear, recovered in his mind
From all those horrors, teaches now at some
Great university. His course—*Cordelia*—
Has students by the thousands every term.
At course's end, he takes his students out,
Points to the clouds and says You see, you see her!
And every one, unable not to cry,
Cries and agrees with him, and he is solaced.

O King, you should retire and drink your beer!
And Hamlet you should leave your happy island
And wear, with fair Ophelia, Denmark's crown.

*Shakespeare Amended*

## WHY SHOULD DENMARK GRIP MY MIND

Why should Denmark grip my mind
When all delights upon this shore I find?
Denmark with its freezing rain
And my father's dying pain
My false mother and her lover—
No, all that, is over, over!
Blue transparence of this sky
Where it would even be sweet to die
Upon the midnight without caring
Merged with love and all love's daring
Breasts lips eyes legs arms and belly
Turning senses into jelly
Why go back to Denmark's numbing
Sleets and snows? Say I'm not coming!
Poor Ophelia's dead and buried.
Sweet Belinda, we are married
By the breeze the sand the foam—
They shall be our hecatomb.

*Shakespeare Amended*

## IF I AM TO BE PRESERVED FROM HEARTACHE AND SHYNESS

If I am to be preserved from heartache and shyness
By Saint Catherine of Siena,
I am praying to her that she will hear my prayer
And treat me in every way with kindness.

I went to Siena to Saint Catherine's own church
(It is impossible to deny this)
To pray to her to cure me of my heartache and shyness
Which she can do, because she is a great saint.

Saint Catherine of Siena, if this song pleases you,
Then be good enough to answer the prayer it contains.
Make the person that sings this song less shy than that person is,
And give that person some joy in that person's heart.

*Masters of the Sun and Sea*


## SONGS ARE ABOUT DEATH

Songs are about death
And life is about stopping
For a while.
Time is about death
And space is about stopping
For a while.
Thought is about death
And sight is about stopping
For a while.

*The Unicorn*


## ALLEGHENY MENACES

Allegheny menaces
But B and O declares
We are very happy people
With our Railroad Shares!

Bought at half a dollar
Mounted now to ten

582

We shall soon be able to
Go back to Gottingen again

And see the varied flowers
Green and white and blue
And walk about the German streets
As the rich people do!

Tuskegee is flighty
Western is a gem
Buy them right and sell them right
And we'll go home again!
*New Times, New World*


## THIS LIFE WHICH SEEMS SO FAIR

This life which seems so fair
Is like a bubble blown up in the air
By sporting children's breath
Who chase it everywhere
And life is like a market
Open at six a.m.
To which nobody comes
They don't know it's a market
And life is like a gun
Carried in someone's pocket
It shoots the bubbles from the air
And closes down the market.
*New Times, New World*


## LO WHERE HAUSSMANN COMES, SEE WHERE HE COMES

Lo where Haussmann comes, see where he comes
To put these projects into execution!
What is that sound I hear? the sound of drums?
No it is Haussmann and the execution
Of his great project, tearing up the streets
Which, as we witness, he completes—
To widen the Champs Elysées
And Paris make, in every way,
The equal of Imperial Rome—

See him, now where he comes!
To shuffle little streets like cards
And deal them out as boulevards,
Avenues shining straight and wide
With a park on every side,
Brilliant streets that radiate
At a white and lovely rate
To Denfert or Passy slim as a bar!
Woods at Boulogne and Vincennes
And at Buttes-Chaumont for workingmen—
Oh, see where Haussmann comes, see where he comes!
*Angelica, or Paris in the Nineteenth Century*


THE BANQUET SONG

Ah, sweet Banquet, lovely Banquet
From your seats you get your name
From the bench, banchetto, banquette
But from love you get your fame
Love and drink and song and friendship
We extol you from our benches!

Banquet, Banquet, holy Banquet
Here the spirit is transcendent
Joined by wine and wit and laughter
No one soul is independent
All are joined in one enormous
Vision of the life before us!

Ah sweet Banquet thank you thank you
Banquet hear our glasses ring
We shall do our best to make you
A fiesta'd everything!
Such a Banquet as has never
Been and which will last forever!
*The Banquet*


LET'S POUR COCA COLA ON THE PRIEST

Let's pour
Coca Cola

On the Priest
While he's asleep!

This day is long
The cherries blossom
Life is strong
And he's asleep!

Each temple garden
Awakes from sleep
The sand is strong
In shining mist.

Let's go, pour
Coca Cola on
The Priest
While he's asleep!

*Don Juan of Kyoto*


I AM DEATH I'LL TAKE THE HAND

I am Death I'll take the hand
Of Borodin the baker
Alfred Schmitz the organ maker
And Jolie la Villette, the sailors' friend.
You turn away. Oh come and dance
The dance is life, and all your life,
And you had better know—
O doctor, O professor,
Young fop or fashion model, where you go
Is where my will directs
To that place where there is no sex
Nor any sport nor holding court
Nor bright ship sailing into port
For each is there alone.

*Summer Vacation*


DOES THE SUN USE YOU

Does the sun use you
Dead friend

To re-charge its light?
Do those waves
Out there
Have the curls of your hair?
Did you give back to the skies
The deep blue of your eyes?
Has your wit, your wonderful conversation
Become a science in other minds?

*Summer Vacation*


IN ANCIENT TIMES

In Ancient Times
The Swedish coast was like a desert place
Snow blossomed, and the surf

We had a King,
A Senate, and a City,
Several cities, everything.

Everything, but not
What that near Future brought,
Inspired Oxen!

Peace they gave us and
The Great
Society of Love! They gave us Love!

Happy the Swedish nation
All her days
Happy sensation
Oxen children everywhere
We will become the most beautiful
People on earth
Especially our women
Beautiful from loving oxen
What truly are oxen
But men of great worth
Transformed to four-legg'd creatures
With bestial naïve features
But these are changed by love!
Oh this is a time of triumph

586

And a time for celebration
The oxen came to Sweden
They guide us to the future
To future love!
The oxen bring us power and bring us love!

The Strangers from the Sea

## THE TRUE LIFE

"The true life
Is the life of the ancestors
And the true village
Is the village under the ground."

Come with me to this village!
Beginning to go under the ground
We see the new life
Of seeds sprouting

"Come with us up from the ground
To the village of breathable air!"

Under the Savanna's Blue Sky

## MIGHT I BE THE FIRST

Might I be the first
I would not be worst
I should have the chance
To make my country dance
Yet if I should fail
How my face would pale!
I will risk it all
Bless me, heaven's ball,
All revealing sun,
But tell not my fears to anyone.

We must make raids, raids, raids,
Raids on the English supplies!
Raids in the morning
And raids at night,

Raids in the evening, by candle light
We must make raids!

Raids for clothing
And raids for food
To do the Revolutionary
Army good!
We must make raids
Raids! raids!
Oh raids on the English supplies!
                    *George Washington Crossing the Delaware*


## YOU WANT A SOCIAL LIFE, WITH FRIENDS

You want a social life, with friends,
A passionate love life and as well
To work hard every day. What's true
Is of these three you may have two
And two can pay you dividends
But never may have three.

There isn't time enough, my friends—
Though dawn begins, yet midnight ends—
To find the time to have love, work, and friends.
Michelangelo had feeling
For Vittoria and the Ceiling
But did he go to parties at day's end?

Homer nightly went to banquets
Wrote all day but had no lockets
Bright with pictures of his Girl.
I know one who loves and parties
And has done so since his thirties
But writes hardly anything at all.
                    *Brothers and Friends*


## WHAT MAKES THIS STATUE NOBLE-SEEMING

What makes this statue noble-seeming
Is the emphasis upon
The upper portions of the face

And not the lower ones.
The sensuous mouth
Is scarcely emphasized at all
Rather the eyes and nose
Both of the Intellectual part and not
Too near the animal-seeming
Kiss-conceiving and germ-breathing
Mouth, yet, Grecian girl, it seems to me
You and I are breathing
Not from the architectural head
Or forehead's gradual slope. Instead
We're breathing through the mouth.
I'm out of breath!
I want you! That or death!
I want your mouth, your breath!

*Two Worlds*


## A LA COCONUT SCHOOL

A la Coconut School
Tous étaient mayas—
On portait le maya costume
Et puis on avait coûtume
De manger des mets mayas,
Et de boire le vin des Indes.

Students, students, demand
When you become woman and man
To revisiter ces écoles
To come back to these schools!
For the best that any life can
Is by the past to make reprimands—
Were we ever just fools?

At the American School
Everyone was American—
In jeans they played it cool
No one was patrician.
They danced the Fourth of July
As the years passed by.

Oh and surely it's good to demand
To return to one's school

Where maybe one teacher was cool
But not more than a rubber band
Where the girls were as tall as the boys
And had mutual sexual joys
Although smoking was contraband
And past one a.m. making noise!

A l'école Coleridge
Everyone was Dorothy Wordsworth
Certains fûrent Keats
And some were Shelley
Mais l'instruction journalière une fois accomplie
Ces identités s'en étaient allées.
But by the end of the teaching day
These identities had gone away.
Gone, gone, gone away
But to be resumed the next day
Dorothy John and Percy Bysshe
Assumed and cast-off, at the teachers' wish!

Oh, to go back to the Schools
With all that we know today!
The teachers we thought were such fools!
The hours and hours of play!
On était un peu ridicule
And went riding about on a mule
With a pleasure undreamed-of today
Bonheur aujourd'hui même pas revé!
                              *How Life Began*

# NEW ADDRESSES

# To "Yes"

You are always the member of a team,
Accompanied by a question—
If this is the way the world ends, is it really going to?
No. Are you a Buddhist? Maybe. A monsoon? Yes.
I have been delighted by you even in the basement
When asking if I could have some coal lumps and the answer was yes.
Yes to the finality of the brightness
And to the enduring qualities of the lark
She sings at heaven's gate. But is it unbolted? Bolted? Yes.
Which, though, is which? To which the answer cannot be yes
So reverse question. Pamela bending before the grate
Turns round rapidly to say Yes! I will meet you in Boston
At five after nine, if my Irishness is still working
And the global hamadryads, wood nymphs of my "yes."
But what, Pamela, what does that mean? Am I a yes
To be posed in the face of a negative alternative?
Or has the sky taken away from me its ultimate guess
About how probably everything is going to be eventually terrible
Which is something we knew all along, being modified by a yes
When what we want is obvious but has a brilliantly shining trail
Of stars. Or are those asterisks? Yes. What is at the bottom
Of the most overt question? Do we die? Yes. Does that
Always come later than now? Yes.
I love your development
From the answer to a simple query to a state of peace
That has the world by the throat. Am I lying? Yes.
Are you smiling? Yes. I'll follow you, yes? No reply.

# To Life

All one can say with certainty about anything that has you is "It moves!
Hey, wait a minute! Look, it's moving! Look
At it, it's moving! It must have life!"
No, that's only an electric charge—it's attached to a battery!
"No, that's life!" The wind blew it halfway across the street—
Or, from one edge of the table to another. It's not alive.
"Yes, it is! It moved by itself!
It has life! It's starting on a journey! Or is in the middle of one! Or near
    the end!"
Is it you who fill me up so? Is it you who are carrying me away?
Tell me how you manage to do that, also, with all the other people?
You must be very busy, very powerful, and manic, why
Do you want to keep up such a huge organization? What ought one to do
    in you
And with you? You give rocky lessons at best.
It would be good to find out from you
If you have some purpose aside from seeming meaningless
To adolescents and appearing marvelous
Beyond all accounting to those who are in love.
You're famous for being horrible, wonderful, irreplaceable
And also incomprehensible. I read Raymond Roussel trying to figure you
    out
I read Stendhal and Henry Green and Italo Svevo and listen to *Don
    Giovanni*
In the Greek torso I find you but you aren't there.
Without you there's no suffering and no dancing at the beach.
I have no husband, says the would-be bride. But she has you.

# To the Ohio

You separated my hometown from Kentucky
And south of us you deftly touched Indiana. Ohioans drove back over you
With lower-priced (untaxed) beer and Bourbon in the trunks
Of their cars to take to Cincinnati and get drunk
Less expensively than with Ohio purchases. In my teenage years
I drove over you in the other direction—to Campbell County—
To gamble, to the Hotel Licking to look at the pretty young prostitutes,
    and drink six-point-seven-percent Hudepohl Beer.
Your heyday had come when I was ten. We were down in the basement
To see if you were there yet. You flooded! You overflowed your banks!
Everything was wet
For miles around you. You were in the papers, trees stood in you up to
    their faces. Men rowed
Boats from one side of a street to another. Doctors
Ran around the city giving typhoid shots. I kept a scrapbook
A big one, of newspaper coverage of you
That was so much admired for its pasted-on white and pink clippings
I was happy about it for a month.
You reappeared beneath the *Island Queen*—five years later—
Which steamed up you to an amusement park—Coney Island,
Named after the one in New York—with Kentucky on your other side.
Leaning over the rail, I looked at it and you, a muddy divider
Between wild good times and the regular life, Kentucky and Ohio—
From one you took your name, and from the other, then, your meaning.

# To My Father's Business

Leo bends over his desk
Gazing at a memorandum
While Stuart stands beside him
With a smile, saying,
"Leo, the order for those desks
Came in today
From Youngstown Needle and Thread!"
C. Loth Inc., there you are
Like Balboa the conqueror
Of those who want to buy office furniture
Or bar fixtures
In nineteen forty in Cincinnati, Ohio!
Secretaries pound out
Invoices on antique typewriters—
Dactylographs
And fingernail biters.
I am sitting on a desk
Looking at my daddy
Who is proud of but feels unsure about
Some aspects of his little laddie.
I will go on to explore
Deep and/or nonsensical themes
While my father's on the dark hardwood floor
Hit by a couple of Ohio sunbeams.
Kenny, he says, some day you'll work in the store.
But I felt "never more" or "never ever."
Harvard was far away
World War Two was distant
Psychoanalysis was extremely expensive
All of these saved me from you.
C. Loth you made my father happy
I saw his face shining
He laughed a lot, working in you
He said to Miss Ritter
His secretary
"Ritt, this is my boy, Kenny!"
"Hello there Kenny," she said
My heart in an uproar
I loved you but couldn't think

Of staying with you
I can see the virtues now
That could come from being in you
A sense of balance
Compromise and acceptance—
Not isolated moments of brilliance
Like a girl without a shoe,
But someone that you
Care for every day—
Need for customers and the economy
Don't go away.
There were little pamphlets
Distributed in you
About success in business
Each about eight to twelve pages long
One whole series of them
All ended with the words
"P.S. He got the job"
One a story about a boy who said,
"I swept up the street, Sir,
Before you got up." Or
"There were five hundred extra catalogues
So I took them to people in the city who have a dog"—
P.S. He got the job.
I didn't get the job
I didn't think that I could do the job
I thought I might go crazy in the job
Staying in you
You whom I could love
But not be part of.
The secretaries clicked
Their Smith Coronas closed at five p.m.
And took the streetcars to Kentucky then
And I left too.

# To Piano Lessons

You didn't do me any good
But being with you
Was like walking up the stairs
Of a building whose attic was June
How much promise there is in the arpeggios!
If I could do only one
Fine, I was arpeggio-capable
As the notes themselves are music-capable
And beauty-capable and capable
Of ripping into pieces by means of art
Any previous aspect or attitude.
I thought if I could by art
And practice, really hard work,
Get to you really the way I
Walked into you, piano lessons,
I could make something wonderful
Of what I had felt and done
With my pitifully short existence
Of too much rush—
But I never did. Thanks, anyway; you were a partner
In an enterprise
That didn't work. We lost but have moved on.

# To Stammering

Where did you come from, lamentable quality?
Before I had a life you were about to ruin my life.
The mystery of this stays with me.
"Don't brood about things," my elders said.
I hadn't any other experience of enemies from inside.
They were all from outside—big boys
Who cursed me and hit me; motorists; falling trees.
All these you were as bad as, yet inside. When I spoke, you were there.
I could avoid you by singing or by acting.
I acted in school plays but was no good at singing.
Immediately after the play you were there again.
You ruined the cast party.
You were not a sign of confidence.
You were not a sign of manliness.
You were stronger than good luck and bad; you survived them both.
You were slowly edged out of my throat by psychoanalysis
You who had been brought in, it seems, like a hired thug
To beat up both sides and distract them
From the main issue: oedipal love. You were horrible!
Tell them, now that you're back in your thug country,
That you don't have to be so rough next time you're called in
But can be milder and have the same effect—unhappiness and pain.

# To Kidding Around

Kidding around you are terrible sometimes
When I feel that I have to do it
Suddenly behaving like an ape, piling up snow on top of a friend
When I know that isn't going to win her heart;
Screaming for no reason very loud, eating in a noisy way,
Running and barking as if I were a dog through the dimly lighted streets
Frightening the inhabitants, bashing myself into the cut-outs
Or mannequins in a store-window display, and yelling Boffo!
I am having so much fun
Seemingly. But isn't this a faithless seeming?
For I'm a joker, an ass
And I can't stop being
Ridiculous, my tongue against the window
Vlop vlap I can't get it loose
It's frozen here!
How can I ever say what's in my heart
While imitating the head butts of a rhinoceros
Or the arm spans of an octopus
I am nothing but a wretched clown
All manner
Of humiliating things.
Like a far-off landscape.
Icy women who loom like towers.
Yet sometimes you are breathtaking,
Kidding around!
To be rid of the troubles
Of one person by turning into
Someone else, moving and jolting
As if nothing mattered but today
In fact nothing
But this precise moment—five thirty-one a.m.
Celery growing on the plains
Snow swirls in the mountains.

# To Carelessness

You led me to sling my rifle
Over my shoulder when its bayonet was fixed
On Leyte, in the jungle. It hit a hornets' nest
And I fell down
Screaming. The hornets attacked me, and Lonnie,
The corporal, said "Soldier get off your ass!"
Later the same day, I stepped on a booby trap
That was badly wired. You
Had been there too.
Thank you. It didn't explode.

# To Some Buckets

Waiting to fill you, buckets,
One morning it was afternoon
Then evening, all the same except
One time when I filled you
And carried you to the apartment
In which a dog was sitting
I forget its name. He drank thirstily
And well I brought you
To other places too with always
A strain, hurting my arms
For you are heavy you
Are heavy with water filled
Whether it was on Leyte
That I carried you
To fellow soldiers
Or up to the blankets, from the sea,
To some who were too hot. It makes
For giddiness to
Concentrate on you
Concentric buckets—senseless—
You lend your sides to the soul.

# To World War Two

Early on you introduced me to young women in bars
You were large, and with a large hand
You presented them in different cities,
Made me in San Luis Obispo, drunk
On French seventy-fives, in Los Angeles, on pousse-cafés.
It was a time of general confusion
Of being a body hurled at a wall.
I didn't do much fighting. I sat, rather I stood, in a foxhole.
I stood while the typhoon splashed us into morning.
It felt unusual
Even if for a good cause
To be part of a destructive force
With my rifle in my hands
And in my head
My serial number
The entire object of my existence
To eliminate Japanese soldiers
By killing them
With a rifle or with a grenade
And then, many years after that,
I could write poetry
Fall in love
And have a daughter
And think
About these things
From a great distance
If I survived
I was "paying my debt
To society" a paid
Killer. It wasn't
Like anything I'd done
Before, on the paved
Streets of Cincinnati
Or on the ballroom floor
At Mr. Vathé's dancing class
What would Anne Marie Goldsmith
Have thought of me
If instead of asking her to dance
I had put my BAR to my shoulder

And shot her in the face
I thought about her in my foxhole—
One, in a foxhole near me, has his throat cut during the night
We take more precautions but it is night and it is you.
The typhoon continues and so do you.
"I can't be killed—because of my poetry. I have to live on in order to
 write it."
I thought—even crazier thought, or just as crazy—
"If I'm killed while thinking of lines, it will be too corny
When it's reported" (I imagined it would be reported!)
So I kept thinking of lines of poetry. One that came to me on the beach on
 Leyte
Was "The surf comes in like masochistic lions."
I loved this terrible line. It was keeping me alive. My Uncle Leo wrote to
 me,
"You won't believe this, but some day you may wish
You were footloose and twenty on Leyte again." I have never wanted
To be on Leyte again,
With you, whispering into my ear,
"Go on and win me! Tomorrow you may not be alive,
So do it today!" How could anyone ever win you?
How many persons would I have had to kill
Even to begin to be a part of winning you?
You were too much for me, though I
Was older than you were and in camouflage. But for you
Who threw everything together, and had all the systems
Working for you all the time, this was trivial. If you could use me
You'd use me, and then forget. How else
Did I think you'd behave?
I'm glad you ended. I'm glad I didn't die. Or lose my mind.
As machines make ice
We made dead enemy soldiers, in
Dark jungle alleys, with weapons in our hands
That produced fire and kept going straight through
I was carrying one,
I who had gone about for years as a child
Praying God don't let there ever be another war
Or if there is, don't let me be in it. Well, I was in you.
All you cared about was existing and being won.
You died of a bomb blast in Nagasaki, and there were parades.

# To Living in the City

I was surprised!
You had bars on the palms of your hands
And places to buy neckties
It seemed by the millions
Rudy Burckhardt cast his line
Of photos onto roofs and chimneys
Meyer Liben
Drove his car up and down
Stopping it to
Lean out and talk to women
This was nineteen-forties
New York. With Delmore
Schwartz and Paul
Goodman in it. James Laughlin
Published everyone
While you and I
Met the poet Jean Garrigue
In Sam Abramson's bookstore
Which was I had been
Told the only place to buy
Henry Miller's
*Tropic of Cancer* and
She was very pretty
Wearing bright
Red lipstick
A jacket, pants, and a tie.
"Jean Garrigue! You're
The poet!" I said. And "That am I!"
She knowingly
Replied. All right,
Living in the City,
I'm for you! I said
To myself and
Later when poetry,
Desire for fame and love
And anonymity and
Full-fledged Communism
Attracted me to you
I found an apartment

With Miriam and Peggy in it
And Miriam said to me one night
I think you'd like my roommate, Peggy.
Miriam was right.
Later, West Tenth Street
Was right. Charles
Street and Greenwich
Avenue were right. Cold-water
Living rooms and soot
Floating through bright
Hard-to-push-up windows
On Third Avenue
Were right.
A woman waits
For me on West
Seventeenth Street I
Run down to my parents
Who are honking the car
We're supposed to drive home
To Cincinnati together there's
No hope! Kenny! my
Father says. Look at you
You're covered with
Lipstick! *Beato me!*
This was farewell
To being anyplace else. I
Wanted you. We've
Been together every night
Now, almost, for fifty years.

# To My Twenties

How lucky that I ran into you
When everything was possible
For my legs and arms, and with hope in my heart
And so happy to see any woman—
O woman! O my twentieth year!
Basking in you, you
Oasis from both growing and decay
Fantastic unheard of nine- or ten-year oasis
A palm tree, hey! And then another
And another—and water!
I'm still very impressed by you. Whither,
Midst falling decades, have you gone? Oh in what lucky fellow,
Unsure of himself, upset, and unemployable
For the moment in any case, do you live now?
From my window I drop a nickel
By mistake. With
You I race down to get it
But I find there on
The street instead, a good friend,
X—— N——, who says to me
Kenneth do you have a minute?
And I say yes! I am in my twenties!
I have plenty of time! In you I marry,
In you I first go to France; I make my best friends
In you, and a few enemies. I
Write a lot and am living all the time
And thinking about living. I loved to frequent you
After my teens and before my thirties.
You three together in a bar
I always preferred you because you were midmost
Most lustrous apparently strongest
Although now that I look back on you
What part have you played?
You never, ever, were stingy.
What you gave me you gave whole
But as for telling

Me how best to use it
You weren't a genius at that.
Twenties, my soul
Is yours for the asking
You know that, if you ever come back.

# To Psychoanalysis

I took the Lexington Avenue subway
To arrive at you in your glory days
Of the Nineteen Fifties when we believed
That you could solve any problem
And I had nothing but disdain
For "self-analysis" "group analysis" "Jungian analysis"
"Adlerian analysis" the Karen Horney kind
All—other than you, pure Freudian type—
Despicable and never to be mine!
I would lie down according to your
Dictates but not go to sleep.
I would free-associate. I would say whatever
Came into my head. Great
Troops of animals floated through
And certain characters like Picasso and Einstein
Whatever came into my head or my heart
Through reading or thinking or talking
Came forward once again in you. I took voyages
Down deep unconscious rivers, fell through fields,
Cleft rocks, went on through hurricanes and volcanoes.
Ruined cities were as nothing to me
In my fantastic advancing. I recovered epochs,
Gold of former ages that melted in my hands
And became toothpaste or hazy vanished citadels. I dreamed
Exclusively for you. I was told not to make important decisions.
This was perfect. I never wanted to. On the Har-Tru surface of my
    emotions
Your ideas sank in so I could play again.
But something was happening. You gave me an ideal
Of conversation—entirely about me
But including almost everything else in the world.
But this wasn't poetry it was something else.
After two years of spending time in you
Years in which I gave my best thoughts to you
And always felt you infiltrating and invigorating my feelings
Two years at five days a week, I had to give you up.
It wasn't my idea. "I think you are nearly through,"
Dr. Loewenstein said. "You seem much better." But, Light!
Comedy! Tragedy! Energy! Science! Balance! Breath!

I didn't want to leave you. I cried. I sat up.
I stood up. I lay back down. I sat. I said
But I still get sore throats and have hay fever
"And some day you are going to die. We can't cure everything."
Psychoanalysis! I stood up like someone covered with light
As with paint, and said Thank you. Thank you.
It was only one moment in a life, my leaving you.
But once I walked out, I could never think of anything seriously
For fifteen years without also thinking of you. Now what have we
    become?
You look the same, but now you are a past You.
That's fifties clothing you're wearing. You have some fifties ideas
Left—about sex, for example. What shall we do? Go walking?
We're liable to have a slightly frumpy look,
But probably no one will notice—another something I didn't know then.

# To Testosterone

You took me to the Spanish Steps
Then we walked up to the top of them and looked down.
Having looked down from there, we walked down
To about the middle of the curving Spanish Steps
And, for a moment, sat down.
But there was nothing doing.
Some cigarette packages lay on the nearby steptops.
The sides were a beige white, running up and down.
No woman in sight
And no one getting in our way, either,
To rouse you from your sleep
Of twenty centuries, the one you always fall into,
And nothing to wake me up, either,
Although I was completely awake in the banal sense
Of knowing where the post office was and the Piazza di Spagna
That was just below. Not far, the Piazza del Popolo
Held the possibility of people, but, I thought,
Less promisingly than where we were might go.
We stayed on the Spanish Steps till almost ten—
I talked to a few people, you slept—and then went sadly home.

The next day however you were very lively
You got up before I did and bought the railroad tickets
That would take us to Naples. "Come on, let's go!" you said
But I was barely awake.
Be calm! "But only to act or to sleep is my nature," you say. "Let's
Use the tickets, take the train; forget
This random tune, and get something done!"
Now leading me to the station—a ravishing Roman girl! "Let's stay here!"
You murmur when my foot is already on the step
Of the *Stazione Termini*. All right, I agree
But my hand is full of tickets and my mind of dismay,
Confusion and dismay. You have started to make me angry
By the way you're making me anxious, which is another thing you do.
Stop it, I say. You stop. You appreciate travel the way I appreciate eating
    lunch.
I do remember Barbara, in Parma.
Exhilaration, riding on your horns, is never far away.

# To Driving

Wherever you went, there were woods,
Driveways, cars, and places to have a picnic! And attention to you,
    Driving,
Meant less attention to the one beside. Soon she'd be driving
And I would look outside. Without you I'd not ever have seen
The underhalf of Louisiana green
And red and white, or have had the place to ask my father the questions
I did about driving. He said You must stay on the road.
Increasingly, as a trip goes on,
You become the main thing it is and rightly so. What would we do
Without you there, quick and slow, dreaming both interior and exterior—
Without your assurance that "Wherever I am, there you shall be
Whether in the Sahara or Vermont. You stand by me
And I will stay with you, for I am Driving,
Memory that, whenever stopped, can be renewed."

# To Jewishness

As you were contained in
Or embodied by
Louise Schlossman
When she was a sophomore
At Walnut Hills
High School
In Cincinnati, Ohio,
I salute you
And thank you
For the fact
That she received
My kisses with tolerance
On New Year's Eve
And was not taken aback
As she well might have been
Had she not had you
And had I not, too.
Ah, you!
Dark, complicated you!
Jewishness, you are the tray—
On it painted
Moses, David and the Ten
Commandments, the handwriting
On the Wall, Daniel
In the lions' den—
On which my childhood
Was served
By a mother
And father
Who took you
To Michigan—
Oh the soft smell
Of the pine
Trees of Michigan
And the gentle roar
Of the Lake! Michigan
Or sent you
To Wisconsin—
I went to camp there—

On vacation, with me
Every year!
My counselors had you
My fellow campers
Had you and "Doc
Ehrenreich" who
Ran the camp had you
We got up in the
Mornings you were there
You were in the canoes
And on the baseball
Diamond, everywhere around.
At home, growing
Taller, you
Thrived, too. Louise had you
And Charles had you
And Jean had you
And her sister Mary
Had you
We all had you
And your Bible
Full of stories
That didn't apply
Or didn't seem to apply
In the soft spring air
Or dancing, or sitting in the cars
To anything we did.
In "religious school"
At the Isaac M. Wise
Synagogue (called "temple")
We studied not you
But Judaism, the one who goes with you
And is your guide, supposedly,
Oddly separated
From you, though there
In the same building, you
In us children, and it
On the blackboards
And in the books—Bibles
And books simplified
From the Bible. How
Like a Bible with shoulders

Rabbi Seligmann is!
You kept my parents and me
Out of the hotels near Crystal Lake
In Michigan and you resulted, for me,
In insults,
At which I felt
Chagrined but
Was energized by you.
You went with me
Into the army, where
One night in a foxhole
On Leyte a fellow soldier
Said Where are the fuckin Jews?
Back in the PX. I'd like to
See one of those bastards
Out here. I'd kill him!
I decided to conceal
You, my you, anyway, for a while.
Forgive me for that.
At Harvard you
Landed me in a room
In Kirkland House
With two other students
Who had you. You
Kept me out of the Harvard clubs
And by this time (I
Was twenty-one) I found
I preferred
Kissing girls who didn't
Have you. Blonde
Hair, blue eyes,
And Christianity (oddly enough) had an
Aphrodisiac effect on me.
And everything that opened
Up to me, of poetry, of painting, of music,
Of architecture in old cities
Didn't have you—
I was
Distressed
Though I knew
Those who had you
Had hardly had the chance

To build cathedrals
Write secular epics
(Like *Orlando Furioso*)
Or paint Annunciations—"Well
I had David
In the wings." David
Was a Jew, even a Hebrew.
He wasn't Jewish.
You're quite
Something else. "I had Mahler,
Einstein, and Freud." I didn't
Want those three (then). I wanted
Shelley, Byron, Keats, Shakespeare,
Mozart, Monet. I wanted
Botticelli and Fra Angelico.
"There you've
Chosen some hard ones
For me to connect to. But
Why not admit that I
Gave you the life
Of the mind as a thing
To aspire to? And
Where did you go
To find your 'freedom'? to
New York, which was
Full of me." I do know
Your good qualities, at least
Good things you did
For me—when I was ten
Years old, how you brought
Judaism in, to give ceremony
To everyday things, surprise and
Symbolism and things beyond
Understanding in the
Synagogue then I
Was excited by you, a rescuer
Of me from the flatness of my life.
But then the flatness got you
And I let it keep you
And, perhaps, of all things known,
That was most ignorant. "You
Sound like Yeats, but

You're not. Well, happy
Voyage home, Kenneth, to
The parking lot
Of understood experience. I'll be
Here if you need me and here
After you don't
Need anything else. HERE is a quality
I have, and have had
For you, and for a lot of others,
Just by being it, since you were born."

# To Consciousness

We didn't pay much attention to you at the barn,
Though without you we would probably have been caught.

# To Jewishness, Paris, Ambition, Trees, My Heart, and Destiny

Now that you all have gathered here to talk with me,
Let's bring everything out into the open.
It's almost too exciting to have all of you here—
One of you physically and another spiritually inside me,
Another worn into me by my upbringing, another a quality
I picked up someplace west of here, and two of you at least fixed things
    outside me,
Paris and trees. Who would like to ask the first question?
Silence. Noble, eternal-seeming silence. Well, destiny, what do you think?
Did you bring Jewishness here or did it bring you, or what?
You two are simply smiling and stay close together. Well, trees and Paris
You have been together before. What do you make of being here
With Jewishness, my heart, ambition, and destiny? It's a frightening, even
    awe-inspiring thing,
Don't you think so? Ambition you've been moving my heart
For a long time—will you take some time off now?
Should we go to lunch? Just sit here? Or, perhaps, sing
A song about all of you. "Including you?" one of you speaks for the first
    time
And it is you, my heart, a great chatterbox all the same! And now you,
    Jewishness, chime in
With a Hebrew melody you'd like us to enjoy and you Paris and trees step
    out
Of the shadows of each other and say "Look
At these beautiful purple and white blossoms!" Destiny you wink at me
    and shrug
A shoulder toward ambition who (you) now begin to sing
"Yes, yes it will include all of us, and it is about time!"
Jewishness and ambition go off to a tree-greened-out corner
And start their confab. Destiny walks with Paris and me
To a house where an old friend is living. You, heart, in the padded dark as
    usual,
Seem nonetheless to be making a very good effort. "Oh, this stirs me,"
    you say, excitedly—
"To be with Jewishness and trees and destiny at the same time makes me
    leap up!"

And you do. Ambition you return but don't take hold.

Destiny, you have taken my heart to Paris, you have hidden it among these trees.

Heart, the rest of this story is yours. Let it go forward in any way it needs to go.

# To the French Language

I needed to find you and, once having found you, to keep you
You who could make me a physical Larousse
Of everyday living, you who would present me to Gilberte
And Anna and Sonia, you by whom I could be a surrealist
And a dadaist and almost a fake of Racine and of Molière. I was hiding
The heavenly dolor you planted in my heart:
That I would never completely have you.
I wanted to take you with me on long vacations
Always giving you so many kisses, ma française—
Across rocky mountains, valleys, and lakes
And I wanted it to be as if
Nous faisions ce voyage pour l'éternité
Et non pas uniquement pour la brève durée d'une année boursière en
    France.
Those days, and that idea, are gone.
A little hotel on the rue de Fleurus
Was bursting with you.
And one April morning, when I woke up, I had you
Stuck to the tip of my tongue like a Christmas sticker
I walked out into the street, it was Fleurus
And said hello which came out Bonjour Madame
I walked to the crémerie four doors away and sat down.
I was lifted up by you. I knew I couldn't be anything to you
But an aspiring lover. Sans ego. It was the best relationship
Of relationships sans ego, that I've ever had.
I know you love flattery and are so good at it that one can hardly believe
What you are saying when it is expressed in you.
But I have loved you. That's no flattering statement
But the truth. And still love you, though now I'm not in love with you.
The woman who first said this to me nearly broke my heart,
But I don't think I'm breaking yours, because it's a coeur
In the first place and, for another thing, it beats under le soleil
On a jeudi or vendredi matin and besides you're not listening to me
At least not as you did on the days
I sat around in Aix-en-Provence's cafés waiting for you
To spark a conversation—about nothing in particular. I was on stage
At all times, and you were the script and the audience
Even when the theatre had no people in it, you were there.

# To Friendship

Puberty was the Norman Conquest
By the language of love I thought you'd be suppressed
But you hung in there. You've stayed with me for sixty years.
You prevented nights lonely
To the point of desperation. You embarked on projects.
You took trips. You bravely quarreled, made up, and sat down again.
You saved a third person. You went into a ditch. You examined causes.
You started magazines and ate turkeys. You went to the clinic. You gave
    advice
Endlessly, the tag-end of gossip. You discussed violence, money, and
    vulnerability.
Egotism was one of your major topics. You left a third one standing on a
    bridge
By your overabsorption in yourself. You familiarized with France.
A glass wall covered with blue and white ribbons made you laugh. You
    sent home for wives,
Husbands, brothers, sisters, and girlfriends. You felt you were the best.
You delivered encomiums. I have images of you moseying down sidewalks
And images of you boisterous and drunk. Sunlight admired you
And so did travel and evening. You gave sleeping a rest, by conducting
    seminars
On variations of yourself until almost dawn.
You are consoling about age and approaching extinction. You keep out of
    bed and leap from apartments
But are caught in a net. The traffic kicks you
Into high gear. You live criticism of life. You quiet the motion
Of barricades rising. You've lasted, in these ways,
Longer than love, which you haven't supplanted.

# To Orgasms

You've never really settled down
Have you, orgasms?
Restless, roving, and not funny
In any way
You change consciousness
Directly, not
Shift of gears
But changing cars
Is more like it. I said my prayers
Ate lunch, read books, and had you.
Someone was there, later, to join me and you
In our festivity, a woman named N.
She said oh we shouldn't do
This I replied oh we should
We did and had you
After you I possess this loveable
Person and she possesses me
There is no more we can do
Until the phone rings
And then we start to plan for you again
And it is obvious
Life may be centered in you
I began to think that every day
Was just one of the blossoms
On the infinitely blossoming
Tree of life
When it was light out we'd say
Soon it will be dark
And when it was dark
We'd say soon it will be light
And we had you.
Sometimes
We'd be sitting at the table
Thinking of you
Or of something related to you
And smiled at other times
Might worry
We read a lot of things about you
Some seemed wrong

It seemed
Puzzling that we had you
Or rather that you
Could have us, in a way,
When you wished to
Though
We had to wish so too
Ah, like what a wild person
To have in the Berkeley apartment!
If anyone knew
That you were there! But they must have known!
You rampaged about we tried to keep you secret.
I mentioned you to no one.
What would there be to say?
That every night or every day
You turned two persons into stone
Hit by dynamite and rocked them till they rolled,
Just about, from bed to floor
And then leaped up and got back into bed
And troubled you no more
For an hour or a day at a time.

# To the Italian Language

I will never forget
The first time I heard you
And understood a few words.
I was determined to learn you
And I did.
I learned to say
Yes, thank you.
Where is the bank?
I have only been in Venice
For several days.
We went to Rome together
And I remained
Your servant.
You knew much more than I
About everything except
American jokes
And the details of the lives
Of a few of my friends.
Aside from that, you dominated
Especially in the domain
Of aesthetic precision
And how big or small things were
Or were both at the same time
I lectured in you in Torino
In a large theater
Filled with one thousand people, Italians
All who knew you better than I
Yet who listened to you in me
And came out, so they said, *"contenti."*
How happy I was
And later to be in bed with you
And to know that next day I would ride
Through the snow half a day in a train
To Florence where I would speak in you again—
So glad to, after all my practice sentences,
My lists of verbs, my stuttering conversation
With the young woman on the train
Near Milano
In fact on the very same *rapido*
Ten years before.

# To Knowledge, My Skeleton, and an Aesthetic Concept

We're sitting around, as usual
Hotcha-nothing-to-do sort of summer
Afternoon-evening and you, Skeleton, aching a little
Ask for a song
From An Aesthetic Concept. You, Concept, explain
That no songs today but, rather, discussion
Of you and then say
What do you think, Knowledge? You
Lounging in a corner, pull up your knees
To your robust chest and say Listen
To both parts and make a conclusion.
A few friends are dropping over
As lazy as we. I say Knowledge your answer didn't
Make very much sense and you say
(To Skeleton) Have some tortelloni. It's
Good for you. And Aesthetic Concept
You're humming a tune that in some way bears yourself out.
I go out to get some coffee and Skeleton
You with me. You say, you know, Knowledge
Is knowledge but all the same
It would be good to hear a song don't you agree
It would help get some of these cricks out of me.
Skeleton, Concept, and Knowledge, all on a summer's day
Turned evening thirty-five years ago
When gin drinks were still popular, the acanthus was blossoming
And each of you said what you felt you had to say
No matter the consequences either to head or to heart.

# To Tiredness

You took me by surprise
In the Church of Santa Sofia
I fell asleep
On a bench there
And then afterwards
Didn't like walking to the new
Destination, our hotel.
I was amazed by you in Houston
Where I was tired all the time
Though I pepped up to go with Sherry
To gamble and drink all night
And afterwards my poems blew out the back
Of the car in which we were speeding
Back to my hotel so I wouldn't be deathly
Tired the next day though I was
Very very tired
Exhilarated all the same
At what I had done to defeat my life's
Apparent intentions
By using time all night
In a destructive way.
You, tiredness, helped me fight
My way back to sanity.
Without you, next day would be last night
Also I might be dead
You've saved my life
Not once but many times.
As long as you don't come
Before I get to the place
Where I'm going to need you,
You're all right.

# To the Island of Hydra

When I sat
Wherever I sat
It was you.
At times I was standing
Also on you.
In walking
I went
From one area, or aspect,
Of your surface
To another
Without falling down
To the rocky sea below
(Oh, your violet forehead,
Your elbows of ceaseless rips!)
Humorous, and undeveloped
You then were
(Though now I hear
You go about the Aegean
Offering tour plans
To ambitious operators)
We had a plan
With youth! With
Sunlight days! With energy!
With uncertain tampering
With crucial yet exquisite things!
With the rabbits hopping over you!
With the tar gabling your sea!
Of stony and of unstony beach!
We worked out a method
Simple as obvious—
I would open the door
Of the house and you close it
Three times a day, about
One hundred times—
Then I could be sure
To stay for a month on you
Which is what I desired.

# To Marijuana

There is one wonderful moment
That I remember, when I had smoked you
I was sitting in front of a fire
In a fireplace and I was crazy about a woman
A new (i.e., recently appeared to me) human
So crazy that to show how great I was, it was,
Unmade I was, it was, I threw my glasses (eyeglasses)
Into the fire. When I went to look for them
Sometime after, they were gone and I was happy
Happy as I have ever been. If you could give me such dramatic glances
All life long I'd surely be a pothead but I also like
To wake up in the morning fresh and strong
And to write poems with my glasses on—
Without them, I'm unable to see.
Therefore I'm not sure what you should be to me,
Marijuana, in the times that are yet to come—
Merely a memory? I can remember the hum
And the catch in my throat your sensations present to me—
I don't know if that's enough—perhaps occasionally
A new bout with you, in the name of appetite, or love,
And occasionally bad (I'd guess) poetry—but then you never know, do
    you?
In any case, thank you for that throwing thing,
For that eagle's wing, away from my reasonable beak.

# To My Old Addresses

Help! Get out of here! Go walking!
Forty-six (I think) Commerce Street, New York City
The Quai des Brumes nine thousand four hundred twenty-six Paris
Georgia Tech University Department of Analogues
Wonderland, the stone font, Grimm's Fairy Tales
Forty-eight Greenwich Avenue the landlady has a dog
She lets run loose in the courtyard seven
Charles Street which Stefan Wolpe sublet to me
Hotel de Fleurus in Paris, Via Convincularia in Rome
Where the motorcycles speed
Twelve Hamley Road in Southwest London O
My old addresses! O my addresses! Are you addresses still?
Or has the hand of Time roughed over you
And buffered and stuffed you with peels of lemons, limes, and shells
From old institutes? If I address you
It is mostly to know if you are well.
I am all right but I think I will never find
Sustenance as I found in you, oh old addresses
Numbers that sink into my soul
Forty-eight, nineteen, twenty-three, o worlds in which I was alive!

# To Walking, the French Language, Testosterone, Politics, and Duration

You who are so often with me when I am moving
From one place to another and you whom one hundred million speak
In all parts of the planet, and you who motivate the branchless race so
   much,
You for whom victory is everything, all these you take into account.
The mind races to you sometimes at such moments and then races back.

I don't think I could live without you, happily, nor truly excellently
   without you.
I can't even consider giving you back. I don't know where I got you
And I want to hold on to you, in any case, no matter what harm you
   may do
But I can largely control you. You on the other hand like many others I
   would efface
If you weren't deemed necessary sometimes by the rest to create more
   good in you.

You whom I can stop by standing still; you, by saying nothing;
You, who stop first for me; you, whom I will never marry;
You whom we can only represent, by a tree, or by a wall—
Give me back the first times I encountered you!
All of you found me clumsy, except you, who simply found me brief.

# To Sleep

Great comrade woman of existence, brava sleep!
How many times I've come to get you
And you weren't there!
Now I have a woman friend who helps me find you
But in those days
When my life was lonely and illicit
When it didn't seem to matter
If I were up or not, nor at what hour,
Then sleep you were a tyrant
And a woman that I followed
From week to week from town to town
Not stalking but walking
In earnest pursuit of you sleep
Until happily you passed out or I fell down.

Now that I think of you
I feel fond. But what are you really?
Are you some exiguous palmfrond
Capitulated by merriment back out of and into existence?
Were you always the goblet from which a few inspired ones
Drank that liqueur that offered them their sublimest poems?
Will you offer them equally to me, sleep
Or have you already done so? Will you be more than fair? This morning I
    feel
As the gondolier advances like a rope's continuingly pulled-at knot
That you may be, and I think with gratitude
Of what we together still might do.

# To the Roman Forum

After my daughter Katherine was born
I was terribly excited
I think I would have been measured at the twenty-five-espresso mark
We—Janice, now Katherine, and I—were in Rome
(Janice gave birth at the international hospital on top of Trastevere)
I went down and sat and looked at the ruins of you
I gazed at them, gleaming in the half-night
And thought, oh my, My God, My goodness, a child, a wife.
While I was sitting there, a friend, a sculptor, came by
I just had a baby, I said. I mean Janice did. I'm—
I thought I'd look at some very old great things
To match up with this new one. Oh, Adya said,
I guess you'd like to be alone, then. Congratulations. Goodnight.
Thank you. Goodnight, I said. Adya departed.
Next day I saw Janice and Katherine.
Here they are again and have nothing to do with you
A pure force swept through me another time
I am here, they are here, this has happened.
It is happening now, it happened then.

# To Angelic Circumstances

God bless you, angelic circumstances
That put me in Rome, at the instant Katherine
Was born, then two months old
How we exulted
To know she would be three
Then four by which time Paris
Was the city of our mirth
For Baby Katherine ruled the trees
And two banks the Champs-Elysées
And the dim bark of the chestnut trees
Of Luxembourg when she was good
Or bad and ruled the echoing breeze
That ruffled the sad students' hair
As they walked through the Cité Universitaire
I remember the bare
Knees of being completely there
And adequately seeing
That what was there was really there
And when the bus came felt like transfigured being
We got on it and there was still air
The blest air that we breathe!

# To Experience

You hung out with me till I was eleven years old
And then you started going elsewhere.
At noon I came upon your shining face
Clearly in an opposing situation.
Oh, Experience, you've become "experience with girls"
I said. Later you were "experience with jobs," "experience of travel"
    "experience of the world"
And then you again became just plain Experience.
Do you have any experience? people said
Or Have you had much experience? Or
The great thing is experience. Have you had
That kind of experience? I said to myself well I have you
But are you adequate, to which you said
In reply, It's more or less up to you. I remember being proud of having
    gotten married
And also of being psychoanalysed and of having spent two years in France.
These were experiences
No one could deny. But you were subtle, asking
But are you having me REALLY or have you had?
I am never so deceiving as when alone
With an accepted cultural artifact, say, like marriage,
Or living in France. What REALLY happened to you, was it
Real? Was I with you, even when you were sleeping, all the time?
I don't know, Experience. I don't know, I guess you were.
And through the long woods come the short dresses of the trees—
THAT was an experience. No, you said. Then, yes.
People may be going to study us like rooms
Of a known palace but minor titillation is all that they will find.
Is the mole's experience but the stone's not?
Aspect in which you make us stale and weary,
Aspect in which you make us very happy
As when climbing over mountains. To have covered the whole range—
Well, what is it? To have gone down that long hill with one's love
Making out in the car—because dangerous was more experience?
You are a bringing of outside into inside but also I have to say
It's the other way around. Around and around we go
And we want you to be new. They come in from the suburbs to find you
And go out on the ocean and into the war zone.
We know we're starting to get you when "pop! pop!" we hear!

Is it always best to have you, or not? It is by far the best to have me.
What about innocence? don't you destroy that? It comes and goes.
I'm not just physical, mind you. I am also love—
And moral judgment and decision amidst indecisions
And the sheer crack of the look of the mountains on the soul.
You know all that. Yes I do. Is there a way to NOT have you?
No, but when repeated, insolently, neurotically perhaps, I tend to roll up,
Coil into a ball and you won't feel anything there
Although you know you possess me, like a fascinating rock. Of which the
    secret—
Is that I need the present in order to breathe.
Without new consignments of me I might as well not be. Angel, farewell!
I'm no angel. I'm with you if you ring or if you crack the bell.

# To Life, Breath, and Experience

Can any of you exist without the others,
Or does one of you mean all?
No experience without life and breath,
But are there breath and life without experience?
Does a just-born ant have experience?
Experience, here is the ant
You see if you can see
How much of you it has.
Breath, you are listening close.
Life, you lean back in your chair.
Soon it will be noon
And suddenly you three go
To the Cemetery Bar
To have a quick one,
And then, when you come out
Of the dark inn bar into the glaring sunlight,
You don't notice that someone is gone
Who was just standing there
Making a witty remark or looking along
The map edge to find out some location.

# To Fame

To be known outside one's city and one's nation
To be known outside one's life! By means of you,
Bella and bruta Fama, talk, public opinion.
If only you bore more the semblance
Of recognition of achievement!
Instead you nod and flounce
Around, you are
Co-animate with feathers
You traipse off with strangers
You sing the song
You've sung thousands of times.
At fifteen I married My Lord You
I decided I was a poet
You, Shelley, and I went into my later life
And the three of us still stayed separate
I was at my desk, Shelley was in the library, you were out drinking or
    dancing. I wrote
"Fame, daughter of Terra, false one and fairest
Of all the sisterhood of fake inventions and intentions
Come stay with us a while, my friends and me—
We have invented a new kind of poetry." What a rush to the heart
And what a rush to the newsstands, if you come! But you are gone.
One person in a billion perhaps has you forever, and even that person
Is lifeless, though you promised something else.
Norris Embry said to me on Hydra one morning, when I was being
Supersensitive and profound on an unimportant subject,
"Kenneth, you're Rilking!" and there you were.

# To My Fifties

I should say something to you
Now that you have departed over the mountains
Leaving me to my sixties and seventies, not hopeful of your return,
O you, who seemed to mark the end of life, who ever would have thought
  that you would burn
With such sexual fires as you did? I wound up in you
Some work I had started long before. You were
A time for completion and for destruction. My
Marriage had ended. In you I sensed trying to find
A way out of you actually that wasn't toward non-existence.
I thought, "All over." You cried, "I'm here!" You were like traveling
In this sense, but on one's own
With no tour guide or even the train schedule.
As a "Prime of Life" I missed you. You seemed an incompletion made up
  of completions
Unacquainted with each other. How could this be happening?
  I thought. Or
What should it mean, exactly, that I am fifty-seven? I wanted to be always
  feeling desire.
Now you're a young age to me. And, in you, as at every other time
I thought that one year would last forever.
"I did the best possible. I lasted my full ten years. Now I'm responsible
For someone else's decade and haven't time to talk to you, which is a
  shame
Since I can never come back." My Fifties! Answer me one question!
Were you the culmination or a phase? "Neither and both." Explain! "No
  time. Farewell!"

# To My Heart As I Go Along

I'm sorry you feel lonely.
You are hidden, all right, but you are very lively.
You give a rat-a-tat-tat to the plainest music.
Do you see—of course you see nothing—I'll make you aware—
I mean, how do impressions get down to you, unequal-equal heart,
    anyway?
My nerves send them down. And my brain gives the nerves
Their perfect instructions.
A friend of mine likes women's thighs better than anything.
What do you think, heart? I do notice you are beating like anything!
What about breasts? What about this old sweetheart? Now you are sad,
Well, not exactly—but you give off a slow, thudding beat.
Women make you happy and unhappy, if those words apply. And so do
    writing and public recognition.
You'd like to be in the body of a well-known and adventurous person,
Wouldn't you, heart? Meanwhile you have been battering along
I think, and not, for the past few moments, paying me much attention.
Fear, a little thud in you reminds me. How about fear?
"Fear is a guest in the villa who heads straight for my room
With a razor!" So we protect each other. On the top of the mountain
Or when I almost fell on the subway tracks, you were there
Learning remedial English to say to me "Watch out!" You spoke to me in
    Yiddish
At the firemen's ball but I couldn't understand you.
"Look at that horse! Watch out for the oblong! Vanquishing woman over
    there!"
Do you note that the world has changed since you began
Your tattoo beneath my chest bone? I would guess that, if you do, you
    don't care.
"Life is pretty simple," you say, "and, besides, I have my work to do.
I am beating out the rhythm for the whole shebang.
Besides which I have to do more than could be guessed at,
Given the so-called 'inner life'—"
Heart, it is good to hear you murmuring. By the way,
When I was a child, my mother told me I had a "heart murmur." Do you
    remember that?
"I heard of something. I do remember going to the doctor. He would tap
    on your chest
But was it a murmur he was looking for? You always say I murmur."

I guess that would have been a different kind, beating heart.
Perhaps walking a few miles would do for you today—
Souls-uniting one, deft one, roof one, architectural
Supervisor, your reactions are so quick sometimes and signals!
Little rabbit down there, being in the branches of my blood system, hobo
    in hiding,
Track worker, ever up to repairs that may need to be made, why does the
    wind blow?
Whose cameras are clicking in the leaves?
Pit pat pit pat. In North America I first encountered you
By pressing one hand against that part of my chest where I thought you
    were.
Boom kaboom "That is your heart." Scare. What is it?
Do I need it? Can I harm it? Can I lose it? How must I take care of it?
    Would something else be better in its place?
What is the good of it? Is there any bad of it? Is it bigger than someone
    else's is? Are all of them the same? You were pumping away,
Of course. I've become used to you. But you still have your surprises.
Why are you on my left side, for example? "The audience sees it as the
    right side."
Still it's stage left. You give prestige to that hemisphere of the body.
So, thud, we go along, thud, an example
Of unity and of disunity in one, or, like Ostia Antica
Or Pompeii, a city and not a city, a dump and not a dump,
Present and past together, with thuds for liaison.
I sometimes feel my life too cautious and circumstance-laden
And I want to be incendiary, like you! "No, you don't want that.
I'm too repetitive. My work is too repetitive. Let's talk of something
    else—
Perhaps of your student days, in Aix-en-Provence, at the Chevaliers'
    house—" Okay. "One dark light green
Afternoon Tootsie Chevalier came out of her house
To join you as you gained composure on the seat of your bicycle
Saying *Je t'ai apporté à manger*—d'you think she loved you
Just a little bit or not at all? I know that I was beating
Fairly rapidly during this largely unknown forgotten event. But not by
    me."
What do you mean, harp? And why do you want to keep gladdening
Me by entertainments? Was this Tootsie you're referring to
The desirable Madeleine? "Aye me, I think so. But what did you do but
    depart

And cleansed the afternoon. That night when Eddy came home he
    suspected nothing
Because there was nothing to suspect. I gave you happiness at the stars
    then
And sexual entertainment for your blood, almost constantly."
You were a great creator and interpreter of dramas, it's true.
And when the political events at Columbia got really hot
You were battering in me when I got up to talk at the meeting
Of old professors to try to dissuade them from going out to stop "the
    community" from crossing Campus Walk.
"I didn't give you any words, though; you had to think of them yourself."
I said "Stop!" mainly. "What are you thinking of? Et cetera." "I
    remember
Quieting down but having a few good beats from that afterwards, too."
You were with me in the army when I thought some enemy soldier was
    moving
Outside my tent—it turned out just to be a duck.
"I remember being excited." You hammered. And now you're hammering
    once again. "Oh, I have the reactions
All right, but it's you who give them to me, even by this curious talk
We're having today, which rattles me forward,
Sideways and back, till I hardly know how to stop
My agitation." In the days, not too un-recent,
When lost love was the staple of my life, I heard you coming
From smiles, from frowns, from telephone calls away.
Your roar was deafening. What I think now
Is that if I seek you a little bit by swimming, by reading, by traveling,
Even by some mild flirtation, it is to keep you down,
Contented, not saving up all your energy to consume
My whole well-being with a bomb. Heart, you can be frightening!
"Once again I have to tell you: the doer isn't I, it's you."
Liar! Collaborator! Friend! We'll drink some coffee
on this hot afternoon, and see what then.
The night promises to be cooler, and Orion may find Orso in his den
Of brilliance, as beneath my breastbone I found you.

# To My Heart at the Close of Day

At dusk light you come to bat
As Georg Trakl might put it. How are you doing
Aside from that, aside from the fact
That you are at bat? What balls are you going to hit
Into the outfield, what runs will you score,
And do you think you ever will, eventually,
Bat one out of the park? That would be a thrill
To you and your contemporaries! Your mighty posture
Takes its stand in my chest and swing swing swing
You warm up, then you take a great step
Forward as the ball comes smashing toward you, home
Plate. And suddenly it is evening.

# To Duration

I found you in the old temple and in breasts and shoulders.
I found you in the midnight weather. Duration, you aren't a lost cause—
It's a strange reassurance that you give.
"You don't have me but you partake of me," you say
"In your connection to the rest of humanity and in your ability to
    detect me
In this old Assyrian temple and in these walls
That haven't yet fallen over." It's best that you stay as you are!
"I had no intention of changing, nor could I do so if I wished.
There's no way the Atlantic Ocean could last only the same amount of
    time
As a quail's egg, for example." Holding such an egg in your hand
You laugh at me. "You humans have an escape, though
Everything is fluid; it's possible that nothing is what it seems.
But may all be in the transitory mind." Hearing you tell me this idea—
That is, having this idea in myself—
That has been around for such a long time, at least since the ancientest of
    Hindus,
I close the door on our conversation
And assume that the world is more or less as it seems
And that a great many things do last much longer than I
And that you are one of them.

# To Scrimping

You always attached yourself to my arm when I went out shopping.
I have kept my eye on you,
As the result of a recent loss, I think due to you.
I should never scrimp on friendship,
Generosity, sweetness—that is a law
I need to have engraved in my cerebrum
As in a library wall!
Scrimping, you are out, or should be out,
Except in this: that trying to save a little may do me good
When I am emotionally exhausted or completely blown out.
I am a tire with my wheel dependent on you, Scrimping,
Then. But mostly I would like to have you off
My hand, my chest, my wrist. I want to excel now at spending
Whatever I can, then you can take me in your cab
And drive me, for nothing! into the sod.
Does that seem too depressed? Scrimping, it's not.
I'm totally serious. It's a very positive idea to give our all
Before they place us upright in the wall
And scrape the mortar on. Scrimping, then what will you say?
Save up? Nonsense! Like me, even with me, you'll be hidden away.

# To Insults

I used to, to some degree, live by you. When
I needed one of you, you were ready,
You'd come forth nasty, direct, and intending to wound.
Ah, what a great satisfaction
For the space of a second you gave!
You're illustrious among certain connoisseurs—
Swift breath intake shows they're excitedly aware.
You're dangerous! Your victim may be injured
Severely and/or, stirred to retaliation, strike back
With physical force. As astonishing to watch as a car wreck
Sometimes your occurring and your effects! When you originate in me
I'm afraid, as if I'd violated some promise
For the pleasure of your uncivilizing heat. How, ever again,
Regain the territory of friendship, of decency, even?
(You do have one praiseworthy quality.
That you're absolute and can clean out a place
Of its accumulated junk, though only rarely, if ever,
Are you a necessity.)
Some children are adept at you, and French courtiers
Apparently were. The gods and the very powerful don't need you.
"Our Saviour was never known to smile," wrote Baudelaire.
Neither did He use you.

# To High Spirits

You have taken the vodka
That I was probably
Saving for tomorrow.
Go on and take it
For there's more enterprise
In waking naked.

# To Competitiveness

Competitiveness you went down to Testosterone Village last night
And got loaded. What was I supposed to do with you today,
This morning, when you tried to get me into a fight
With my own dog, for god's sake, over getting
To the newspaper first? Sometimes you aren't useful—
However at others I relax into your arms, sure that you'll take care of me
As long as I'm inventive enough. To make my moves
And to keep those moves a secret until I've won!
To be the champion of battles! To win all day
And not lose one! To take home the gasping prize to my lair in the
   conceited mountains!
To be the best bear! The loudest lion! The most oak-clocked owl!
It's probably foolish to tell you this, but be careful.
You're standing in a road full of other examples of you
And are as likely to get knocked down as to come home whole.

# To the Unknown

Though we don't know anything about you,
Even a slight change in you excites us—we want to get married.
We change jobs. We change countries. We open a book
We close it, still not knowing you. We find there's more and more of you.
Millions of things. You sit back and easily
Let one by one go. Still, you remained and remain again immense.
Some have painted you, but it was only tiny squiggles.
How could we show much of you? I have a standing date with you,
But so does everyone, at the end. By that time, we'll know nothing
And then you'll be ordinary again, as you were at the start.
It was finding out something that made you grow.
As soon as one knows, for example, that one friend has a name
One slowly becomes aware there must be billions of names
One could never know, and you came close to me and said,
"It hardly matters. But there are some things sweeter still,
Much much sweeter, that also you may never know
Unless you find them in me." "Where are you? How can I be
Closer to you?" I said. I was a small person
And you—was it oddly?—made me feel grand,
Important as any of the great ones,
Who knew, and didn't know, you, as well. We were, in regard to you,
    partners.
In you the voices of all living creatures are heard
Like found objects. Perhaps your idea of meaning
(I'm assuming you have one) is to let things migrate
From one place to another until there is no more motion.
If there is some way to find out more about you,
Let me know in advance, and I will come down to meet you
As far as the open part in which you live.

# To One Thing after Another

View, I had you once in Madagascar and once or twice in Nepal
Three times in Burgundy a hundred and forty times in Rome
Fifteen hundred in Paris and countless times at home.
Starting, you are always here when the end is pre-eminent.
End, you are a glass ribbon that won't bend. Crowd, you give silence to
 the soul.
Morning, you've lifted my spirits, Sanskrit, you've pulled a style down.
Hills, are you satisfied with what is already known?
Loads of coal, why are we waiting? There is time to warn cities and
 swings.
Solidity, the fire announced you but said you were dying.
Whole cities, you commence; old cities, you relent. If all of you—
 concepts, objects,
Cities, panoramas, gulfs—have ears to hear with—
That is the question, whether anything not human needs words. Someone
 proclaimed
Some years ago, and the idea had considerable success,
That if people talked to their plants they would find them blooming
Better than ever—but you, manifold subjects,
Do you profit from that in any way?
What lines of talk light bright light under doorsills
Give sun enough to an old battering ram
Or incessantly thudding steam engine device?
Whose lingo is going to unfrustrate the lemons
In a cold year when tangled in their own white blossoms
They stretch the morning's ears? Is hearing possible?
Do you, odd clouds, remember
Anything the diva sang or said? Did you, floorboards, retain a clenched
 feeling after the opera?
Cork subtitle, do you profit from what is read
Aloud to you, this titillating morning? And, gross overshoes,
Do you like to share my laugh? Venice, are you still my town?
Do you, shortcomings, like to lie in the grass
And hear lovewords spoken by old folks? If I were a giraffe,
You say, custom-built car, but in fact you've said nothing.
I am left here in the solitude of the Carpathians.
Will you, mountains, listen to me and jar a few old beliefs?

Does it do any good to be an elixir of hopelessness, Russia?
Nothing seems more natural than berating you, mittens,
For not staying firmly on hands, but humor is a restriction.
You, melancholy casino, remain closed until they tell you to open—
They, seasons, in a car.

# To the Past

In every microsecond of the present, you're here
It doesn't seem fair that you are
But fairness is not a judgment that you'd make
And behind my shoulders you begin to shake
A cape or blanket and if I stop and run out to the car
It doesn't matter, you are still there.
Driving along through you, I think, what can undo you?
At all parties for you, everyone is always dying.
As soon as we go to sleep you eat our food
And smoke our cigarettes, then, acting lazy,
Wake us and say, "Go on, this day is yours. I'm going to take a break,
A day-long rest." But you are lying.
You can't help yourself, but neither can we.
Together, mighty past, we dominate things.

# To Destiny

You could be to be a rock
Or a rock star. An elephant. A ride in a canoe
That concludes with a faster heartbeat for all involved.
You could be a pestilence or a courtship or a seminary.
You're bound to have a limited plot; but say, what is it?
You are an old idea not talked to so much any more. People have figured
    out
What they think they're doing. You seem to some a DNA roustabout—
If anything. A hand of yours is raised to interrupt me:
"If you tear the building down, what will you do with the stones? I am
    Destiny!
Don't try to outwit me." But—there are things I want you to tell me.
Does it matter if I go on drinking? Should I stay married or not? Who or
    what
Is my redeemer if anything or anyone is? Does it matter if I keep working
    or not? Where should I live?
Am I meant to amend, and to attend on, other lives?
Won't you, yourself, fly off to younger souls
Who promise fatter progeny. Have you already done so, recently?
"No," you roar, "I am still here. And the answer to all your questions is
    that it doesn't matter—
As far as I'm concerned you might as well eat this tub of butter,
Fly in that damaged plane, go off with that woman,
Sleep on a bed of fire and work all night instead of during the day.
Your questions are misdirected. I'm the future. What you do now doesn't
    matter
To me or to anyone else in my unknowable establishment."
No wonder hardly anyone speaks to you any more. "I know. It's useless."
Still, thanks for what I already have. "Not my doing—I'm the 'shall-have'
    man."

# To Some Abstract Paintings

I was learning from you how to develop
A certain kind of elation in regard to non-objects,
And then you went away.
I laughed at and with you.
Painters collapsed in you and they smacked you
Out and around in gobs of red and blue. Now anyone who tries to trap
   you
Finds something else.
You promised there was a meaning inside the meaning
That surpassed the meaning or would even come up with a new one
That everyone would see.
That didn't happen. But there's the longing
Created in those you leave behind you
The sense of which remains on the canvas
On canvas after canvas after canvas.
Thanks for showing them to me.
Those who created you grew old. Most died.
You survive, you live on as a sort of aside
To our age, to which you say,
"Beauty is abstract, abstract beauty. That is what
We paintings know and what you may never know." We collect you.
We may not know what we're seeing when we see you—
But it is something—
In your red and green parade. A practitioner says,
"I hate those colors!" He uses white and blue.
Then it isn't the flag of Greece he makes, but you.

# To Various Persons Talked to All at Once

You have helped hold me together.
I'd like you to be still.
Stop talking or doing anything else for a minute.
No. Please. For three minutes, maybe five minutes.
Tell me which walk to take over the hill.
Is there a bridge there? Will I want company?
Tell me about the old people who built the bridge.
What is "the Japanese economy"?
Where did you hide the doctors bills?
How much I admire you!
Can you help me to take this off?
May I help you to take that off?
Are you finished with this item?
Who is the car salesman?
The ocean's not really very far.
Did you come west in this weather?
I've been sitting at home with my shoes off.
You're wearing a cross!
That bench, look! Under it are some puppies!
Could I have just one little shot of Scotch?
I suppose I wanted to impress you.
It's snowing.
This racket is annoying.
We didn't want the baby to come here because of the hawk.
What are you reading?
I care, but not much. You can smoke a cigar.
Genuineness isn't a word I'd ever use.
Say, what a short skirt! Do you have a camera?
The moon is a shellfish.
Who are you, anyway?
I want to look at you all day long, because you are mine.
Might you crave a little visit to the Pizza Hut?
Thank you for telling me your sign.
I'm filled with joy by this sun!
The turtle is advancing but the lobster stays behind. Silence has won the
    game!

Well, just damn you and the thermometer!
I didn't know what you meant when you said that to me.
It's getting cold, but I am feeling awfully lazy.
If you want to, we can go over there
Where there's a little more light.

# To Breath

There is that in me—you come Sunday morning to entertain my life
With your existence. I am born and my mother warms me
She warms me with her self while you circulate through me
And fill me with air! My mother is so young
To have to deal with an entire existence, mine, apart from hers!
She needs you to replenish what's there—
Gala you, who stretch the seams.
Without you, the millions of joys of life would be nothing,
Only darkness, no pages in the book. In love you're there quickly
In the race through the forest, in the dangerous dive from the rock.
I have often sensed you at parties
The girls come up to the boys and all of them breathe
You're awake for them even while they sleep.
What I want you to do for me is this:
I want to understand certain things and tell them to others.
To do it, I have to get them right, so they are hard to resist.
Stay with me until I can do this.

Afterwards, you can go where you want.

# To Old Age

You hurried through my twenties as if there were nowhere to look
For what you were searching for, perhaps my first trip to China.
You said, "I love that country because they love everything that's old
And they like things to look old—take the fortune cookies for example
Or the dumplings or the universe's shining face." I said,
"Chopsticks don't look old," but you were hurrying
Past me, past my love, my uncomprehended marriage, my
Nine or ten years nailed in the valley of the fools, and still you were not
    there,
Wouldn't stop there. You disappeared for a year
That I spent in Paris, came back to me in my father's face
And later in my mother's conversation. You seemed great in the palm trees
During a storm and lessened by the boats' preceding clops.
Looking at a gun or at a tiger I never thought I was standing facing you.
You were elsewhere, rippling the sands or else making some boring
    conversation
Among people who scarcely knew each other. You were left by Shelley to
    languish
And by Byron and by Keats. Shakespeare never encountered you. What
    are you, old age,
That some do and some do not come to you?
Are you an old guru who won't quit talking to us in time
For us to hang up the phone? You scare me half to death
And I suppose you will take me there, too. You are a companion
Of green ivy and stumbling vines. If I could break away from you
I would, but there is no light down in that gulch there. Walk with me,
    then
Let's not be falling . . . this fiery morning. *Grand âge, nous voici!* Old age,
    here we are!

# A POSSIBLE WORLD

# Bel Canto

The sun is high, the seaside air is sharp,
And salty light reveals the Mayan School.
The Irish hope their names are on the harp,
We see the sheep's advertisement for wool,
Boulders are here, to throw against a tarp,
From which comes bursting forth a puzzled mule.
Perceval seizes it and mounts it, then
The blood-dimmed tide recedes and then comes in again.

Fateful connections that we make to things
Whose functioning's oblivious to our lives!
How sidewise news of fight from darkness springs,
How blue bees buzz from big blooms back to hives
And make the honey while the queen bee sings
Leadbelly in arrangements by Burl Ives—
How long ago I saw the misted pine trees
And hoped, no matter how, to get them into poetry!

Stendhal, at fifty, gazing, as it happened,
On Rome from the Janiculum, decided
That one way he could give his life a stipend
Was to suspend his being Amour's fighter
And get to know himself. Here he had ripened,
Accomplished, loved, and lived, was a great writer
But never had explored in true detail
His childhood and his growing up. So he set sail

Composing *La Vie de Henry Brulard*
But in five hundred pages scarcely got
Beyond his seventeenth year, for it is hard
To take into account what happens here
And fit it all onto an index card.
Even one moment of it is too hot,
Complex and cannibalistically connected
To every other, which is what might be expected.

Sterne's hero has a greater problem, never
Getting much past his birth. I've had a third one.
My autobiography, if I should ever

Start out to write it, quickly seems a burden,
An I-will-do-that-the-next-time endeavor.
Whatever life I do write's an absurd one
As if some crazy person with a knife
Cut up and made a jigsaw puzzle of a life.

In any case a life that's hardly possible
In the conditions that we really live in,
Where easy flying leaps to inaccessible
Mountainy places where love is a given
And misery, if there, infinitesimal,
Are quite the norm. Here none by pain is driven
That is not curable by the romanza
That's kept in readiness to finish any stanza.

Whatever, then, I see at this late stage of
My life I may or may not have stayed ignorant
Of that great book I've strained to write one page of
Yet always hoping my page was significant.
Be it or not, for me and for the ages,
I leave it as it is. Yet as a figurant
Who has not stopped, I'm writing in addition
More lines to clarify my present disposition.

One person in a million finds out something
Perhaps each fifty years and that is knowledge.
Newton, Copernicus, Einstein are cunning;
The rest of us just rise and go to college
With no more hope to come home with the bunting
Than a stray dachshund going through the village.
However, what a treat our small successes
Of present and of past, at various addresses!

To be in all those places where I tarried
Too little or too late or bright and early,
To love again the first woman I married,
To marvel at such things as melancholy,
Sophistication, drums, a baby carriage,
A John Cage concert heard at Alice Tully—
How my desire, when young to be a poet
Made me attentive and oblivious every moment!

Do you remember Oceanview the Fair?
The heights above the river? The canoes?
The place we beached them and the grass was bare?
Those days the sand bars gave our knees a truce?
The crooked line of pantry shelves, with pear
And cherry jam? And Pancho, with his noose?
Do you remember Full and Half and Empty?
Do you remember sorrow standing in the entry?

Do you remember thought, and talking plainly?
Michel and I went walking after Chartres
Cathedral had engaged our spirits mainly
By giving us an insight into Barthes.
Michel said he was capable of feigning
Renewed intentions of the soul's deep part,
Like this cathedral's artificial forces
That press a kind of artless thought into our faces.

And yet—The moor is dark beneath the moon.
The porcupine turns over on its belly
And new conceptions rap at the cocoon.
Civilization, dealing with us fairly,
For once, releases its Erechtheum
Of understanding, which consoles us, nearly.
Later we study certain characteristics
That may give us a better chance with the statistics.

How much I'd like to live the whole thing over,
But making some corrections as I go!
To be a better husband and a father,
Be with my babies on a sled in snow.
By twenty I'd have understood my mother
And by compassion found a way to know
What separates the what-I-started-out-as
From what-I-sometimes-wished-I-was-when-in-the-mountains.

To be once more the one who what was worthy
Of courtship courted—it was quite as stressful
As trying to, er, as they say, give birth to
A poem and as often unsuccessful,
But it was nice to be sublime and flirty

With radiant girls, and, in some strange way, restful.
I could be everything I wasn't usually—
And then to get somebody else to feel it mutually!

In poems the same problem or a similar.
Desire of course not only to do old things
But things unheard of yet by nuns or visitors
And of the melancholy finch be co-finch
In singing songs with such a broad parameter
That seamstresses would stare, forget to sew things,
Astronauts quit the sky, athletes the stadium
To hear them, and the rest of what they hear be tedium.

Such wild desires, I think it's recognizable
Are part and parcel of the Human Image
And in a way, I'd say, no less predictable
Than Popeye's feelings for a can of spinach.
Yet if we're set on course by the Invisible,
All predetermined, what about the language
That teases me each morning with its leanings
Toward the Unprogrammed Altitudes beyond its meanings?

Are you, O particles, O atoms, nominatives
Like Percevals and Stendhals, set in motion
By some Ordaining Will that is definitive?
Is this invading chill and high emotion,
This tendency to know one is regenerative,
Is this, all, tidal take-home like the ocean?
Be what you may, my thanks for your society
Through the long life I've had, your jokes and your variety,

The warmth you've shown in giving me a temperature
That I can live with, and the strength you've shared with me
In arms and legs—and for your part in literature,
What can I say? It is as if life stared at me
And kissed my lips and left it as a signature.
Thank you for that, and thank you for preparing me
For love itself, and friendship its co-agent.
Thank you for being this, and for its inspiration.

# A Review

Pure finality of bedding—
Intellectual life—
This article to reassure me—
Others are alive—
Then unexpectedly awake
Middle of the night—
What are they thinking—
Afraid? Probably. Succeeding
At something? Likely—
All night
Breathing, rain.

# A Momentary Longing
# to Hear Sad Advice from One Long Dead

Who was my teacher at Harvard. Did not wear overcoat
Saying to me we walked across the Yard
Cold brittle autumn is you should be wearing overcoat. I said
You are not wearing overcoat. He said
You should do as I say not do as I do.
Just how American it was and how late Forties it was
Delmore, but not I, was probably aware. He quoted *Finnegans Wake* to me
In his New York apartment sitting on chair
Table directly in front of him. There did he write? I am wondering.
Look at this photograph said of his mother and father.
Coney Island. Do they look happy? He couldn't figure it out.
Believed *Pogo* to be at the limits of our culture.
*Pogo*. Walt Kelly must have read Joyce Delmore said.
Why don't you ask him?
Why don't you ask Walt Kelly if he read *Finnegans Wake* or not.
Your parents don't look happy but it is just a photograph.
Maybe they felt awkward posing for photographs.
Maybe it is just a bad photograph. Delmore is not listening
I want to hear him tell me something sad but however true.
Delmore in his tomb is sitting. People say yes everyone is dying
But here read this happy book on the subject. Not Delmore. Not that
    rueful man.

# Mountain

Nothing's moving I don't see anybody
And I know that it's not a trick
There really is nothing moving there
And there aren't any people. It is the very utmost top
Where, as is not unusual,
There is snow, lying like the hair on a white-haired person's head
Combed sideways and backward and forward to cover as much of the top
As possible, for the snow is thinning, it's September
Although a few months from now there will be a new crop
Probably, though this no one KNOWS (so neither do we)
But every other year it has happened by November
Except for one year that's known about, nineteen twenty-three
When the top was more and more uncovered until December fifteenth
When finally it snowed and snowed
I love seeing this mountain like a mouse
Attached to the tail of another mouse, and to another and to another
In total mountain silence
There is no way to get up there, and no means to stay.
It is uninhabitable. No roads and no possibility
Of roads. You don't have a history
Do you, mountain top? This doesn't make you either a mystery
Or a dull person and you're certainly not a truck stop.
No industry can exploit you
No developer can divide you into estates or lots
No dazzling disquieting woman can tie your heart in knots.
I could never lead my life on one of those spots
You leave uncovered up there. No way to be there
But I'm moved.

# To Buddhism

How calmly and gently you approach me in Thailand
And propose that we sit down and talk
In the pollution and in the heat, that we find a little fresh air, shade, and
    talk. You
Explain some principles—I already know a few of them
From my college days when I subscribed to a periodical named *Cat's Yawn*.
    A Zen periodical,
It was so named the editor said because those words make no sense. I
    didn't
Understand why he said they made no sense. However, I was drawn to the
    koans.
You tell me about the two different vehicles
And the life of Gautama, which I know. You show me statues. Of which
The golden Sleeping Buddha is the most celebrated, though I find more
    moving
The riverside cliff statue carved in Bingling Si (in China)
Amazing! But where would I fit into you or you into me? It won't happen.
Reluctantly, I lose you, never having had you. This is so much in line
With what *Cat's Yawn* said about you and with what you told me
That I imagine its making you smile.

# A Schoolroom in Haiti

In Haiti, Port-au-Prince, a man walked up and down the school hallways
    carrying a bull whip.
Oh, he never uses it, the school administrator said. Its purpose is only to
    instill good discipline in the students.
They were from fourteen to seventeen years old,
Boys in white shirts and white short pants. They stood up
And wouldn't sit down till the Minister of Education
Beckoned to them to do so.
They concentrated very hard on the ideas they were being given for
    writing poems.
After the officials left, they started writing their poems in Creole.
After four or five days they were asking to come forward and sing to the
    rest of the class these Creole poems. They did so.
This experiment was never repeated. The government became even more
    repressive.
One poem begins "B is for black, Bettina, a negress whom I dote on."
The assignment was a poem about the colors of the vowels or the
    consonants in the manner of Rimbaud.
What has happened to those poems? What has become of those students?
I have the poems in New York. In Haiti I had asked to teach ten-year-olds
    but I had been told
They won't be able to write well enough. The reason was they didn't
    know French,
Not well enough to be able to write poetry. Their native language was
    Creole,
The language they spoke at home, but at the Lycée Toussaint L'Ouverture
And every other school, the instruction was in French.
They were stuck behind the French language. It loomed over them a wall
Blocking out everything:
Blocked mathematics, blocked science, blocked history, blocked literature
While Creole stayed back with them, cooking up poetry
But that was all. For the most part, except for a few rich boys
Who could afford to study French in the afternoons
They were left fatally behind.

# The Expansive Water

Out in the middle of the ocean
The first time
How gray and strong the expanse of water looks
This is my first time on the ocean.
I don't get seasick. At least,
I don't think so. "Greek sculptures
On certain Greek vases, low-relief ones,
Like the coast near Bari, show more a sea-struck
Kind of reality than I have ever felt
In here. Out there—" But the young woman to whom I was talking
Seemed to have lost interest. "What is
Your name?" I asked. "Ellen," she said, turning away
To join her companions at the bar.

Later when I talked to Ellen she was not interested.
Then when I talked to her later than that she was interested.
Everyone else was seasick but Ellen and me.
I hope the storm lasts, I said.
This remark was not a success. Ellen didn't care for my kind of
    conversation.
What are you looking for in someone else? I said to Ellen
And she said, Give me the ring and tell me you want a baby.
Whoaaa! I said. We've just met.
The storm died down. Ellen is walking along the gangway with someone
I think I may have seen in an old movie
But it is only a much younger counterpart to such a person,
John Gilbert, but anyway he is much too good-looking
For me to have as competition. Still, "Ellen," I cried, "I'll give you a
    baby!"
Kenneth, she says, you exaggerate! It's a nice day
And I am in the midmost of my youth!
Hey Ellen, says "John Gilbert," and they walk on.

# La Ville de Nice

O harbor for the rich and poor
O plain yet evanescent
O married man and paramour
O peacock born of pheasant

The first time that I walked through your
Streets, still to the earth a present,
Twenty years old, on tour,
Once near my ear a husky pleasant

Voice intoned "Est-ce que tu
Ne voudrais pas la joie?"
Not knowing what to do,
I went to my hotel, l'Hôtel du Roi

Saying that surprising word (la joie)
And kept on saying it until
I'd gone from Nice to Cannes
And then kept traveling on.

# Topiary Couple

The trees on the left side of the garden
Had been trimmed so that their outline resembled
A man and a woman making love.
The woman was very beautiful.
The man had a hatchet in his hand
By which it could be guessed that he was George Washington.
A cherry tree grew freely at his side.
But the woman did not seem to be Martha Washington!
What would George be doing, even as a tree, with another woman?
This was the wild side of his life
When, freed from Presidential responsibilities,
He could chop down trees and make love to women as he wanted—
Great joy, at this thought, wells up in the gardener's heart.

NOT-MARTHA
  Oh, a divorce between desire and reason,
  A cumulative state, like those cherries we eat
  When all's in blossom and we take
  The next day's sufferance for the mules of now.

GEORGE WASHINGTON
  Not-Martha, you have hit on a pretty tape.
  Amusing to be with like a grape
  I would carve us into every shape
  If I could really wield this hatchet—

The trees on the left side of the garden
Become more than topiary this one time.
Talking to each other they found an idle thing.
That could be an ideal thing.
They went on talking far into the night
And during the next hundred days
Until finally George Washington said to not-Martha-Washington
"It's time to be again what once we were!"
But they, trees, remain fixed, no return, from branches and leaves.

# Behavior in Thailand

Walking
Up to someone to be introduced
I remember
The book on Thai etiquette I read
Never point with your finger
Or your hand, only with your head
As in soccer, with head—or foot.

It's the booming of Bangkok's traffic
And the very bad air
Pollution gives this late twentieth century
A bad name. Pollution. The great thing
Is that it (pollution) is curable
No one has even started to cure it here.

This royal dwelling has many European characteristics
Its construction is fairly recent
European innovations were considered exotic in Thailand
A hundred, even fifty years ago
Such innovations for example as a functioning bathroom.
One non-European characteristic
Is the elephant's-foot umbrella stand in the hall.

The Oriental Hotel
Is a real palace
It has two hundred bathrooms
It sits by the river
And is a grand hotel
And doesn't have an elephant's-foot stand.

A huge sleeping Buddha
Lying on his side
Is made entirely of gold
Worth inestimably more to his worshippers
Than he would be on the currency exchange
He is here, instead of there.

Buddhist monks
About seventeen to twenty-two years old
Saffron-robed, they brush past passersby on the road

As if they were the money, themselves,
The world was spending
Continually helping itself to improve.

Thai women have a historical attitude
It happened therefore it will happen again
It makes one feel like a diamond-covered wren
Of platinum-glazing oxygen
To do it again
Means being in the center where one was sent
Millions (perhaps) of years ago along with men.

The hot streets say to my feet
Sit down
But the scalding bench says
You had best get back up
And keep walking
Because here on us, it's hell.
Bright clouds whiz past.

In one kind of Buddhism (Mahayana)
You get credits for good actions
And this can help you escape from life
I.e., the life cycle which is so unsatisfactory
One such action is paying for the release of a little bird
Which will be captured again at once and recaged, and its freedom sold to
    someone else
To do this costs five baht, forty cents.

Over here, across the river
Is another city!
A water-filled half
Not streets but canals—
Here, what's reflected (houses, markets, persons)
Is all—almost all—that you see.

On one hot corner
Whatever you see
Will be there again
With not the same people
And you are not the same
But the baby will be born.

# On the Acropolis

It doesn't seem as though we could die up here, does it?
The Acropolis is so old that death on it seems superfluous.
So we can afford to take some chances—
Leap off the wall! Bash statues with our heads!

God smiles down at the Acropolis. It's a good church
But with the wrong idea. Then he is distracted by his children
Scattered among the chambers of the sea.

Old friends, I am thinking of you still.
You built the Acropolis but you didn't build it for me.

The Acropolis has a uniform
That no schoolboy can wear because it is invisible.
"It goes to the Periclean School!"

When I first came to Greece
I was twenty-five years old
And I've learned so little since
That the Greeks already knew!
Almost nothing!
I don't know why this is—
Mathematics, astronomy
All have remained dim to me—
I should have applied myself!
My "life" got in the way
But what was in my life
Inimical to Greece?

Those who put me off by their irony
Are unlike the Acropolis.
Or at least unlike the way it seems.
If the whole Acropolis were ironic,
I mean an ironic comment,
It would be a huge joke
Enjoyable frightening and laughable-at without end!

Go to look at it at sunset when it's PINK
My guidebook said. Good advice about anything, I suppose.

Or, after some road has been mended, when it smells like tar.
"When you are in love, go hear your beating heart."

Aeschylus and Socrates
Used to sit and chat up here
On the old rocks beneath the fight of the very old sun
And one of their frequent subjects was
How young or old they felt or were.
"I am getting on, Socrates," says Aeschylus.
"Oh no," cries Socrates, "you still look like a boy!"

Plato would walk up here when he was tired
And talk to the alas-dead Socrates—
"Master I have come to a wall
And with statues and columns beyond it. What should I do?
"Keep walking," the dead one counsels,
"And walking and walking, until the end.
You know it, know what to do—you are my best pupil."

What a car would do on the Acropolis
I can't imagine. But a deer or a beaver could
Build a home here while the light turned red
And sank into the Aegean.

The "wave of the future"
Never waved over the Acropolis
It was never in any sense prophetic
Or meant to be prophetic
Of what was to come.
As long as the original lasted
The present was the only time.

Acropolis, Acropole, Acropolexis,
*Acro*—high, outermost, ultimate, never taken, undivulged,
Single-hearted, far, furious, added to *Polis*, city
High-up city, but what a curious city you are
With more god-objects per second than people in the street!

Greek people who are used to it
Say, "Oh, up there!"
On the great wall
A thousand miles of moonlight

Wrote Li Ho.
The Acropolis you can see all at once—
The Parthenon its nose
The Erechtheum its mouth
The Propylaea (entrance stairs) its teeth.

You can't find a glass of water
On the Acropolis or in Notre Dame
Or on the Great Wall of China. No use trying! There just isn't one there!

There are also no comic books on the Acropolis.
Though there are some on the subject of the Acropolis.
I buy a few down below, on the city's streets,
HELLAS KOMIKS and E PARTONIKI.

The tyrant Pisistratus used it for a fortress
To boss the life-loving Athenians until five hundred twenty-seven B.C.
At which time there was only one temple up here, the Hecatompedon.
About face! Present
Arms! You're under arrest! You have nothing but Persian papers, no good
    up here!

On Mount Athos you could be a Persian
Or a Thessalian or a Macedonian but you couldn't be a woman—
The slightest evidence and off you go! No females allowed—
Not even a butterfly or a squirrel.

"I have a guest over at my house."
But it isn't Apollo
I'll bet
And is it Hermes Trismegistus by any chance?
Apollo FLAYED someone
For competing with him in music.
How horrible, cruel, and sadistic (it was Marsyas).

As for Diana the punishment for seeing her naked was losing your eyes
Your liver and your heart. You were a dead Achaean
Never again to walk by the Aegean.

Yet they say it would be better for us
If we had this kind of mythology of our own
Instead of Daniel Boone and Jimmy Carter—

I look up at the sky and I see a constellation
Of Jimmy Carter signing an antipollution bill
And of Hermes tearing the insides out of a bear!

And to deal with the horrible tangle inside me
I don't know which to choose. Lucky, we have both.

The giant Athena statue
Gave the Persians pause.
Persian Number One said
If they have a goddess as great as that—
And Persian Number Three said
You're right! We'd better go!
Fast! Persian Number Two
Applied for citizenship
To become an Athenian.

It rains on the Acropolis I don't get wet
I am an American
The rain is twenty-five hundred years ago.
No one lives on the Acropolis tonight but the Acropolis Rat.

Acropole! Out of the earth
Came your marble, out of the sea
Came your earth, out of the air
The gods and goddesses
Who have been with you since you were zero years old!

The Acropolis has a strong format:
Temple, temple, temple, you have it up to here!
Gorgeous sources of divine misinformation,
One after another, blather blather blather, idiocy of the sky.

"The Acropolis has been
Removed from serious contention
By the historical operation
Of di-ectomy: removal of the gods."
So says the report.
But who is writing it?

# Zones

When you have enough time
You can do it again and again
And that is how you make a forest
With each one the same
In being different
From all the others. You
"Really want to get something done"
How many trees, then, do you include in the forest?
The day isn't over
And the night isn't over
On the contrary the day has just begun
With a hooting and whistles
And a lark's clerical swirl
A pristine hopscotch of the scattering woodland repeats.
This doesn't reveal anything obvious
But rather gives a discrete
Powerful complicated understanding. Nature,
Which gives us the forest, is it wide
Or narrow from an absolute point of view?
It won't fit into a wheelbarrow;
And neither will time—
It has too many zones, as in the forest
Each tree has its own
And is its own
Dawn, morning, noon, evening, night.

# A Changing China

I won't come with you, she said, to your demonstration.
She was afraid of becoming too admiring of what I did.
Later I met her at the Friendship Store.
We ate a dozen dumplings made with dog.
The handbook has illustrations
Of different breeds.
Here a collie, proud and tall,
Here a scotty, fun and small,
And the German Shepherd so munificent,
The cocker spaniel so glad to greet.
Three nights at the Peace Hotel.
It was filled with peace.
Peace rambled through its walls
Its stairways were peaceful its bathrooms were peaceful,
Everything seemed peaceful in the Peace Hotel
Now replaced by a more modern one called Golden Dog,
*Le chien d'or, er shaiku ai ny pan.*
I've lost the name and address
Of a Chinese writer held in house detention
Which some other writers gave me.
It's illegal, it's dangerous
If they find I had it I may be done for
I am hidden in the bamboo.
Big Business
Is coming to China
But Business that changes the score
China can hardly catch its breath any more.
I wasn't arrested I found the piece of paper.
Outer lobby there is a display of glass insects.
A bird flying over Kunming
Where the Fahrenheit temperature averages sixty-five
In the air of this unjust time.
In each room here is a hogshead made of bar glass.
Overseas Chinese are sleeping in the basement
And the stone five hundred feet high is topped by a bell.
Forgave its attitude toward dogs

After all we eat lobsters
Come here my little pet
Ah! Thlunk! The lobster is dead.
He lies in the Huang Po river basin with a stone for a head.
"No firecrackers in the chamber" the sign in each room.

# Day and Night in Kuala Lumpur

The Malays, who are in the majority, are Muslims.
The Chinese, who have a lot of the money
To be found in the country, are Buddhists, twelve percent
Of the population is Indian, and they are Hindus.
The Muslims have a giant mosque
In the middle of Kuala Lumpur surrounded by cloverleaf-highway-type
    curve-offs,
A big line of bathrooms, for "cleansing" and
A number of minarets. The Chinese, Buddhist
Temples have music and smoke, and a great number
Of Buddhas because the more Buddhas there are the better will be
One's good fortune. The way some poets have a great many poems,
Collectors a great number of paintings, actors a great many roles
Or as a person may quite simply wish for a great many lovers or friends.
The Muslims, that is the Malays, rule the state. And the teaching
In high schools is in Behasa Malayu and you hardly have a chance
To get a state job if you are not a Malay, a Muslim.
One is born into one's religion here as into one's skin,
As into a tour group one can never forsake.
The Malay Sultans are exempt from laws,
They thrive in cool palaces. One sultan just cut off his gardener's head
With a sword because he displeased him in some way and legally nothing
    can be done. In K.L.
Gigantic high-rises shoot up everywhere
Full of offices and computers and Malay folk
Doing the financial work of Europe, America, and Japan. And if one longs
    for the village
(The panang), as the guidebooks say all Malaysians do ("they are
    essentially a forest and riverside people")
One goes there on the weekends. And in the soft arms of someone one
    goes to sleep.

In the Hindu park outside K.L. the monkeys
Are abundant and have quite a time! They line the great big stairways
That go up to the Holy Caves and they try to steal things from anyone
    who climbs up them. Often they succeed.
From me they get a Kleenex and from Karen nothing but she had nothing
Protrusive that they could get their hands on.
These monkeys' hands are essentially all fingers with no unnecessary part,
The fingers almost all bone.

They (monkeys) give to Kuala Lumpur its closest equivalent to
   Disneyland
But they are alive and have religious significance.
Anyone, any dead person, that is, might now be a monkey, which may be
   the reason
These monkeys are protected. It is as if Christians
Had Damned Souls and Saved Ones running along the stairs
Of their cathedrals and churches! However, one doesn't want to stay
Among these animals for long. Now, attired in batik,
Some persons go out, but many, many stay in, because it is so hot—
Although there is a big stuffed Santa Claus in a Chinese novelty store
   downtown.
Malaysia has had its life cycle interrupted. Universal modern technology
   has butted
Its nose arms and shoulders into the front window of the car.
What to do about it? So much has happened. So much has been suffered.
   So much has sweated, swatted, and wept. In batik then they go out
In the polluted hydrogen, oxygen, nitrogen, and all—And the Americans
   are here in their shirts
And the Japanese and the Germans in their shirts
And the French and the Italians in their sleeves
And the British who used to run the whole show
And built the railway station, for example,
Strictly according to Empire specifications:
It has a slanting roof capable of withstanding a large accumulation of
   snow
Snow that has never fallen in the Malay Peninsula. But now the British (as
   rulers) have gone
Taking their social classes and cricket games with them.
Their "club" remains, but it's no competition for the mosque
Any more, or even for the monkeys. You see a green lawn,
A white building, and that's it.
Malaysia, lying next to Thailand, has a sad reputation
For its atmosphere and for the non-jollity of its people.
The Thais are happier. As soon as you cross the border you can see it.
Even the pollution in Bangkok seems friendly
Compared to the pollution in K.L.; yet both are killers. Malaysia's poet
   laureate
Has a long white beard. He is writing a poem
About the contrasts of the high-rises and the villages,
In three-faithed Kuala Lumpur of the beautiful name.

# Proverb

*Les morts vont vite*, the dead go fast, the next day absent!
*Et les vivants sont dingues*, the living are haywire.
Except for a few who grieve, life rapidly readjusts itself
The milliner trims the hat not thinking of the departed
The horse sweats and throws his stubborn rider to the earth
Uncaring if he has killed him or not
The thrown man rises. But now he knows that he is not going,
Not going fast, though he was close to having been gone.
The day after Caesar's death, there was a new, bustling Rome
The moment after the racehorse's death, a new one is sought for the stable
The second after a moth's death there are one or two hundred other
    moths
The month after Einstein's death the earth is inundated with new theories
Biographies are written to cover up the speed with which we go:
No more presence in the bedroom or waiting in the hall
Greeting to say hello with mixed emotions. The dead go quickly
Not knowing why they go or where they go. To die is human,
To come back divine. Roosevelt gives way to Truman
Suddenly in the empty White House a brave new voice resounds
And the wheelchaired captain has crossed the great divide.
Faster than memories, faster than old mythologies, faster than the
    speediest train.
Alexander of Macedon, on time!
Prudhomme on time, Gorbachev on time, the beloved and the lover on
    time!
*Les morts vont vite*. We living stand at the gate
And life goes on.

# At Extremes

I had a dream about a polar bear
He seemed to want to inform me about something.
I have had a psychoanalyst but I have never had a soothsayer.
Even if my soothsayer were a polar bear I would not believe her (or him).
The men I see giving speeches in the public square know nothing at all
About anything I care about except how to move crowds
They like to move crowds the way Shelley wanted the West Wind to
    move his product.
Each might go and live with Janice in Florence in nineteen fifty-four.
Each might wake up some early spring morning oddly wishing to eat a
    piece of hard candy.
A former student of mine is doing very well, I hear, but his chronic anxiety
Makes him dissatisfied and unhappy, fearful that people don't appreciate
    him.
Well, some people appreciate him but he isn't satisfied with that.
He is sufficiently intelligent and ambitious but he gets headaches.
He will not go to Florence to live with Janice in 1954.
I am the only person in the whole history of the world ever to have done
    that.
No one knows when he or she is going to die. The polar bear probably
    never thinks about it.
He is wholly committed to life, unlike my former student,
Unlike Janice, unlike me. We are all committed to the life product.
What power is there in having done something once and then knowing
    automatically that it is for all time!
One, wearing a bathing costume of white featuring red dots, politely
    smiles,
If you don't try to come on to me I will show you the cliff
At which dolphins jump, but I couldn't promise
I used to say you don't need the sun when you travel first class
We were living in Greece unswayed by politicians
But we could be mightily moved by changes in the economy
Janice said to me one very hot summer day look at my feet
I said they're nice She said I didn't mean that, you silly
I mean look at all the tar on them from being on this beach
At that time there were no houses close to the sea.
You have to go back to your house.
You sleep there. Hotels are invented.
A hotel is where when you go there they have to let you in

If a room is available and you can convince them you can pay.
Michelangelo leaves Florence. He is just a man.
Ruskin and Michelangelo face each other across an oaken table.
When you are free it is hard to decide what is best.
There are no rooms in the hotel.
But now there is one. It hasn't been swept recently.
There is dust on the floor.
Gratefully, Michelangelo Antonioni sinks into a deep slumber.
Four of his great films are already made and another one is to follow.
The sheep were the best men at the sheepflies' wedding.
A noun perturbs an adjective with its slightly superior social class.
I'm the thing itself, the noun says.
Stay in love said Michelangelo and Antonioni woke up. Being bareheaded
    was serious business
In an arctic wind.
We were in good physical condition and not depressed.
We were fifty percent men and fifty percent women
We were afraid that half of us might be squid.
The nouns, wishing to be pampered, call the adjectives back
But it is the verbs, here by this thundering surf, that are triumphant.
Octopus come bearing blue-hatted children on their backs.
In a hotel you may sometimes find geniuses around
Probably they won't speak to you unless they need company.
Children clamber up to the roof of the hotel
Silently one of them wishes he or she were an octopus
Then one would be one's own village maybe one's own city
How could I have need, a child thinks, for anyone then?
The bird flies over the gray, deserted porch of the hotel.
I am the only one who saw Miss X at four-fifteen in the afternoon on June
    2nd for the first time while attempting in a slight fit of nervousness to
    light up a Camel.
You are difficult to smuggle through customs.
Gypsy romance makes its appearance.
Everyone was fairly well satisfied—or almost—with someone else,
Even the ones who listen to the speakers and the one who walks around
    the city with his hands behind his back.
In Vinalhaven the old-timer's baseball game proceeds—
For some people, "reality" is represented by a prostitute, just plain
    business. Get down to facts.
The facts are that when you are fourteen or fifteen you want sex.
In some way or another you are going to get it.

686

By what process this turns into something with dominion over your life is
  unknown.
Theories abound. Small-town railroad stations. Bus stops. Inventions to
  replace teeth by glass.
Winter is ignorance. She picks the rose apart, trembling, with life in her
  fingers.
The polar bear swims toward the dam. He is part of a continuum.

# Possible World

Peach Peach Peach

Tarzam

# MONDO HUMP

Black          Kenneth

MONDO HAMPER

Reach Reach Reach                                          reach, reach

                 Don't you know

    Sentence

                          along the beach

                  MONDO SEVERANCE

Mondo Universal Collectivity
Mondo aggrandizement
Mondo nothing left to teach

                       MONDO SENTENCE

      plague
                                               trunk
                 sunned
    TAKE

                                        MONDO RESUMP-
                                               tion

         WIRY, VALLEY, CABLE, AIRY

              MONDO Completes

                   BUMP

MONDO OF CARRY
MONDO OF TEACH
           the sun


      MONDO IS SUNBURNED DAIRY

Kenneth fled because of sacred thinking

    Mondo of unfloored beach

Scared he is walking
Unprepared he is walking
      UN
          KNOWING

          that ALL

                            answers
                        are within
                            his reach
        They are in

              his STOMACH
they are in his eyes and thoughts

    WILL power

                        beds
        poison ivy

     A street of balls a horse of sounds a dachshund of
                  breathing sighs
     BABBLING
       Those Wonderful WOMEN
Dog-hooked                  SOUNDS
     Ever to be Seen,
         Embraced AGAIN
  How?

         Cause event effect

MONDO

      back
         the
     in                             basement
             Meantime

                                          AGREEABLY

           singing

        seaside BUMP

                 MONDO

           MONDO SIMMER
                      MONDO GLASS

"You can't beat that you just can't compete with that," said
             holding out to catch
                                 WHAT?

MONDO Hamper          Gallery,
            Cannery
                                        MONDO Slump


In a bright summer air a curious mondo

                                gravithump
                Haste!

        A bear, a trump
                genius
        the letters of the world
                        Mondo extreme


                Crying Hump


            crying personal seaboard faces


                aqua log
                        aqua log series thump



                                        Mondo Hump


        Invites   gladness   alights     madness
                        Mondo
Desert fastness
                        Mondo
                                invites fastness
                                        Mondo
            Serene

# VOX

Vox when we are living together

# POP

VOX POP

Pop when we are living together vox
opposed to capital punishment
slavery of fruit trees

Poppop the voices of the people          when we looked out
banister
Vox let the people have a voice                     over
saying

## VOX    POP

we used to live there, all three
of that, mixed Kenneth
In whose dark dentyne shop
Liberty Bell for panters
VOX POP
Living well for theatres of three
VOX entertainment
and lively winter west
pop
Pop
Pop
Pop    Pop
pop

## BLACK BOARD MONDO

all aboard

Mondo Peach

flowering

VAGUE and BUMP
                    hummingbird

mondo some
You were wearing your see-through Adam-and-Eve fox costume

I watched the labels come
Remove the dome

Abelard and Eloïse     1968 to nineteen ninety-one

Astrid and Helicon
                                Mondo

whatever
            nineteen eighty
But You

Mondo SUNK
        and influence
Affluence MONDO
                        mondo Scum
                                        on pond
in nineteen eighty-two I find you

# MONDO

summers      cocktail trees
Avenidas in which by shortcut brain dense populace

### EVENING THOUGHTS
dense popular mondo

### FOOL

To have been so brainless ivy cat fool
Iridium fool
Shot fool
Claxon seam tennis

Summer Hearts

### MONDO

SHE

said            why NOT
explain
I can                          but not

Why

Won't                      her

We used to go there

raising great hotels
ONCE

WE WALKED

all

PAR over
is

LOOKING FOR A BUMP

Arabian foot-chase

I plodded out a fire
in a vacant lot

MONGREL

*Mongrels* is unhappy

BLISTERS TRACE

extreme Himalaya park

MONDO

to
voting          sleep apart          BOMB

At this moment SHE

Boisterous rovers
To other civic entities than ours
Have tendency to revitalize
Ancient and tricky orders
Of fan-tailed architectures
To surmise
That these are somehow better than ours
Is, as they say, to "wick the general"
As it is to "non-inflate the bed"
A bird harbors
That stone's distaste
For being what it was stopped by
Being bad.

Holes in the city walls

SUFFERING

BLACK
          GREEN
                    RED
                         WHITE
                                   ORANGE
                                             MIDDLE
                                                       SUN

          apparently in tails
          apparently in jeans
          apparently in sober attire
          apparently glad, and in good health

                                             ALL THE PEOPLE
               ALL THE PEOPLE

                         who have wanted things spread out

                                             And they say

          "I don't do that kind of

                         work"

Blue baby baboon helmets on holiday

               Go under the deck

               "I don't know"

MONDO

Finally you can do anything except not            DIE

EVEN                                       be at rest

BENEATH

# HOPPO

Mondo Breath

Grace

Celestial mondo

This is the reason you wore

She wore

Waited

A Possible World

•  •  •

# To a Bug

Insect on high
Now as on propeller plane
Down
To this glass's rim.
My wife's
Here and my friend Jean
Claude Vignes

I must
Swat you
Away

I wrote an opera libretto
In this Paris "apartment"
It's awfully small
To be called an apartment
Bug
You who from on high
Swoop down
May find it a department

Very big
A part of France
Or the bald heads
Of a university
Of silence
Where they allow
No (such) flies!

But the air is bigger
Go away
Oh no, now
Jean Claude
Wants to
See you
Janice
Does too. She says
"Kenneth, stop! wait!
It's an

Unusual housefly
One actually
Very rare in our day!"

"Oh!"
Jean Claude
Says. (And I
Considered you
Just a fly! Here

Have a piece
Of our
Cake)
Janice says
No, not
That. Instead

She brushes
You away
Then you're
Out

The window
No
More in our
Flat we
Can
Eat lunch
At last she
Says a
Very
Interesting bug

Seen one in

I've

A Vermeer

Not on!

Says

Jean Claude

A Ter Borch

Or is it

You know

The one

Children in it

In red

Janice said

Where now

Fly?

With the five

Dressed

"Oh!"

"Ah!"

Will you

# Variations at Home and Abroad

It takes a lot of a person's life
To be French, or English, or American
Or Italian. And to be at any age. To live at any certain time.
The Polish-born resident of Manhattan is not merely a representative of
    general humanity
And neither is this Sicilian fisherman stringing his bait
Or to be any gender, born where or when
Betty holding a big plate
Karen crossing her post–World War Two legs
And smiling across the table
These three Italian boys age about twenty gesturing and talking
And laughing after they get off the train
Seem fifty percent Italian and the rest percent just plain
Human race.
O mystery of growing up! O history of going to school!
O lovers O enchantments!

The subject is not over because the photograph is over.
The photographer sits down. Murnau makes the movie.
Everything is a little bit off, but has a nationality.
The oysters won't help the refugees off the boats,
Only other human creatures will. The phone rings and the Albanian
    nationalist sits down.
When he gets up he hasn't become a Russian émigré or a German circus
    clown
A woman is carrying a basket—a beautiful sight! She is in and of
    Madagascar.
The uniformed Malay policeman sniffs the beer barrel that the brothers
    of Ludwig are bringing close to him.
All humanity likes to get drunk! Are differences then all on the surface?
But even every surface gets hot
In the sun. It may be that the surface is where we are all alike!
But man and woman show that this isn't true.
We will get by, though. The train is puffing at the station
But the station isn't puffing at the train. This difference allows for a sense
    of community

As when people feel really glad to have cats and dogs
And some even a few mice in the chimney. We are not alone

In the universe, and the diversity causes comfort as well as difficulty.
To be Italian takes at least half the day. To be Chinese seven-eighths of it.
Only at evening when Chang Ho, repast over, sits down to smoke
Is he exclusively human, in the way the train is exclusively itself when it is
    in motion
But that's to say it wrongly. His being human is also his being seven-
    eighths Chinese.
Falling in love one may get, say, twenty percent back
Toward universality, though that is probably all. Then when love's gone
One's Nigerianness increases, or one's quality of being of Nepal.
An American may start out wishing
To be everybody or that everybody were the same
Which makes him or her at least eighty percent American. Dixit Charles
    Peguy, circa 1912,
"The good Lord created the French so that certain aspects of His creation
Wouldn't go unnoticed." Like the taste of wheat, sirrah! Or the Japanese.
So that someplace on earth there would be people who were
Writing haiku. But think of the human body with its arms
Its nose, its eyes, its brain often subject to alarms
Think how much energy, work, and time have gone into it,
To give us such a variegated kind of humanity!
It takes fifteen seconds this morning to be a man,
Twenty to be an old one, four to be an American,
Two to be a college graduate and four or five hours to write.
And what's more, I love you! half of every hour for weeks or months for
    this;
Nine hundred seconds to be an admirer of Italian Renaissance painting,
Sixteen hours to be someone awake.
One is recognizably American, male, and of a certain generation. Nothing
    takes these markers away.

Even if I live in Indonesia as a native in a hut, someone coming through
    there
Will certainly gasp and say Why you're an American!
My optimism, my openness, my lack of a sense of history,
My distinctive facial muscles ready to look angry or sad or sympathetic
In a moment and not quite know where to go from there;
My assuming that anything is possible, my deep sense of superiority
And inferiority at the same time; my lack of culture,
Except for the bookish kind; my way of acting with the dog, come here
    Spotty! God damn!

All these and hundreds more declare me to be what I am.

It's burdensome but also inevitable. I think so.

Expatriates have had some success with the plastic surgery

Of absence and departure. But it is never absolute. And then they must
bear the new identity as well.


Irish or Russian, the individuality in them is often mistaken for
nationality.

The Russian finding a soul in the army officer, the Irishman finding in
him someone with whom he can drink.

Consider the Volga boatman? One can only guess

But probably about ninety percent Russian, eighty percent man, and
thirty percent boatman, Russian, man, and boatman,

A good person for the job, a Russian man of the river.

This dog is two-fifths wolf and less than one-thousandth a husband or
father.

Dogs resist nationality by being breeds. This one is simply Alsatian.

Though he may father forth a puppy

Who seems totally something else if for example he (the Alsatian) is
attracted

To a poodle with powerful DNA. The puppy runs up to the Italian boys
who smile

Thinking it would be fun to take it to Taormina

Where they work in the hotel and to teach it tricks.

A Frenchwoman marvels at this scene.

The woman bends down to the dog and speaks to it in French.

This is hopeful and funny. To the dog all human languages are a perfumed
fog.

He wags and rises on his back legs. One Italian boy praises him, "Bravo!
canino!"

Underneath there is the rumble of the metro train. The boy looks at the
woman.

Life offers them these entangling moments as—who?—on a bicycle goes
past.

It is a Congolese with the savannah on his shoulders

And the sky in his heart, but his words as he passes are in French—

"Bonjour, m'sieu dames," and goes speeding off with his identity,

His Congolese, millennial selfhood unchanging and changing place.

# Flight

The rocketship was waiting. I had to get on it.
It flew me away from the gardens,
It flew me away from the lake, the deliberate Como,
It flew me away from the strolls in the sun.
It didn't go very far but merely brought me
To a place where a few years previous
I had sat down writing some letters.
The rocketship hardly needed
Its rocket parts to do this, an ordinary plane would have done.
It took me to Hydra fifty years ago
If it didn't need rockets now, it needed them then.
I had no idea where I was going
The rockets made it sure I landed there
The island surrounded and supported by rocks
There were Norris and the waterside restaurant Msieu Oui-Oui's,
There were Dion and the ants in the courtyard
There was a large church bell and no water
(No wells) till the water boat came with its hose
There was Margaret there was Margaret's face
No opera and no concert
But lofty conversation, white bricks
A wall-hanging of *The Return of Odysseus*
No cars and no lawyer and no doctor
And the rocketship waiting again.

# A Big Clown-Face-Shaped Cloud

You just went by
With no one to see you, practically.
You were in good shape, for a cloud,
With perhaps several minutes more to exist
You were speaking, or seemed to be,
Mouth open wide, talking, to a
Belted angel-shaped cloud that was riding ahead.

# Roma non basta una vita

1

Kate, to Mario. You seem so happy. How can that be, when you've told
   me how depressed you are?
Responds Mario: I am so sad that I have come out on the other side. Ha
   ha.
On this other side spring flowers are visible,
Daisies and morning glory and poppies, a million poppies.
People smoke these in order to have veesions,
Mario says. Kate, then, Yes, I know, tell me.
M: You have to pass a church examination before you become an airmeet
   (hermit).
They recently have an airmeet who is crazy, perhaps from being on this
   drug
But maybe not. In any case he is crazy. He is appearing on the television
To tell of his psychawtic adventures so they are banning this theeng
That anyone, even a crazy one, should become an airmeet.
Mario: drives at eighty miles an hour. All passengers: experience fear.
   Kate:
Mario, stop! We aren't really on the other side! We're still in ordinary
   reality
And we don't want to die. Mario says I must have been dronk on the
   pawpie. I am sorry. I go slowly now.
Returning from the other side, he is sad again, but we get back.

2

The priest comes to bless the apartment.
There is magic in the air.
If we don't we may have bad luck.
The church could set fire
Or send out hooligans to wreck our sweet apartment.
No they wouldn't do that.
Meanwhile he is blessing.
He has already blessed the table at which you sit
Thinking of world history and of where we may go
Tonight. And now he is blessing the bed

I swear he is and now he passes out of sight
To bless the garlic on the terrace. He's right
To bless the windows
It's through them the poetry comes in
Blessing with fresh air the day and night
The priest is all set to go now
After the kitchen bless you and goodbye
A small token Grazie and may the Lord give you peace
I love this apartment. So, I think, do you. It's just right
For a blessing
On this contemporary, laid-back day.


3


Nothing is more striking than an airport
When, on a sparkling summer's noon,
You suddenly realize
That if the physician smokes beware
Of an updraught hitting you in the eye.
The airport is as beautiful as a plank
Thrust out over the water so you can see
Where you are going to, if not destined to, dive
You'll also see
Not a reflection of the world you leave behind
That has so violently to be reconsidered.


4


To see Rome's buildings and its history
I walked through the whole city and its streets
Unbothered by the traffic and the cars.
I said, lost in self-consciousness and thoughts
For Rome one life and span are not sufficient
To take its ancientness and forums in
One needs more than one's time and one's existence
To know the great piazzas and the fountains.
This promenade and leisure I'll remember
As part of something else, quiet and thinking,

Not let the future blur what comes to pass.
Saying which, I closed up the day and book
Of what there was, that spring and afternoon.


5


Here I am waiting for Mario in the gran caffè
On the Piazza del Popolo he is forty minutes late.
Arriving hand outstretched from his little car he says
I am sorry to be so late but it took much
Longer than I have expected. So many of the streets are forbeeden—his
    religious view
Of the traffic plan of Rome.

Sitting down, he tells me of his imaginary girlfriend (fidanzata)
A Spanish girl he invented and corresponded with
After a trip to Spain when he was in his twenties.
He in fact didn't have a fidanzata and, embarrassed about this lack,
Invented Paloma, to impress his friends. The correspondence he said
Was quite romantic and very hot and he enjoyed the letters
He wrote and those he received, on different stationery.
Where is Paloma now? Huh hah, I don't know he says. Maybe still in
    Spain, maybe not.


6


Better one day as a lion
Than one hundred years as a mouse.
Mussolini's theory
Which gives rise to doubts.
After this one day
You would be a dead lion
Or a live mouse
It would be the same thing.
Who is not part mouse
Except when Love is at the throttle
Or when we have drunk from the bottle
To a nice excess.

Or when a lion stirs in us at injustice
Unfairness, criminality, the pitiable
Then we may band together
And fight that as citizens.
Is Blake in agreement
With the ill-starred Benito?
No, Blake was in the private sector
And had no gangs of ruffians
Vulgar and full of hate. His lions
Were tigers of magnificence
Not rowdies for the fascist state.
Better one day as a giraffe
Than fifteen as an aardvark
May be easier to action,
Is harder to understand.


7

Francesco says to Jeanne (in French)
It was a lovely evening. Of course you did invite two people who represent
    to me
All that I find most disgusting and appalling in Rome, and are the reasons
    I have left it.
These were two Roman aristocrats Francesco detested. Aside from that
(*A part ça*) everything was perfect. Much laughter (though not by Jeanne,
And barely by Marcello, but after a while, some) followed by a delighted
    discussion
Of the phrase "*A part ça*," which seemed to refute if only slightly
What another friend said about why Italians didn't buy his novels,
"There is no irony in this country, none at all!" At least, I thought so.


8

In Rome where I was often lonely
Romans when they have met you and think they may, just may, like you
If you're so forward as to suggest you might meet some time
For lunch or for a drink, characteristically say
Si. Ci telefoniamo, or ci sentiamo, which means

Yes. We shall telephone each other. Which means
That if nothing even a shade more appealing should turn up
If I haven't lost your number and if I remember who you are
I may phone you; but, when that happens, it doesn't mean
You two will meet, but only that a ci-telefoniamo again
Will swing through your chest like icicles
Giving you an impression that the real, true social life
Of actually being with Romans is about to begin.


9


Mario says (twelve years ago) that the end of communism is a great
    tragedy
For the intellect because now there is no place to turn
From the evils of capitalism.
He is waiting for something else.


10


Here you are in this miserable city in this wretched restaurant
Where you don't want to be at all (in fact we were in a mediocre outdoors
    restaurant in
The Campo de Fiori which wasn't such a bad
Place to sit though it was awfully hot, even at eleven at night).
You're here because of thees woman. Ah! I rejoiced, feeling suffering
But I have written about this conversation someplace else ("Talking to
    Patrizia," in *One Train*).
Patrizia said. So thees woman did she come back to you?
Are you then together now? No I said. Both our lives have changed.
    Patrizia says
I weel sand you my *Collected Poems*. You know when I start going through
    the papers
All over my apartment
I am finding some surprising good ones. Buona notte good night.
About a friend of hers who was supposed to meet us, Patrizia says E un
    ombra
She is a shadow you can never catch her!

Alla Rampa, O restaurant
At which I sit with Jeanne and Marcello
And with Julian Beck and Judith Malina
On this late April night
When we have just come down from the Villa Borghese
Where one named Robert or (Jeanne) "Roberto"
Has given a concert on the piano
And where Marcello tells me
Of his strange life as a conductor
He knows he will be in Geneva in two years
For seven days and in Como in two thousand and five,
New York in September, et cetera
He has to live in the future with a hard hand on the past
(The scores of opera) and the present (not going mad)
And Julian and Judith tell me for the first time in thirteen years
Or thirty, I can't remember, they have their own apartment
They are doing a Living Theater stint in Rome
And for some reason they've been given, or found, an apartment
Can I imagine that, all those years without one's own place to live!
Yes I can imagine it and there is talk about the concerto
And then the evening comes to an end. I'm fifty three.
I look up at the beautiful night sky.

I used the wrong word
To explain the presence of Karen in my apartment
To Alessandra the cleaning woman,
Saying *la mia suocera* instead of *la mia cognata*
(My mother-in-law instead of my sister-in-law)
*Ah, la bella giovane!* Alessandra said
Or *E bella e giovane*, I didn't understand which
But knew as soon as I'd had time
To think it over, that I'd made a big mistake.
This kind of mistake I thought irreparable
Even though the apartment had been blessed.
The Father should have blessed my Italian vocabulary I said
To a window in a room where no one was present but me.

In San Pietro in Montorio
You can hardly stand up.
In the eternally flowing Tevere
You can't sit down.
In the Vatican you can eat cake
But you can't wear shorts.
Today you are turned away
From Saint Peter's and from coming before your God.

Mario comes over to the apartment
To put on his one-man show
About the Italian film magnate Dino di Laurentiis.
Mario once worked for him
He seats himself behind a table
And puts on a Dino di Laurentiis mask.
He presents di Laurentiis as vile and corrupt.
Mario likes this kind of character
For his plays. Another of his one-man shows is Mussolini
Which has a considerable success.
To what extent do you think you, Mario,
Are like—Ha ha Mario says. Maybe you are right. I have been theenking
  of this.
Maybe you are right ha ha but maybe you are not.
It's true Mario that you always cut them down.
I try to, Mario says. The first play of his I'd seen
Years earlier was called *Felicità*.
Felicita is a beautiful girl who brings happiness
Everywhere she goes and as a result all is destroyed.
So then who is this one Mario says.

## 15

Rome is asleep. Finally.
But we are still up. Then, wildly,

The sound of a motor scooter. Rome
Isn't asleep. And we are up.


16

My daughter was born here and jokingly hoped
There would be a plaque
Commemorating this fact in front of the hospital
As there is in my heart.


17

Feathers, leathers above Roma it is all cardiography!
Chinese lanterns won't melt the snow (contemporary Russian poetry)
I am your vagabond and you are my faithful behind. Emerald tax!
    Seasons!
Whatever is below Rome is below the earth. Dynamites and traffic
    patterns.
No friend even knows I exist. Loneliness is my political party Veblen is
    my op-ed
Whose is the harp? Calendulas a-coming. Face of glitz.
But is it my own moaning that I hear? Never believe a dock rat. I am your
    peer.
Yes, I look into the objects. No, this contrariness is mine!
Time is absolved by it. Wreckers come on the scene. Self cognizance,
Self pity, all in one freaking sheaf. But I am of cosmogonies
As you are, bella Roma, of the days. Now both let's roll.


18

My new play Mario tells me which I have not yet wreeten
Is about an Italian who decides to becawm a Mooslim.
All of the Italian artists and intellectuals were communists
And when there is no more communism they do not know what to do
So they try the New Age, meesticeesm, pheesical feetness, Yoga, etc.,

But that dawsn't work. Then they deescawver the Mooslims.
They can be against capitalism again.

19

Dawn light not quite over the Victor Emmanuel Monument
But first late-night dawn streaks and we six standing there
The moon, the noon-gray fight remembered not,
Or living in memory only. Ugly sledge-
Hammer effect of this pile of stones on the heart
And on the brain. Moving down toward the ruined deserted theater
Overwhelmed by the energies of creation
Could be anywhere (I suppose)
But happens to be here.
With what result? Blue. Rose.
So comes the dawn.

# Paradiso

There is no way not to be excited
When what you have been disillusioned by raises its head
From its arms and seems to want to talk to you again.
You forget home and family
And set off on foot or in your automobile
And go to where you believe this form of reality
May dwell. Not finding it there, you refuse
Any further contact
Until you are back again trying to forget
The only thing that moved you (it seems) and gave what you forever will
    have
But in the form of a disillusion.
Yet often, looking toward the horizon
There—inimical to you?—is that something you have never found
And that, without those who came before you, you could never have
    imagined.
How could you have thought there was one person who could make you
Happy and that happiness was not the uneven
Phenomenon you have known it to be? Why do you keep believing in this
Reality so dependent on the time allowed it
That it has less to do with your exile from the age you are
Than from everything else life promised that you could do?

# The Unfinished

A beautiful young woman with eyes like a leopard's
Walks past and
She does what a beautiful woman does. She indemnifies reality
From the stones and the Sundays to the hardest hit;
She makes malleable reality
So it will fit on a further beam. She unravels mutuality
So that it's tucked in a single seam. She is not Mrs. Bailey
My schoolteacher in the third grade,
Although of such truths poetry is made. I would not gladly
Live in a world without her, but that is fate.
She may be married to Tarzan. She may be Brendetta the Milk Maid.

# The Moor Not Taken

Desdemona had her choice of numerous Moors.
But she chose Othello.
Why do I say "but"? Because Othello was a killer.
True, he had to be made jealous before he killed her
But how could anyone do that but a killer?
If we had been Desdemona, I am sure,
We should have chosen another Moor.
About five feet eleven, not Shakespeare's, another.
We get to talking and I ask him, finally, about the Moors
He says they don't really exist any more,
That the people of Morocco are no longer Moors
And do not recognize themselves in the person of Othello.
Your coffee was very good he said, and thanked me and went away,
Centuries too late to be taken, either by Shakespeare or by Desdemona.

# Thor Not Taken

You have many good qualities, Ingrid said,
But I want my husband to be a Christian
And you still believe in the Norse gods, Thor the most outrageous.
I love you, love you, he said. But I cannot leave my gods.
Take me without Thor, he said. She quavered. Is that possible?
A child played with a set of wooden rabbits on the floor.
She remembered it fondly. The game set had been given to her by her
    grandfather, Bryggen-Thor.
Is that possible? she again said. The rabbits stayed the same while the girl
    grew up.
Now she was a woman. The cold wind blew against her ears.
Is it truly possible? she said. That I could have you—without Him?
Aye, merry, he said. And that day Christianity began its conquest of
    Norway,
Of sad Sweden, proud Denmark, and the Greenland isles.

# Movement

Why did I take my life in my hands to see a few fish
And some gigantic cakes of ice
And to meet a few South American writers?
I could have imagined all this without coming here
And slightly increased my chances of staying alive.
I used to think it didn't matter how long I lived
But I didn't know how it did matter how much I saw
And could write about and how many people I met.
I'll have to take my life in my hands again now to go back
From life "down here"
I say "down here" because of the way it is on the map.
I have gone mainly east and south because that's where everything was
    that I wanted to see.
Finally, when I was almost sixty I went west, to China.
Where were things I wanted to see but I hadn't known
I could get to with my physical presence
Which is everything, the reason for life.

# Primus Inter Pares

### DAPHNIS AND CHLOE

To be the first ones there.

### DOG ON THE DOCK

To be the first one there.

### THE FACE IN THE SUN THE TASTE OF WHEAT

To be the first one there.

### CANVAS

To be the first one there.

### FORLORN LOVE, YOU IRREPLACEABLE COMMODITY, LET ME GO

To be the first one there.

### PERSON IN A CLOUD

To be the first one there.

### WE SPEND HALF A LIFE

To be the first one there.

## AMALFI, TORN BY THUNDERSTORMS, IS WRECKED AND IS NO LONGER THE DESIRABLE RESORT IT ONCE WAS

To be the first one there.

## THE LESSON COMEDY GAVE US

To be the first one there.

## THE TRAIN STARTED UP BUT I WAS RELUCTANT

To be the first one there.

## BYRON AS AN ACROBAT

To be the first one there.

## SHOO FLY SHOO FLY AND OTHER GAMES AND ANOMALIES

To be the first one there.

## ORDERLY CAFÉ

To be the first one there.

## MUDDIED WATERS

To be the first one there.

## JANUARY. EMISSARY. GOODNIGHTS

To be the first one there.

## LATCHKEY

To be the first one there.

## DECORATIONS REPEATED MANY TIMES

To be the first one there.

## CLEMENCY

To be the first one there.

## SHEEP FILLING ALL THE SPACE AROUND A HARBOR

To be the first one there.

# Relations

*La comtesse de Pierre, née de Mac-Mahon*
*Se promène sur le boulevard Mac-Mahon*
H. J. M. LEVET, *Cartes Postales*

Julie, there was the time
You went on the *De Grasse* with E. E. Coulihan
Unknowing. He, a student, and you, met
One night, ship's ball, a party
For those not seasick. And you danced,
Oh how you danced!
And on deck afterwards, kisses
By the slippery dozens, and hands
Clutching the waist and back. Valery Larbaud
Admires Levet and goes to visit
His apartment rue Caulaincourt, the way R. Padgett
Three years back visits the provincial home of Reverdy
What different poets. For Levet
Fancy duds, white nights, a lot of women and a few poems.
For Reverdy a lot of poems and almost nothing else.
My grandfather
Gets dressed up in a blue serge suit, smiles.
He died (too)
He is a contemporary
Of Levet the first part of his days, of Reverdy the second.
Larbaud and he are exactly contemporary.
Coulihan dies young, age about forty.
You didn't forget him, and Coulihan didn't forget you.

Countess Julie, now, born a de Mac-Mahon,
Goes walking on the Boulevard Mac-Mahon,
The Arc de Triomphe visible
From where her family cemented its name.

# Barking Dogs in the Snow

Barking dogs in the snow! Good weather is coming!
Good weather is coming to barking dogs in the snow.
A man changes only slowly. And winter is not yet past.
Bark, dogs, and fill the valleys
Of white with your awful laments.

# A Memoir

This "dys-synchrony" one feels
    In reading other people's memoirs
My life was not like that. But your life was
    Your nationality and your "class"
Apparent in every sentence
    If not in every word
So, I think, if I write mine
    Everyone will know me
As the street runs past when it is well planned
    Another street, to which it was the alley
But is now a confirmed street all its own
    Frank O'Hara said to me
One thing that cannot be taken away from us
    Is Panavision
The next year I went to Rome
    When I read or even think of the memoir of the stone
It exhilarates, and deprives me
    Of my own voice, the major word collection
Of mine in my own time
    Greek columns rolled
As far as Selinunte
    On the pastel fly
I could hardly include an erg of former energy
    Without its being analyzed by myself
The clothes of all who walked past me
    Contained other bodies than mine!
For they came one at a time
    It is the study of languages
Of the polar bear heart
    Weeks passed, I felt silly,
Useless, above all lonely, and apart
    A heap of nothing
Rivers have names because there are few of them
    Mud puddles generally none
Smell of the Tuileries
    Glass hat racks attributing
What shall I put in my memoir
    Kansas City
Got off bus to get a haircut there

Wearing a cowboy hat Kitty
You loved me with something to spare
Opened to brightness
I thought I saw you down at the ship
You did
I invented the airplane
I said My gawsh! in a way
That people loved I walked Niagara Falls
Hit my shoulder and you'll see
Gray's *Anatomy*
Combining at a party
The boy the girl and the dog
The old man
I hang in the air as if by accident
Totally dependent on the social contract
And the good will of others
And the evanescent spirit
I am here
Love is there
Life is here
Summer there
So no one's is a valid-to-ponder-about life
Only the shallows
Of the green, at first, ocean,
Then its purpler blues
I married into a family of indefinite objects
When I was two years old
Indefinite stars above me
Indefinite life my mother
Obscure relation to the sum
Of all those people around me
Indefinite desk indefinite chair
Vague flowers, vague tub, vague mirrors, pianos
I see my grandson, Jesse, now
Marrying the same world.
The roof pays taxes
Its tiles its taxes to the sun
I thought that love is
A burning product
But now I see
That it is random particles

One treatise about lunch is worth a thousand about hepatitis
                    Until you have hepatitis
White is thrillingly indifferent
                    To red, but blue is this rake
Secrets lost like forests
                    Oh from what branch
Of tyrannosaurus have we fallen
                    "In nineteen fifty-two I went left"
"In nineteen eighty-five
                    I turned right"
I felt answerable
                    To one purity and then to another
A bear cub
                    Seen in Cincinnati
A tiger in Minneapolis
                    I was sorry to have missed you
However without knowing about it
                    You should never let your woman dance
With another man! the short guy—Indiano
                    In Guatemala sometime in the seventies
An ocean trumping
                    Its waves on the flush of the sand
Macho mysteries unavailable to me
                    Lessons I learned later
Which are by then useless
                    Seeing hearing Johnny Somebody
She was the best friend
                    Of anyone who knew her
The blue tops
                    Of the kitchen cabinets
The storm
                    When it came we were both away
Who, as retro as a trumpet
                    Leading a parade, is the other guy?
A film by René Clair
                    Runs past me waving its arms
Times waiting in line at the Cinema
                    Des Swans
In wit is pleasure
                    Also in wind is pressure
Across the street is the
                    Now across countries steal

O Italian girl in London
                Oh Italian girl
I hope you have
                Forgotten me
I give back what I have taken
                In return I want nothing
The birds walked over the
                Roof on which the dog is barking
Beeping to keep awake, cars coming
                With temperatures halcyon of increase
Different idols doing it
                The prize in the coffee
You can't get it out
                As known to myself when awake
And she said, Let's go away
                Engines on hillside to my right
Pomona on my left *en plein air*
                The doves in the tree Whingo!
Nineteen thirty-seven
                There is much less of me
Nineteen eight
                No existo
Nineteen eleven
                Much the same
Nineteen ninety-seven
                Bumps! Foghorns! Shepherds!
Owl attacks,
                Supernumerary fogs and yet
Nineteen ninety-nine
                Dawn Nineteen fifty-three
A song, Guy Béart tells me,
                Needs to contain three things
Intellectual interest for the man
                Sentimental interest for the woman
And fun for the child
                A "sexist" idea
That year glorious summer came
                On five spring evenings
Supernumerary lists
                Lists for the young and the aged
I've seen old people standing in holes
                That bulldozers left in the concrete

Others assailed by diamonds
>Curiosity about anthills

How many stares at Greek
>Without learning a word of it!

Apollo and Thespia
>There was my life as a life

I thought without Greek I can't lead it
>I think without Greek I have led something else

Of Italians there was Poliziano
>One among many

Or several at the door
>I bring home the book *Tutte le poesia italiane*

She cries (Janice)
>"All of Italian poetry!"

Greedily we attack it but it
>Is the complete poems

Only of Poliziano
>Chi non sa come e fatto el paradiso

Guardi Ipolita mia
>Negli occhi fiso

That's great Janice said I
>Said Yes isn't it great

We then won't have to nominate
>Any more heroes for our sensibilities tonight, we have
>Angelo

I once thought "Am I Angelo" I then thought
>"Angelo makes masterpiece

After masterpiece
>Alas I am not Angelo

I am reading work of Angelo
>Songs cease. Begin and cease."

On the desk in the chair and in bed
>Ipolita's eyes

Whose values seem ever to increase
>Until finally

Raymond Chandler and Poulenc take to the wall
>In superior agitation

Mickey Mouse and Rumi
>Take to the wall

And all of the Berber nation
>Grandma and clipboard stick to the wall

If you can get in this you can get out of it

Type of reaction meanwhile raccoon
All sweetness is gone
Meaning some sweetness (I have known so far)
Is gone
You Hotel de Fleurus is gone
English grammar is gone
As for French you "have to dream in it"
Try to make things cease
Without even whispering
On a pillow that book lay lighting
Up the whole bed Janice said stay in bed
It is worth clocking for
Then is all sweetness
I wondered if anyone would ever
Love things in the same way
Some did even many I wasn't the only one
A shower head an oyster
Catching it is enough
While—a bedroom window at their scene
I throw the bicycle up
In the air then catch it I am so young
Volatile evergreen
Keep walking sensations in shoulders
Plus throat You travel too much
M. Gallimard said to M de G
You flatter yourself too much
I spoke to myself
Her strangeness
His confusing ways
Her supposed militancy
His regret
Her natural poses
You want everything
As one
When we left it was the market still there?
This problem of Berkeley's
That is itself so unreal
Gravity goes to sleep so does plywood in the wall
Its tenure like a baby's is long
O life of the Piltdown
The High Renaissance
Somebody up there has done something!

M's sister comes down to the bar
I am humming with praise
We are under the covers
It is the time of the jazz age
That succeeded the other
Muggsy Spanier and Bunny Berrigan
I've flown around the world
In a plane
Discovering Communism
Karl Marx does the dishwork
Hegel lives on in memory
In any event the Marxists helped
The good people to escape
Later we would form an army
Beside some ludicrous pump
It created
I had (we had) to undiscover it again
Okay! Janice said let's
Read all of Poliziano
I found three poems
I might almost be able to read
"Chi non sa come"
And two others
The rest were too
Unpossessed by our vocabularies
Roland jumped up
From his intriguing chanson
We never spent much money
We were thoughtful and lost
Whereas Poliziano
Once he entered the diplomatic service
Angelo hello
I am plenty of these
Everyone is an envelope
Inside which one is hiding
Some trees
At last I am feeling in love
The murderous rise of the ship
Tormenting the created water
In any case once he did
Entered the service
At twenty-six

Had so little time to write poems
That except for a few official occasions
He stopped
But what would old Poliziano have written
"I live under seven stars
As an eagle might
*Mais attenzione!*"
Would this high-thinking-feeling Italian man
Even recognize my presence in the street
Well I had others Janice and I drink tea
So keep reading him ignorant
Intellectual (relatively) wandering
Through a culture
Someone is singing
On the landing below
The arc strike of a pen on paper
Doesn't put one in the show
However much we try
Like the moon I have tried to be everything
Except to be that
Completely other impossible
Said the bite professor waddling
Jane Henderson's clear stained rose
You are the substitute for that
With no vultures it is raining
I wrote down Hawk I wrote
Then hog I wrote then hock I wrote
You are the substitute for that!
Don't get so excited,
Moving away from the Maison des grands clichés
You'll spy a building on your right
You may find worth entering
But don't go there yet it's your tomb!
The forsythia weathers the trip
This rose (envelope)
Is bright
This (rose) letter is breathing
I passed their schoolhouses wanted to teach
Radiator central
Telling
Dangerous friends everything
Needing no further work

                    The friend who
Constantly reappeared
                    In dreams, as I
Had wished him to be
                    Though still a puzzle
He was, too, when alive
                    But this time I knew
That he was dead and put back together
                    I was always afraid
He would fall to pieces again
                    And threw my dog in the air
May have hurt him when he fell down
                    Fear resuscitated
He is himself again
                    To walk out and see Jenna
In her white two-piece tumbling tutu
                    We can graduate from college
Together I said and off we went
                    To Yankee Stadium and the Bronx Zoo
Grace Paley walking past my apartment
                    In a march against injustice
Lionel Abel philosophizing on a bar stool
                    Jim Dine mangiatore dei suoi colori (eating his paints)
Larry Rivers installing some pipes
                    In a lower East Side apartment, waiting
A bus comes by containing
                    The even-handed breeze
Maria Teresa Cini wobbling
                    When the elevator comes to a sudden stop
And saying
                    A poet should never see an apartment like this
John Ashbery gets tight
                    Noel Chatelin smacks him
With a five hundred franc bill
                    The Life of the Bee
M. says in Paris
                    Probably your real life is here
Since you like it so much
                    That it's almost unnatural
And N. said
                    Here in Rome you will find the true life
Down around the stadium

Waking and out looking at those old stones
 I thought that maybe she was right
The stone life one admires
 A little and then a lot
Then some sprinkling afternoon with sunshine not at all
Your real existence is with us your friends
 J. putting her jacket on backwards
Makes us laugh
 The great archway
With her necklace of brilliants
 Naked J.T.
Already done justice
 The real life maybe the real life
Is sex
 The hills are the main civilization
The old woman holds the pup
 Tightly in her fragile arms for it is snowing
Noon, luck, days on a planet
 Is the one room where lovers stand apart
I was once one of those
 As you keep laughing about at breakfast
How could you ever have been
 Town grapefruit town breakfast
I have to go back to Penn Central before daybreak
 Train leaving at dawn
The smell of cold artillery and mixed up rifles
 Gives way to several novels by Booth Tarkington
I came to a place where there were a lot of birds
 Not alien forms
Oh well Past is past (James Schuyler)
 Whereas the future
Do you dream about it much
 I never think about the future
She says
 Scratching a mirror of her dress
Catwalking the incumbency, matador
 Here is thy sling
Aboveboard there is a tourniquet sliding
 Halfway between some ditch dock doors
We are through playing there
 The past is an energy without thought
All proposals about it are vipers

You take the first egress and I'll get lost

The banners

That told not of triumph

But of the opening of an audio equipment store

The ten lost driveways of Venice

Never to be thought of or stored

In memoria universalis

Recognition of the spring signs

The first note of the violin

Sappy happy hibiscus

The lanterns of lips and of tongue

I secretly or not so secretly wanted to sail

An orchestra island

Catastrophic tour

But instead lay insolvent

To play bingo

With a foreign correspondent

Your student grant money amounts to more

Than here is paid to a bank president

How about some coffee

Asked the rugs

Is Turkey that invisible?

I wondered myself

Walking up the grass

Highway a middle precedent

Wandering down this slope

Hearing about hideaways to have been

The way Trollope wrote *Phineas Redux*

And *The Eustace Diamonds* and Balzac wrote *Père Goriot*

Interest in blackmail

Or sleeping on top of Harry's Bar

Loved Sciascia's *The Day of the Owl*

The rhythms of fingers

Re-write Beethoven's Fifth Symphony

Nor Mozart's hammerklavier quartet

Newton and Tito and Felix the Kat

Heroes planned to protect disorder

What poor man is the champion

Who denies old age?

Coincided we look around

For the parallels that make good arches

A stadium more than a tree

A compromise with Lorenzo the Magnificent
One day a kitten falls in a well
And is rescued by Dionysius
Which is the full name of Dion
Of Hydra age five
My daughter is a friend of his
My memoir for a moment gets fat
And glows if impossible to write
Walking around as if with gods in that garden
And demigods themselves were our persons
For fifteen minutes it was light
The dogs of darkness carried in
Waking up I thought "I am forty"
But actually I was fifty
Paul Klee painting with delight
On a very small scale like a jitney
Feel memorially enclosed in the night
When we walked it together
The "ho-ha!" of walking
Beats the "who-ha" of sleeping
In the piranha tank
Said Leonard circa twentieth century
I want the moon to be my problem
All the time
Who would deny that
The circus said
I mean the varied voices of the circus
That I heard in Paris
Janice stringing out clothes on a line
And the cat, the poor cat
In the well-bottom
Not every man is fortunate enough
To visit Corinth
With its agora of up-for-sale beauties
The Greeks, worried, I remembered
Bones and muscles are not but almost enough
We'd also need divine hindsight
To be born then
Children's footprints on the marble
Pages stuck
In the machine
Of the unpainted square

Water turning into icicles
Woman being the scoreboard of man
Four wins and one baby
The showplace of stardom
Numbered, the Tigris and the Euphrates
Man being the showplace of woman
Castigated scored rebuked
And the best conversation of the time
When I'm awake am I available
Protons! my friend murmurs we have to go out
And get this down
Envy encamped against people
Bitterness encamped against people
Bees that made sense
To purpose in the sand
You lifted your head up
And I sat down at night
How do the Frenchies do it?
Said Rory circa nineteen seventy-eight
Ambusculating Paris
Right shadows on trees
Overcoats planned not by headlights
But coasts of butterflies
The sheep god damn this tavern
A rumor of foresight
After the drinks and news came out
Not Africa but could have been
I love that country
That country is not in sight
They do it by theories
Immaculate conceit
When I went to bed
O material objects
Stones made of sunlight
It would appear
Better
Maybe Ipolita
Outliving her golden age
Treachery was in the air
From best beloveds it was still there
Planked me into some residencies of my life
Okinawa hand grenades

Columbia the tests
Fiery life as a patient of psychoanalysis
                    My freebooting life as an expatriate
Pardon me will you open that door
                    Time-mates of Pluto or of Theophrastus
I am busy don't bother me please
                    Existence among friends as amidst idiots
Or hornets or pleasing angels
                    Habituation to paying by the mule
A wayward assumption
                    When Janice felt lost
It was easy but I had to find her
                    She was also a supreme self
As was Katherine
                    Who was in my arms
I felt Let us no longer take up arms
                    One against the other
I thought for at least ten years afterwards
                    I've wasted my life I didn't stay in Paris
In fact my life went ho ho ho
                    And flattened itself out in New York
I could have made a memoir that was all loss
                    Lost Marina lost marriage lost Paris lost inspiration
I would live in this Memoir for days
                    But a birthday was obvious
Became all too clear
                    I hadn't wasted my life because it wasn't wasted
My head was in my hands
                    But I was only thirty-five
Never to slump again
                    In quite that same fashion
Suddenly the universe is awake
                    You used me up but I was a dog
In nineteen eighty-six
                    Scared book ambitious for experience
Besides the laments that were wasted
                    Came back and back and back
Inglorious afternoons
                    Spent near the bump shack
A woman's favorite tune
                    Sung next to me in the unCadillac
That joy of hand touching

Grave genius
I felt always
        For two or three minutes a month
Did I thought "These will stay"
        Commanding?
There was plenty of time
        A man and woman lost in the jungle
Hardly wasting their time until they get out
        But she saying It is wasted
Wasting my time eating and drinking
        Because there is only one life
The memoir shows how not it
        Existence to promise is
No one can lead it
        Except by arriving too late
But then you have it
        And this palaver is foolish
One thing could make me happy
        Two things could make me glad
To have intelligence enough to find
        A third thing
And so forth
        Until I had
The billion elements gyrating from central
        Self
To make useful one third of a day
        And its ready existence in the soul
As defined by Mitsugo
        "Garden of flash seasons"
But we grow cold
        Eating and drinking just to be waiting
For those millions of things to come
        So give me five I'll
Be happy
        Give me fourteen my mind be on a roll
One agora in a blue cashmere sweater
        Three agoras (pl?) in white angora sweaters
Nineteen steam chimneys away
        The board with a nail in it
Each is precious
        Being of course evanescent
I don't give up

I take the boat
It is full of Carpaccios!
Seventy Saint Ursulas
The bargains are overflowing
The peach tree gets what it can
It gets blossoms and peaches
And the kindly stares of the populace
This "middle-aged" man is crying
The peach tree gets that too
So life is wasted from the beginning
There is no way to use enough life
Not by excess can you do it
Nor by sparely imagining
Maybe only by working your way through it
Like voltage or a rabbit
But the dream is that there is one
I think of the past woman to help move this one on
And destroy it with vivacity
Why do you wish to see more things
Act as if you were thirteen years old
Prepare to see Hamlet
Is superficial
I want to be a song
Tendency to walk over here city
Now dormant or as they say asleep
While waiting with everybody else
To see what comes
I regarded the malignancy as only fear
It would have to be written about too
The memoir
Is a raincoat
A seed
A nothing
Saint Joan is not in it
One fraction of humanity
Making a huge difference
Imaginable to me at fifteen
Though not much later
Photocopying machines and General de Gaulle
Are not in it
In yours maybe but not in mine
Robert closes the door

The steeplechase is beginning
This rope has the smell of the Regatta
Ave opera
The elephant's foot
There won't be much traffic
Janice said
I said There isn't any
There was very little
Tom was a suit
She had wanted to wear
Waking up and walking though the streets
A far cry from Gene Kelly
In *Les Demoiselles de Rochefort*
Dancing all around the harbor
A pale sheep
The whiskey or the brandy
The coke stand wouldn't take us in
It was very warm out even the stones
Having no old-fashioned significance
This is prohibited by language
Also by boys and girls in long shirttails
The sea cancels out the least resistance
That wallet the breeze great medicine birth
Everywhere I look
To sneak back on my experience
Life what an eroded stone you are
And plant you with gasps of poetry
Now that I can face them directly
These streets and these alleys not my own
When I went to the Rome opera
That bent it
You have a beautiful head
The young woman said
She was headed into a life of resentment
And contentment
If I thought What do I know
I started a memoir
What do I care
If she imagines silence?
It won't work from over this way
She has had a new baby
The memoir is five feet two

But no longer
Enduring what we tell each other
                    I am a fragment
Would you, lilac, put in a school
                    Of this morning
Vanish from those
                    Hot lips forever
That stake and seal your mortality
                    And to whom would I be speaking
If all signs were you?
                    Get only so far
Then the general trail of humanity
                    Soon there's no more speaking
But have worked on whatever there was
                    An honest face
Asking a quiet question
                    In some culture at five a.m.
Or the cannon's boom
                    The darkness seems more and more ridiculous
Vigorously on its way
                    But not yet a fixed idea
This existence like another
                    Taking place

# INDEX OF TITLES

# INDEX OF FIRST LINES

# INDEX OF FIRST LINES

A NOTE ABOUT THE AUTHOR

Kenneth Koch published many volumes of poetry; all of the shorter poems are collected in this volume. His short plays, many of them produced off- and off-off-Broadway, are collected in *The Gold Standard: A Book of Plays* and *One Thousand Avant-Garde Plays*. He also wrote several books about poetry, including *Wishes, Lies, and Dreams; Rose, Where Did You Get That Red?*; and *Making Your Own Days: The Pleasures of Reading and Writing Poetry*. He was the winner of the Bollingen Prize (1995) and the Bobbitt Library of Congress Poetry Prize (1996), a finalist for the National Book Award (2000), and winner of the first annual Phi Beta Kappa Poetry Award (2001). He was named Chevalier dans l'Ordre des Arts et des Lettres by the French government in 1999. Kenneth Koch lived in New York City with his wife, Karen, and taught at Columbia University.

A NOTE ON THE TYPE

This book was set in Janson, a typeface long thought to have been made by the Dutchman Anton Janson, who was a practicing typefounder in Leipzig during the years 1668–1687. However, it has been conclusively demonstrated that these types are actually the work of Nicholas Kis (1650–1702), a Hungarian, who most probably learned his trade from the master Dutch typefounder Dirk Voskens. The type is an excellent example of the influential and sturdy Dutch types that prevailed in England up to the time William Caslon (1692–1766) developed his own incomparable designs from them.

Composed by Stratford/TexTech,
Brattleboro, Vermont

Printed and bound by Berryville Graphics,
Berryville, Virginia

Designed by Soonyoung Kwon